GREG MILLER is a national security reporter for the *Washington Post*. He was among the *Post* reporters awarded the 2018 Pulitzer Prize for Investigative Reporting for the news organisation's ground-breaking stories on Russia's interference in the 2016 presidential election and the resulting investigations of the Trump campaign and administration. He was also part of the team awarded the 2014 Pulitzer Prize for Public Service for coverage of American surveillance programmes revealed by Edward Snowden. He is co-author of the book *The Interrogators*, and in addition to the United States and Europe has reported in Afghanistan, Pakistan, Morocco and Turkey.

A *Washington Post* Notable Work of 2018

'The most comprehensive account of the Trump-Russia story to date ... Miller trots expertly through this troubling tale'
Sunday Times

'A lucid and startling account ... the clearest account yet of what Russia actually did'
The Times

'How Clinton became Putin's enemy after she attacked the legitimacy of Russian elections has been well told ... But no one has done a better job than Miller of describing the vastness of Russian efforts to destroy her'
Guardian

'Damn good ... Miller's book paints on a broad canvas, showing readers the full arc of an incredibly complicated political tale ... Miller's account ... is highly persuasive'
Washington Post

12923994

'May read like a greatest hits of America's horror show at the hands of a leader unfit to confront the threat of Russian interference'

Kirkus

'Penetrating … Well-paced but rich in detail, Miller's narrative is one of the best of the many new books on this evolving saga. His treatment of Trump's possible obstruction of justice in trying to influence investigations by former FBI director James Comey and other intelligence officials is especially good'

Publishers Weekly, Starred Review

'An integrated synthesis – a solid account that goes back many years to get elements of a full picture' *New York Journal of Books*

'We cannot understand what happened in the 2016 election, Russia-gate or the imploding Trump presidency by reading the 24-hour digital news on our phones … Fortunately, we still have a simple technology invented nearly six centuries ago: books. Greg Miller has written a damn good one'

KAI BIRD, winner of the Pulitzer Prize

ALSO BY GREG MILLER

The Interrogators: Inside the Secret War Against Al Qaeda

THE

APPRENTICE

TRUMP, RUSSIA

AND THE SUBVERSION OF

AMERICAN DEMOCRACY

GREG MILLER

WILLIAM
COLLINS

William Collins
An imprint of HarperCollins*Publishers*
1 London Bridge Street
London SE1 9GF

WilliamCollinsBooks.com

First published in Great Britain in 2018 by William Collins
This William Collins paperback edition published in 2020
First published in the United States by Custom House,
an imprint of HarperCollins*Publishers*, in 2018

1

Copyright © 2018 by W P Company LLC

Greg Miller asserts the moral right to be identified
as the author of this work in accordance with the
Copyright, Designs and Patents Act 1988

A catalogue record for this book is
available from the British Library

ISBN 978-0-00-832578-7

All rights reserved. No part of this publication may be
reproduced, stored in a retrieval system, or transmitted,
in any form or by any means, electronic, mechanical,
photocopying, recording or otherwise, without the
prior permission of the publishers.

This book is sold subject to the condition that it shall not, by
way of trade or otherwise, be lent, re-sold, hired out or otherwise
circulated without the publisher's prior consent in any form of
binding or cover other than that in which it is published and
without a similar condition including this condition being
imposed on the subsequent purchaser.

Set in Bembo Std
Printed and bound in Great Britain by
CPI Group (UK) Ltd, Croydon

MIX
Paper from
responsible sources
FSC™ C007454
www.fsc.org

This book is produced from independently certified FSC™ paper
to ensure responsible forest management.

For more information visit: www.harpercollins.co.uk/green

To Rebecca, Katie, Peter, and Cole

For Mom and Dad

CONTENTS

Part Five

PROLOGUE

THE WARREN OF CUBICLES WAS SECURED BEHIND A METAL door. The name on the hallway placard had changed often over the years, most recently designating the space as part of the Mission Center for Europe and Eurasia. But internally, the office was known by its unofficial title: "Russia House."

The unit had for decades been the center of gravity at the CIA, an agency within the agency, locked in battle with the KGB for the duration of the Cold War. The department's prestige had waned after the September 11 attacks, and it was forced at one point to surrender space to counterterrorism operatives. But Russia House later reclaimed that real estate and began rebuilding, vaulting back to relevance as Moscow reasserted itself. Here, among a maze of desks, dozens of reports officers fielded encrypted cables from abroad, and "targeters" meticulously scoured data on Russian officials, agencies, businesses, and communications networks the CIA might exploit for intelligence.

Deeper inside was a conference room adorned with Stalin-era posters of heroically depicted Soviets, muscled soldiers and workers striding across fields or factories under the hammer and sickle. The room, swept routinely for listening devices, was the scene of increasingly tense meetings in the months leading up to the 2016 presidential election, as senior agency officials sought to make sense of a series of disconcerting reports. In late July, the agency had gained access to an extraordinary stream of information showing that Russian president Vladimir Putin was himself directing the "active measures" operation aimed at disrupting the U.S. presidential race. U.S. intelligence partners were also warning Russia House about worrisome contacts between Russian figures and campaign associates of the Republican nominee.

Donald Trump's vigorous displays of admiration for the Russian leader only made things more bewildering. He routinely praised Putin and even seemed to enlist Moscow in an effort to hack his opponent's email account. The question was, why? Taking a hard line against Russia was the politically winning move, and yet Trump seemed subservient.

Unlike any presidential candidate in memory, Trump had shielded his finances from public scrutiny. He refused to release his personal tax returns. His business empire was a labyrinth of separate companies registered under different names. Many of those he had done business with hid their identities behind corporate shells. Some of his most prominent developments were deep in debt, though how deep and to whom was nearly impossible to discern.

During the campaign, there was consolation in the idea that Trump's unsettling behavior toward Moscow was a product of inexperience—a problem that would be contained when he was surrounded by smarter advisers or wouldn't matter anymore once he lost. But those inside U.S. spy agencies were privy to alarming secrets that were not so easily shrugged off. Among them was that the Kremlin was actively seeking to help elect Trump.

Russia House was the point of origin for that assessment, which would later be embraced by the U.S. intelligence community and infuriate the 45th president. The Kremlin's objectives began with sowing discord in American democracy, but broadened in mid-2016 to backing a specific candidate—who at this moment, his second day as leader of the free world, was making his way toward CIA headquarters.

President Trump had barely been in office twenty-four hours when his motorcade departed the White House grounds for the nine-mile trip to the CIA's Northern Virginia campus. The clouds and cold that had dampened Inauguration Day lingered over a city littered with the debris of America's post-election divide—pro-Trump memorabilia, inauguration programs and celebratory banners along the parade route; broken windows and burned vehicles on blocks where protesters had clashed with police in riot gear. Trump's arrival in the White House had been followed by a women's march that drew a crowd three times larger than the inaugural audience,[1] and now throngs of pink-clad activists watched the caravan accelerate through the D.C. streets. Their gestures toward the motorcade, countered by some salutes from Trump supporters wandering Washington, reflected in the thick tinted glass of the president's passing car.

The street-side crowds dissipated as the line of vehicles left downtown, crossed into Virginia, and followed the Potomac River north, turning onto the main route through the suburb of McLean and then past the zigzagging barricades that guard the entrance to the CIA. The agency occupies a sprawling, leafy campus in Northern Virginia enclosed by miles of electrified fence. At the center of the property is a seven-story building with a row of glass doors opening onto an iconic marble lobby—with the CIA seal inlaid in the terrazzo floor—frequently depicted in movies.

The CIA welcome for Trump would be cordial, even warm, but it was by now well known that the agency was responsible for a series of highly classified reports that had helped trigger an FBI investigation of Russia's interference and ties to associates of the president. And Trump had made no secret of his growing belief that the CIA and FBI were engaged in a coordinated effort to damage his presidency before it had even begun. His blistering attacks on intelligence agencies had only intensified as he prepared to take office. He disparaged their conclusions about Russia's involvement in the election and accused them of deliberately sabotaging him by leaking a document that had come to be known as the "dossier." That collection of memos, compiled by a former British intelligence officer, contained dozens of unproven but explosive allegations about then-candidate Trump's ties with Russia. Among the most salacious was that he had consorted with prostitutes during a 2013 trip to Moscow for the Miss Universe pageant, paying women to defile a hotel room where President Barack Obama had once stayed.

The dossier's contents had been in circulation in Washington newsrooms for months, disseminated not by spy agencies but the private opposition research firm that had commissioned the reports. Their unsubstantiated assertions had gone mostly unreported in the press until U.S. intelligence officials told Trump about the dossier two weeks before he was sworn in. When its contents were published on BuzzFeed, Trump lashed out on Twitter. "Intelligence agencies should never have allowed this fake news to 'leak' into the public," he said. "One last shot at me. Are we living in Nazi Germany?"

The sting of that slur was acute. The CIA's lineage traced to World War II and the creation of a spy service whose mission was to help Allied forces defeat the same Nazis that Trump now invoked. The agency's precursor, the Office of Strategic Services, was disbanded after the war, but a statue of its founding director, General William "Wild Bill" Donovan, still stands in the agency lobby. Trump likely knew little of that history—or for that matter of the record of CIA abuses and corresponding reforms that had transpired during the intervening decades—and would never retract the insult. Many presidents had clashed with the CIA, but the relationship had never taken such an ugly turn before a commander in chief had even taken office.

No one knew what Trump would say when he addressed the crowd that awaited him, but one thing was certain: he would not be brought into Russia House.

THE TRIP TO LANGLEY HAD BEEN PLACED ON THE PRESIDENT'S CALendar weeks earlier by Reince Priebus, the White House chief of staff. Priebus, a political operative grounded in the Republican Party establishment, had mapped out the new president's first days down to the hour, a detailed schedule that was to set a breathtaking pace and serve as an example of the urgency and ambition of the new administration. The CIA was the first government agency on Trump's itinerary, a decision designed in part to assure the GOP establishment that Trump would settle into office and be "presidential," which for Republicans entailed being a staunch defender of the country's national security institutions. More important, the Trump team hoped that the visit could avert an unnecessary rift with an agency whose unique aura and authority had proven seductive to previous presidents but was also capable of fierce bureaucratic combat—even against occupants of the Oval Office.

Trump stepped out of his armored car at 2:06 P.M. in an underground parking garage and was greeted by a CIA leadership team in flux. Now-former director John Brennan and his deputy had resigned once Trump took office, so Meroe Park, who had served for more than three years in the number three role, was officially in charge of the agency and its 20,000 employees. Park (the first woman to hold the reins as director, albeit in an acting capacity) held the job for just three days—long enough for Trump's pick as CIA chief, Republican congressman Mike Pompeo, to be confirmed.

Park escorted the president into the Original Headquarters building, an H-shaped structure that opened when John F. Kennedy was president. Trump was then taken by golf cart—an accommodation he required even for short distances—to a futuristic command post that operatives of Kennedy's era could hardly have imagined.

The CIA's Predator operations floor is a dazzling theater of high-tech warfare. Concentric rows of computer terminals face a wall of high-definition video screens. The ambient lighting is darkened to allow analysts to focus on footage transmitted halfway around the world from aircraft (the early Predators now largely replaced with larger, more powerful Reapers) equipped with cameras and missiles but no cockpits. The number of CIA drone strikes had plunged since the early years of the Obama administration, the peak of the covert war against Al-Qaeda, but the use of unmanned aircraft was still significant. The viewing can be monotonous—countless hours of surveillance over dusty patches of remote terrain in places including Pakistan, Yemen, and Syria. But moments of engagement are dramatic.

The sight of missiles streaming toward a target is particularly adrenaline-inducing to the newly initiated, and the agency often brings those it most wants to impress to the Predator display, with highlights of successful strikes cued up. Trump appeared suitably enthused, though puzzled by what he regarded as undue restraint. When told that the CIA flew surveillance flights over Syria, but that only the military conducted strikes—an Obama policy meant to return the agency's focus to its core espionage mission—Trump made clear he disagreed. When the agency's head of drone operations explained how the CIA had developed special munitions to limit civilian casualties, the president seemed nonplussed. Shown a strike on a Taliban compound, Trump noticed that the militants had scattered seconds before the explosion. "Can they hear the bombs coming?" Trump said. "We should make the bombs silent so they can't get away."

Agency officials had been given just three days' notice that Trump had planned to visit CIA and would deliver remarks; they had scrambled to make preparations that typically take weeks. An email to the workforce had offered tickets to the first four hundred employees to respond, a move that helped to ensure the new president would encounter a friendly crowd since the event was being held on a weekend. The agency readied a teleprompter, hoping the president would work from a prepared text. But the White House sent word at the last minute to scrap the screens—Trump would speak off the cuff.

THERE ARE NUMEROUS LOCATIONS AT CIA HEADQUARTERS SUIT-able for a speech, among them a cavernous hallway lined with past directors' portraits and a semi-spherical auditorium known as the Bubble. But the risers for Trump's visit were placed before the agency's most hallowed backdrop: a marble wall on the north side of the main lobby marked by six rows of hand-carved stars, 117 in total at that time, each representing an agency officer killed in the line of duty. The number had grown by at least forty since the September 11 attacks, reflecting the toll of the wars in Iraq and Afghanistan. The constellation had gained three new hand-chiseled stars just months before Trump's visit, commemorating a trio of paramilitary officers killed in eastern Afghanistan in 2016. The names of many of the dead are entered in a grim ledger that rests beneath the field of stars, protected by an inch-thick plate of glass; the goatskin-bound volume also contains blank spaces for those whose identities and CIA missions remain classified.

The wall is, to the CIA, Arlington National Cemetery in miniature, a sacred space. In addition to somber memorial services when new stars are unveiled, the setting has been used for ceremonies marking momentous agency events, including the culmination of the hunt for Osama bin Laden. It has also been a backdrop for presidents. In 2009, Obama stood before the stars for a first visit that was also uncomfortable. As a presidential candidate, he had called the CIA's post-9/11 interrogation methods torture. Once in office, he ordered the agency's secret prisons dismantled, and directed that the legal memos used to justify their operation be made public. Obama defended those decisions to a wary audience that he acknowledged viewed him with "understandable anxiety and concern." But he also spoke of employees' sacrifice and courage, describing the stars behind him—eighty-nine at the time—as "a testament to both the men and women of the CIA who gave their lives in service to their country." Even those who considered Obama hostile to the agency (and there were many) respected his recognition of so many lives lost.

As the ceremony for Trump got under way, Park was first to the podium, telling the new president that "hundreds more" agency employees wished to attend but were turned away for lack of space. "It means a great deal that you chose to come to CIA on your first full day as president," she said.

Vice President Mike Pence was next to speak, and hit all the politically expedient notes. It was "deeply humbling," he said, to appear before "men and women of character who have sacrificed greatly and to stand before this hallowed wall, this memorial wall, where we remember 117 who paid the ultimate sacrifice for our freedom." He then set the table for Trump, saying he knew the new president was "going to make America safe again," and that he had "never met anyone with a greater heart for those who every day, in diverse ways, protect the people of this nation through their character and their service and their sacrifice."

Trump took the stage in a striped blue tie and, though indoors, a topcoat that fell below his knees. "There is nobody that feels stronger about the intelligence community and the CIA than Donald Trump," he said as he stood facing the bronze gaze of Donovan's statue. The agency would get so much support under his administration, he said, that "maybe you're going to say, 'Please don't give us so much backing.'" He vowed to rid the world of terrorist groups and assured employees that their new director, Pompeo, was a "total star."

The speech to that point seemed on track. Park and other agency officials appeared to exhale, gaining confidence that their fears—a confrontation, an attack on the Russia analysts, another Nazi slur— would not materialize. Then midway through his fifteen-minute appearance, without any pause or outward sign, Trump changed course. Abandoning discussion of anything relevant to the agency, he set off on a riff about how youthful he felt—"thirty, thirty-five, thirty-nine"—and described the size of his crowds during the final days of the campaign—"twenty-five thousand, thirty thousand people, fifteen thousand, nineteen thousand." He falsely claimed to hold the record for *Time* magazine covers, and teased that he would help build a new room at CIA so that "your thousands of other people that have been trying to come in" would have the privilege of seeing him next time. Drifting into solipsism, Trump called members of the media "the most dishonest human beings on earth" for refusing to acknowledge the "million, million and a half people" he said had attended his inauguration the previous day—an erroneous claim off by a factor of four.

Hard-core Trump loyalists in the crowd stayed with him, standing throughout, cheering the taunts and boasts. But others began to shift uncomfortably, and CIA veterans who read his remarks or watched them online recoiled. There is no shortage of braggadocio at the CIA, an agency regarded by other U.S. intelligence services as permanently afflicted with a superiority complex. But in that setting, between the flags that frame the memorial wall, the display of rampant egotism felt offensive. A CIA veteran called Trump's address "one of the more disconcerting speeches I've seen." Another called it a "freewheeling narcissistic diatribe." Brennan, whose career at the agency spanned twenty-five years, issued a statement later that day describing Trump's appearance as a "despicable display of self-aggrandizement." The president, Brennan said, "should be ashamed of himself."

Members of Trump's entourage had a different reaction: the applause and ovations persuaded his handlers, including Priebus, that the president had made headway in mending his rift with the CIA, and possibly had begun to win over the agency workforce. Pompeo, according to aides, saw the dynamic in reverse: that through ovation and flattery the workforce had begun to win over a president who craved adoration. Either way, Trump's team considered his appearance at CIA a success.

During his speech, Trump directed applause to two of his closest aides, both sitting in the front row. "General Flynn is right over here. Put up your hand. What a good guy," Trump said of his national security adviser, Michael Flynn. A retired Army general who had been one of Trump's most vocal campaign supporters, Flynn was by then already under FBI investigation for omitting large foreign payments from his financial disclosure forms. Within days, he would also be questioned by FBI agents over his troubling post-election contacts with the Russian ambassador to the United States. Next to get presidential praise was Priebus: "Reince. He's like this political guy that turned out to be a superstar, right?" Trump said of his chief of staff, who was already struggling to tame the chaos of the Trump White House and was soon, like Flynn, banished.

Absorbed in self-adulation and grievances, Trump was blind to a stunning array of problems, some in plain view from the CIA stage: the failings of a national security adviser he'd insisted on hiring despite warnings; the existence of a larger agency workforce beyond this clapping, self-selected crowd that would be profoundly disturbed by his vainglorious performance; the fragments of intelligence being assembled in that very building that would help expose a web of connections between his campaign and Russia, and feed into investigations that would threaten his presidency.

Trump's ability to see these perils was impaired by his own unfamiliarity with the norms of governance, his insecurity and narcissism. Other presidents had varying levels of these traits, but none had ever possessed such a concentrated combination. These qualities had been on display from the start of his campaign. But now, against a backdrop that symbolized the profound burden of presidential responsibility, his shortcomings seemed suddenly and gravely consequential.

In the reality show that had propelled him to great fame, Trump was depicted as a business titan with peerless instincts—a consummate negotiator, a fearless dealmaker, and an unflinching evaluator of talent who forgot nothing. Week after week, contestants competed for the chance to learn from a boardroom master—to be, as the show's title put it, his apprentice.

In the reality that commenced with his inauguration, Trump seemed incapable of basic executive aspects of the job. His White House was consumed by dysfunction, with warring factions waiting for direction—or at least a coherent decision-making process—from the president. His outbursts sent waves of panic through the West Wing, with aides scrambling to contain the president's anger or divine some broader mandate from the latest 140-character blast. He made rash hiring decisions, installing cabinet officials who seemed unfamiliar with the functions of their agencies, let alone their ethical and administrative requirements. Decorated public servants were subjected to tirades in the Oval Office and humiliating dress-downs in public. White House documents were littered with typos and obvious mistakes. Senior aides showed up at meetings without the requisite security clearances—and sometimes stayed anyway. Trump refused to read intelligence reports, and he grew so visibly bored during briefings that analysts took to reducing the world's complexities to a collection of bullet points.

The supposedly accomplished mogul was the opposite of how he'd been presented on prime-time television. Now he was the one who was inexperienced, utterly unprepared, in dire need of a steadying hand. Now he was the apprentice.

The word, of course, has another connotation, one acutely relevant when it came to Donald Trump: an aspect of servility. Trump's admiration for the leader of Russia was inexplicable and unwavering. He praised Putin, congratulated him, defended him, pursued meetings with him, and even when talking tough, fought virtually any policy or punitive measure that might displease him.

Like any trained intelligence operative, Putin understood the manipulative power of playing to someone's insecurities and ego. On cue, he reciprocated with frequent praise for the president he had sought to install in the White House. The CIA experts in Russia House saw through these ploys, but they now worked for a president who couldn't be persuaded of anything by an agency he believed was engaged in a plot to discredit him.

It's hard to imagine that even a master manipulator like Putin would have anticipated the full success of his operation. Not only had he sabotaged Hillary Clinton, but he had also helped install in the Oval Office someone who—by virtue of his fragile ego, disdain for democratic norms, and volatile leadership—compounded the impact of the Russian campaign. In the months that followed Trump's visit to CIA headquarters, his administration would be tarred by scandals political and personal, a rate of White House dismissals unparalleled in history, and investigations into possibly illegal actions by the president, his family, and his team. Trump's decisions sometimes seemed as if they were designed to erode American effectiveness or standing, be it in government or on the world stage. Again and again he would belittle America's closest allies—Britain, Canada, France, Germany, and Australia—all the while praising Russia's strongman.

In so doing, Trump was extolling an authoritarian with an abysmal record on human rights. A significant number of Putin's critics have ended up dead, most prominently Boris Nemtsov, an opposition politician who was shot multiple times as he walked near the Kremlin in 2015. Others included Natalya Estemirova, the human rights activist who was kidnapped in Chechnya and found shot in the head; Anna Politkovskaya, the crusading journalist who was shot in her apartment building as she returned home; Sergei Yushenkov, the politician who was shot while investigating a possible government role in the bombing of an apartment building; and Alexander Litvinenko, the former security services officer who died an excruciating death in Britain when his tea was laced with polonium-210, a radioactive substance. Particularly among those who had spent decades in the shadows at secret war with the USSR and then Putin's regime, Trump's obsequious manner was horrifying—and mystifying.

After concluding his speech, Trump was whisked out of the building and back to his car for the return trip to Washington. The CIA crowd thinned as crews began stacking chairs and breaking down risers. That week, something occurred that officials had seen only in the aftermath of a CIA tragedy. Flowers began to accumulate at the foot of the Memorial Wall on Monday, as the agency returned to work. By week's end there was a small mound of bouquets placed by employees who passed by the stars in silence.

THIS IS THE STORY OF ONE OF THE MOST STUNNING AND ALARMING instances of political malfeasance in American history: the successful efforts of a foreign government to influence the results of a presidential election, and the president's potential obstruction of justice after his tainted victory. What was indisputable was that a foreign government had successfully infiltrated our democracy, pushing the election toward the candidate it favored. What now also seems indisputable is that, almost immediately after the Mueller Report was submitted to Congress, Trump directly attempted to do exactly what his critics claimed he had done with Russia: cut a criminal quid pro quo deal with a foreign government to benefit his own political standing. As this book reveals, Trump campaign goings-on in the Ukraine were always key to the collusion investigation. Evidence is also mounting that just as Trump has blocked government officials from cooperating with Congress, the Mueller investigation was badly hampered by a similar White House strategy. Trump and his allies seem increasingly desperate to hide the truth about his relations with Ukraine and Russia. He would not want you to read the pages that follow.

PART
ONE

PART
ONE

CHAPTER 1

THE HACK

THE GEOGRAPHY AND HISTORY OF THE NETHERLANDS—ALWAYS in the shadow of great powers—forced it to become quietly effective at espionage. And while the Dutch intelligence service, known as AIVD (which translates to General Intelligence and Security Service), cannot match the global reach of the CIA or MI6 (Britain's Secret Intelligence Service), and its officers may never compete for screen time with Jason Bourne or James Bond, it kept its focus on Russia even as the United States was diverting intelligence resources to terrorism after the September 11 attacks.

With one of the largest and fastest internet hubs in the world, the Netherlands had become a pass-through point for cyber criminals, particularly from Eastern Europe. Dutch spies, as a result, became particularly adept at operating in cyberspace, relying on that capability to monitor online crime as well as the resurgent threat posed by Moscow. In 2014, AIVD accomplished a digital feat of David-and-Goliath proportions, the agency's cyber unit penetrating a hacking syndicate linked to Russia's foreign intelligence service, the SVR. The Dutch gained access not only to the group's computer systems but to the surveillance cameras mounted above the entrance to its lair, capturing clear images of the Russian hackers as they filed into what they'd always thought was a secure space in the heart of Moscow. Analysts used the images in some cases to identify individual hackers, gradually compiling a roster with their names, the handles they used online, and grainy photos.

The AIVD had achieved what cyber spies call "exquisite access." It was in the process of carefully exploiting this penetration a year later that the Dutch began to see a suspicious new stream of data flowing into the SVR system. AIVD spies traced its origin to a Democratic National Committee server in Northern Virginia.

The DNC functions as the war chest and back office of the Democratic Party, raising money and helping to field and fund candidates across the country. In presidential races, it oversees the party's primaries, its debates, its convention, and the process of selecting its nominee for president. The breach of its systems was at that stage almost imperceptible, intermittent signals between a pair of computers on opposite sides of the Atlantic. In reality each ping was a silent betrayal, an expression of obedience by a DNC server to a distant machine secretly working for the Kremlin.

The Russian hackers' forays into the DNC network had easily eluded the organization's security, but U.S. intelligence agencies also failed to see the breach, even though the hackers behind it were already well known, having pulled off a spree of attacks in previous months on high-profile targets including the Pentagon, the State Department, and the White House—operations the Dutch had also detected and warned the Americans about. Certainly the DNC wasn't as alarming a target as those repositories of U.S. government secrets, but the failure to detect the intrusion would mean that by the time it was first noticed by the DNC, Moscow was already tunneling toward troves of material, including internal DNC emails and research files, that it would use to sow chaos in the U.S. election.

The Dutch relayed what they had learned to the National Security Agency, the massive U.S. spy organization responsible for all forms of electronic espionage. The AIVD turned over images of the hackers, IP addresses (numeric codes that correspond to specific computers on the network), and other information that the NSA was able to corroborate.

From that moment in 2015, the scale of the Russian operation and its consequences for the United States would only expand. But at the time, U.S. officials saw the alert about the penetration of the DNC as falling into the category of conventional espionage, the sort of data gathering that Russia, China, and every other country with enough hacking capability—including the United States—pursues. Such probing of government, institutional, and corporate networks was so persistent and aggressive by state-level hacking enterprises that the adversaries involved acquired distinct reputations. The Russians were seen as the most sophisticated and—ironically, given how the year would play out—adept at hiding their tracks. China was "noisier," less concerned with getting caught. While improving, Iran and North Korea were second-tier players. Attacks on think tanks and political organizations like the DNC were a problem, but defending against them was not necessarily the job of the U.S. government, which had enough on its hands fending off the equally frequent assaults on higher-stakes targets: classified networks, black budget programs, weapons designs.

Protecting those assets required constant vigilance. In November 2014, less than a year before the DNC attack, the White House experienced a Russian offensive so brazen that American officials saw it as a turning point in Kremlin tactics. The hackers gained entry with a common "spearphishing" ruse—sending bogus emails with disguised links or attachments that, once clicked, led to a malware-infested site set up to gather passwords and other sensitive information. The most striking aspect of the intrusion wasn't that Russian hackers got into a White House network—in this case an unclassified email system that allowed White House staff to correspond when the issue at hand wasn't sensitive, such as writing your husband that you'd be home late, or a congressional staffer that you'd received her letter. What was exceptional was how they reacted when confronted in that digital space by American cyber defenders. Rather than retreat and move on as the Americans patched holes, the Russian operatives stayed and fought. Every time the Americans severed the Russians' connection to the malware they had installed—key to their survival inside the White House network—the intruders managed to repair the link or create a new one.

The NSA team had a remarkable penetration of its own: through secret "implants"—the software equivalent of a Trojan horse, bits of pre-positioned code—the Americans were able to monitor the Russians' computers and see their adversaries' every move in advance, as if watching them wheel new weapons into position before firing. The advantage proved decisive, but only after a protracted fight. At a 2017 security conference, Richard Ledgett, who was deputy director of the NSA at the time, described the battle as the online equivalent of "hand-to-hand" combat and a game changer unlike any the agency had ever waged.

The DNC penetration detected by the Dutch did not prompt such a daring showdown. The information was noted on internal NSA report logs and shared with other agencies, including the FBI. On August 6, 2015, an agent from the FBI's Washington, D.C., field office called the DNC's front desk and asked to speak with the "person in charge of technology." Inevitably, he was transferred to the computer help desk and put in touch with an IT contractor, Yared Tamene.

FBI special agent Adrian Hawkins told Tamene that there were signs of compromise in the DNC system and provided some computer IP addresses that he said would help to locate the intrusion. But the address was the one the DNC used for its entire network—tied to more than a thousand laptops, servers, and phone lines. Tamene was a former college math instructor who had been an IT consultant at the DNC for four years but was no cybersecurity expert. He had heard plenty about how individuals were conned out of their passwords by hackers pretending to be from the government, a bank, or a credit card company, and was wary. He pressed Hawkins to provide proof of his position, but remained unswayed by the agent's attempts to convince him.

The call lasted several minutes, as Hawkins outlined in somewhat cryptic terms the bureau's concerns about the breach. He wanted to know whether the committee had detected the intrusion on its own and done anything about it. Tamene hesitantly acknowledged that the committee had endured some phishing attacks, but dodged detailed questions about the organization's staff and systems. Hawkins then offered the first hint—although an indirect one—that the bureau suspected Russia. Check for malware associated with "the Dukes," he said, an industry nickname for the hacking group with ties to Moscow. Tamene seemed unfamiliar with the moniker but agreed to have a look. After hanging up, he and a colleague did a quick internet search, read up on the group's methods, and performed a cursory search of DNC log files. They found nothing and Tamene couldn't help wondering whether he had fallen for a prank. Tamene informed his supervisor, Andrew Brown, the DNC's chief technology officer, of the incident.

The disconnect persisted through subsequent interactions—that is, when both sides managed to connect at all. In October, two months after he first called the DNC, Hawkins left a series of voice mails for Tamene, who ignored them, later explaining he had nothing new to report. Behind the scenes, he appealed to Brown for help, telling him, "We need better tools or better people." A month later, in November, the FBI agent finally got through, only to be told by Tamene that the DNC network appeared clean. Hawkins countered by again providing the DNC address, saying it was "calling home" to Russia. Tamene took this warning more seriously. He and his team began exploring whether there were gaps in the DNC's defenses—bad search parameters, problems with the firewall—that were preventing the IT department from detecting the intrusion. But again, his follow-up checks yielded no evidence of compromise. It would later turn out that the FBI's internal deliberations were so slow that by the time Hawkins had permission to pass along one IP address, the Russians had switched to another.

All of this back-and-forth had given Russia's hackers another three months inside the DNC servers. In all that time, the FBI's Hawkins had not seen fit to raise the matter with top officials at the DNC. Nor did they learn at this stage from their own staff: because of the tech team's failure to find evidence of the hack, Brown evidently felt no need to sound internal alarms.

The bureau's failure to contact a single official above Tamene would later be deemed by the DNC to be an unfathomable lapse. The FBI, for its part, felt it had tried repeatedly to warn the committee—in fact, Hawkins was so frustrated by the difficulty in getting through that in December 2015, he went to the low-slung DNC building on a quiet street two and a half blocks south of the Capitol. He asked the security guard in the lobby to be on the lookout for Tamene, and to stop him and have him call the bureau.

After months of frustration, the FBI pushed for a face-to-face meeting. In February 2016, Hawkins, Tamene, and two of his IT colleagues arrived at Joe's Cafe, in Sterling, Virginia, thirty miles west of the DNC's Washington office, but a ten-minute drive from the DNC's data center in Loudoun County.

There in Joe's Cafe, Tamene's lingering uncertainty about Hawkins's FBI credentials finally subsided when the agent produced his badge. More important, Hawkins also produced a set of computer logs from a day in December showing precise time stamps that enabled the DNC to narrow its search for suspicious activity. He listed penetrations of other targets by the Dukes and recommended a tool that could help detect intruders on DNC systems. In a February 18 email, Hawkins even provided IP addresses associated with the DNC intrusions—data that traced the attack back to its origin in Russia.

AFTER FINALLY CONVINCING THE DNC TECH TEAM THAT THE breach was real, Hawkins urged them not to block those Russian incursions. Take modest steps to protect sensitive data, he said, but don't disrupt the correspondence between the two systems or make any moves that would let Russia know its operation had been discovered. Though counterintuitive, this would allow further monitoring and avoid sending the hackers into hiding or, in a worst-case scenario, wiping the system of data to cover their tracks—leaving a barren, broken network. But it also left more time for Russia to make off with more data.

Tamene and his team went back to search their firewall logs. Again, nothing. They continued to wonder whether it was all a hoax, mischievous hackers merely "spoofing" DNC addresses online and making the FBI think the committee's defenses had been pierced. Nevertheless, for the next couple of months, the FBI continued to alert the DNC about possible intrusions. In March, one of Hawkins's colleagues, FBI special agent Lafayette Garrett, emailed the DNC tech team twice, alerting them to phishing attempts aimed at committee staffers; thus prompted, the committee's tech team was able to repel the forays. A month later, Hawkins asked Tamene for copies of computer logs that might help the FBI see which IP addresses were connecting to the DNC network. Tamene said he needed to ask the DNC's lawyers.

On April 26, Hawkins was put in touch with Michael Sussmann, a former prosecutor who handles cyber cases at the DNC's law firm in Washington, Perkins Coie. Sussmann urged DNC executives to approve the FBI's request, saying that the logs would be part of a classified investigation and kept from the public. "They really are helping you," he explained in an internal email. But by then it was already too late. Critical opportunities to contain the damage had been squandered—by FBI agents who took too long to get past the DNC help desk and by committee staff who failed to grasp the growing danger or get the attention of committee executives.

AS ALL OF THIS WAS GOING ON, HILLARY CLINTON WAS BEING PUMmeled by additional digital trauma.

Clinton's use of a private email account while serving as the nation's top diplomat between 2009 and 2013 had been a self-inflicted political wound that hobbled her candidacy from the outset. The practice had been unearthed by Republicans as part of an intensely partisan congressional inquiry into one of the most tragic events of Clinton's State Department tenure—a 2012 attack on two American compounds in Benghazi, Libya, in which the U.S. ambassador, J. Christopher Stevens, and three other Americans were killed.

Congress is equipped with an array of oversight committees to investigate such events, and a whopping seven of them did. They found security breakdowns and unheeded warnings but no evidence to substantiate incendiary claims that the Obama administration had blocked a viable rescue mission or engaged in a cover-up. The Republican leadership, however, created an additional panel—the House Select Committee on Benghazi—with a deep budget, broad authority, and cynical mission that was inadvertently revealed long afterward by one of its architects.

"Everybody thought Hillary Clinton was unbeatable, right?" House majority leader Kevin McCarthy, a California Republican, said in a Fox News interview in September 2015 as the presidential campaign was heating up.[1] "But we put together a Benghazi special committee, a select committee. What are her numbers today? Her numbers are dropping. Why? Because she's untrustable. But no one would have known any of that had happened, had we not fought."

The Benghazi committee was by no means the first to politicize a catastrophic event overseas, but the effectiveness with which it did so altered the dynamic in Washington. The name of the coastal Libyan city became a political shorthand—like Watergate or Whitewater—for a scandal that Clinton couldn't shake. But it wasn't any particular decision she had made about State Department personnel or facilities in Benghazi that proved most politically damaging. Instead it was the committee's discovery as it assembled documents that Clinton had used a private email server while serving as secretary, and that the department had only a portion of her official correspondence.

Russia undoubtedly took note of this dynamic as it mounted its election interference campaign. And many of the partisan impulses that were sharpened by the Benghazi experience would resurface in 2016, impeding the United States' ability to deliver a united response.

Clinton's use of a nongovernment email server—@clinton
email.com—had first been revealed in 2013 by a Romanian hacker
who went by the name Guccifer. But the committee zealously dug
further into the matter. Led by South Carolina Republican and
former federal prosecutor Trey Gowdy, the panel noticed that messages to and from the secretary were being routed not through classified State Department systems but rather a server in the basement
of the Clintons' home in Chappaqua, New York.

Under congressional pressure, the State Department sent letters
to Clinton and her predecessors asking them to produce any work
emails still in their possession. (Former secretary of state Colin
Powell had also used a private email account.) In December 2014,
Clinton's lawyers arrived at the department with twelve boxes
filled with hard copies of more than thirty thousand messages. But
she withheld another thirty-one thousand, insisting that while they
were stored on her system they pertained to personal matters, including her daughter's upcoming wedding and mother's funeral,
and were "not related in any way to my job as Secretary of State."
Having concluded this, she had then erased the emails she deemed
personal.[2]

It was a decision that played straight into decades-long depictions
of Clinton as secretive and duplicitous when it came to conceal-
ing the family's alleged misdeeds. The committee was, reasonably,
outraged that she had deleted a massive stockpile of messages without allowing any outsider to review what was being destroyed.

The controversy remained under wraps until *The New York Times*
broke the story several months later, on March 2, saying Clinton's
use of private email "may have violated federal requirements that
officials' correspondence be retained," and reignited lingering concerns about the Clintons' "lack of transparency and inclination toward secrecy." Immediately, the Clinton campaign was on its heels.

A week later, in a tense press conference, Clinton said that in using her private email address she had "opted for convenience," and acknowledged that "it would have been better if I'd simply used a second email account." Republicans rushed forward with sinister interpretations, implying that she was hiding incriminating messages about Benghazi or other scandals. The panel issued a subpoena for all of her communications, hoping to stave off any further email destruction. At the same time, the State Department came under court order to start publicly releasing batches of Clinton emails after they had been internally reviewed. The result was a disaster for Clinton—monthly dumps for the media to sift through, generating a seemingly endless stream of stories on the very issue that Trump and Putin would come to see as one of her most acute vulnerabilities.

State Department investigators subsequently determined that "classified information may exist on at least one private server and thumb drive that are not in the government's possession." Because some of the sensitive information in the emails belonged not to State but to spy agencies, the inspector general for the entire intelligence community examined a sample of forty Clinton emails and found that at least four contained classified material. He then relayed that finding to the Justice Department. The fallout from that referral would be devastating to her chances of becoming president.

IN THE SPRING OF 2016, NEARLY A YEAR AFTER THE DUTCH HAD ALERTED Washington to the penetration of the DNC, a second wave of Russian hackers converged on Clinton-related targets. These new intruders were working not for Russia's foreign intelligence service, but its military spy agency: the Main Intelligence Directorate of the General Staff, otherwise known as the "GRU." Long seen as inferior to other Russian services, the GRU had invested heavily in cyber capabilities and had raised its standing in the Kremlin through one successful hacking operation in particular.

The head of the Russian military, General Valery Gerasimov, had delivered an address in 2013 that American spies studied closely.[3] Reprinted in a Russian publication called the *Military-Industrial Courier*, the speech spoke of a new era of hybrid warfare, one in which "the role of nonmilitary means of achieving political and strategic goals has grown, and, in many cases, they have exceeded the power of force of weapons." The GRU had tested this theory in Ukraine in 2014, where it used a series of cyberattacks to shut down telecommunications systems, disable websites, and jam the cell phones of Ukrainian officials before Russian forces entered the Crimean peninsula.

After the Russian military had seized control of key Crimean facilities, GRU turned its information warfare troops loose to rally public support among Crimea's largely ethnic Russian population to break with Ukraine and support annexation by Moscow. To do so, GRU psyops teams blitzed social media platforms, including Facebook and the Russian-language social network VKontakte, with fake personas and pro-Russian propaganda. In one week alone GRU cyber teams targeted dozens of Ukrainian activist groups, hubs of protesters on social media, and English-language publications, sowing confusion and creating the impression of a groundswell of support for Russian intervention.

Three years later, the GRU joined the Putin-ordered operation to damage or defeat Clinton. Working out of a building on Komsomolsky Prospekt in Moscow, a GRU cyber-operative named Aleksey Lukashev sent a spearphishing email to Clinton campaign chairman John Podesta on March 19, 2016. Lukashev had used a popular online service for shortening website addresses to help mask his baited missive and make it look like a legitimate security notification from Google. The breach was enabled when one of Podesta's aides saw a supposed security warning from Google and had asked a computer technician to evaluate it. "This is a legitimate email," the technician wrote. "John needs to change his password immediately." With the ensuing mouse click, Russia gained access to a trove of messages stored on Podesta's account.[12] Within two days, Lukashev and his GRU unit had made off with more than 50,000 emails.

Lukashev was part of a GRU hacking group designated by its unit number, 26165. That same month, the hackers began probing the DNC network for gaps in defenses, seemingly oblivious to the fact that another Russian intelligence service was already rummaging through the files. U.S. spies said it was not uncommon for Putin to unleash separate agencies on the same target. In April, the Russian unit found an indirect route into the DNC system, stealing the computer credentials of an employee at a sister organization, the Democratic Congressional Campaign Committee, which occupied the same office and worked to help elect congressional candidates. Another spearphishing operation did the trick, luring the DCCC employee into clicking a link that effectively gave the GRU the keys into the network.

Once inside, Lukashev's group installed a program known as X-Agent malware on at least ten DCCC machines, enabling them to steal passwords and data from other employees, and even monitor their keystrokes and take photos of their computer screens as they typed away unsuspectingly. The hackers tried to hide their tracks by transmitting the pilfered information to a server the GRU had leased in Arizona (paid for not with rubles or dollars but with bitcoin cryptocurrency). By April 18, the GRU used its access to the passwords and files of the DCCC—some of whom also had access to the DNC network—to sneak across a digital bridge into the main party organization's network.

In April, GRU operatives registered a new internet domain— dcleaks.com—after discovering that the first address they wanted, "electionleaks.com" was already taken.

For all its advances, the GRU made a number of costly blunders that would help U.S. investigators reconstruct the incursion. The Russian hackers often used the same computers, email addresses, and phony online accounts for multiple transactions related to the operation—registering the dcleaks.com domain, accessing URL-shortening services, and facilitating bitcoin payments.

Those clues would be collected and revealed nearly two years later. But even at the time, the GRU arrived inside the DNC system with all the stealth of a cymbal crash. At long last, the committee's overmatched security team finally encountered an intruder that its systems could detect.

The GRU's hackers were "like a thunderstorm moving through the network," recalled one investigator involved in the case. "They were actively compromising systems. They were remote access-ing into systems in the middle of the night. They were deleting logs. They were opening up files on administrators' desktops. They were archiving massive amounts of files." At one point, the GRU crew began stashing pilfered material in a massive single file, pre-sumably to make it easier to drag out when the raid was done. But they stuffed so much into the single container that it crashed the system they had set up to export their stolen data in the first place. Left behind, the copy of the busted file provided investiga-tors a comprehensive inventory of the loot—but no firm sense of how much other material the GRU might have captured in other smash-and-grabs.

On April 29, little more than two months after the February Joe's Cafe meeting between special agent Hawkins and three members of the DNC's IT group, Tamene's team of contractors saw strange activity on the network. He promptly notified his supervisors at the DNC and—after so many months deflecting calls from the FBI—dialed Hawkins to inform him of what he had found.

It had now been eight months since the FBI had first reached out to the DNC.

CHAPTER 2

PUTIN'S TROLLS

V LADIMIR PUTIN, A NATIVE OF LENINGRAD, NOW ST. PETERS-
burg, was born in 1952 in the lingering shadow of World
War II. His father had been badly wounded in combat and his
mother barely survived the 900-day siege of Leningrad when the
Nazis tried to starve the city into surrender. The death toll in Leningrad was 640,000, including one of Putin's brothers. Both parents got factory jobs after the war and Putin grew up in a walk-up
communal apartment building where he recalled chasing rats in the
stairwells. "There was no hot water, no bathtub," Putin said many
years later. "The toilet was horrendous. It ran smack up against a
stair landing. And it was so cold—just awful—and the stairway had
a freezing metal handrail." A bright boy, Putin attended a school
for the city's best students. He also studied judo, earning a black
belt, a skill that invested the diminutive young man with a quiet
confidence.

After earning a law degree at Leningrad State University, Putin
joined the KGB in 1975. "I was driven by high motives," he said of
his choice of profession. "I thought I would be able to use my skills
to the best of society." He had an undistinguished career, however,

making it only to the rank of lieutenant colonel. He served in counterintelligence, monitoring foreigners in Leningrad, and then as an officer in Dresden, a backwater assignment, where he almost certainly attempted to recruit Westerners who came to East Germany. With the fall of the Berlin Wall, Putin returned to his native city and attached himself to the administration of the reformist mayor, Anatoly Sobchak, one of his old law professors. A fluent German speaker, Putin established a reputation as a competent but colorless bureaucrat who worked well with foreigners. His real skill was his ability to vault upward, almost unnoticed, on the coattails of powerful patrons.

In 1996, after Sobchak lost his reelection bid, Putin moved to Moscow, holding a series of positions in the administration of President Boris Yeltsin, until he was appointed director of the FSB, the intelligence and security agency that was rebuilding its power following the dismantling of the KGB. In August 1999, Putin was appointed prime minister in the chaotic Yeltsin administration, marked by the increasing decrepitude and alcoholism of the president. When Yeltsin resigned on December 31, 1999, Putin—looking very much like a nervous, pale junior staffer—became acting president. He won election to the post three months later with 53 percent of the vote.

The rich and powerful around Yeltsin had backed Putin's rise because they believed he was malleable, but Putin, as ruthless as he was cunning, viewed them as a threat to his rule. He gradually used the powers of the state and the court system to bring the oligarchs under control, imprisoning those who crossed him and seizing their property. The man who'd once seemed destined for the background became the new tsar, and the country's media, also brought to heel, portrayed the vigorous Putin as the embodiment of Russia's revival, a state that he had returned to its proper place as a global power able to rival the United States—"the main enemy," in the parlance of the KGB.

Seen from Moscow, the operation to sway the U.S. election had a long prologue. It was carried out by a regime that has fine-tuned the politics of grievance into a sophisticated propaganda weapon. Putin believes the United States engineered the breakup of the Soviet Union, eagerly plundered the fallen empire's spoils, and has been using its influence ever since to keep Russia weak. His innovation has been to sharpen and magnify those charges into his raison d'état—and to point to them to show why responding to U.S. aggression was not only justified but a necessity.

His resentments, nurtured over many years of perceived slights and betrayals, had found a particular focus in his animus for Hillary Clinton. As Russians voted in the parliamentary election on December 4, 2011, videos documenting widespread fraud at the ballot box rocketed around the internet. The next day, Clinton offered her view on the sidelines of a conference in Bonn, Germany. "Russian voters deserve a full investigation of all credible reports of electoral fraud and manipulation," she told reporters. "The Russian people, like people everywhere, deserve the right to have their voices heard and votes counted."

As she spoke, activists in Moscow were readying a protest of the election results in the city center. They had registered an expected five hundred attendees with the police; five thousand showed up, the biggest anti-government demonstration of the Putin era. The frustrations of an urban middle class that increasingly yearned for not just material well-being but also for political freedom burst into the open. It would take months for the protests, which soon drew some hundred thousand participants, to subside.

Putin was furious. To him, the fact that the first protests erupted just hours after Clinton's remarks was far from a coincidence. His

German biographer Hubert Seipel described Putin's anger that day as a seminal moment in shaping his disdain for Clinton and his conviction that the United States sought regime change in Russia.

"I saw the first reaction of our American partners," Putin told supporters a few days later. "The first thing the secretary of state did was to characterize and evaluate the elections and say that they were dishonest and unfair, even though she had not yet received the materials from the [election] observers. She set the tone for certain actors [in] this country—she gave them a signal. They heard that signal and, with the support of the U.S. State Department, began their active work."

Putin would survive the challenge and eagerly start pushing back—with the same tools he accused the West of using against him.

FEBRUARY 2016 BROUGHT ST. PETERSBURG SNOW FLURRIES AND ICE fog, a curtain of crystals in the frigid air. The districts that hug the northern bank of the Neva River had for decades been dotted with factories that rose during the nineteenth century. The area had seen its fortunes fade with the Soviet Union's collapse. But its tree-lined streets, historic apartment buildings, and green spaces had maintained their charm, and the closed factories gradually gave way to office buildings beckoning a digital-friendly generation of Russians and internet start-ups.

The shuttered factories had been well situated alongside the ancient waterways that braided Russia's intersection with Europe. But now, with steamships replaced by fiber optics, those with enough know-how, funding, and cleverness could access different sorts of currents. The firm that leased the four-story building at 55 Savushkina Street seemed to be among this new breed of Russians who in their own modern ways were following in St. Petersburg's mercantile tradition.

The name of the company, the Internet Research Agency, sounded vaguely impressive if uninspired. A street sign in front of the building warned cars to slow down for children crossing on the next block. A short stroll away, on a verdant island in the Neva, were tennis courts, a museum, and a palace overlooking the water that served as a summer retreat for Tsar Alexander I. Not that the tech-savvy employees of the Internet Research Agency had time for such diversions. Each morning they filed in for cubicle-bound jobs that combined two of their generation's consuming pastimes: crafting posts for social media and clicking refresh to see whether their creations had gone viral.

On February 10, 2016, as the fog outside thickened, employees received new instructions for an important project. An internal memo directed the company's "specialists" to devote their social media skills to a single target—the U.S. presidential election. The aims were explicit: "use any opportunity to criticize Hillary and the rest (except Sanders and Trump—we support them)."

The Internet Research Agency memo represented a distillation of a remarkable effort only alluded to in the company's name. Since its founding, the agency had devoted inordinate attention to studying the political climate in the United States, with special focus on issues that seemed to strike deep emotional chords with Americans—guns, Islamist terrorism, and race. By April 2014, the firm had set up a special department for what was referred to internally as the "Translator Project," an effort to infiltrate America's dominant social media platforms—YouTube, Facebook, Instagram, and Twitter. And unlike the costly stratagems of the Cold War— planting sleeper agents, recruiting and running Western turncoats, launching satellites and spy planes, underwriting proxy wars—the disruptive potential of the internet was vast and unbelievably cheap.

The project required an immersive understanding not only of the way Americans interacted online but also the fault lines of the country's political landscape. In June 2014, two of the company's employees boarded flights for the United States. Aleksandra Krylova and Anna Bogacheva spent the next three weeks crisscrossing America, making stops in at least nine states, including California, Texas, Michigan, Louisiana, and New York. Posing as tourists, the travelers studied the contours of the country's charged political atmosphere. The report they compiled upon their return was valuable enough that the agency sent another employee on a subsequent excursion, in November, to Atlanta, for a more focused, four-day mission whose purpose remains murky.

Even by tech start-up standards, the Internet Research Agency had an unusual business model. There were normal-seeming departments—graphics, data analysis, search-engine optimization—but no evident source of revenue. Nor were there any meetings with clients; the agency's "research" was all consumed in-house. And yet it had kept adding employees, hundreds of them, with an annual budget in the millions of dollars.

The firm's founder had no apparent background or expertise in online ventures. The incomplete accounts of his life indicate that Yevgeny Prigozhin was born in St. Petersburg in 1961 and appeared headed for athletic glory as a cross-country skier before being imprisoned in 1981 for crimes including robbery. After his release amid the Soviet Union's 1991 collapse, Prigozhin opened a hot dog stand, but the move that truly altered his fortunes in Russia came seven years later, with his purchase of a rickety vessel that he turned into a floating food establishment. New Island Restaurant, as it was called, attracted a different category of clientele—most notably another St. Petersburg native, Vladimir Putin. Prigozhin endeared himself to the future Russian president with an attention to detail and a willingness even as proprietor to engage in the more quotidian aspects of running a restaurant. Putin "saw how I built my business starting from a kiosk," Prigozhin said in an interview with a St. Petersburg magazine. "He saw how I was not above serving a plate."

The connection ultimately helped position Prigozhin for a series of lucrative catering contracts, supplying food to schools in St. Petersburg and the Russian military. (His bond with the increasingly powerful politician paid off in other ways, too: in 2002, Putin brought world leaders, including President George W. Bush, aboard the New Island for meals taken while drifting along the city's waterways.) Those deals led to even greater riches as Prigozhin branched out, earning billions from contracts that came to include providing soldiers for hire to guard oil wells in Syria. Prigozhin family social media accounts offered glimpses of sprawling estates, private airplanes, and Yevgeny's adult children cavorting on a luxury yacht. As he ascended into the ranks of the Russian oligarchs, the entrepreneur who so impressed Putin by personally busing dishes acquired the nickname "Putin's cook" and was soon handling other kinds of dirty work.

According to a top-secret NSA report issued more than a year after the U.S. election, the Internet Research Agency conducted information warfare along several fronts. One was referred to internally as "govnostrana"—which the NSA translated as "crap country"—and referred to attacks meant to damage a nation's reputation and sap its citizens' confidence. This effort involved the creation of two types of trolls (the term for online provocateurs), one focused on influencing public opinion by amassing loyal followings, and another that used teams of four or five people to churn out a mass volume of posts to overwhelm any competition from those posting contrary opinions.

In a February 2018, interview with *The Washington Post*, Marat Mindiyarov, a teacher by training, explained that he began working at the agency in late 2014 because it was close to home and he needed to make money during a stretch of unemployment. "I immediately felt like a character in the book *1984*," he recalled. The agency, he said, was "a place where you have to write that white is black and black is white. Your first feeling, when you ended up there, was that you were in some kind of factory that turned lying, telling untruths, into an industrial assembly line." Others hired at the Internet Research Agency described their assignments and the atmosphere there as similarly Orwellian. Lyudmila Savchuk, an activist and journalist who infiltrated the Internet Research Agency in 2015 as part of an investigation of the outfit, said, "Their top specialty was to slip political ideas inside a wrapping that was as human as possible."

Like many employees at the agency, Mindiyarov's main tasks involved producing pro-Putin propaganda for Russian-speaking audiences, particularly to drum up support for Russia actions in Ukraine. A former Soviet republic, Ukraine had since the fall of communism struggled to balance its close cultural and economic ties to Moscow against a desire to build a more independent and Western identity, developing democratic institutions and pursuing closer ties to Europe. That struggle had first taken on a frightening new dimension in 2004. During that year's presidential campaign, reform candidate Viktor Yushchenko had become badly disfigured after ingesting what authorities later determined was a near-lethal dose of the same dioxin used in Agent Orange, a poisoning that few seemed to doubt had been carried out by the Kremlin. Yushchenko survived only to lose the race to a rival politician, Viktor Yanukovych, who was seen as a puppet of Moscow.

Amid evidence of widespread electoral fraud, Ukraine had been convulsed by prodemocratic protests that came to be known as the Orange Revolution. It was one in a series of popular uprisings inside and outside Russia that unnerved Putin, who came to suspect clandestine interference by the United States. A revote ordered by the country's supreme court reversed the disputed outcome, handing the election to Yushchenko. Putin looked to the Russian military and intelligence services to undermine the democratically elected leader, and some of the strategies that did just that would be models for his later intervention in the American presidential contest.

Yushchenko was unable to fully stabilize the country, and after five years the pro-Moscow Yanukovych regained power. Drawing upon (and paying heavily for) the advice of an American consultant, Yanukovych lasted four years before an uprising removed him from office. Moscow responded to the disintegration of the government it backed by sending in Russian forces—the insignias stripped from their green uniforms—to begin dismembering the country. Russia annexed the Black Sea peninsula of Crimea and sent arms and "volunteers" from the ranks of its own military to bolster pro-Russia separatists in eastern Ukraine. Putin claimed that Russian speakers in Ukraine needed to be protected in the wake of a nationalist revolution, but much of the world saw the Russian invasion as a violation of international law and Ukraine's sovereignty.

When Russia's currency began tumbling under crippling sanctions imposed by the United States and the European Union, Mindiyarov was enlisted in a campaign to post glowing comments on Russian news sites and online magazines. "I was writing that everything was the opposite: how wonderful our life was, how wonderful it is that the ruble was strengthening . . . that sanctions were going to make us stronger and so on and so forth," he recalled.

Days at the agency were divided into two twelve-hour shifts, Mindiyarov said, with quotas requiring employees to deliver 135 website comments per shift, 200 characters apiece. "You come in and spend all day in a room with the blinds closed and twenty computers," he said, adding that he was paid 40,000 rubles, or about $800, a month after Russia's currency crashed in late 2014.

It was decent money at a time when Russia's economy had been crumpled by Western sanctions.

Mindiyarov said he wasn't involved in the "Translator Project," but knew there were other sections of the company aimed at an audience in the United States. An unnamed troll told an independent television station in Russia that Internet Research Agency employees were told to engage with Americans online and "get into an argument in order to inflame it, and rock the boat." The troll said their orders by 2016 were to specifically attack Clinton. "The main message is: aren't you tired, brother Americans, of the Clintons, how long have they been around?" the station quoted the troll as saying. To ensure that their use of English was seamless enough for online political debate, employees in St. Petersburg watched the Netflix drama *House of Cards,* a show about a corrupt American pol who rises to become president.[1]

As an English speaker, Mindiyarov had been approached to apply for the "Facebook department," where pay was twice as high. (The employees who emerged from that section for smoke breaks were younger, hipper, with newer phones and better haircuts.) But Mindiyarov was tripped up by the entrance test: his English wasn't strong enough to pass as native in the rapid-fire encounters of social media, where you had to be fluent even in American idioms. In response to the essay question "What do you think of Hillary Clinton?" he wrote that she seemed to have a strong chance to be the next U.S. president. It was unclear, he reflected later, whether the answer itself was disqualifying or merely the caliber of the English he used to articulate it.

THE WEEKEND OF THE WHITE HOUSE CORRESPONDENTS' ASSOCIAtion Dinner at the start of May was supposed to bring a momentary respite from the pressure of the presidential campaign. Many Washington insiders, including senior officials at the DNC, would be donning gowns or tuxedoes for the annual bash near Dupont Circle. The so-called nerd prom always attracts an influential if eclectic crowd—cabinet secretaries, cable news anchors, and a smattering of Hollywood stars. Five years earlier, with Trump in attendance, Obama had mercilessly taken full advantage of the chance to return fire on the reality TV star who had used his fame to fan a baseless conspiracy about the president's place of birth. The jokes mocked Trump's ego and boorishness, and as the audience roared, Obama's target was visibly annoyed, so much so that some would later wonder whether that moment of humiliation had motivated him to mount his own serious run for the White House.

Saturday night's event, Obama's last as president, was expected to have a more valedictory tone for the Democrats, but the prospect of another Democrat in the Oval Office come 2016 also provided reason to celebrate. Preparation for the pre-event parties was already under way on Friday when DNC executive director Amy Dacey learned for the first time around four P.M that the committee's network had been penetrated. Immediately she picked up the phone and dialed Michael Sussmann at Perkins Coie.

"We've had an intrusion," she told him. The contract IT team first thought they could contain the damage and keep the committee's systems up and running, she explained, but it seemed obvious they were overmatched, especially if the bureau's suspicions proved correct and the hackers were Russian. Finally Tamene and his team were getting it: the DNC was in big trouble. "They were mature enough to know that they couldn't fight the Red Army," Dacey said.

While still on the phone with Dacey, Sussmann fired off a text to Shawn Henry, a former top cyber official at the FBI who had left the bureau to take a top job with a Silicon Valley cybersecurity firm, CrowdStrike. With his shaved head and dark suits, Henry would never be mistaken for a member of the hacker crowd, but he had been on the front lines of previous election-cycle cyberattacks. In 2008, he was in charge of the FBI cyber division when Chinese officials hacked the computers of the presidential campaigns of John McCain and Barack Obama, looking to steal intelligence that would give them insight into how each man would steer U.S. foreign policy regarding China.

As the White House Correspondents' Dinner and a weekend of follow-up events got under way in Washington, Sussmann formally moved to enlist CrowdStrike to protect the DNC. The intrusion and the plan to counter it were to be kept secret from most DNC staff. "You can't let the attackers know you know they're there," Sussmann instructed Dacey. "You only have one chance to raise the drawbridge." If the hackers were tipped off, they could destroy logs and wipe their tracks or worse—steal piles of data while making a scorched-earth retreat. Most Democrats would party in blissful ignorance of the potential nightmare going on back at their national committee headquarters.

For the DNC, the timing was terrible. Half a dozen primaries had just ended, with Clinton taking a commanding lead, but the coming weeks formed a brutal final sprint, with potentially decisive contests in ten states, including Oregon, Indiana, and California. The Democratic National Convention, the committee's showcase event, was twelve weeks away. The party had picked Philadelphia for the 2016 event, and 50,000 people were expected to attend, including about 5,000 delegates, with millions more watching on television.[2] The DNC's staff was working around the clock planning for the general election. It was also an intense period of political maneuvering. Supporters of Bernie Sanders, the senator from Vermont, were already suspicious that a party apparatus held tightly in the Clinton family grip had sought to deny them the nomination, and the internal debates about candidates, strategies, fundraising, and campaigning were detailed in thousands of internal DNC emails, spreadsheets, and other files—all residing on a computer system that might have been thoroughly compromised by Russia.

"You had staff running full tilt, gathering research on the Republican front-runner, Donald Trump," Dacey recalled. "You had an intruder inside the system who was interested in that opposition research, and a convention to plan for. It was the perfect storm."

By Friday, May 6, CrowdStrike had worked with Tamene's team to install stronger threat detection system software. Immediately it turned up troubling evidence of two Russian hacking teams—the newly discovered, "noisier" intruder as well as the quieter one that the FBI had long warned the DNC was already inside.

U.S. intelligence agencies had for years been reluctant to publicly identify hacking groups by country out of concern that doing so would jeopardize sources as well as run the risk of complicating diplomatic relations. When they wanted to signal publicly that a nation-state was behind a cyber campaign, they adopted the euphemism "advanced persistent threat," or APT. The term had been coined in 2006 by an Air Force intelligence officer looking for a way to pass information to defense contractors getting hammered by a specific set of foreign hackers, without revealing the classified detail that the country behind the assault was China. It had then spread to cyber firms in the private sector and now was used throughout the industry. A Chinese cell known as People's Liberation Army Unit 61398 had carried off a string of thefts of intellectual property and commercial secrets from American and European defense contractors, and engaged in espionage against countries including the United States, Canada, India, and Israel as well as against the United Nations. They were so prolific and brazen that like graffiti artists, they sometimes left telltale signs of who they were, lines of computer code that sometimes included nicknames such as "Ugly Gorilla." Unit 61398 became known as APT1.

The teams rummaging through the DNC machines were known from previous intrusions on other targets and already had their designated monikers: APT 28 and APT 29. CrowdStrike had its own branding conventions using animals to represent various countries. Chinese groups were pandas, while the label for the Russian teams was based on a symbol associated with that country for centuries: the DNC hackers were dubbed Fancy Bear and Cozy Bear.

CrowdStrike was confident that Fancy Bear—the later arrival at the DNC—was an extension of the GRU. Cozy Bear's affiliation was less clear. CrowdStrike suspected that it was tied to Russia's domestic intelligence service, the FSB. But U.S. intelligence agencies had for years been certain that whatever the name—Cozy Bear, APT 29, or the Dukes—the team was an extension of Russia's foreign intelligence service, the SVR.

The original Cozy Bear DNC hack had taken place so long ago that log files were difficult to come by, but with what they could find, CrowdStrike investigators began to reconstruct the intruders' actions. The Cozy Bear crew had been disciplined and patient. They had compromised the DNC's email, chat, and internet phone systems. They had set up an automated mechanism so that every time a DNC employee got an email, a copy was forwarded to Cozy Bear. The unit stole passwords and log-ins for system administrators, but behaved cautiously with these keys, never gorging themselves on data they could access, always minimizing the chances of getting caught. The April newcomer, however, had no such manners—it foraged without restraint.

Investigators saw no indication the two teams were working together or were even aware of one another's presence, though they did seem to target separate areas of the network: Fancy Bear went after research files, at one point making off with a trove of opposition material on Trump, while Cozy Bear focused on emails and chats. The bottom line was clear: the committee and many of its internal secrets had been utterly exposed. Yet in calculating the damage, DNC leaders and investigators relied on an assumption that seemed reasonable: that while whatever information the Russians had taken might be mined by Kremlin analysts, it wouldn't be exposed publicly. Cozy Bear, after all, had attacked other nongovernmental organizations and defense contractors as well as foreign governments and political organizations. "This is a sophisticated foreign intelligence service with a lot of time, a lot of resources," Henry concluded. "There's no doubt this is a nation-state targeting a United States political system. What are candidates thinking about? What are they developing? What are their strategies? It's classic espionage." And classic espionage meant not revealing to the world what had been stolen, if for no other reason than it would jeopardize subsequent efforts.

Having taken measure of the breach, the experts began drafting a plan to kick the hackers out. Doing so would require rebuilding entire systems, resetting passwords, and picking a time to shut the network down. On an aggressive timeline, the operation could be carried out starting around May 20. But DNC leaders were reluctant to disrupt the network at a time when the party's nomination had not yet been secured, so a date was set for the three-day Memorial Day weekend, when it would be easier to take the system offline without cutting into work time or raising suspicions. Yet while Clinton's lead was commanding, Bernie Sanders was still in the race and drawing energetic crowds. The DNC leadership decided it was better to wait even longer and ensure that the contest was clinched. CrowdStrike held off, scheduling the work for mid-June.

During that stretch, the Russians amassed more emails that appeared to show DNC bias in favor of Clinton—not only old correspondence, but new messages written during the stretch when the DNC could have been in cleanup mode. And because the hacking was still being kept secret, nobody outside the inner circle had any sense that they should be more cautious than usual when sending emails and documents. On May 21, Mark Paustenbach, a committee communications official, wrote to a colleague, "Wondering if there's a good Bernie narrative for a story, which is that Bernie never ever had his act together, that his campaign was a mess." Other damaging emails had been written before CrowdStrike had even had enough time to conclude the attack was being carried out by Russians. For example, on May 5, a committee staffer emailed Paustenbach and Dacey suggesting a way to call voters' attention to Sanders's faith. "It might make no difference, but for KY and WVA can we get someone to ask his belief. Does he believe in a God," wrote Brad Marshall, the DNC's chief financial officer, who had lived and worked for years in Kentucky. "He had skated on saying he has a Jewish heritage. I think I read he is an atheist. . . . My Southern Baptist peeps would draw a big difference between a Jew and an atheist." This was way beyond the official DNC position, which was that the organization was there to help all Democratic candidates without favor toward any in particular. Marshall added in a second email that it came down to the "Jesus thing." Dacey replied: "AMEN." Dacey later insisted that she had meant her remark not as affirmation of the plan but to express understanding of the venting by her staff. Regardless of intention, it was a comment that would later add fuel to a fire.

On Monday, June 6, Clinton clinched the Democratic nomination, making history as the first woman in the United States ever to be selected to represent one of the two major parties in a presidential contest. Breathing easier that their secret had held for five weeks, the DNC leadership finally turned to the task of getting rid of the intruders. But as plans took shape for what the cyber team called "Remediation Weekend," officials knew that word of Russian penetration of a major party was unlikely to hold. Sussmann, the lawyer, recommended preempting this possibility by contacting a reporter at *The Washington Post*.

ON WEDNESDAY, JUNE 8, ELLEN NAKASHIMA WALKED A FEW BLOCKS from *The Washington Post*'s building on 13th and K Streets to Sussmann's office at Perkins Coie. In a sixth-floor conference room, she met Dacey for the first time. Henry was there, too, along with Sussmann. The three of them proceeded to tell her about the dramatic events of the preceding month. Dacey was no expert in cyberattacks, but she was intent on making sure that people knew what happened and understood the stakes.

On the evening of Friday, June 10, after the DNC staff had gone home, a crew of about ten committee technology workers, including Tamene, as well as a separate team of CrowdStrike investigators, arrived at committee headquarters for Remediation Weekend.

The crew worked Friday, Saturday, and Sunday, pausing for only brief stretches of sleep. The entire DNC network was shut down. To keep the mission secret, the committee had told employees the unusual arrangement was required for a system upgrade. The process was tedious and repetitive. The committee had collected hundreds of laptops from staffers—some of whom fretted that this meant their jobs were at risk because Clinton was taking over the party leadership. The remediation team piled the devices in stacks, side by side, on a large rectangular table in a first-floor conference room. Each laptop had to be reimaged, a manual process consisting of wiping the hard drives clean, reinstalling the operating system, and clicking through a series of tiresome fields to select the correct language, time zone, etc. Meanwhile, a parallel team backed up terabytes of committee data to a clean collection of servers. Every laptop, once reimaged, had to have its data restored.

By Sunday night, the project was finished, and Dacey, who came into the office to check on the work, breathed a sigh of relief. In appreciation of the magnitude of the operation, one of Crowd-Strike's founders, Dmitri Alperovitch, a Russian-born expert with degrees from Georgia Tech, showed up to take his exhausted team to dinner at a Brazilian steakhouse. Monday morning, the network was back online, the laptops, with new software running to detect any return of the Russians, redistributed.

DNC officials had shared their account with Nakashima on the condition that it not be published until the committee's networks had been secured. She began composing a draft of the article and made plans with editors to put the story online on Monday, June 13. But on Sunday the twelfth, as the DNC team was completing its scrub, devastating news broke in Florida: Omar Mateen, a twenty-nine-year-old security guard, had opened fire in the packed Pulse nightclub in Orlando, killing forty-nine people and wounding fifty-three others—then the deadliest mass shooting by a single gunman in U.S. history.

The *Post* put the hacking story off for an extra day. At 11:30 A.M. on Tuesday it appeared atop the paper's website, opening, "Russian government hackers penetrated the computer network of the Democratic National Committee and gained access to the entire database of opposition research on GOP presidential candidate Donald Trump."[3] The article emphasized that the hackers had been expelled from the DNC's systems over the preceding weekend and quoted a range of officials and experts casting the intrusion as a classic case of cyber espionage. Moscow, it was agreed, was far more likely to hoard the stolen material and mine it for insights that could provide critical leverage in global affairs. The prospect that Russia would wage an unprecedented campaign of information warfare—sowing doubt about the democratic process, damaging the candidacy of Hillary Clinton, and ultimately seeking to help elect Donald Trump—was beyond imagining at that moment. Kremlin spokesman Dmitry Peskov quickly denied any Russian involvement.

On June 15, within twenty-four hours of the *Post*'s story, the website The Smoking Gun posted a story saying it had been contacted by an "online vandal" using the name Guccifer 2.0. Elaborating on a blog site, he claimed to be flattered by accounts depicting the operation as "sophisticated," insisting that "in fact, it was easy, very easy." He insisted he was not Russian, but a Romanian who had chosen his moniker partly to honor his hacking predecessor Guccifer but also because he loved the Gucci brand. "I'm a hacker, manager, philosopher, woman lover," he proclaimed. But in online correspondence with journalists, his persona seemed to crack. Posed questions in Romanian by the journalist Lorenzo Franceschi-Bicchierai, writing for the online tech publication Motherboard, Guccifer 2.0's responses came back in fractured syntax that seemed to betray a reliance on Google Translate. In subsequent exchanges, his online personality seemed to shift, suggesting more than one hand was operating the Guccifer 2.0 persona.

To establish his credentials, he passed along a collection of pilfered DNC documents. The files included internal memos and a list of donors that catalogued six-figure contributions to the party from, among others, movie star Morgan Freeman, director Steven Spielberg, and Hollywood executive Jeffrey Katzenberg. Guccifer 2.0 referred those interested to the DCLeaks website that GRU hackers had set up in April and where even more DNC material was now placed. The document that got the most attention was a 237-page collection of DNC opposition research.

Marked *confidential,* "Donald Trump Report" was a sprawling catalogue of Trump's perceived political vulnerabilities, recounting his privileged upbringing, his lawsuits and bankruptcies, affairs and broken marriages, vacillating party affiliations, crass comments about women, fierce verbal attacks on Muslims, penchant for falsehoods, and alleged racism. "One thing is clear about Donald Trump," read the file's first sentence. "There is only one person he has ever looked out for and that's himself."

To Democrats, all of this added up to a portrait of an ideal opponent, someone who by any conventional standard had to be considered unelectable. But damning as it was, the material laid out in the document was, for the most part, already widely known. If Democrats were hoarding any bombshells, they weren't listed in the pages of its "Donald Trump Report."

Guccifer 2.0's message labored to divert suspicion from Russia. "Hi. This is Guccifer 2.0 and this is me who hacked Democratic National Committee," it said. The writer offered a brief account of his or her exploit, explaining that it involved breaching "mail boxes of a number of Democrats" and then exploiting the information to get "into committee servers." The hacker claimed to have been inside the DNC network for more than a year and stolen "thousands of files and mails."

In reality, Guccifer 2.0 was a GRU creation, an online persona operated by the same hackers who had rampaged through the DNC and DCCC networks. On June 22, one week after Guccifer 2.0's debut, the Russian hackers behind this online puppet got a message from an eager ally in their unfolding operation against Clinton: WikiLeaks. The organization, determined not to watch from the sidelines, urged Guccifer 2.0 to send "any new material here for us to review and it will have a much higher impact than what you are doing." Weeks later, WikiLeaks was pleading again for access to the trove, saying, "if you have anything Hillary related we want it," noting that the Democratic convention was rapidly approaching and unless the digital saboteurs intervened "she will solidify Bernie supporters behind her."

THE UNITED STATES AND WIKILEAKS HAD BEEN IN A STATE OF OPEN hostility since the group in 2010 published half a million military records from Afghanistan and Iraq and approximately 250,000 diplomatic cables. That release triggered a criminal investigation of WikiLeaks and indirectly led its Australian founder, Julian Assange, to seek asylum in Ecuador's embassy in London. Assange had been accused of sexual assault in Sweden and said he feared that if he was extradited there to face charges, he would be ultimately transferred to the United States, regardless of the outcome of any court proceeding in Sweden.

Yet while WikiLeaks professed to be concerned only with demolishing the wall of secrecy maintained by the powerful, its publication of confidential information—couched as a moral imperative—has been consistently amoral, with no concern for how such revelations might damage those whose names turned up in the material. Without notable regret they have publicly released a wealth of personal data belonging to people who have little to do with their larger political causes, including credit card numbers, medical records, and Social Security numbers.

Assange, who has hosted a talk show on RT, the Kremlin's propaganda channel, has made no effort to hide his own disdain for the United States or his relish at the prospect of its downfall. With "a faint smile," he told *The New Yorker* in 2017 that the American empire might finally be collapsing. Although Assange denied that Russia was his source for the DNC emails, he has never much cared how he obtains what he publishes. "If it's true information, we don't care where it comes from," he once said. "Let people fight with the truth, and when the bodies are cleared there will be bullets of truth everywhere."[4] That disregard for sources was matched by an increasing affection for authoritarian leadership (including his own of WikiLeaks) that would eventually place him firmly in the pro-Trump camp.

After a series of failed attempts to transfer the stolen documents to WikiLeaks, Guccifer 2.0 sent the organization an email with an attachment—"wk dnc link1.txt.gpg." It arrived on July 14 with instructions on how to unzip the trove. Four days later, WikiLeaks responded that it had accessed "the 1 Gb or so archive" and would begin publishing "this week."

CHAPTER 3

MOTHS TO THE FLAME

AVOIDING THE MAIN LOBBY AS A SECURITY PRECAUTION, DONALD Trump was escorted through a loading dock, into a freight elevator, and up to *The Washington Post* publisher's suite on the ninth floor. As he made his way into a March 2016 meeting with the paper's editorial board, the Republican candidate walked past historic plates of the *Post*'s front pages lining the walls. On them were headlines that marked Hitler's rise to power, America's plunge into World War II, and the U.S. blockade of Cuba as the Soviet Union sought to install nuclear weapons a hundred miles off the coast of the United States.

Trump had from the beginning faced profound doubts about his qualifications to handle such harrowing events. Even within his own party, there was concern that his disposition and ideas—backing torture, praising Putin, criticizing European allies—were themselves threats to international stability. As Trump took a seat in the *Post* conference room, overlooking Franklin Square Park in downtown Washington, he had two objectives: to quiet these doubts and introduce a credible foreign policy team.

The paper's opinion writers had been told in advance by the

campaign that if asked about foreign policy advisers, Trump would make news. When the question came at the outset of the interview, Trump feigned ignorance about this bit of stagecraft.

"Well, I hadn't thought of doing it, but if you want I can give you some of the names," he said, turning to a piece of paper for this purpose. He proceeded to read a list that raised not a glimmer of recognition among the writers, some of whom had covered foreign policy for decades. Several participants would say later that Trump himself seemed unfamiliar with the individuals he introduced.

Of the five names that Trump listed, only one would actually end up working in his administration: retired lieutenant general Keith Kellogg, who had commanded the Army's 82nd Airborne Division and held a senior job with the Coalition Provisional Authority in postwar Iraq, would end up chief of staff on the National Security Council. Two others had fleeting associations with the campaign and résumés that raised eyebrows: Walid Phares had ties dating to the 1980s to militant Christian groups in Lebanon and anti-Islamic views; Joseph Schmitz had resigned as inspector general at the Pentagon amid allegations of obstructing investigations of political appointees.

The final names on Trump's list were virtual unknowns.

"Carter Page, PhD," Trump said, glancing at his list. "George Papadopoulos, he's an energy and oil consultant, excellent guy."

In fact, Page was a familiar figure to only one corner of the national security establishment in Washington: the FBI agents in charge of investigating Russian espionage.

THAT TRUMP FELT COMPELLED TO PRESENT THIS ROSTER WAS A reflection of the pressure brought by his surging candidacy but also the extraordinary isolation of his campaign. By March, Trump could no longer be dismissed as a long shot or a joke. He had stockpiled delegates with convincing victories in a string of primaries, and vanquished all but two opponents in the Republican field: U.S. senators Marco Rubio of Florida and Ted Cruz of Texas.

Both senators seemed incredulous to find themselves losing to a reality television star. "I will do whatever it takes, I will campaign as hard as it takes, I will stay in this race as long as it takes," Rubio told a crowd of seven thousand supporters in Atlanta on February 27, 2016. "A con artist will never get control of this party." Two weeks later, after Trump claimed a massive haul of delegates on Super Tuesday and captured Rubio's home state of Florida, the chastened senator was done. Cruz soon bowed in defeat as well.

Yet many in Washington were not so ready to acquiesce. Candidates with momentum like Trump's ordinarily exert a gravitational pull on the powerful in their parties, attracting donors and would-be advisers eager to position themselves for influence with, or jobs in, a new administration. With Trump, however, the inverse was happening: the closer he got to securing the nomination, the more determined many of the most experienced and respected policymakers affiliated with his party were to reject him.

On March 2, as the dust from Super Tuesday was still settling, a collection of 122 self-described GOP national security leaders published a letter online vowing "to prevent the election of someone so utterly unfitted to the office." The missive was signed by a roster of Republican loyalists, some of whom had held senior positions in government, others regarded as influential advisers and columnists. The petition was drafted by Eliot Cohen, who had served as counselor to Secretary of State Condoleezza Rice in the George W. Bush administration. Other signatories included Michael Chertoff, former head of Homeland Security, and Dov Zakheim, who had held senior positions at the Pentagon.

The letter excoriated Trump, saying that his views were so "unmoored" that he veered from "isolationism to military adventurism within the space of one sentence." His support for resuming the use of torture on terror suspects was "inexcusable," and his "hateful, anti-Muslim rhetoric" needlessly inflamed tensions across the world. The letter noted that his "admiration for foreign dictators such as Vladimir Putin is unacceptable for the leader of the world's greatest democracy." It concluded with a stab at his supposed business acumen. "Not all lethal conflicts can be resolved as a real estate deal might," the letter said. "There is no recourse to bankruptcy court in international affairs."

The next day, Mitt Romney, the 2012 Republican nominee, gave a scathing speech opposing Trump's candidacy, declaring that his foreign policy was "alarming allies and fueling the enmity of our enemies." Trump, Romney said, was a "phony, a fraud," a candidate "playing the American people for suckers." Two weeks later, party insiders gathered at the Army and Navy Club in downtown Washington to devise plans to block Trump's nomination and potentially launch a third-party bid. The "never Trump" movement would intensify in the coming months, ultimately to no avail.

Trump's decision to announce his team of foreign policy advisers on March 21 at the *Post* was meant to arrest the intraparty revolt. But the anonymity of those included on his roster only reinforced the impression of a campaign bereft of experience or expertise. The résumés of Page and Papadopoulos were laughably thin.

Public records showed that Papadopoulos had graduated from DePaul University in Chicago in 2009, lived in London for a stretch, and then worked as a research assistant for the Hudson Institute, a conservative think tank in Washington. His few writings, including several op-eds for Israeli news sites, focused on Greece, Cyprus, and Israeli natural gas holdings in the eastern Mediterranean. On his personal LinkedIn page, he highlighted his role as a representative to the 2012 Geneva International Model United Nations, a mock exercise in global diplomacy for high school and college students. It was the sort of credential one might include on an application for an internship, not present as a qualification to advise a potential president. (The UN claim may also have been dishonest—others at the Geneva event that year have no record or recollection of him attending.)

Page had more seemingly legitimate experience. A 1993 U.S. Naval Academy graduate, he had worked at Merrill Lynch before starting his own company, Global Energy Capital, in Manhattan. He claimed affiliations with respected think tanks including the Council on Foreign Relations, a New York–based organization that counted a dozen former secretaries of state among its members.

Hidden at the time, apparently even to Trump, were more disconcerting aspects of his background. Just days before the candidate's meeting with the *Post*'s editorial board, Page had been questioned by the FBI—not for the first time—about his ties to Russian intelligence. In fact, by that point the bureau had been tracking Page, intermittently, for at least three years in connection with an FBI probe of a Russian spy ring in New York.

Page was aware of the bureau's interest. Back in June 2013, he had met with FBI agents at New York's Plaza hotel (once owned by Donald Trump until indebtedness forced him to sell), insisting that his contacts with Russians were related to "my research on international political economy" and that any documents he had provided related to the energy business. He made it clear that he was doing the FBI a favor by assisting them voluntarily because, he said helpfully, "it seemed to me that the resources of the U.S. government might be better allocated toward addressing real national security threats, particularly given the recent Boston Marathon bombing."

As part of their surveillance, the bureau had lengthy transcripts of Kremlin agents describing their efforts to recruit and manipulate Page. Portions of those transcripts appeared in a 2015 com-

plaint filed in the Southern District of New York—referring to
Page anonymously as "Male-1." The Russians' conversation had
been captured by a listening device the FBI had planted on a binder
the Kremlin operatives had unwittingly carried into a conference
room. They spoke of Page with undisguised scorn, frustrated and
amused by his seemingly clueless behavior.

In his encounters with Page, Victor Podobnyy had cast himself
as someone who could help the American pursue energy-related
business deals in Russia. In reality, Podobnyy was an SVR agent
posing as an attaché at the Russian mission to the United Nations.
He marveled at Page's affection for Russia and said of his American
mark: "I think he is an idiot and forgot who I am. Plus he writes to
me in Russian [to] practice the language. He flies to Moscow more
often than I do."

Page later told the FBI that he had met Podobnyy in January
2013 at an energy industry conference in New York. The Russians
regarded Page's interest in oil riches as a vulnerability. Page "got
hooked on Gazprom [the largely state-owned oil and gas company]
thinking that if they have a project he could be rise up," Podobnyy
explained in the exchanges intercepted by the FBI, referring to the
Russian energy giant. "It's obvious that he wants to earn lots of
money," he concluded with a laugh.

On another recording, a different Kremlin operative, Igor
Sporyshev, who was working undercover as a trade representative
of the Russian Federation in New York, complained that the cha-
rade they were running would eventually mean that he would have
to get involved with the bumbling American. Podobnyy brushed
him off, saying that he would continue to "feed him empty promises" and eventually cut Page loose. "You get the documents from
him and tell him to go fuck himself."

Page did provide documents to the Russians, though he later
claimed to reporters that he had shared only "basic immaterial

information and publicly available research." He added that he furnished "nothing more than a few samples from the far more detailed lectures I was preparing at the time for the students in my Spring 2013 semester, 'Energy and the World: Politics, Markets, and Technology' course which I taught on Saturdays at New York University." (Page, an adjunct professor at NYU, had twice failed to defend his PhD thesis at the University of London before finally earning his doctorate.)[1]

In the end, the FBI probe had limited results. The two Russians caught speaking about Page were protected from prosecution in the United States by diplomatic immunity. A third, however, was under what intelligence agencies call "non-official cover"—that is, using phony private sector credentials rather than working out of an embassy or consulate. Evgeny Buryakov, who posed as an executive at Vnesheconombank, a Russian development bank, was arrested and convicted of espionage as part of a broader case in which Page was only a small player. Buryakov served a thirty-month sentence before he was released in 2017 and deported to Russia. Page was never accused of wrongdoing, in part because the bureau was never sure that he knew he was interacting with Russian spies.

His brush with the FBI did nothing to diminish his enthusiasm for Russia. In the ensuing years Page continued to travel to Moscow, pursue business deals there, and publish articles and blog posts that read like Kremlin talking points. In one remarkable 2014 piece for *Global Policy*—a scholarly publication of Durham University in England—Page praised a particularly controversial Putin ally. Igor Sechin was Russia's former deputy prime minister and chairman of the Rosneft energy conglomerate. He was also one of the oligarchs sanctioned by the United States to punish Russia for its intervention in Ukraine. Page wrote of Sechin with reverence, saying that he had "done more to advance U.S.-Russian relations than any individual in or out of government from either side of the

Atlantic over the past decade." A year later, Page likened the rationale behind the American sanctions to one of the nation's darkest
legacies, equating the effort to dissuade Moscow from meddling
in other countries to an 1850 guide on how to produce "the ideal
slave."

In December 2015, Page sought a volunteer position with the
Trump campaign by reaching out to Ed Cox, the son-in-law of
former president Richard Nixon and the chairman of the New
York State Republican Party. Cox, who was directing would-be
volunteers to many of the GOP candidates, helped Page get an appointment with Trump campaign manager Corey Lewandowski.
When Page arrived at Trump Tower, he encountered an overwhelmed political operative who interrupted their conversation repeatedly to answer calls on a pair of incessantly ringing cell phones.
Lewandowski took Page next door to the office of Sam Clovis, a
conservative talk radio host from Iowa serving as the Trump campaign cochairman.

After a cursory background check that involved little more than
a Google search, Clovis added Page's name on the list of advisers
that Trump carried into his meeting with the *Post*.

Former colleagues, business associates, and teachers struggled to
make sense of Page's new profile. His adviser at the Naval Academy
recalled a student who was a striver, opportunistic but eccentric. "I
always found him a little out of place," said Stephen E. Frantzich,[2] a
political science and history professor who supervised Page's work
on a research paper. Page was a "geeky kid, a good writer and hard
worker" who displayed no particular interest in Russia. Yet Page
claimed in an interview decades later that he was specifically drawn
to the academy after seeing two officers in naval uniforms standing in the background on television coverage of U.S.-Russia arms
negotiations in the 1980s. Page, then a teenager in Poughkeepsie,
New York, said, "I came in off the street on my skateboard and I

watched the summit meetings between Reagan and Gorbachev." The naval uniforms made him think "that's interesting, maybe that's some kind of way of getting involved and helping out."

After five years in the Navy, which included an assignment as an intelligence officer for a UN peacekeeping mission in Morocco, Page devoted himself to chasing riches. In 2004, he moved to Moscow for the position with Merrill Lynch. The title he was given, vice president, sounded more glamorous than the tasks it entailed— planning meetings and drafting papers for the firm's principals. But Page later depicted himself as a heavy hitter, setting up transactions involving billions of dollars and serving as an adviser to Gazprom. Sergey Aleksashenko, chairman of Merrill Lynch Russia at the time, described Page's claims as outlandish and said that he reacted to hearing Trump had named him an adviser by "laughing, because he [Page] was never ready to discuss foreign policy."

Page left Moscow in 2007 and made his way to New York, where he continued to embellish his Moscow business record and social life, even claiming to have had a long-term romance with a Bolshoi ballerina. His company, Global Energy Capital, had a website decorated with stock photos of oil derricks and the Manhattan skyline, but listed no employees or clients. In interviews, Page spoke of working in a midtown Manhattan skyscraper that shared an atrium with Trump Tower. In reality, the office he occupied was a windowless room rented by the hour in a corporate coworking space.

For Page, the stars suddenly aligned when a billionaire businessman declared he was pursuing the nation's highest office with no standing entourage of advisers. Trump's views of foreign policy were at best a work in progress, but on one subject he spoke with a clarity that Page found intoxicating: Trump was more overtly enamored of Russia than any candidate to compete for one of the major American political party nominations in a century.

"I believe I would get along very nicely with Putin," Trump said in July 2015, shortly after announcing his run. He was speaking at a forum in Las Vegas when a Russian graduate student in the audience—a woman named Maria Butina, who would be charged two years later as an unregistered Russian agent who had infiltrated conservative circles—asked how he would alter the U.S. relationship with Moscow. "I don't think you'd need the sanctions," Trump said. "I think we would get along very, very well."

AS THE ELECTION APPROACHED, THE TRUMP CAMPAIGN ATTRACTED figures who were more recognizable to party veterans, though regarded as damaged or discarded by the establishment. Veteran campaign strategist Paul J. Manafort and retired three-star U.S. Army general Michael Flynn were both from middle-class New England backgrounds—Manafort's family had started a construction company in Connecticut and Flynn was one of nine children, the son of a retired Army sergeant and a schoolteacher, on the shore of Rhode Island. Each had ascended the ranks of core American institutions, Manafort the Republican Party and Flynn the U.S. military. But neither had ended those associations entirely on his terms. Manafort had drifted to the margins of Republican politics after the 1990s and focused on chasing riches overseas. Flynn had been forced to resign the last position of his military career, head of the Defense Intelligence Agency, over concerns with his leadership failings. The Trump campaign offered an unexpected shot at redemption, a chance to restore their reputations and position themselves either for a return to power or profit in the private sector.

Manafort and Flynn had one other thing in common: a charitable view of Russia's role in the world and a willingness to take money from sources close to the Kremlin.

This approach had already made Manafort rich. After decades at the center of American politics—serving as a senior adviser to the presidential campaigns of Gerald Ford, Ronald Reagan, George H. W. Bush, and Robert Dole—he had turned his attentions to a surging demand for lobbying firepower among despotic regimes overseas. His qualms were minimal and his qualifications substantial: his decades in Republican back rooms had given him a deeply embedded network of government contacts. His experience running campaigns and his intricate knowledge of modern polling and messaging positioned him as the go-to consultant for autocrats willing to pay huge sums for skills that would help them fend off any rivals but also apply a veneer of American-style democracy in otherwise rigged contests.

The foreign clients Manafort represented had risen or clung to power through corruption and bloodshed. Among them were Philippines president Ferdinand Marcos and Angolan guerrilla leader Jonas Savimbi. Manafort's firm took so much money from sources in those countries and others, including Nigeria and Kenya, that he was referenced repeatedly in a scathing 1992 report called "The Torturer's Lobby" by the Center for Public Integrity, a nonprofit investigative organization.

Manafort moved into an even more lucrative echelon through his work in Ukraine on behalf of a candidate and party with extensive ties to Putin. After the revote that put Yushchenko into office, his Moscow-backed opponent, Yanukovych, spent the next six years plotting to claim the presidency he'd narrowly lost with the help of a new ally: Manafort. The price tag was staggering and largely hidden from public view. For his services recasting Yanukovych and his Party of Regions (deceivingly) as pro-Europe reformers, Manafort and his company collected millions, much of it laundered through a web of overseas accounts. Manafort would later disclose in one filing that his firm had pocketed more than $17 million in a single two-year stretch, but that was only a part of the payout—*The New York Times* in 2017 obtained secret ledgers kept by the Party of Regions showing an additional $12.7 million in undisclosed cash payments to Manafort's company from 2007 to 2012, meaning that from this one client Manafort had brought in nearly $30 million.

Over a decade, Manafort and his subordinates hid vast sums from U.S. authorities through a dizzying array of front companies, avoiding taxes by routing payments from secret accounts in Cyprus—essentially wiring money to pay bills in the United States without ever reporting the income. From 2008 to 2014, according to a Justice Department indictment, Manafort channeled $12 million from overseas accounts into the United States through a titanic shopping spree: $520,440 to a Beverly Hills clothing store, $163,705 for Range Rovers, $623,910 for antiques, $934,350 for rugs. And those were just the incidentals: Manafort shifted millions more from Cyprus to assorted trusts and limited liability corporations to buy homes in Manhattan, Brooklyn, and the Washington, D.C., suburbs.

Manafort used his Ukraine connections to pursue lucrative deals with oligarchs. Among them was the $18 million sale of Ukraine's cable television assets to a partnership assembled by Manafort and Oleg Deripaska, a Russian oligarch close to Putin, around 2008. Manafort denied taking illicit payments and depicted his consulting work in Ukraine as part of an honest effort to democratize the country and elevate its prospects of joining the European Union. Yet after Yanukovych prevailed in his 2010 bid to be Ukraine's new president, the evidence of his brutal rule and lavish lifestyle at the expense of ordinary Ukrainians was hard to conceal. If Manafort was uncomfortable working for a leader who had little love for democracy or human rights and a visible affection for Putin, it did not show.

Three years after taking office, Yanukovych—under intense

pressure from the Kremlin—rejected an agreement that would have moved Ukraine closer to membership in the EU, which many in the country wanted. Instead, he agreed to take a cash infusion from Russia and edge away from Europe in favor of lashing Ukraine's political and economic fortunes to Moscow. The nation erupted in a new wave of unrest: protests in the capital city of Kiev spread across other parts of the country and degenerated into riots, clashes with police left dozens of people dead, and government authority teetered on collapse. Fearing for his life, Yanukovych fled the country in February 2014 for the safety he could find only in his true base of support: Russia.

The crisis in Ukraine, such a distant consideration for most Americans, was in hindsight intricately connected to what happened in 2016 in the United States.

For all his projections of strength and security, Putin is deeply insecure about his hold on power, and particularly anxious that a revolt like that in Ukraine could bring his own end. A senior U.S. official who served in Moscow during the Obama and Trump administrations and had contacts in the Kremlin said that Putin's anxiety is profound and macabre. After the deposed Libyan dictator Muammar Gaddafi was dragged from a culvert in 2011 by an angry mob, sodomized with a bayonet, and shot, Putin watched footage of the gruesome incident repeatedly. It was a graphic demonstration of the outcome he most feared, and one that he was convinced had been set in motion by the U.S. intervention in Libya and could occur, if he were not vigilant, in Moscow.

The 2014 unrest in Ukraine intensified Putin's paranoia, and he again suspected manipulation by Washington, particularly after seeing the State Department's top official on Russia, Victoria Nuland, handing out sandwiches to protesters.

Russia retaliated by releasing an intercepted phone call between Nuland and the U.S. ambassador to Ukraine in which she expressed irritation with Europe's slow response to the unfolding crisis. "Fuck the EU!" she said. The release caused minor diplomatic embarrassment but had a greater significance. Spy agencies steal such signals routinely but usually guard them jealously to ensure that the victim doesn't discover the breach. In this case, the Kremlin had taken a piece of intelligence and "weaponized" it—something it would undertake on a far grander scale two years later.

The ignominious departure of Yanukovych and the collapse of his political party cut off a massive flow of cash to Manafort. That was only the beginning of his problems. The FBI had begun probing payments surrounding his work in Ukraine, and agents interviewed him twice, first in 2013 and again a year later. The scrutiny made it risky for Manafort, his revenue plummeting, to reach for the money he'd stashed overseas.

Manafort's dealings with Russians also began to catch up to him. Deripaska, the oligarch he'd worked with on the $18 million cable television transaction, became convinced that he'd been cheated by Manafort and began a years-long campaign in courts to get his investment back. Deripaska sought entry into the United States but, fortunately for Manafort, was denied a visa because of his alleged links to organized crime.

Despite hemorrhaging funds, Manafort was unable or unwilling to stanch spending on a lifestyle that by now included homes from the Hamptons to Palm Beach, vacations in the South of France, a horse farm in Florida, and projects for his filmmaker daughter. Instead, he turned to even more legally dubious financial maneuvers, taking out multimillion-dollar loans on properties he'd acquired with money he'd never reported as income. A later criminal indictment accused him of submitting doctored financial statements, diverting loan proceeds, and lying about credit card bills as part of a sprawling scheme to dupe banks.

His personal life was also spiraling out of control. In late 2014, he was caught cheating on his wife of thirty-six years, according to a trove of text messages exchanged by his daughters that was stolen by hackers (possibly Ukrainians seeking revenge on Manafort) and posted online. In the messages his daughters—Andrea, who was then twenty-nine, and Jessica, then thirty-three—spoke of their father with a mix of sympathy and revulsion. Andrea hinted at the financial crunch her father was facing, complaining that he was "suddenly extremely cheap" in conversations about her wedding budget and strapped by a "tight cash flow." They expressed admiration for his accomplishments but described him as manipulative and cravenly dishonest. In the most damning passage, Andrea bluntly acknowledged the moral stain of the Manafort fortune. "Don't fool yourself," she wrote to her sister. "The money we have is blood money."

The affair appeared to add to the financial strain. According to the texts, he had rented a $9,000-a-month apartment as well as a home on Long Island for his new girlfriend, a woman thirty years younger than him. When the affair was exposed, Manafort agreed to couples counseling. After that failed, he checked into a therapy facility in Arizona, where he often sobbed during daily ten-minute phone calls home.

These were the circumstances of the man Trump would turn to in 2016 to lead his campaign.

EARLY THAT YEAR, MANAFORT SAT DOWN AT A COMPUTER AND began typing a memo to pitch his services. "I am not looking for a paid job," he wrote, aware of Trump's miserly impulses and volatile tendencies toward paid subordinates. The two-page missive, which he delivered through a mutual acquaintance, recited his experience running conventions and wrangling GOP delegates presenting himself as someone who could head off the threat of a convention coup. He also cast himself, remarkably, as a Washington outsider, an exile of the swamp Trump had vowed to drain. Finally he noted that he lived in Trump Tower—unit 43G—and claimed that he had once helped Trump quiet the skies over his Mar-a-Lago estate in Florida by lobbying the Federal Aviation Administration.

Former colleagues, mindful of the problematic sources of Manafort's riches, warned him of the scrutiny that would accompany a return to the political spotlight. But Manafort was unswayed—Trump was his kind of guy. On March 29, eight days after Trump's meeting with the *Post* editorial board, Manafort was brought on board.

MANAFORT JOINED AN OPERATION SO BEREFT OF FOREIGN POLICY expertise that one campaign official summarized the search criteria in stark terms: "Anyone who came to us with a pulse, a résumé, and seemed legit would be welcomed."

Only one early Trump backer exceeded those expectations, bringing with him the kind of credentials that would ordinarily have been welcomed by any campaign. Michael Flynn's patriotism, sacrifice, and distinguished service were beyond dispute. In the fifteen years since the September 11 attacks, he had spent almost as much time deployed to Afghanistan and Iraq as he had spent with his family in the United States. The Army traditionally favors officers who rise up by leading combat units, but Flynn had climbed the service's intelligence ranks. His ascent to three-star general was a reflection of his effectiveness as an officer, but also the realities of a new era of conflict. Against amorphous terror and insurgent networks, the ability to process streams of data from drones, captured militants, and their laptops and cell phones was often more important than overwhelming force.

Flynn helped design a lethally effective combination of these ingredients. In concert with General Stanley A. McChrystal in both Iraq and Afghanistan, he worked to compress a nightly cycle of raids by commando units followed by rapid exploitation of information gathered at the scene. The data was used to generate targets for the next round of raids, often within hours, a tempo that proved devastating to insurgents. The approach helped pull the war effort out of a tailspin at a time when Al-Qaeda's franchise in Iraq had driven the country into a sectarian bloodbath. In 2006, forces under McChrystal and Flynn decapitated the Al-Qaeda network, tracking its leader in Iraq, Abu Musab al-Zarqawi, to a village north of Baghdad and ending his insurgent career under a pair of 500-pound bombs.

When McChrystal was given command of the war in Afghanistan in 2009, he again turned to Flynn as his top intelligence officer. While deployed, Flynn co-authored a twenty-six-page article that delivered a blistering critique of America's cluelessness about the cultural and religious complexities of the conflict. Titled "Fixing Intel," it was published by the Center for a New American Security, a Washington think tank. Flynn's report was seen by some as self-serving but it burnished his reputation as an unconventional thinker.

When McChrystal's career was derailed over a troubling profile in *Rolling Stone* magazine, Flynn returned to Washington to take what many regard as the top job in his specialized field, running the Defense Intelligence Agency, a spy service that caters to the needs of the military from a base across the Potomac River from Reagan National Airport.

Then it was Flynn's turn to implode.

He'd arrived at DIA with ambitious plans to reorganize the agency around geographically focused centers and to upgrade its overseas collection capabilities to more closely resemble those of the CIA—in effect, to raise DIA above its reputation as a backwater among U.S. intelligence agencies.[3] He warned any who resisted his agenda that he would "move them or fire them."

But Flynn, who had helped devise the formula for subduing insurgent organizations, seemed overwhelmed by the complexity of the organization he now led. From the outset, the hallway murmurs were that he was struggling to adapt outside the supportive structure of McChrystal's combat apparatus, where orders were executed with the snap of a salute and the mission was both clear and all-consuming. The DIA, by contrast, was a sprawling agency of 17,000 employees, half of them civilians. Its mission was diffuse, its structure bureaucratic, and its rhythms nothing like the raid-exploit-raid repetition Flynn knew on the front lines. Subordinates left meetings confused by his instructions; members of Congress were alarmed by his inability to answer basic questions about the agency's budget. Flynn made so many unfounded pronouncements—about the Islamic State, North Korea, and other subjects—that aides coined a term for his puzzling assertions: "Flynn facts." Senior aides began warning the director of national intelligence, James Clapper Jr., a gruff Air Force general who had spent half a century around U.S. spy agencies and was now in charge of all of them, as well as the Pentagon's top intelligence official, Michael Vickers, that Flynn's disruptive approach was damaging morale.

As the months passed, Flynn's views about Islam appeared to harden, and he became fixated on Iran. He pushed analysts to scour intelligence streams for hidden evidence of Iran's ties to Al-Qaeda, connections that most experts considered minimal, and search for proof of Iranian involvement in a variety of events where there seemed to be none, including the 2012 attacks on U.S. compounds in Benghazi, Libya. No matter the evidence, Flynn kept pressing, always seemingly convinced of connections to the country he considered America's greatest enemy.

The DIA chief had an inexplicable admiration for another American adversary, however. In June 2013, Flynn traveled to Moscow for meetings with General Igor Sergun, his counterpart at the GRU, the military intelligence agency that three years later would help disrupt the U.S. election. Prior DIA chiefs had made similar visits, but Flynn was convinced that he had been accorded special treatment and developed a rapport with the Russians that might enable a cooperative breakthrough.

Flynn "was brought into the inner sanctum," recalled U.S. Army brigadier general Peter Zwack, who was the U.S. defense attaché in Moscow and accompanied Flynn throughout his three-day visit. Flynn was allowed to lay a wreath at Russia's Tomb of the Unknown Soldier. He was taken to the GRU's gleaming modern headquarters on the outskirts of Moscow, where—in a remarkable gesture—he was invited to deliver an hour-long address on U.S. counterterrorism methods to a collection of majors and colonels who, Zwack surmised, "had never before encountered an American intelligence general."

That evening Flynn hosted a dinner for Sergun at Zwack's residence at the U.S. embassy, decorated with a LeRoy Neiman painting of Red Square. The assembled officers began raising glasses of vodka, culminating in a final toast to making "the airlocks fit," a reference to the 1975 joining of the Apollo and Soyuz spacecraft. Sergun returned the gesture the next night by hosting a dinner for Flynn at the historic Sovietsky Hotel, providing the American general a personal tour of the room where Stalin's son had lived.

Flynn saw such promise in the encounter that he returned to DIA and began planning a reciprocal visit that would bring Sergun and his GRU entourage to the United States. He continued to pursue the idea even after U.S.-Russia relations went into a protracted skid over Moscow's military incursions into Ukraine. Eventually Flynn had to be told by his bosses to abandon the plan—an intervention that only added to their growing vexation with him.

DIA directors are expected to serve terms of at least three years. But by early 2014, Clapper and Vickers had had enough, and told Flynn that his troubled tenure would run out after two. Flynn, only fifty-five, was forced to retire.

Flynn's wife, Lori, wore a festive floral dress with a lei around her neck to his farewell ceremony on August 7, 2014, as if anticipating the coming freedom that she and her husband, an avid surfer, were soon to enjoy. And Flynn, in an Army dress uniform draped with the many medals he'd won during his career, ended his remarks to the five hundred in attendance at DIA headquarters with an expression more associated with sailors than soldiers, a wish for "fair winds and following seas."

Beneath the surface, he seethed.

FLYNN'S REMOVAL HAD BEEN DELAYED BY MONTHS TO ALLOW HIM to make one final move up in rank and secure his third star. Despite that accommodation, Flynn became increasingly bitter toward those he blamed for his ouster. He began claiming that he was pushed out not because of any leadership deficiencies, but because Obama and his top aides "did not want to hear the truth" that Flynn was speaking about militant Islam. He started a company, Flynn Intel Group, a consulting and lobbying firm that pursued international clients willing to shell out six-figure sums for his overseas expertise and access in Washington. He also began working on a book—half memoir, half call to arms against Islamists—with the neoconservative author Michael Ledeen. Flynn joined a speakers' bureau and began making appearances on Fox News, NBC, CNN, and other cable news channels. The outlet that seemed most eager to provide a platform for the forced-out former general was RT, an international English-language television channel funded by the Russian government.

"There is a saying I love: truth fears no questions," Flynn said in one of his RT interviews. He may have loved the saying, but, as it would turn out, didn't always adhere to its message.

PAGE, PAPADOPOULOS, MANAFORT, AND FLYNN CAME TO THE CAM-
paign from different directions, but each saw their association with Trump as a way to reach or recover influence. At the time there seemed little downside. If Trump won, a job at the White House or elsewhere in his administration wasn't out of the question. If he lost—as seemed almost inevitable—the contacts they made and attention they got could only enhance their post-election fortunes.

Moths to Trump's flame, all four would end up burned, whatever futures they envisioned eventually reduced to a single imperative: staying out of jail.

AS TRUMP GAINED MOMENTUM IN THE REPUBLICAN RACE, HE BE-
gan facing pointed questions about how he could continue heaping praise on Putin when so many of the Russian leader's adversaries ended up disfigured or dead. Trump's defiant responses were un-like anything ever uttered by a major party candidate. "I think our country does plenty of killing also," he said in mid-December 2015 on MSNBC's *Morning Joe* program. Putin is "running his country and at least he's a leader, unlike what we have in this country." Two days later, on ABC, Trump said that murdering journalists would

be "horrible. But, in all fairness to Putin, you're saying he killed people. I haven't seen that. I don't know that he has . . . I haven't seen any evidence that he killed anybody."

The consistency of his deference to Putin seemed out of character: whether on social media or standing before a packed arena, Trump seemed incapable of stringing together more than a few sentences without insulting or demeaning a rival, a demographic, or an entire country. Unscripted and unapologetic, Trump often seemed to offend even when he didn't intend to. Yet, with Putin, Trump was disciplined and on-message, never even inadvertently critical.

The pattern was perplexing to Trump's political adversaries as well as national security officials in Washington. Some saw his early statements about Putin as the uninformed comments of a political neophyte, someone who had only a cursory understanding of world affairs. It was Trump being Trump—staking out a provocative position that he might abandon when it became politically advantageous to do so, or better-informed advisers got through to him.

As Manafort, Page, Papadopoulos, and Flynn came on board, the Trump campaign's entanglements with Russia—and questions about their purpose—intensified. The search for answers would eventually occupy U.S. intelligence agencies, committees in Congress, and a team of FBI agents and prosecutors led by special counsel Robert S. Mueller III. Before those organizations were fully engaged, however, there was a far smaller, independent inquiry under way.

CHRISTOPHER STEELE HAD PERSONAL EXPERIENCE WITH THE ruthless side of the Kremlin that Trump could not bring himself to see, stationed in Moscow in the early 1990s under diplomatic cover for Britain's Secret Intelligence Service.

Steele and Putin were nearly espionage contemporaries, Steele in Moscow, after the Soviet Union collapsed, while the future Russian leader was based in East Germany for the KGB when the Eastern Bloc began to unravel. Putin was permanently scarred by what had happened when the Berlin Wall came down in 1989. Crowds stormed the Dresden offices of the East German secret police and then turned their attention to the nearby headquarters of the KGB. Putin, by his own account, radioed a Red Army tank unit to ask for protection. "We cannot do anything without orders from Moscow," came the reply. "And Moscow is silent." Putin, sickened by the fecklessness of his government, returned to Russia and had begun pursuing a career in St. Petersburg politics when Steele arrived in Moscow. Their paths would intersect several times in the ensuing decades.

THE SOVIET UNION WAS IN ITS DEATH THROES AT THE START OF Steele's Moscow assignment, and he would witness the hammer-and-sickle flag lowered for the last time, opening a chaotic new era for Russia and the former Soviet republics. Steele had joined MI6 after graduation from the University of Cambridge, where his success as a student allowed him to transcend his family's working-class roots. His father worked for the United Kingdom's weather service; a Welsh grandfather had mined coal. Steele excelled at Cambridge and became president of the prestigious debating society, the Cambridge Union. His path to espionage began when he saw a newspaper ad seeking applicants interested in overseas adventure. Only when he responded did Steele learn the ad had been posted by MI6.

Steele had seemed poised for a series of foreign assignments when his undercover career was derailed. During a four-year posting in Paris in the late 1990s, he was one of dozens of British spies whose true identities were published online by a disgruntled former MI6 agent.[4] Steele came back to MI6 headquarters in London and rose up the intelligence service's ranks until, in 2006, he was placed in charge of its Russia desk.

He was soon greeted with a brutal demonstration of the Russian intelligence service's resurgence under Putin, then in his sixth year as president. That November, Alexander Litvinenko, a former FSB officer and Putin critic who had defected to Britain, was taken to a hospital with a mysterious ailment. British authorities concluded that he had been poisoned by a cup of tea laced with radioactive polonium. Three weeks later he was dead. Putin issued a statement of mock remorse, saying, "Mr. Litvinenko is, unfortunately, not Lazarus."

Steele was put in charge of the MI6 investigation. His findings contributed to a broader official UK inquiry that took nearly a decade to finish and release to the public. It concluded that Litvinenko's murder had "probably" been ordered by Putin. To Steele, there was never any doubt.

For all of his expertise and accomplishments, Steele had his detractors, and his departure from MI6 in 2009 was interpreted by some as a sign that he had realized that he was not likely to rise any higher in the spy agency. He also faced a personal crisis: his wife, with whom Steele had three children, was gravely ill—British press reports said she had cirrhosis of the liver—and died later that year.

After his retirement, Steele launched a London-based consulting firm, Orbis Business Intelligence Ltd., an increasingly common path for ex-spies whose contacts and inside knowledge of foreign governments and markets were in demand among corporate clients. One of Steele's first contracts had him working for the English Football Association on an investigation into corruption at FIFA, soccer's global governing body. U.S. investigators were also involved, eventually filing corruption charges against fourteen soccer executives. As a result of this partnership, Steele found himself working closely with FBI agents and sharing his research with the Justice Department—developing relationships that he would turn to again as troubling Russia connections began to surface in an American presidential election.

Steele's involvement with that election began with a June 2016 call from Glenn Simpson, a former *Wall Street Journal* reporter who had founded his own private research company in Washington, Fusion GPS. Steele and Simpson had met years earlier when Simpson was an investigative reporter for the *Journal* based in Brussels and pursuing stories about Russian organized crime and its spread into Europe. One of Fusion's business lines was opposition research, a euphemism for digging up dirt on political candidates.

Fusion had initially been hired in late 2015 to investigate Trump's business record—including any ties to Russia—by the *Washington Free Beacon*, a conservative paper. It was an unusual move for a news organization: media outlets generally don't pay for stories, let alone hire private investigative firms to root around in politicians' or celebrities' lives. But the *Beacon* in this case was doing the bidding of one of its prominent funders, Paul Singer, a wealthy New York investor and major GOP donor who at the time was determined to stop Trump from winning the party's nomination.

The money for Fusion dried up as Trump racked up wins in major primaries and establishment candidates including Jeb Bush and Rubio were forced from the race, but Simpson found a new source of support: Perkins Coie, the law firm representing the DNC as well as the Clinton campaign. With Trump's praise of Putin already an issue, Perkins Coie was intrigued by Fusion's tantalizing early reports and eager to pick up the tab, via DNC funds, to see what else the company could find on the Republican candidate and the Kremlin.

The new funding stream enabled Fusion to expand its probe.

The firm's research typically involves scouring public records, court filings, and media reports to produce a comprehensive profile of a subject—much the way Simpson had worked as an investigative journalist. To scrutinize Trump's ties to Russia, public records searches wouldn't be enough. Simpson needed sourcing that could get him closer to the Kremlin, and turned to the ex-British spy he had met in Brussels.

Steele signed on with Fusion in early June 2016. "I didn't hire him for a long-term engagement," Simpson later testified before Congress. "I said take thirty days, twenty or thirty days, and we'll pay you a set amount of money, and see if you can figure out what Trump's been up to over there, because he's gone over a bunch of times, he said some weird things about Putin, but doesn't seem to have gotten any business deals." Steele was told the client was a law firm but not which one or its connection to the DNC. The ex-spy, his biography undoubtedly known to Russian intelligence, never entered Russia himself as part of the investigation. Instead, he worked through a collection of cutouts— intermediaries used to relay communications without raising suspicion. Among them were native Russians both in and out of the country who were already on contract with Orbis and in position to make contact with their own sources, some of them close to influential oligarchs or the Kremlin.

Steele and Simpson expected to turn up information tying Trump to shady business operatives, accessing unsavory sources of money, or otherwise entangled in Moscow's ubiquitous corruption. But from the start, the information that flowed back to Orbis from Steele's network of sources was more fundamentally unnerving, alleging that the Kremlin had spent years cultivating Trump, not necessarily as a future presidential candidate but an influential American sympathetic to Moscow; that Russia was providing helpful information to the Trump campaign; and that Russian intelligence possessed compromising information on Trump and episodes of sexual perversion during his 2013 Miss Universe trip to Moscow.

Verifying some of the most salacious leads would prove elusive for legions of reporters and investigators for the next two years. But in some ways the most alarming report from Steele's sources proved accurate and prescient: in one of the first entries of what became known as the "Steele dossier," he warned that Russia was waging a covert influence campaign aimed at disrupting the 2016 election and defeating Clinton.

He also almost immediately came across disturbing information about Carter Page.

ONCE ON THE TRUMP TEAM, PAGE BEGAN GRANTING INTERVIEWS in which he presented himself as the campaign's "Russia adviser." He played up his business ties to Moscow and urged campaign officials to have Trump make contact with the Kremlin. His status with Trump earned him a speech invitation from the New Economic School in Moscow, a prestigious institution where Obama had once given a talk. In May, Page emailed others on the campaign to propose that Trump go in his stead "if he'd like to take my place and raise the temperature a little bit."

In June, Page used his credentials as a member of the Trump campaign to attend an event at Blair House, a historic residence just across Pennsylvania Avenue from the White House where foreign guests of the president often stay. At a gathering for Indian prime minister Narendra Modi, Page startled the assembled foreign policy experts and academics by praising Putin as a stronger leader than Obama, and vowing U.S.-Russia relations would recover when Trump was in office.

In the ensuing weeks, Page had a flurry of interactions with campaign officials about his pending trip to the Russian capital. He sent emails submitting drafts of his speech and asking for feedback from campaign manager Corey Lewandowski, spokeswoman Hope Hicks, and J. D. Gordon, a former naval officer serving as a foreign policy adviser.[5] At a dinner for members of Trump's national security team at the Capitol Hill Club, a watering hole for Republicans, Page greeted Alabama senator Jeff Sessions and told him he was heading to Russia in a matter of days. The campaign maintained that he was going to Russia on his own, and not as a Trump representative. But organizers of the New Economic School event made clear that they were not necessarily interested in the independent opinions of Page.

"Carter was pretty explicit that he was just coming as a private citizen, but the interest in him was that he was Trump's Russia guy," said Yuval Weber, a Harvard professor who said he was with Page for much of his time in Moscow, and whose father, Shlomo Weber, was the rector at the New Economic School and had extended Page the invitation.

Page's July 7 remarks in Moscow were astonishing. "Washington and other Western capitals have impeded potential progress through their often hypocritical focus on ideas such as democratization, inequality, corruption, and regime change," he said. He cited the Occupy Wall Street movement, the Bernie Madoff scandal, and the collapse of Enron as evidence of irreparable cracks in the American system. Putin, by Page's account, was a force for global enlightenment, fostering a system of international relations "focused on mutual respect, equality and mutual benefit and tolerance, and access to resources."

Page kept the same campaign advisers apprised of developments on his trip in a series of emails. Relaying an apparent interaction with Russian deputy prime minister Arkady Dvorkovich—chairman of the board of the New Economic School—Page said

Dvorkovich "expressed strong support for Mr. Trump and a desire to work together." In a July 8 email to Gordon and another campaign adviser, Tera Dahl, Page said he would "send you guys a readout soon regarding some incredible insights and outreach I've received from a few Russian legislatures and senior members of the presidential administration."

Manafort, meanwhile, moved to exploit his new position. Two weeks after being brought on as campaign adviser, he emailed his most trusted employee in Kiev, Konstantin Kilimnik, who, according to U.S. officials, also had long-standing ties to Russian intelligence. Citing his new connection with Trump, Manafort asked, "How do we use to get whole?"

The messages between Manafort and Kilimnik were written in deliberately cryptic fashion, but references to "OVD" made clear that one of Manafort's top priorities was to find a way to settle accounts with Oleg Vladimirovich Deripaska, the Russian billionaire who had accused Manafort in a Cayman Islands court proceeding of taking money intended for the cable television properties in Ukraine as well as other investments, then failing to account for the funds. (In the messages Manafort and Kilimnik appeared to use the Russian delicacy "black caviar" as code for sums of cash.) A Manafort spokesman would later claim that the emails reflected an "innocuous" effort to collect debts owed by assorted Eastern European business associates. If so, Manafort seemed to go to significant lengths to obscure that legitimate purpose.

Deripaska has been among the Russian leader's closest allies for years. Leaked U.S. diplomatic cables described Deripaska in 2006 as "among the 2–3 oligarchs Putin turns to on a regular basis" and a "more-or-less permanent fixture on Putin's trips abroad." His ties to Manafort went back almost as far. In 2005, Manafort sent a memo to Deripaska pitching the aluminum magnate on a plan to engage in lobbying and other activities to advance Russia's interests in the former Soviet republics, according to an Associated Press investigation. As part of this effort, Manafort offered to lobby the U.S. and other Western governments to help oligarchs in Ukraine hold on to assets looted from the state, to extend his consulting work into Uzbekistan, Tajikistan, and Georgia, and to help pro-Russian entities develop "long-term relationships" with Western journalists. Deripaska denied that he ever enlisted Manafort for such work, but acknowledged in a 2017 defamation lawsuit against AP that the two had business arrangements dating back to the mid-2000s.

On July 7, while Page was in Moscow and Trump was on the verge of securing the GOP nomination, Manafort sent another email to Kilimnik, asking him to relay a message to Deripaska offering secret updates from inside the campaign. "If he needs private briefings," Manafort wrote, "we can accommodate."

Despite his flimsy résumé, Papadopoulos was in some ways the most resourceful in cultivating contacts with the Kremlin. More than the others, he appeared to be doing so at the direct bidding of the Trump campaign.

Ten days after Trump introduced Papadopoulos as an "excellent guy," the newcomer took part in a disjointed meeting of the Trump foreign policy brain trust at the still-under-renovation Trump Hotel in Washington. The session—the only known gathering of the group that Trump attended—was convened by Gordon, the campaign adviser, and presided over by the future president.

Photos of the meeting show Trump seated at the head of a table in a disheveled room with stacked dishes and poster-size photos of the Trump Hotel interior positioned on easels, presumably for those overseeing the final phases of construction. Trump was surrounded by at least ten advisers, including Sessions at the far end of the table. Page was not present. Papadopoulos, sporting a fresh haircut and a blue suit, was shown leaning forward attentively, his elbow resting on the black tablecloth. There is no record or transcript of the conversation that transpired. But witnesses said that Papadopoulos astonished those assembled by announcing, upon introducing himself, that he could arrange a meeting between Trump and Putin. It was a staggering assertion for someone who never worked in government, had apparently never been in Russia, and had no recognizable diplomatic or foreign policy credentials. The assembled advisers seemed unsure how to respond, and neither endorsed the idea nor shot it down.

AFTER A BRIEF STINT AS A FOREIGN POLICY ADVISER FOR GOP CANdidate Ben Carson, who had also been desperate to fill his roster, Papadopoulos found his way aboard the Trump campaign after an interview with Clovis, who had also brought in Page. The campaign cochairman saw an eager volunteer and gave him a fateful bit of advice on how to ingratiate himself with the candidate. Clovis told his latest recruit on March 6 that one of the campaign's central foreign policy goals was to improve relations with Russia. Papadopoulos had made significant if indirect contact with the Kremlin in a matter of weeks.

While traveling in Italy on March 14, Trump's "excellent guy" met Joseph Mifsud, an academic from Malta with mysterious ties to senior officials in Russia. Mifsud took little interest in the lowly think tank researcher until he noticed Papadopoulos's name in press coverage of Trump's *Washington Post* meeting. Mifsud quickly set up a meeting in London, where he introduced the fledgling Trump aide to a woman from St. Petersburg, Olga Polonskaya, who he falsely claimed was Putin's niece.

Papadopoulos reported to Clovis that he had made rapid progress on arranging "a meeting between us and the Russian leadership to discuss U.S.-Russia ties under President Trump." "Great work," Clovis replied, though he noted that the idea would have to be discussed more widely among senior officials in the campaign.

Papadopoulos and Mifsud remained in touch frequently over the next month by email and Skype. On April 18, Mifsud connected the young Trump aide to Ivan Timofeev, the program director of the Russian International Affairs Council, a government-backed think tank. Timofeev had substantial ties to the Kremlin, serving as program director of the Valdai Club, an annual foreign policy conference in Russia attended by Putin. According to U.S. prosecutors, Timofeev also served as an undeclared proxy for the Russian Ministry of Foreign Affairs.

A few days later, on April 26, Mifsud relayed tantalizing information to Papadopoulos. Having just returned from the Valdai event, Mifsud said that he had learned that Russia had "dirt" on Hillary Clinton, in the form of thousands of emails. It was three months before the first batch of DNC files would be dumped online.

FLYNN HAD MET TRUMP FOR THE FIRST TIME BACK IN AUGUST 2015, a year after his DIA ouster. The retired general said he had received a call from Trump's team and agreed to a meeting at Trump Tower. The conversation was scheduled for thirty minutes but went for ninety.

"I was very impressed. Very serious guy. Good listener," Flynn recalled. "I got the impression this was not a guy who was worried about Donald Trump, but a guy worried about the country." Trump's positions on a range of issues—support for the use of torture, suspicion of European allies—were in complete opposition to Flynn's previous statements on those subjects. But the men shared hard-line views of Islam, an unusual affinity for Russia, and a deep resentment of the current president, both feeling he had disrespected them.

"I found him to be in line with what I believed," Flynn said.

Flynn had interactions with several GOP candidates, and for a time served as an informal adviser to Carly Fiorina. But as he moved more visibly into the Trump camp, Flynn got a remarkable offer from RT: an invitation to a gala in Moscow celebrating the network's tenth anniversary. Flynn would be paid $45,000—money he would later fail to disclose on federal forms—and would be seated at a VIP table next to Putin, though he would later say he didn't know about that arrangement in advance.

Before the trip, Flynn had stopped by his former agency, the DIA, for a courtesy classified briefing on Russia. Agency officials said Flynn did not disclose the nature and purpose of his Moscow visit, and that when photos surfaced of Flynn wearing a black tie and seated next to Putin, his successor at DIA, Lieutenant General Vincent Stewart, was so furious that he imposed new restrictions on sharing information with former agency executives. On the morning of the December 10 event, Flynn sat for an extended interview with Sophie Shevardnadze, a prominent correspondent for RT and the granddaughter of the former Soviet foreign minister. Flynn seemed uncomfortable in that setting, onstage before a Russian audience, asking at one point, "Why am I here? I'm sort of in the lair."

In many of his media appearances, Flynn had a tendency to fault U.S. leaders for lacking an adequate understanding of global problems without being able to articulate a coherent position or prescription himself. Even so, his words to Shevardnadze must have sounded encouraging to the Kremlin. "The U.S. can't sit there and say, 'Russia, you're bad,'" Flynn declared. The two countries need to "stop being like two bullies in a playground. Quit acting immature with each other." Later, he added, "My wish is that we figure out a way strategically to work together."

While in Moscow, Flynn also sought meetings with U.S. officials, including the CIA's station chief, the highest-ranking intelligence officer in the country. Out of courtesy, the station chief agreed, only to find himself being lectured by Flynn on how the United States was mishandling its relationship with Russia and needed to "ease back," according to a U.S. official briefed on the exchange. When Flynn pressed for a follow-up meeting the next day, the CIA officer became concerned that Flynn had met with Russian officials and had more unwanted advice to impart or, worse, information he wanted to collect. The station chief said no.

THOUGH THE CAMPAIGN WAS GAINING A PRO-RUSSIA ELEMENT, NO one seemed more enamored of Moscow than the candidate himself. At a Trump rally in San Jose on June 2, 2016, he bristled at mounting criticism of his affection for Russia, mocking those, including many in his own party, who had begun calling on him to disavow his praise for Putin.

"Then Putin said, 'Donald Trump is a genius, he's going to be the next great leader of the United States,'" Trump said. (Putin, when asked about Trump in December, had actually called him "colorful" and "talented" while saying "it's not our affair to determine his worthiness.") "No, no, think of it," Trump continued. "They wanted me to disavow what he said. How dare you call me a genius. How dare you call me a genius, Vladimir. Wouldn't it be nice if we actually got along with Russia? Wouldn't that be good?"

One day after Trump's San Jose appearance, his son Donald Trump Jr. received an email offering "some official documents and information that would incriminate Hillary and her dealings with Russia and would be very useful to your father." The message came from Rob Goldstone, a music publicist with ties to the Trump family as well as to a Russian pop star, Emin Agalarov, whose father, Aras, had made billions in construction contracts under Putin. The elder Agalarov had partnered with Trump to bring the Miss Universe pageant to Moscow in 2013.

Goldstone's email had some garbled information. He claimed that the older Agalarov had gotten the information on Clinton after meeting "the crown prosecutor of Russia," although there is no such position in Russia. He added that "this is obviously very high level and sensitive information but is part of Russia and its government's support for Mr. Trump."

Trump Jr. neither tripped over the odd reference to the crown prosecutor nor the remarkably explicit offer of campaign assistance from the Kremlin. "Thanks Rob I appreciate that," he replied. "I am on the road at the moment but perhaps I just speak to Emin first."

America's main adversary for nearly a century was offering damaging information, almost certainly obtained through illicit means, to subvert the U.S. process for selecting a president. There are many ways that Trump Jr. might have responded. He could have ignored the email, directed it to the campaign's lawyers, or placed a call to the FBI. But he did none of those things. Instead, he wrote back with unambiguous enthusiasm. "If it's what you say I love it," he said, "especially later in the summer."

PART

TWO

———

CHAPTER 4

"I BELIEVE YOU HAVE SOME INFORMATION FOR US"

C ANDIDATES ALWAYS SEEK SYMBOLIC BACKDROPS AT MOMENTS of political embarkation. Ted Cruz chose a Christian college in Virginia for his announcement that he was entering the 2016 race. Jeb Bush wore shirt-sleeves at a state college in Miami. Bernie Sanders declared his candidacy on the grounds of the U.S. Capitol. Clinton released a two-minute video that devoted more screen time to images of everyday Americans taking on new challenges than to the prohibitive favorite to be the next president.

On June 16, 2015, Donald Trump had entered the presidential race on a gilded escalator. Without taking a step, he descended into a crowd of cheering supporters in the baroque lobby of Trump Tower.

A monument to excess, Trump Tower was an unlikely setting for the launch of a populist campaign. But it was inconceivable that Trump would begin anywhere else. The center of his self-created universe, with his palatial residence and his business offices on the skyscraper's upper floors, the building is a fifty-eight-story man-ifestation of the image he spent his entire life cultivating: that of a dealmaker and business titan who transformed a family empire of unglamorous apartment complexes into a global brand synonymous with success and opulence.

The tower also served as a symbol of the vaunted boardroom savvy that Trump promised to bring to Washington. Certainly the breadth of his properties and the ubiquity of his brand were evidence of undeniable business talent—for seizing opportunity, sizing up people, and of course, selling himself. But like the tower's marble and metallic veneer, the Trump aura has always masked a less regal reality. Behind the glittering name were repeated bankruptcies, racial discrimination claims, unpaid contractors, class action lawsuits, and financial entanglements with the criminal and corrupt. Beneath the tale of spun gold were opinions and a pattern of behavior that without the offsetting charms of wealth and fawning media attention would have led to ostracism. Discrepancies about the building's true dimensions (he claims it has sixty-eight stories, ten more than actually exist) speak to a life premised on falsehood.

From childhood, Trump had been perceived as egotistical and a bully. As an adult, his views of women and minorities, as well as his vision of the American dream, seemed stuck in a bygone era, unaltered by the social movements that otherwise defined the majority of his generation and the politics of his hometown. Like anyone in high-end real estate, Trump was prone to exaggeration and self-aggrandizement. But he seemed to take these traits to extremes, habitually overstating—and outright lying—about the size of his fortune, the measure of his charity, even the ratings of his reality show. When he wasn't making such claims directly, he would impersonate imaginary characters in phone calls to journalists, describing "Donald Trump" with a cascade of superlatives and fabrications.

These tendencies were on display from the outset of Trump's

campaign. As he stepped onto a stage draped with American flags, he dispensed with the clichés of announcing one's candidacy—the faint praise of political rivals, the lofty rhetoric about hope, unity, and higher purpose. Instead, he delivered a diatribe that depicted America as a global laughingstock and presented himself as its only viable savior, a role he said he was willing to suspend his luxurious life to accept.

Many voters would be repulsed by the fact that Trump made no effort to subdue the coarse aspects of his personality or refine his message to avoid insulting entire demographic categories. But to others, it made him appealingly unscripted. In a field of candidates whose positions and even personalities were shaped by polls and focus groups, Trump stood out as strikingly authentic no matter the factual inauthenticity of many of his claims.

Trump's opening speech was actually more honest than most to the extent that it was a remarkably accurate reflection of who he was as a person and what he would be like as president. He opened with a stream of falsehoods. He claimed a turnout of "thousands" to see his announcement, though reporters counted hundreds—some of them movie extras hired for the occasion; he said that America's gross domestic product had plunged "below zero," when it was well into the trillions and even its growth still registered positive; he accused the U.S. government of having spent $5 billion on the troubled website used by citizens to enroll in the subsidized health insurance program known as Obamacare, for which he offered no evidence.

His spurious depictions of the country's finances were matched by extraordinary exaggerations of his own. He touted a personal net worth exceeding $9 billion, and brandished a supposed balance sheet verifying this total drawn up by a "big accounting firm" that he declined to name. In fact, he had overstated his net worth by at least a factor of two, according to the most reliable estimates,[1] and had opened his bid for the presidency with a version of the falsehood he had probably told most frequently in his public life.

Trump had long been utterly obsessed with his standing among America's richest people, and often had gone to extraordinary lengths to cheat his way up such rankings. In 1984, smarting over *Forbes*'s decision a year earlier to value his holdings at $200 million—a fifth of what he claimed in interviews with the magazine—Trump waged a campaign to influence the next round of tabulations. He courted one of the main reporters on the project, twenty-five-year-old Jonathan Greenberg, with invitations to his office and company parties. He threw fistfuls of fictitious data at *Forbes*, claiming the Trump family owned more than 23,000 apartments worth $40,000 apiece. (Greenberg's scrutiny found only 8,000, perhaps worth an average of $9,000.)

At one point, Greenberg took a call from a supposed Trump subordinate named "John Barron," who sought to persuade the journalist that he failed to fully grasp the scale of Trump's empire. Barron told Greenberg that Trump had taken possession of the majority of his father's assets—a falsehood revealed later by family legal filings—and that because of the consolidated holdings Trump should be considered a billionaire. Greenberg made recordings of the odd conversations with Barron, and they made clear Barron was just Trump trying to alter the cadence of his voice.[2] *Forbes* saw through the ruse, at least in part, assigning Trump a net worth of $400 million. More rigorous scrutiny showed that even $400 million vastly overstated Trump's wealth, so while the magazine had rejected the outrageous figures pushed by Trump and his phony alter ego, it still had moved him up. "This was a model Trump would use for the rest of his career, telling a lie so cosmic that people believed that some kernel of it had to be real," Greenberg later wrote. It "led to future accolades, press coverage, and deals. It eventually paved a path toward the presidency."

The most poignant moment in Trump's opening speech came when he spoke of his father. Fred Trump was the son of Friedrich Trump, a German immigrant who had been a barber and then a hotel manager and moved the family to a house on Jamaica Avenue in Queens and began accumulating money and properties in the burgeoning borough. Friedrich died during a flu epidemic when Fred was only twelve, leaving his family with the seeds of their future fortune. His widow, Elizabeth, managed the budding real estate business she renamed E. Trump & Son. Fred grew up to take the reins of the company, and as New York's population and economy boomed, he turned its focus toward building sprawling apartment complexes. In the 1920s, vast tracts of Brooklyn and Queens were undeveloped. It was an auspicious and lucrative moment, and Fred Trump made the most of it.

"I started off in a small office with my father in Brooklyn and Queens," Trump said during his announcement speech. "I learned so much just sitting at his feet playing with blocks listening to him negotiate with subcontractors."

That father was a stern figure with streaks of his own vanity—neighbors recalled marveling at the Cadillacs in the family driveway with *FCT* license plates. The cars were the least of it: Donald grew up in a faux southern plantation twenty-three-room mansion in the Jamaica Estates neighborhood of Queens, surrounded by the trappings of wealth, including a chauffeur and a cook.[3] Trump attended the nearby private Kew-Forest School, though poor grades and surly behavior later prompted his father to send the teenager to an upstate New York military academy.

The combination of Trump's privileged upbringing and extraordinary ambition facilitated his future success, but it possibly stunted his development in other ways. Little about his background, for example, was conducive to racial sensitivity or an ability to empathize with the less fortunate. Class pictures from his childhood are even more lacking in diversity than the overwhelmingly white male cabinet he assembled as president. And while Fred Trump may have been a professional inspiration for his son, his views on race appear to have been less than enlightened. In 1973, the family firm was sued by the Justice Department for "refusing to rent and negotiate rentals with blacks." (The Trump organization marked applications with a *c* for *colored*.)

Donald had stepped into the family business after earning a degree at the University of Pennsylvania, with ambition beyond his father's low-rent apartment empire. That made fighting back the Justice Department not just a matter of the moment but his future, and he enlisted attorney Roy Cohn, infamous for his role as a top lawyer to Senator Joseph McCarthy in the 1950s anticommunist purges in Washington (which came much closer to an actual witch hunt). With the no-holds-barred Cohn steering them through the crisis, the Trumps fought back, filing a countersuit alleging false and misleading claims. The dueling suits ultimately ended in a settlement requiring the Trumps to refrain from further discrimination and place ads in newspapers assuring renters of all races they would be welcome. Cohn's scorched-earth approach had a lasting influence on the twenty-seven-year-old Trump. Among the lessons was that truth could be drowned out by counterclaims and legal threats, and that the Justice Department wasn't to be treated as an enforcer of enlightened laws or stalwart of American democracy. Sometimes it was the enemy, and you fought it.

EVIDENCE OF RACIAL ANIMOSITY WOULD CONTINUE TO FLARE UP throughout Trump's career, and he would establish himself as the most xenophobic mainstream presidential candidate in recent history. The United States, he said, had become "a dumping ground for everybody else's problems." He directed a stream of vitriol at America's southern neighbor. "When Mexico sends its people, they're not sending their best," he said. "They're sending people that have lots of problems, and they're bringing those problems with us. They're bringing drugs. They're bringing crime. They're rapists." That Trump's buildings existed largely because of the labors of thousands of immigrants seemed irrelevant to him.

"He used to say, 'Donald, don't go into Manhattan. That's the big leagues,'" Trump said of his father in his announcement speech. "I said, 'I gotta go into Manhattan. I gotta build those big buildings.'" With his father's financial backing, Trump was able to take that leap. In 1975, he embarked on his first big deal, reaching an agreement with the Hyatt chain to acquire a tired 1919 hotel, the Commodore, in midtown Manhattan near Grand Central Terminal, and transform it into a gleaming Grand Hyatt. It was a springboard to all the deals that followed.

In the ensuing decades, the deals got bigger and Trump got richer, but six times his companies entered bankruptcy, including after his misguided acquisitions of Atlantic City casinos, a luxury airline, and the legendary Plaza hotel. Debts and real estate reversals cost him access to conventional capital, as leading financial institutions increasingly refused to lend to him. In the late 1990s Trump was forced to turn to less discriminating sources of funds, most prominently Deutsche Bank. The German firm—Europe's largest investment bank—had embarked on a major expansion into real estate lending and faced mounting suspicion that it was allowing itself to serve as a conduit of illicit cash for Russian oligarchs. Trump's financial disclosures during the election showed he owed $360 million to Deutsche Bank, which by then was under multiple investigations for money-laundering schemes and massive mortgage-related fraud. Three days before Trump was sworn in as president, Deutsche Bank reached a $7.2 billion settlement with the Justice Department.[4]

Trump had always borrowed heavily in building his empire, calling himself the "King of Debt." It was a common strategy in real estate development, using others' money to reduce risk and multiply buying power, launching more and larger projects in the hope of collecting commensurate rewards. "He always used other people's money, not cash," said Barbara Res, who was a senior executive for Trump in the 1980s. "He always got somebody to put up funds for him. To put up the money. And he put up the brilliance."[5]

Then in the mid-2000s, he abruptly changed course. The Trump Organization went from being a builder of high-end real estate, one that acquired properties and oversaw construction, to a licensing operation that took hefty fees from other developers for permission to affix the Trump logo on their hotels and condos. The king of debt also went on an inexplicable cash-spending binge, buying instead of building. In the nine years before running for president, he spent more than $400 million in cash on an assortment of properties, including a $12.6 million estate in Scotland, several homes in Beverly Hills, and $79.7 million for golf courses in Scotland and Ireland.[6] He then plowed more millions into renovating and maintaining these properties, often, curiously, at a substantial loss.

A private company, the Trump Organization provided no explanation for how it had emerged from such financial peril in position to spend such sums. Trump "had incredible cash flow and built incredible wealth," his son Eric said. "He didn't need to think about borrowing for every transaction . . . It's a very nice luxury to have."

The shift toward licensing revenue was propelled by an unexpected break. In 2002, Trump was approached by the producer of the *Survivor* series on CBS to take part in a new reality show dubbed *The Apprentice*. Trump saw the tremendous promotional potential. ("My jet's going to be in every episode," he said.[7]) Trump began slapping his brand on a motley array of products, including menswear, steaks, vodka, and get-rich-quick classes at Trump University that would end in yet another class action lawsuit.

Even as his business evolved, Trump still saw himself as a real estate tycoon. His search for partners willing to pay millions merely for the use of the Trump brand—while shielding the American mogul from virtually all the financial risk—led him far from Manhattan into murky overseas terrain. Trump-branded projects in Azerbaijan, the Republic of Georgia, Brazil, and Indonesia put the future president in business with multiple individuals and companies suspected of money laundering, political corruption, and other categories of fraud.[8]

Russia had drawn Trump's attention for decades. He pursued numerous deals to build a skyscraper in Moscow, starting in 1987 when he traveled to Russia to survey potential sites as part of a proposed partnership with the Soviet government.[9] He tried again in 1996, announcing plans for a $250 million "Trump International" complex, and several times more in the ensuing decade.

None of those projects materialized. But while Trump could never gain a foothold in Moscow, Russian money began flowing out of the country and finding him. Endemic corruption under Putin had created an entire class of kleptocrats, loyalists enriched by the diversion of money extracted from the country's oil and mineral wealth as well as other formerly state-owned assets. Many sought to move their mounds of currency overseas in case the Kremlin sought to grab them back, and money began surging into Trump's portfolio.

In the United States, Trump-branded properties were increasingly sustained by an influx of cash from questionable foreign sources. His children Donald Jr. and Ivanka came under investigation for their promotional claims and the financing surrounding a forty-six-story condo hotel in Manhattan's SoHo neighborhood built with substantial backing from investors from the former Soviet Union. Hundreds of condos at Trump-branded beachfront towers in South Florida were purchased by limited liability corporations—entities that mask the true owners' identities, a perfectly legal arrangement but one that can conveniently be used to hide the conversion of illicit cash into Western assets. Among the buyers who did disclose their identities, at least five dozen had Russian addresses or passports. All told, they spent a combined $98.4 million on sixty-three condos.[10] In 2008, the future president sold a Palm Beach estate to a Russian oligarch for $95 million, just four years after buying it for $41 million. His son Donald Trump Jr. said that same year that "Russians make up a pretty disproportionate cross section of a lot of our assets."

These dim corners of Trump's empire mostly escaped the attention of a public captivated by the blinding glare of his brand. His rambling announcement speech was widely ridiculed by political experts as proof that his campaign was just another vanity project, that Trump wasn't even making any pretense to be a serious candidate. But away from Manhattan and the Beltway, voters saw a Midas who might be able to transform a troubled American landscape. With their budding adulation, Trump began planning to take possession of a more prestigious piece of real estate: the White House.

Trump made only passing reference to Russia in his 2015 announcement speech, though months later he was secretly pursuing yet another potential deal to build "Trump Tower Moscow." The project was spearheaded by Trump's lawyer, Michael Cohen, and a Russian-born associate, Felix Sater, who had an office in Trump Tower and carried Trump-branded business cards. (Sater had spent time in prison for stabbing a man and had separately been convicted of fraud. Aiming to reduce his sentence, he became an FBI informant.)

"Our boy can become president of the USA and we can engineer it," Sater wrote to Cohen in a November 2015 email touting the project.

Sater and Cohen would continue to pursue a Trump Tower Moscow deal deep into 2016, apprising Trump of their progress even as he moved closer to securing the Republican nomination for president. Trump never told voters that as he campaigned to represent America's interests in the world, he was secretly seeking a potentially lucrative real estate venture in Russia, a project in which planners discussed offering the penthouse as a perk to Putin.[11]

ALMOST EXACTLY A YEAR LATER, TRUMP TOWER WAS THE SETTING for a far smaller gathering kept secret from the public.

On June 6, 2016, music promoter Rob Goldstone circled back to Trump Jr. by email, asking when he might be free to speak with Emin Agalarov, whose father had helped bankroll the Miss Universe pageant in Moscow, "about this Hillary info." Trump Jr. then engaged in a flurry of messages and calls with both Goldstone and Agalarov. Phone records obtained by congressional investigators show two calls between Trump Jr. and Agalarov, one at 4:04 P.M. and another at 4:38 P.M., though it was unclear whether they spoke or exchanged voice mails.[12]

Within that thirty-four-minute time frame, Trump Jr. made or received another call, though with whom remains a mystery. (Phone records showed the number as "blocked.") Democrats in Congress would wonder whether Trump Jr. had conferred with his father—whose Trump Tower residence had a blocked number—over how to proceed. In testimony before congressional committees, Trump Jr. professed not to remember whom he'd spoken with.

Trump Jr. and Agalarov—whose developer father was sometimes referred to as the "Trump of Russia"—connected by phone again on June 7. That afternoon, Trump Jr. spoke with both Manafort and his brother-in-law, Jared Kushner, another scion of a wealthy real estate family who had married into the Trump clan and become part of the candidate's inner circle. Trump Jr. wanted Manafort and Kushner to attend the meeting. He then emailed Goldstone to set a time and place: "How about three at our offices?"

In later testimony, Trump Jr. would claim that he did not know the names or backgrounds of those being ushered into a suite of offices on the twenty-fifth floor of Trump Tower on June 9. The event was marked on his calendar only as "Meeting: Don Jr./Jared Kushner." Trump Jr. said Kushner and Manafort knew even less about the guests or their purpose, and had been asked merely to "drop in." But the fact that Trump Jr. coordinated schedules with them and insisted on their attendance suggests that he saw the meeting as important enough to convene his father's top aides.

The meeting occurred as planned on June 9, though the time was bumped to four P.M. Trump Jr., Kushner, and Manafort found themselves sitting across a large conference table from Goldstone and four Russian-speaking associates. Among them was a lawyer, Natalia Veselnitskaya, with ties to senior officials in the Kremlin; Rinat Akhmetshin, a Russian-American lobbyist; Ike Kaveladze, a U.S.-based executive in the Agalarov company; and an interpreter.[13]

Veselnitskaya's ties to the Kremlin are unquestioned if hard to accurately assess. She had earned a law degree in Moscow, worked in the office of a Russian prosecutor, and represented a roster of influential oligarchs—including a railway magnate who faced money-laundering charges in New York. "I am a lawyer and I am an informant," she would later say in a television interview.[14]

But Veselnitskaya was best known in the United States for her campaign to overturn a set of banking and travel restrictions imposed on senior Russian officials suspected of human rights abuses. The sanctions were imposed as part of a congressional act named for a Russian lawyer, Sergei Magnitsky, who died in prison in 2009. Magnitsky was incarcerated by the Russian government while working for a U.S.-born businessman, William Browder, who claimed that he had been cheated out of hundreds of millions of dollars in an elaborate Russian tax fraud.

After Magnitsky's death, Browder led a years-long crusade that culminated in the 2012 sanctions. Veselnitskaya became the point person in a Kremlin-orchestrated counter-campaign that involved lobbying members of Congress and orchestrating efforts to damage the reputations of Browder and Magnitsky. (Putin also retaliated by banning American adoptions of Russian children, a move that underscored how few levers are available to Moscow in sanctions showdowns.)

"I believe you have some information for us," Trump Jr. said, getting straight to the point.[15]

Veselnitskaya launched into a meandering discussion about "individuals connected to Russia supporting or funding Democratic presidential candidate Hillary Clinton," Trump Jr. testified later. "It was quite difficult for me to understand what she was saying or why." It eventually became clear that she was referring to a trio of male heirs to the Ziff Davis publishing empire and one of their companies, a firm that had invested with Browder in Russia and come under investigation by Russian authorities.

Trump Jr. scoffed at this supposed "dirt." The Ziff brothers "support everybody—Democrats, Republicans. . . . It cannot be counted as a negative in any way," he said.

At that point, Veselnitskaya pivoted, and began talking about frictions between the United States and Russia over the Magnitsky sanctions.

Manafort kept his head buried in his phone throughout the meeting, leading the Russian team to believe he had paid little attention. In fact, he was typing cryptic notes into the device—"Bill Browder" "Offshore–Cyprus" "Illici"—that track closely with Veselnitskaya's prepared talking points. Manafort's notes taper off as she dove more directly into her case for repealing the Magnitsky Act, suggesting that he lost interest.

Kushner became visibly impatient. He "was very frustrated that he was in this meeting," Kaveladze, the Agalarov employee, testified. At one point, Kushner asked, "Why are we here and why are we listening to that Magnitsky Act story?" The level of his frustration suggested that the meeting was somehow failing to live up to his expectations, a dynamic that is hard to reconcile with Trump Jr.'s claim that Kushner and Manafort had no advance notice of its purpose.

As Veselnitskaya continued to ramble, Kushner stopped her again and said he couldn't follow what she was saying. Rather than summarize or clarify, she went back to the start of her script. Trump Jr. finally cut her off. "We're in the middle" of a campaign, he said, forcing the meeting to a close. "We're extremely busy right now. . . . If we win, then we might get back to you and continue that discussion about Magnitsky."

Veselnitskaya recalled matters somewhat differently.[16] Trump Jr. had prodded her for documents that could hurt Clinton, she said, asking "whether I had any financial records which might prove that the funds used to sponsor the DNC were coming from inappropriate sources." She insisted that "it was never my intention to collect any financial records to that end."

Trump Jr.'s testimony about the meeting months later before congressional investigators would be plagued by implausibly poor memory, such as his inability to recall whom he had spoken to on a blocked number on June 6. Trump Jr. couldn't remember talking to

Manafort or Kushner in advance about the meeting, though phone records showed he had made calls to both. He claimed he couldn't even remember the presence of the Russian lobbyist, Akhmetshin, even though others testified that the Russia native, who had served in a Soviet counterintelligence unit, showed up wearing hot pink jeans with tears in the fabric and a similarly garish shirt.

Trump Jr.'s recollection was clear, however, on one subject: his disappointment. "All else being equal," he said, "I wouldn't have wanted to waste twenty minutes hearing about something that I wasn't supposed to be meeting about."

The Russians were also disgruntled. The group gathered afterward at a bar in Trump Tower and, over a round of drinks, spoke with Aras Agalarov in Moscow. Veselnitskaya took the phone, expressed thanks for arranging the meeting, and indicated that it had gone well. But Agalarov's California-based employee, Kaveladze, called back a few hours later to say that "it was a complete loss of time and it was useless." Even Goldstone apologized to Trump Jr. as he departed the meeting and reported back to Emin Agalarov that "this was the most embarrassing thing you've ever asked me to do."

Trump Jr.'s account of the meeting would undergo troubling revisions a year later when it was first reported by *The New York Times*. At that point, his father had been in office for six months, the investigation of his campaign's ties with Russia was accelerating, and the president's dictation of a highly misleading statement about the Trump Tower meeting—during a crisis management session aboard Air Force One—would be seen by investigators as possible obstruction of justice. Yet even by the benign version of events presented by Trump Jr., the circumstances of the meeting were remarkable: a Russian, apparently unknown to the campaign but dangling a tantalizing offer from the Kremlin, was welcomed into Trump's inner sanctum and met with three of his most trusted aides.

Former CIA intelligence officials, including several who served in Moscow, described the approach by Veselnitskaya as consistent with Russian tradecraft. In their view, the meeting was likely an effort to gauge the campaign's receptivity to secret collaboration with Moscow. Before delivering any incriminating material, the Russians would want to test whether the Trump team would accept it and use it, or report the approach to the FBI.

By that measure, every member of the Trump team passed the test from Russia's perspective. None ever took any steps to report the matter, even months later, after evidence of Russian interference in the campaign became overwhelming. Trump officials also put themselves in legal jeopardy. The law bans any campaign contribution from a non-U.S. citizen. It doesn't have to be cash—an offer of damaging information about an opponent could be of significant value. Aiding a foreign entity seeking to insert itself into a campaign could invite a charge of conspiracy. Trump Jr., who struck congressional investigators as contemptuous in their closed-door interviews with him, was defiant when asked why he hadn't considered an offer of illicit campaign help from the Kremlin problematic.

"I didn't think that listening to someone with information relevant to the fitness and character of a presidential candidate would be an issue," he said. He professed never to have mentioned the meeting to his father, though just two days before the Trump Tower session Donald Trump suggested that damaging information on Clinton was forthcoming.

WHILE TRUMP JR. WAS MAKING ARRANGEMENTS TO WELCOME RUSsian visitors to Trump Tower, the Kremlin was delivering a brutal message at the doorstep of the American embassy in Moscow.

Shortly after midnight on June 7, 2016, a taxi approached the north gate of the embassy carrying a visibly agitated CIA officer. The yellow cab was still rolling when he leaped from the vehicle and lunged toward a pair of glass doors that would usher him back into the safety of sovereign U.S. territory. Wearing a knit cap and dark coat, he managed only a few steps before he was thrown to the ground by a Russian sentry who seemed to have been launched out of a guard shack in the embassy shadows.

The two men wrestled on the concrete for nearly a minute, the American pinned to his back, kicking and writhing toward the embassy entrance. He forced one glass door open with a desperate reach and then flung his right leg across the threshold. Pushing with both feet against the glass, he summoned enough force to send both men skidding across the invisible diplomatic boundary. The Russian, a uniformed member of the FSB, conceded and withdrew.

Russian news shows aired footage of the skirmish captured by security cameras positioned across the street from the embassy. They broadcast the CIA operative's real name, accused him of failing to identify himself, and depicted the Russian guard as a hero who had fought to protect the embassy from what had appeared to be a potential terrorist. The mauled CIA officer left Russia with a blown cover and a broken shoulder.

CIA officials said the beat-down was payback for the officer's success that night in eluding FSB surveillance. But they feared the episode was also meant to convey a deeper warning from the Kremlin: the rules of engagement in U.S.-Russian espionage were taking a ruthless turn.

Harassment of U.S. officials in Moscow had been escalating for years. After arriving in the Russian capital in 2012, Ambassador Michael McFaul was hounded by camera-wielding activists who ambushed him around Moscow with such regularity that they appeared to have hacked into his private calendar. FSB agents kept his family under conspicuous and often menacing surveillance, trailing the car that carried his boys to school, showing up at their soccer games, and sitting behind the family at church. Long after McFaul's wife was known to Russian intelligence, they continued to stop her and force her to step out of her car to produce her passport when returning to the embassy grounds. Nothing comparable was known to have happened to Russian diplomats in Washington.

The level of Russian antagonism toward the United States was excessive but at that point still could be considered an extension of the indignities that were common during the Cold War, when KGB operatives routinely broke into the apartments of American diplomats or slashed tires to intimidate CIA officers and signal their ubiquitous presence. The beating of a CIA officer on the embassy doorstep, however, was unprecedented. It was followed by another frightening episode a month later, when a Russian military helicopter dropped from the sky to make multiple passes over a vehicle being driven by the U.S. defense attaché on an officially declared excursion to a Russian military base near Norway. Aiming a camera through the car's windshield, the rattled Americans captured images of the armed helicopter swooping across the hood of their vehicle.

The ferocity directed at U.S. officials in Russia alarmed Washington, adding to the consternation over Russia's hack of the DNC, its intervention in Ukraine, and military rescue of the Bashar al-Assad regime in Syria. But those were only the visible pieces of an even broader challenge that would be revealed in the coming months.

AFTER WINNING PRIMARIES IN CALIFORNIA AND FOUR OTHER states on June 7, Trump delivered a victory speech in which he said he would soon devote an entire appearance to alleged Clinton misdeeds. "I am going to give a major speech on probably Monday of next week and we're going to be discussing all of the things that have taken place with the Clintons," he said. "I think you're going to find it very informative and very, very interesting."

Trump did deliver a speech on June 13, in New Hampshire, but it was focused on national security. He unveiled no new allegations about Clinton.

Help from Moscow, however, was on its way. The files that Russia had looted from DNC servers—the "dirt" that Papadopoulos heard about in April—would soon be delivered to WikiLeaks. The assist from the Kremlin that eluded Trump Jr. at the Trump Tower meeting was about to materialize.

CHAPTER 5

THE MISSING EMAILS

I HAVE *THE WASHINGTON POST* HERE—THE TOP, TOP, TOP," TRUMP said into his phone as he glanced toward the paper's politics editor sitting in his twenty-sixth-floor office. "He's so big you wouldn't even believe it! And he's a good guy."

Even while wrapping up a call, Trump was laboring to disarm an emissary of his favorite adversary, the press. Weeks earlier, the candidate had banned the *Post* from covering his campaign events. "Based on the incredibly inaccurate coverage and reporting of the record setting Trump campaign," he had declared on Facebook, "we are hereby revoking the press credentials of the phony and dishonest *Washington Post*." Now Steven Ginsberg, the paper's senior politics editor, had come to Trump Tower not to appease the GOP nominee, but to understand what was behind his splenetic outburst.

Trump's New York City office had a distinctly 1980s vibe, with beige carpet, tan fabric walls, and tinted plates of glass overlooking Central Park that are bordered with gold-colored metal polished to a reflective sheen. Family photos cluttered the windowsill, framed magazine covers lined the walls, and stacks of books, articles, and campaign items bearing his name sat in piles on his expansive desk.

For all his bluster, Trump can be remarkably averse to close-quarters conflict, and that day he seemed determined to avoid the meeting's unpleasant agenda. He spent most of the hour-long July 5 session touting his triumphs in the Republican primaries and vaguely extolling the virtues of his campaign vows to prevent Muslims from entering the country, allow racial and religious profiling, and build a wall on the border with Mexico. (Asked to explain "extreme vetting," he replied, "that means you're going to be vetted very strongly.")

Prodded by Hope Hicks, a former model who had graduated from doing PR for Trump's daughter Ivanka's clothing company to serving as a press aide for her father, the candidate finally turned to the subject at hand, accusing the paper of being "really unfair" and "vicious." He cited unflattering headlines and fretted about a forthcoming *Washington Post* biography, though he said he had seen the proposed cover and "it looks nice." Trump was most animated about stories that exposed his false claims about donations to charities, which he declared had "made me look so bad!" For years he had taken credit for huge donations while rarely drawing any money out of his own accounts. He had also failed to follow through on a campaign pledge to give $1 million to veterans until challenged by the *Post*'s David Fahrenthold to provide proof.

Those complaints were as far as he wanted to go regarding the question of whether he had actually done what he'd promised. It was a trademark rambling Trump performance—recorded with his knowledge by Ginsberg—in which the candidate seemed to have little interest in hearing the other side or even any voice other than his own. He seemed to lose interest in the argument over coverage when he realized he couldn't turn it into a negotiation, that

Ginsberg wasn't offering concessions in exchange for a restored credential.

Midway through the meeting, however, Trump's ears perked up. Word came in that FBI director James B. Comey was about to hold an eleven A.M. press conference in Washington. "What's that about?" he said. Realizing that it was likely about Clinton and the investigation of her use of a private email system while serving as secretary of state, Trump began to play out the politics. "I think he's under a lot of pressure," he said of Comey. "Because every lawyer says she's guilty. So many other people have been guilty for far less. I think he's under a lot of pressure.

"Meredith, will you turn on the television at eleven o'clock?" he said through the open door to his assistant. "Turn on Fox." (Amazingly, for a man of his media appetites, Trump seemed to have no television in his office. To watch Comey, Trump and Ginsberg had to walk into the reception area and stand beside a small TV on a shelf.)

"After a tremendous amount of work over the last year, the FBI is completing its investigation," Comey said, launching into an extraordinary fifteen-minute monologue that blindsided the Justice Department, chastised a presidential candidate, and altered the course of the 2016 election in ways that historians will spend years assessing.

Comey buried the bottom line, the bureau's decision on whether Clinton had committed a crime, until the end of his speech. But Trump could sense the political ground shifting in his favor by the minute. "This is bad," he said, mentally calculating the damage to his opponent. "This is bad."

IN LATE JULY 2015, THE FBI HAD LAUNCHED ITS OWN PROBE INTO the missing Clinton emails. The existence of the investigation quickly spilled into public view. Congress had been notified about the referral to the Justice Department, and it took little time for that to leak. Clinton tried repeatedly to dismiss the matter, calling it "another conspiracy theory" and a fixation for the press. "Nobody talks to me about it other than you guys," she said over her shoulder at a pack of reporters.

Comey, a Republican, had spent much of his career at the Justice Department, rising from an assistant U.S. attorney in Richmond to U.S. attorney for the Southern District of New York before becoming deputy attorney general in the George W. Bush administration in 2003. There he established a reputation as a fierce defender of the integrity of the Justice Department, notably in a 2004 hospital-room confrontation with White House counsel Alberto Gonzales and the president's chief of staff, Andrew H. Card Jr. The two White House officials were attempting to persuade Attorney General John D. Ashcroft, who was recovering from emergency gallbladder surgery, to reauthorize a controversial warrantless domestic eavesdropping program. Comey, who was acting attorney general in Ashcroft's absence, had refused to agree to extend the program. When he learned that the White House was attempting to go around him and get the ailing Ashcroft to sign off on an extension, Comey rushed to George Washington University Medical Center, arriving just before Gonzales and Card. When the White House officials entered, the attorney general, already briefed by Comey, raised himself up and said he shouldn't have authorized the program. He then said it wasn't up to him anymore anyway, gesturing to Comey and saying, "There is the attorney general."

Obama appointed Comey to head the FBI in 2013 and succeed fellow Republican Robert Mueller. Comey, less formal than his austere predecessor, was a popular director among the bureau rank and file, but he also had a reputation, behind the "aw, shucks" persona, for being excessively convinced of his own rectitude and judgment—as Clinton was learning.

In October 2015, Comey departed from long-standing practice by acknowledging the investigation in public, creating the extraordinary situation of a sitting FBI director openly talking about the probe of a leading presidential candidate. He told reporters that he was getting briefed on the matter regularly and was confident in the bureau's ability to pursue the case "in a professional, prompt and independent way."

But secretly he already had doubts. A month earlier, Comey left FBI headquarters for a meeting across the street at the Department of Justice, a two-minute trip on foot that took longer in the black bulletproof SUV that the FBI director was required to ride in. Attorney General Loretta E. Lynch had called the meeting to discuss how to navigate the Clinton email probe. She and Comey both had upcoming public appearances in which they would inevitably be asked how their departments were handling the very public referral.

Underscoring the sensitivity of the issue, the meeting took place in a windowless secure conference room in the Justice Department's command center on the seventh floor. Participants dropped their cell phones in a lead-lined box as they entered. Comey was accompanied by his deputy, Andrew McCabe, as well as his chief of staff and general counsel. Lynch had a comparable entourage.

No one thought it politically feasible to refuse to address the issue, but no one wanted to break Justice Department policy against confirming the existence of an investigation. It was a practice grounded in the grave responsibility that came with such prosecutorial power. Lynch tried to thread the narrowest of needles: she proposed avoiding the word *investigation* and instead referring to the Clinton email inquiry as a *matter*.

Lynch's wording may not have been entirely dishonest, but it was undoubtedly an evasive euphemism. Justice officials understood Lynch's instruction not as a way of providing political cover to Clinton but an imperfect means of staying on the right side of department policy. As the meeting broke up, George Z. Toscas, a deputy assistant attorney general who accompanied Lynch, joked with Comey that he was now director of "the Federal Bureau of Matters."[1]

Comey later said that he resisted Lynch's compromise wording, asking, "Why would I do that?" and being told to fall in line: "Just call it a matter."[2] Other participants do not recall him raising any objection or offering an alternative. In any case, Comey acquiesced temporarily, though he eventually pointed to the conversation as one of several factors in his decision to make a solo announcement about the investigation's conclusion. He later wrote acidly that the FBI doesn't "do 'matters.'"[3]

A document of dubious origin compounded Comey's concerns. In March 2016, the bureau obtained a purported piece of Russian intelligence with politically charged contents. Those contents referred to an email Russia had supposedly intercepted between Democratic operatives stating that Lynch had privately assured the Clinton campaign that the FBI investigation would be safely contained. Many in the bureau were convinced the document was fake, created to sow confusion and distrust. Authentic or not, Comey later said he worried that if it ever surfaced, no amount of explaining would dissuade a large segment of the population from believing that the Clinton email probe was fixed.

The credibility of the probe was threatened more urgently in late June by a chance encounter between Lynch and former president Bill Clinton in Arizona. Clinton was at a Phoenix airport after a day of campaign events and fundraising when he learned that Lynch was in another plane parked on the tarmac. Ever gregarious, Clinton wandered over and boarded Lynch's aircraft. Both sides insisted that they merely exchanged pleasantries and updates about their grandchildren without broaching the subject of the email probe. But the impromptu visit created a new crisis for the bureau and the candidate. Comey eventually testified that Lynch's "meeting with President Clinton was the capper for me. . . . I then said, you know what, the Department cannot by itself credibly end this."[4]

In reality, Comey had been quietly discussing for months with other FBI officials how to conclude the investigation and make the bureau's findings public without consulting or coordinating with Lynch—even while taking part in meetings that led Lynch's team to think otherwise. It was usually up to prosecutors, not investigators, to decide the disposition of a case. Lynch, however, had previously signaled that she would abide by the bureau's recommendations, a concession she hoped would ease pressure on her to recuse herself. Comey had interpreted that pledge as granting him power to decide the "matter" himself.

What everyone assumed was the final act unfolded over the Fourth of July weekend. At 8:00 A.M. on Saturday, July 2, while much of the city was still quiet, Clinton and her attorneys arrived at the J. Edgar Hoover Building in Washington. The meeting had been scheduled specifically to avoid press attention. She and her team entered the basement parking garage and took an elevator to the eighth floor. There, in a secure conference room, Clinton spent the next three and a half hours answering questions from a pair of FBI agents.[5]

"They wanted to know how I had decided to use my personal email at the State Department, who I'd talked to, what I'd been told," she recalled. The agents conferred with Comey by phone that afternoon and informed him that there was nothing she said that they believed was demonstrably false. "The view of the team," Comey said, "was 'We're done here.'"[6]

Three days later, Comey blindsided the Justice Department, the Clinton campaign, and the White House. Jennifer Palmieri, Clinton's campaign spokeswoman, was at home in Maryland that day when she got an early morning text from a reporter: "Comey presser today?" She thought it was unusual for Comey to call such an event, especially on short notice, just one day after the July Fourth holiday. "It can't be about us," she said to herself. Clinton "had just met with him on Saturday, and this was Tuesday."[7] With little clue what the day would bring, Palmieri made her way into Washington, meeting Clinton for an event at the National Education Association.

Palmieri's befuddlement was shared by others. The fact that Clinton had met with the FBI days earlier had quickly leaked to the media, but it seemed unlikely that the Justice Department would have come to a conclusion so quickly after interviewing her.

Clinton was onstage when Comey's press conference got under way. There were no screens for her team to watch Comey, so they followed the event on Twitter.

Standing before a set of microphones at the FBI's briefing room, his six-foot-eight frame positioned between two bureau flags, Comey opened by declaring that he had not coordinated his statement with Lynch or anyone else across the administration. "They do not know what I am about to say," he said.

After speaking for a quarter of an hour, Comey finally revealed the bureau's bottom line. "Although we did not find clear evidence that Secretary Clinton or her colleagues intended to violate laws governing the handling of classified information," the FBI director said, "there is evidence that they were extremely careless in their handling of very sensitive, highly classified information." He declared the investigation finished and that Clinton would not face any charges.

Clinton's team had braced for the possibility that Comey would recommend prosecution, a move that would have thrust the campaign into crisis. But as the FBI director launched his blistering critique of Clinton's email habits, Palmieri exhaled. "If he was pursuing anything," that is, urging prosecution, he more likely "would just put out a statement."[8]

Clinton was less sanguine about the development and wanted to "hit back hard" at Comey for trampling the traditional boundaries of his office.[9] But advisers argued against a combative response, emphasizing—wrongly, as it turned out—that the email probe was finally behind them.

"This is a very positive outcome and I'm really grateful that it is happening three weeks before the convention," Palmieri said later, describing her reaction to Comey's statement. Of course, there would inevitably be fallout—Republicans in Congress would convene hearings, Clinton's poll numbers would tumble—but the fallout, it seemed, would be political rather than legal. "This is a good day," Palmieri recalled thinking. "It was still a good day."

IT WAS A BETTER DAY FOR DONALD TRUMP.

By that point in the campaign, Trump had been pounding Clinton on the email issue for weeks. "Hillary Clinton has to go to jail," he said during the San Jose campaign rally in early June. "She has to go to jail," he repeated, then, seeming pleased with his decision to plunge across that ethical boundary, appended: "There, I said that."

A month later, Comey had essentially ruled out that outcome. Even so, the Trump campaign smelled blood. The FBI director's words "were strong enough that we knew we had the building blocks for something that would be sustaining and long term," said Sean Spicer, who at the time was serving as chief strategist for the Republican National Committee.[10] A call for prosecuting Clinton would have been preferable, but the public scolding Comey delivered "was sort of ten degrees off perfect," he added.[11]

Hammering away at that perceived vulnerability became an organizing principle of the Republican convention that got under way July 22 in Cleveland. Every time Clinton's email controversy was raised by speakers, the convention seemed to vibrate with vigilante energy.

Two speakers in particular tapped into this mood, all but endorsing mob rule: Michael Flynn and Donald Trump.

While at DIA, behind the scenes, Flynn had encouraged the partisan Benghazi probe. His hardening views toward Islamists and disgust with Clinton made Flynn perfect for Trump's purposes. Flynn had been a regular presence at Trump's rallies, brought out to lend his decorated military pedigree to the proceedings and whip up the crowds. He was even a rumored vice presidential candidate. It was attention Flynn seemed to relish, though many of his former military peers were troubled by his conduct. Both his longtime mentor McChrystal and the former chairman of the Joint Chiefs of Staff, retired U.S. Navy admiral Michael Mullen, had separately intervened, urging Flynn to tone down his spiteful speeches. Mullen called Flynn's conduct a "violation of the ethos and professionalism of apolitical military service."[12] But Flynn had brushed off the admonitions, and his alliance with Trump gave him a platform to strike back at members of an administration and political party that he blamed for his professional humiliation.

Flynn's wrath was on full display in an alarming speech on the opening night of the Republican convention. "We do not need a reckless president who believes she is above the law," he bellowed, his brow pulsing. He called not merely for voters to reject Clinton but for her to drop out of the race, saying that "she put our nation's security at extremely high risk with her careless use of a private email server."

Chants of "Lock her up!" began to rise from the crowd. Flynn, who had spent thirty-three years in the military, many of them trying to plant the seeds of democratic values in despotic countries and establish institutions of restraint and rule of law, joined enthusiastically.

"Lock her up! That's right! Yes, that's right! Lock her up!" he said, his head bobbing affirmatively. Flynn then uttered words that would haunt him when he later found himself at the mercy of the American system justice: "If I, a guy who knows this business, if I did a tenth—a tenth!—of what she did, I would be in jail today!"

Trump used his acceptance speech to paint a picture of America as a land of untended borders, collapsing industry, surging murder rates, and hidden terror cells. He blamed Clinton for the rise of the Islamic State terror group and the disaster in Benghazi, describing her legacy as one of "death, destruction, terrorism, and weakness."

Trump then went to work on Clinton's most gaping political wound. "When a secretary of state illegally stores her emails on a private server, deletes thirty-three thousand of them so the authorities can't see her crime, puts our country at risk, lies about it in every different form, and faces no consequence—I know that corruption has reached a level like never ever before in our country."

Trump's barrage brought down the house, concluding a convention animated largely by antipathy toward Clinton. His line of attack was about to be joined by a pair of allies that Trump cultivated openly: Vladimir Putin and Julian Assange.

ON JUNE 14, WEEKS BEFORE EITHER PARTY'S CONVENTION, CLINTON and Bernie Sanders arrived separately at the Capital Hilton, a few blocks north of the White House. The two had battled for fourteen months, a contest that pundits had originally dismissed as a mismatch but instead had turned into an exhausting, emotional siege. The self-proclaimed socialist had turned his campaign into a populist movement propelled largely by young voters. Their rowdy enthusiasm for a seventy-four-year-old candidate with a tangle of white hair only seemed to highlight the energy missing from Clinton's rallies. His proposals, including universal health care and free college education, garnered fervent support from the left wing of the party.

The summit at the Hilton was aimed at finding a way to resolve their differences, unite the party, and avoid delivering the November election to Trump. Clinton had just prevailed in the delegate-rich California primary, and Sanders was still stinging from a loss that effectively rendered the nomination beyond his reach. But Sanders still had leverage, with a sizable block of supporters so committed that 28 percent of them vowed they would not vote for Clinton even if she were the only Democrat remaining in the race. The two candidates were tense as they took their seats in a conference room. Clinton brought campaign chairman John Podesta; Sanders was joined by his wife, Jane.

Sanders wanted policy promises before he would consider backing his rival. Clinton offered concessions on health care and education costs, though she stopped well short of adopting his positions. The two candidates left by separate exits around 10:30 P.M. with no agreement on an endorsement, no plan for them to appear at rallies together or otherwise convince his supporters to support her campaign. Nevertheless, both sides described the session as productive, improving the prospects of a peaceful convention.

Preparations for that event were in their final stages in mid-July. Stage crews were finishing work on an elaborate blue set with massive flat video screens floating above a circular platform. Obama, his wife, Michelle, and former president Bill Clinton were polishing speeches that would seek to humanize a candidate who often struggled to connect emotionally with citizens. After the Republican spectacle in Cleveland, Democrats saw a chance to convince voters that only one party was prepared to assume office in January, that only they could be trusted to responsibly wield the power of the presidency.

·Clinton understood the importance of an event that had long stopped serving any meaningful role in choosing a candidate. She recalled the propulsive effect the 1992 Democratic convention in Madison Square Garden had on her husband's campaign, and hoped she would emerge from the 2016 version with similar momentum. But hard as she tried, Clinton could never match the magnetism of her Democratic predecessors or even the authentic appeal of Sanders. Her case to voters inevitably came down to admirable but not necessarily inspirational qualities: competence, preparation, discipline. That reality only added to the pressure heading into Philadelphia to achieve through flawless choreography what her acceptance speech might not: help voters beyond the Wells Fargo Center forget—or at least get past—the doubts and fatigue that accompanied decades in the public eye and a string of scandals.

Those plans were rattled before the convention began.

BY FRIDAY, JULY 22, THE DEMOCRATS HAD GOTTEN THROUGH THE Republican convention, and they felt they'd been successful at countering GOP messages. At DNC headquarters, Lindsey Reynolds, the chief operating officer (number three on the DNC org chart), was in a meeting in a third-floor conference room just down the hall from Amy Dacey's office. Shortly after 10:30 A.M. she got a text message from Dacey: "I need to see you." Usually Dacey added something like "not a rush." Not this time. Reynolds knew something was up. She left the meeting and walked into Dacey's corner office. The executive director was on the phone. She pointed to an email on the screen. The news was grim. WikiLeaks had dumped online 19,252 emails stolen from the DNC's computers—a stock-pile that the anti-secrecy website made searchable by keyword. Assange himself began touting the release that morning: "Are you ready for Hillary?" he asked on Twitter. "We begin our series to-day with 20 thousand emails from the top of the DNC." A short while later, WikiLeaks's own account sent out links to the trove, with hashtags to spread the word on social media: #Hillary2016 and #FeelTheBern.

Reynolds sent out an email convening an emergency meeting of committee staff at headquarters. Nearly a hundred people filed into a conference room and what they were told left them shell-shocked: thousands of their internal emails—some of them private, many containing unfiltered comments about candidates and donors—were exposed to the world. "They were frustrated. They were angry. They felt violated," Reynolds recalled.

The committee and Clinton campaign both cut off staff access to WikiLeaks, fearing that the group might try to track the activity of DNC employees searching the site, thereby helping WikiLeaks home in on what was potentially most embarrassing to the organization. The committee also fretted that WikiLeaks might deposit malware on the computers of DNC staffers searching the trove for their emails.

Calls and texts began flying among top committee officials, Dacey and senior lawyers Michael Sussmann and Marc Elias. The DNC set up a parallel system for searching the cache using Perkins Coie computers, downloading the WikiLeaks trove to a network normally used by the law firm for reviewing sensitive case documents.

For DNC staff, the blowback was immediate and distressing—even scary. People had their cell phone numbers in their signature lines in their emails, and quickly started getting nasty text messages, crank phone calls, death threats, and messages that assailants were outside their houses ready to attack them. One email said: "I hope all your children get raped and murdered. I hope your family knows nothing but suffering, torture and death." There were also ugly text messages signed "Bernie 2016," saying things like "I wish you would go down with the sinking ship that you are." By the end of the week, some were even being signed "Trump 2016." Staffers were spammed with emails. Trollers signed them up to magazines and LISTSERVs. All this as they were about to start the national convention. They couldn't change email addresses and phone numbers because they needed them to maintain ongoing communication with vendors, fundraisers, and organizers.

A team formed to review the emails found that only a few were modified—a date changed, a name taken off. But there were no major changes or fabricated emails mixed into the stack, meaning the DNC's damage containment operation could focus on real messages without worrying that Russia had planted potentially far more incendiary fakes.

The emails were not from Clinton's personal account or her campaign, and contained no revelations that might spark a new scandal about the candidate. But the material was more than enough to inflame existing tensions in the party and generate headlines around the two words most devastating to her campaign: Clinton and email.

The #FeelTheBern hashtag showed that those behind the leak recognized the potential of their material, and the news coverage seized on the fresh evidence of party hostility toward Sanders. The "Does he believe in a God" message showed staff searching for new lines of attack on Sanders. Another urged planting stories in the press that Sanders "never had his act together, that his campaign was a mess." Others were more plainly derisive, snickering at Sanders's campaign releases and dismissing supporters as "Bernie bros."

And then there were messages from DNC chairwoman Debbie

Wasserman Schultz, calling Sanders's campaign manager a "damn liar" and scoffing at the candidate's complaints of unfair treatment, saying his comments were "spoken like someone who has never been a member of the Democratic Party and has no understanding of what we do."

Much of the material could be viewed as venting, the sort of off-hand corrosive remarks that course through any organization. And Sanders wasn't the only target—there was also demeaning chatter about donors and an outburst aimed at Obama for refusing to show up for a fundraiser: "THAT'S f—ing stupid." Some of the sniping about Sanders—a lifelong independent who seemed to relish his spoiler status and chafe at the idea of actually joining the party he sought to represent—seemed understandable. And some of the most embarrassing emails came after Clinton had essentially locked up the nomination, a time of mounting frustration with Sanders for refusing to bow out and lend his support to the inevitable nominee.

The revelations threw the party into open conflict on the eve of Clinton's long-awaited coronation. The emails reinforced the perception that Clinton was prevailing not because of campaign skills or a compelling message, but because decades at the pinnacle of Democratic politics had put her in control of the party machine. The leak provided ammunition to anyone convinced that she was presiding over a process that was thoroughly corrupt.

Trump seized on the email spill. "Leaked e-mails of DNC show plans to destroy Bernie Sanders. Mock his heritage and much more. On-line from Wikileakes, really vicious. RIGGED." Trump's spelling of WikiLeaks was wrong, but his political instincts were not.

Even party stalwarts were disturbed. "The DNC did something incredibly inappropriate here," said Edward G. Rendell, a former DNC chairman and also former governor of Pennsylvania. "It truly violates what the DNC's proper role should be."[13] Sanders supporters, already reluctant to fall in line, seemed on the verge of revolt.

The WikiLeaks dump came as Clinton was heading to Miami to introduce her vice presidential pick, a campaign ritual that can usually be counted on to generate a gush of positive press. Clinton and her running mate, Senator Tim Kaine of Virginia, smiled gamely through an appearance at Florida International University where the newly selected running mate demonstrated his fluency in Spanish before a raucous crowd of five thousand. Behind the scenes, the campaign was in crisis mode.

Wasserman Schultz, whose congressional district straddles the northern boundary of Miami and was there for Kaine's introduction, faced immediate pressure to resign. Campaign chairman John Podesta pulled her aside and made clear that Clinton saw no alternative. But it took her until Sunday to relent, extending the drama until the eve of the convention. In a face-saving gesture, she was allowed to hold on to her title through the duration of the event, even while relinquishing committee controls to Donna Brazile, a longtime Clinton aide named interim chairwoman.

The move helped avert a potentially disastrous opening to the convention. Sanders supporters scrapped plans to stage a series of Monday morning votes aimed at forcing Wasserman Schultz to step down. But the mood remained tense and raw. On the second day of the convention, Sanders sought to tamp down the controversy by urging his rebellious delegates to stand down and back the Democratic ticket. "We have got to elect Hillary Clinton and Tim Kaine," he said. The plea was greeted with boos and even a smattering of "lock her up" chants. Putin's plan to sabotage Clinton was working.

THE TRUMP AND CLINTON CAMPAIGNS IMMEDIATELY BEGAN SPAR-
ring over how to interpret the WikiLeaks dump. Robby Mook,
Clinton's campaign manager, had gone on television from Philadelphia to say that Russia was actively trying to help Trump win,
a claim that at that moment struck reporters and even some intelligence officials as implausible if not hysterical. Manafort called
Mook's allegation "absurd" and insisted there were no ties between
the Trump campaign and Russia.

U.S. intelligence officials seemed not to know what to make of
the early signs of Russian interference. At a security conference in
Aspen, Colorado, director of national intelligence James Clapper
said it was too soon to be certain of Russian intent and expressed
concern about possible overreaction. Clapper said that he had been
taken aback by the "hyperventilation over this" and that Americans need to accept the fact that hacking was now pervasive in near
all aspects of public life and "not be quite so excitable when you
have yet another instance of it."

His view would not be nearly so sanguine when he returned to
Washington and learned of the CIA's intelligence on Putin and his
determination to defeat Clinton.

THE FRANKLIN BAR IS A BLOCK NORTH OF RITTENHOUSE SQUARE,
an urban park in the center of Philadelphia that was mapped out
by William Penn decades before American independence. The
bar borrows its name and ambience from a less illustrious Philadelphia institution than generally assumed. The Franklin Mortgage & Investment Company was a front for one of the most
prolific Prohibition-era bootlegging operations in U.S. history. At
its peak, the company—run by a mobster, Max "Boo Boo" Hoff—
had a hidden headquarters equipped with 175 phones to manage a
distribution ring that netted as much as $5 million a year. Business

for Boo Boo evaporated with the end of Prohibition, but the bar named for his operation simulates the look of a 1920s speakeasy, and thrives on sales of craft cocktails to Philadelphia's elite.

The establishment was almost empty on the humid afternoon of July 26 when Tom Hamburger, a reporter for *The Washington Post*, settled into a quiet corner.

One of the more seasoned members of a distinct Washington breed, investigative reporters who specialize in digging through thick stacks of campaign finance reports and finding sources privy to backstage maneuvers, Hamburger had worked at the *Los Angeles Times* and *The Wall Street Journal*, where he toiled alongside Glenn Simpson before the latter's departure from the news business to found Fusion GPS. Already on the hook to help with multiple unfolding stories that day—most of them tied to the WikiLeaks dump—Hamburger was reluctant to take what seemed like a dubious reporting detour. The meeting at the bar was at the request of a longtime Washington source who was sometimes a font of insight and information and at other times might be looking for a drinking partner with an expense account.

Having ordered a 4:30 P.M. bottle of wine and the first of several plates of appetizers, the source proceeded to lay out claims about Trump and Russia that seemed outlandish. The source said he had obtained information contained in a report by a former Western intelligence operative familiar with Russia, a project that it seemed clear even then was being paid for by Clinton allies. The report was full of disturbing allegations—that Russia had been cultivating and supporting Trump for at least five years, that the candidate had been offered but so far not accepted numerous real estate deals in Moscow, and that the Kremlin had amassed a dossier of compromising material on Trump, including evidence that he had consorted with prostitutes in the presidential suite of Moscow's Ritz-Carlton Hotel.

The claims struck Hamburger as simultaneously frightening and preposterous. It all sounded like a fevered replay of the movie *The Manchurian Candidate*. At the same time, Hamburger and colleague Rosalind Helderman had already been pursuing and publishing stories on the troubling connections between the Trump campaign and Russia. Hamburger pressed for more details and pushed for a chance to speak directly with the intelligence operative in question. The source demurred but said the material was being shared with a select group of Democratic Party officials who were discussing how to pass along the information to law enforcement.

It was months before Hamburger learned Steele's identity, let alone had the chance to meet him. Hours later, but still in daylight, the two men emerged from the bar and Hamburger made his way back to the convention. The *Post* team continued to scour Democratic sources in Philadelphia, as well as national security officials back in Washington, as the convention program pressed on with a lineup of speakers that culminated that night with a nostalgia-inducing appearance by Bill Clinton.

The next morning, the paper's editors and reporters made their way to the downstairs lobby breakfast bar of the Alexander Inn, six blocks east of Rittenhouse Square, for a daily planning session. The *Post* had sent eighty staff members to Philadelphia for the convention, occupying the entire hotel. As they filled their plates and made lists of potential stories, Trump appeared on TV screens in the hotel from a campaign appearance at his Doral golf resort near Miami. The journalists were paying only partial attention to his opening remarks, in which he mocked Clinton for failing to hold a press conference, chastised Democrats for failing to put American flags on their convention dais, and feigned sympathy for Sanders and his treatment by his party. Then came the first question, about Russia and WikiLeaks.

"It's just a total deflection, this whole thing with Russia," Trump said. After years of claiming a close bond with Putin, Trump now said, "I don't know who Putin is," and rejected the case of Kremlin involvement in the leaked emails, saying that "nobody even knows this, it's probably China, or it could be somebody sitting in his bed." All of those words would fade into the realm of the nearly forgotten, however, because of what he said next:

"Russia, if you're listening, I hope you're able to find the thirty thousand emails that are missing," Trump said, referring to the messages that Clinton had deleted from her private server. "I think you will probably be rewarded mightily by our press."

There was a hush in the hotel lobby, broken by the exclamation of a single editor: "Holy shit."

Hours later, GRU hackers for the first time launched spear-phishing attacks against private email accounts used by Clinton's personal office and seventy-six addresses associated with the campaign.

CHAPTER 6

CROSSFIRE HURRICANE

I F RUSSIA WAS LISTENING, SO WAS THE FBI. IN LATE JULY, FBI DI-rector James Comey and a small group of senior advisers were confronting a momentous decision: whether the bureau, having just completed an investigation of one presidential candidate, now needed to turn its agents on the other.

With his words of encouragement to the Kremlin's spies, Trump had done his part to make sure the answer was yes.

Trump and his aides would try to undo the damage of his "Russia, if you're listening" remark, insisting that it had been a joke. But his words echoed ominously through the hallways of the bureau and the CIA. Both were built in part to counter the Soviet and later Russian threat, and both were already in heightened states of alert over the email dump on WikiLeaks, Trump's penchant for praising Putin, and a slender but expanding stream of intelligence on suspicious contacts between Trump subordinates and Russians. And now this.

In the coming months, the search for evidence of coordination between Moscow and the Trump campaign would often focus on cryptic emails, clandestine overseas meetings, and attempts to set up elaborate back channels. And because of a startling piece of information the FBI received from Australian officials the same week Trump encouraged electronic warfare against Hillary Clinton, the possibility of a secret deal between the Trump campaign and Moscow suddenly didn't seem so farfetched.

THE MESSAGE ARRIVED IN GEORGE PAPADOPOULOS'S INBOX JUST weeks after he had been formally announced as a foreign policy adviser to the Trump campaign. "Lovely to meet you George," the effusive email began. "I'd love to catch up and have a chat if you have time." The author was Erika Thompson, a midlevel diplomat in the Australian embassy in London, who had been introduced to Papadopoulos by a mutual acquaintance at the Israeli embassy. Thompson invited the young American, already in London, to meet for "lunch or a beer or a glass of Australian wine—even chicken wings if you like."

After a meeting that apparently included that ubiquitous appetizer, Thompson wrote back: "George! Thanks again for meeting Friday. We both had enormous fun and I'm very annoyed that you're leaving London so soon. So many wings left to eat!" She then, unprompted, offered to arrange a meeting with Australia's high commissioner to the United Kingdom (a term used instead of *ambassador* among members of the British Commonwealth). Even that title understated Alexander Downer's stature: the scion of a dynastic political family in Australia, he had been the country's foreign minister until 2007, finishing an eleven-year term that was longer than any in the country's history. His father had also been high commissioner to the United Kingdom, and his grandfather was one of the signatories of Australia's constitution, a document that was partly drafted in 1897 in a ballroom of the family's North Adelaide estate, a landmark still known as Downer House.

"He's a great contact," Thompson said. "He's been everywhere, knows everyone and loves a good conversation . . . Maybe tomorrow around 6?"

The invitation was a sign of Papadopoulos's dizzying ascent in the foreign policy world—the lowly adviser who months earlier was still listing the Model United Nations on his résumé was suddenly being invited to drinks by a top diplomat in Europe.

Papadopoulos had called attention to himself in London with provocative statements to the British press. In December 2015, Trump, seeking to sound tough on terrorism, described authorities in Europe, where the Islamic State had staged deadly attacks, as cowering in response to the terror group. He claimed, inaccurately, that police in Paris were no longer patrolling dangerous parts of the city and that neighborhoods of London were "so radicalized that the police are afraid for their own lives." Then–Prime Minister David Cameron shot back that Trump's remarks about British police and Muslims in general were "divisive, stupid, and wrong," and said a Trump visit to the United Kingdom would galvanize European opposition to him.

Five months later, in a May 4 interview with the London *Times*,[1] Papadopoulos was asked about the prospects of a relationship-mending meeting between Cameron and Trump, who by then was the GOP front-runner. Papadopoulos noted that the campaign had not received any overtures from Cameron and that if he wanted to be on good terms with a potential Trump administration, it would be "wise for him to reach out in a more positive manner." He added that "an apology or some sort of retraction should happen." The comments were relatively mild but created a stir in the UK, depicted as an ultimatum delivered by a Trump minion.

Trump was still months away from securing the GOP nomination. But Downer had watched Trump run roughshod over the Republican field with an "America First" campaign in which he pledged to tear up long-standing trade partnerships and depicted close allies as parasites. Downer understood that it was pointless to expect a comprehensive take on the Trump worldview from a cipher like Papadopoulos, but if nothing more, it was an opportunity to take the measure of one of the few identified members of Trump's foreign policy brain trust.

Downer and Papadopoulos met late afternoon at the Kensington Wine Rooms, an upscale establishment with a rustic decor just blocks from Kensington Palace and the high commissioner's Hyde Park residence. "We had a drink and he talked about what Trump's foreign policy would be like if Trump won the election," Downer recalled.[2] Australian officials "didn't know anything about Trump and Russia and we had no particular focus on that. For us, we were more interested in what Trump would do in Asia."[3]

Downer was drinking a gin and tonic and doing most of the talking.[4] Papadopoulos struck him as surprisingly young and inexperienced, someone who seemed unlikely to land in a position of real influence in the U.S. government. When Papadopoulos said he was confident Trump would get the GOP nomination, Downer asked what chance the New Yorker had of winning the whole election. Papadopoulos said he thought Trump was a strong candidate and then, in an almost offhand way, made a disturbing remark.

Russia, he said, had "damaging" material on Clinton and was prepared to release it in the final stage of the election.

Papadopoulos didn't treat this revelation with any conspiratorial gravity; he seemed to view it as juicy diplomatic gossip and a means of showing off. He didn't call the material "dirt" or refer to a trove of hacked emails—details he knew from his meeting two weeks earlier with the Maltese professor Joseph Mifsud. Nor did Papadopoulos give any indication that Trump was involved in, or aware of, the Russian plan. "It was just that this guy clearly knew that the Russians did have material on Hillary Clinton," Downer said.

Within forty-eight hours, Downer had filed a detailed report of the conversation to the Foreign Ministry in Canberra. That report, per standard operating procedures, was shared with Australia's main spy service, the Australian Security Intelligence Organisation, known as ASIO. But in a measure of how little weight Downer attached to Papadopoulos's comment about Russia, he treated it almost as an afterthought, mentioning it midway through the report. It was, he later said, "just buried in the cable."

The United States, the United Kingdom, Canada, New Zealand, and Australia compose the world's most exclusive espionage club, a federation known as the "Five Eyes" (FVEY). The level of trust among them is so extraordinary that they cooperate on intelligence operations, share the most sensitive technological developments, withhold relatively few secrets from others in the group, and generally refrain from spying on one another. Even so, the Downer report sat in Australia's files for two months, viewed as intriguing but uncorroborated, nothing to alert the Americans about. At least not yet.

SOME OF THOSE WHO WOULD BE TASKED WITH EXCAVATING THE strange relationship between the Trump campaign and the Kremlin had long been investigating—and busting—Russian spies. And while the relationship between the United States and Russia had warmed since the end of communism, Putin's ascent had begun to reverse that reconciliation. In the summer of 2010, it was as if the Cold War had come out of a twenty-year coma. As temperatures across the country soared on a Sunday in late June, teams of FBI agents fanned out to make a series of simultaneous arrests and dismantle one of the oddest Russian spy rings in recent U.S. history. The ten suspects were dubbed "the Illegals"—an old Soviet term—because they were posing as private citizens rather than Russian diplomats, meaning they had no immunity from American laws. All had gone to extraordinary lengths to embed themselves in American society. Many had spent more than a decade burrowing into false identities, mundane professions, and suburban neighborhoods across the country.

One, a female in her twenties with fiery red hair, presented herself as an online real estate agent. Others worked as an accountant, a college instructor, and a travel agent. One pair of spies lived as a couple in Cambridge, Massachusetts, with their two teenage sons, where the husband earned a degree at Harvard and was employed as a sales consultant while his wife worked as a real estate agent—an arrangement that would partly inspire the popular television series *The Americans*. (Another pair of Russian agents living in Montclair, New Jersey, who had two unsuspecting daughters, were also a source of inspiration.)

Oddly, it was never clear that the illegals actually stole any secrets of value, although one Russian succeeded in meeting a U.S. government employee with a job in nuclear weapons research. Instead, they seemed to function as "sleeper cells," biding their time while maintaining clandestine contact with Moscow Center, the headquarters of the SVR. ("Moscow Center" and "Russia House" were both names coined by novelist and ex-spy John le Carré and later adopted by actual intelligence agencies.)

The FBI had kept the Russian agents under surveillance for years, capturing images of them making "brush past" meetings in which they swapped identical bags with known Russian operatives; using their laptops at bookstores and coffee shops to send coded messages to nearby Russian handlers; and collecting bundles of cash at designated drop sites. Their goal, the FBI said upon announcing the arrests, was "to become sufficiently 'Americanized' such that they can gather information about the United States for

Russia, and can successfully recruit sources who are in, or are able to infiltrate, United States policy-making circles."

Among the small army of federal investigators involved in the case was a rising FBI agent named Peter Strzok. For several years, he served as a Boston case agent tracking the couple in Cambridge who posed as Canadian citizens Donald Heathfield and Tracey Foley, but whose real names were Andrey Bezrukov and Elena Vavilova. He left that office in 2003 but returned to Boston seven years later, brought back by FBI leaders to be involved in the take-down of the illegals in an expression of respect for his early work on the case.

Strzok had grown up in Minnesota, earned a bachelor's and master's degrees at Georgetown, and served as an Army artillery officer before joining the FBI in 1996. His initial focus was terrorism, which surged in priority after the September 11 attacks. Strzok found himself on the front lines of Al-Qaeda investigations—he was the agent who found the rental car the 9/11 hijackers had abandoned at Logan International Airport before boarding one of the planes that was crashed into the World Trade Center. Months later, Strzok was sent to France to investigate the failed plot by Al-Qaeda operative Richard Reid to blow up a Paris–Miami flight with a bomb hidden in his shoe, an aircraft that was diverted to Boston when the explosive failed to detonate.

After his work on the illegals case, Strzok began ascending the bureau's counterintelligence ranks. He spent six years as a supervisor of an espionage squad at the Washington Field Office, which is responsible for hunting spies and moles in and around the nation's capital, a territory that includes foreign embassies and all sixteen U.S. spy services. In 2014, Strzok supervised the investigation of former NSA contractor Edward Snowden, who made off with a vast trove of classified files about U.S. surveillance capabilities that he shared with reporters at *The Washington Post* and *The Guardian* before fleeing first to Hong Kong and then gaining asylum in Russia.

By 2015, Strzok was in line for a coveted job at FBI headquarters that seemed certain to provide a path even further up the leadership ranks. In reality, he was entering the most perilous stretch of his career. Over the next year, he would play a lead role in two of the most politically charged probes in FBI history, involving both major parties' eventual nominees for president. At the same time, he was carrying on an affair with an FBI colleague, Lisa Page, an indiscretion that would be captured and ultimately exposed—along with their views about Clinton, Trump, and FBI bosses—in thousands of texts they sent each other on bureau-issued cell phones.

These treacherous currents converged in July 2016. Strzok was one of the FBI agents who had questioned Clinton about her private email server during her Fourth of July weekend visit to bureau headquarters. He helped compose the statement that Comey made three days later in which he declared that the bureau saw no basis to prosecute Clinton. An earlier draft described her handling of classified information on emails as "grossly negligent." Strzok took out that phrase, which had a specific legal meaning, and replaced it with "extremely careless," a construction that, in hindsight, might also have applied to his own conduct.

With the Clinton investigation seemingly wrapped up, Strzok fell into a funk. "Got the Sunday blues, bad," he wrote on July 10 to Page, a lawyer and senior adviser to FBI deputy director Andrew McCabe. "Maybe it's Midyear post-partum," he said, using a shorthand for "Midyear Exam," the code word bureau officials had adopted to refer to the Clinton probe. "Gotta find something at work to motivate me."[5]

"The next thing," as Strzok later put it, would land in a matter of weeks.

AS SOON AS THE DNC WIKILEAKS DELUGE BEGAN, DOWNER RE-
called his meeting at the Kensington Wine Rooms with a shudder.
"I think we better make sure the Americans are aware of this," he
said to his staff. The ambassador had included Papadopoulos's reference to the Russians' plan to unleash "damaging" information on
Clinton in his report to Canberra, but it was part of a broader communication summarizing his conversation with an inexperienced—
and possibly unreliable—Trump aide. Now it seemed urgent. One
of Downer's aides called the U.S. embassy in London and said that
the high commissioner needed to speak with the ambassador on
something pressing without revealing the subject.

The American ambassador, Matthew Barzun, was away on vacation, leaving his deputy chief of mission, Elizabeth Dibble, in
charge. Dibble was in the final weeks of her thirty-six-year career
with the State Department, with plans to retire and return to the
United States. Her staff told her about the request from Downer
and that the subject was urgent but "not a security affair," meaning it wasn't a life-and-death matter like a terror plot. It was late
morning, within hours of the call, when Downer arrived and was
escorted into Dibble's office, a spacious space on the second floor,
overlooking Grosvenor Square, a royal park in the Mayfair district
of London.

Downer came straight to the point, saying that Australia had
concerning information it needed to relay to the U.S. government
about Russia and the American presidential election. He described
the meeting with Papadopoulos and his reference to material damaging to Clinton. Downer was carrying a piece of paper, a printed
copy of the paragraph from the cable he'd sent to Canberra describing Papadopoulos's reference to Russia and its plan. Dibble
was coming into the subject cold, and initially was under the im-

pression that Russia had already passed material to the Trump campaign. The entire conversation was over in fifteen minutes.

Dibble thanked Downer and within minutes of his departure called the top FBI official at the embassy. The report was relayed through classified channels back to Washington, where it landed with a jolt on the seventh floor of FBI headquarters.

The FBI was by then paying close attention to the proliferating connections between Russia and the Trump campaign. Bureau officials had taken notice of the fact that Paul Manafort and Carter Page were exploiting their new Trump affiliation—Manafort by making contact with his old Ukrainian associate and exploring ways to settle unresolved debts; Page by conspicuously singing Putin's praises and jumping at the chance to deliver a speech in Moscow. The FBI's lingering suspicion of Page was strong enough that Comey took the unusual step of setting up a briefing with senior Obama administration officials at the White House after Page had been named to the Trump team to go over the bureau's concerns.[6]

The FBI was also beginning to absorb the material from Steele. One of his memos included information attributed to an anonymous source—believed to be Russian American businessman Sergei Millian[7]—that "the Kremlin had been feeding Trump and his team valuable intelligence on his opponents, including Democratic presidential candidate Hillary Clinton, for several years." Born in Belarus, Millian had arrived in the United States in the early 2000s and began working in real estate in Atlanta. He went on to found the Russian American Chamber of Commerce, and claimed to have close ties with Trump, calling himself the "exclusive broker" for dozens of Russians buying apartments in Trump buildings in the United States.

Steele's relationship with the FBI went beyond his providing critical information to the bureau that fed into a sprawling corruption probe of FIFA. Steele had also been hired by the FBI to help investigate a money-laundering operation run by alleged Russian mobster Alimzhan Toktakhounov out of an apartment in Trump Tower.[8] As Steele's work for Fusion GPS had progressed, he'd become increasingly convinced he had to pass on what he was learning to the FBI. In his Senate testimony, Simpson, the Fusion executive, said that Steele emphasized the U.S.-UK relationship—"we're your closest ally"—and said he felt "professionally obligated" to share his findings. On July 5—the same day as Comey's Clinton press conference—Steele met with an FBI agent in London.

In the end, it wasn't Paul Manafort or Carter Page—with their extensive entries in FBI case files—that prompted the bureau to finally open an investigation. Nor was it Steele, whose findings didn't reach FBI higher-ups in Washington until well into August. Instead, within days of the bureau's receipt of the Australian report on Papadopoulos, Comey convened a team of advisers referred to internally as "the skinny group"—because membership was so slender—and began mapping out a probe that would again pull the bureau into the minefield of presidential politics. In addition to Comey, the group included his deputy, McCabe; counterintelligence chief Bill Priestap; general counsel James Baker; and Comey chief of staff James Rybicki. There were two other members of the group: Page and Strzok.

The pair used their work phones to hide their affair from their spouses, but almost all of their text messages were archived by the FBI. In that correspondence, Strzok and Page engaged in a running commentary throughout the Democratic and Republican conventions. Neither seemed particularly enthusiastic about Clinton, but both viewed Trump with disdain. "Wow, Donald Trump is an enormous d*ouche," Page wrote on July 19, the night Trump appeared briefly onstage to introduce his wife, Melania, whose remarks were ridiculed over passages that seemed to have been plagiarized from a 2008 convention speech by Michelle Obama. Page described the Trump campaign as a "two-bit organization. I do so hope his disorganization comes to bite him hard in November." Strzok wrote back: "It HAS to, right? Right?!? Panicked."

During the Democratic convention, they talked about how frail Bill Clinton looked and praised the speech by Vice President Joe Biden. They worried that Sanders might bleed support from Clinton, and Strzok said he was more "worried about the anarchist Assanges who will take fed information and disclose it to disrupt." As the Democratic convention came to a close, their correspondence took a more sober turn.

On July 29, Strzok referred obliquely to a "new case" and asked Page if she'd discussed it with McCabe. Two days later, he said he had "mentally moved on to the next big thing," and the two exchanged blistering remarks about Russia. There is "very little I find redeeming" about Russia, Page wrote. "Even in history. Couple of good writers and artists I guess." Strzok, who had spent much of his career at war with the Kremlin, made no such allowances. "F*cking conniving cheating savages," he wrote. "At statecraft, athletics, you name it. I'm glad I'm on Team USA."

Strzok went into FBI headquarters that Sunday, as the temperature climbed into the low nineties in Washington, and sat down at an FBI computer. He opened a form known as an "electronic communication" and typed in the designation for the bureau's counterespionage section. He filled out a "synopsis" required for new cases and typed up some preliminary notes. The computer generated an eleven-character tracking number (in the FBI's system, Russian counterespionage cases begin with the sequence 105). Strzok was also responsible for the investigation's code name. The moniker for the Clinton probe, Midyear Exam, had reflected the sense of pressure and dread in the bureau that accompanied that assignment. This time, Strzok turned to the lyrics of the Rolling Stones, seizing on a portentous phrase for a probe that in time would become a howling squall. As Strzok hit send, "Crossfire Hurricane," the FBI's investigation of Trump and Russia, had officially begun.

TECHNICALLY, THE PROBE WAS NARROW AT THAT POINT OF CON-ception, focused exclusively on what Papadopoulos knew about Russia's plans to sabotage Clinton and whether he had committed any crime. But from the outset, FBI leaders understood the magnitude of this undertaking and where it might lead. The probe had been triggered by what "Papadopoulos had been discussing," Comey wrote.[9] But the real purpose, he said, "was to try to understand whether Americans, including any associated with the Trump campaign, were working in any way with the Russians in their influence effort."

Comey may have understood the stakes, but he failed to anticipate how disastrous his own decisions would be for the bureau and, ultimately, himself. His handling of the Clinton email probe would itself come under investigation and serve as a pretext for his firing. And Comey's tendency to entrust a small team at bureau headquarters for the most politically charged investigations—rather than employ a nearby field office—created a hidden vulnerability that would erupt a year later. It meant that one agent—Strzok—was heading the two most high-profile cases the bureau was handling.

THREE WEEKS AFTER LAMENTING THE CLOSURE OF THE CLINTON investigation, and the ensuing sense of professional letdown, Strzok embarked on an assignment that would be far more consuming, consequential, and treacherous. Even as he completed the tedious computer forms, Strzok was mentally moving through the inquiry's steps. Within forty-eight hours, he and another FBI agent would arrive in London to interview Downer and begin retracing

Papadopoulos's path since he had joined the Trump campaign. The bureau had notified the second-ranking official at the U.S. embassy in London about the agents' pending arrival but had urged her "to keep it quiet," Strzok wrote.

"Damn this feels momentous," he wrote. "Because this matters. The other one did, too, but that was to ensure we didn't F something up. This matters because this MATTERS."

CHAPTER 7

DEEP INSIDE THE KREMLIN

IN EARLY AUGUST 2016, CIA DIRECTOR JOHN BRENNAN CALLED White House chief of staff Denis McDonough. "I need to get in to see the president," Brennan said. There was unusual urgency in his voice.

Brennan had just spent two days sequestered in his office reviewing a small mountain of intelligence on Russia. The conference table at the center of the dark-paneled room was stacked with dozens of binders bearing stamps of TS/SCI (Top Secret/Sensitive Compartmented Information) and code words that corresponded to the most sensitive collection platforms aimed at the Kremlin. There were piles of "finished" assessments—analytic reports that had gone through layers of review and revision and were the agency's equivalent of an article ready for publication. But Brennan had also ordered up what agency veterans call the "raw stuff"—the unprocessed underlying material that forms the pieces of any intelligence puzzle.

Long after the end of the Cold War, Moscow remains among the most forbidding espionage environments. CIA officers face constant surveillance and elaborate Russian countermeasures that can make it almost impossible to determine whether a recruited spy is legitimate or secretly still loyal to the Kremlin. The agency scrapes together fragments of intelligence inside the Russian capital almost any way it can think of—informants, listening devices, surveillance cameras, and computer implants are only the most obvious approaches. Even then, the risk of exposure inside Russia is so great that the CIA focuses a large share of its intelligence gathering efforts on Russian travelers and sources far from Moscow.

Clearing his schedule, Brennan pored over all of it, his door closed, staying so late that the glow through his office windows remained visible deep into the night from the darkened driveway that winds past the headquarters building's main entrance. Brennan had gone through a similarly immersive exercise at other times of tectonic shift, including when the Islamic State supplanted Al-Qaeda as America's main terror threat. The WikiLeaks dump less than two weeks earlier suggested another such moment was at hand.

One development was a particular source of alarm to Brennan. In late July, Russia House delivered a bombshell—intelligence that reached deep inside the Kremlin revealing that Putin himself had authorized a covert operation aimed at destabilizing the American presidential election. The information came from two separate highly sensitive streams of intelligence, and captured the Russian leader, in his own words, declaring the operation's objective: damage Clinton and help elect Trump.

By then, the Russian connection to the WikiLeaks dump was public. The FBI knew that both the SVR and the GRU had penetrated the DNC's computer network and made off with thousands of files. The fact that those files had ended up splayed out online was also a pretty clear sign that the Kremlin had departed from the standard espionage playbook. But the intelligence on Putin was a breakthrough. The former KGB agent is one of the most elusive espionage targets in the world, avoiding electronic communications and conducting state business from secure chambers in the Kremlin. His inner circle, composed of loyalists who themselves are under constant FSB scrutiny, is nearly impenetrable. To gain insights into his intentions or instructions to Russia's spy services was, as one former CIA operative put it, the espionage equivalent of "the Holy Grail." Even today, U.S. officials have obscured details about the agency's sources, saying that their exposure would jeopardize key capabilities and potentially put sources in harm's way.

Putin's involvement made clear that Russia's spy agencies weren't merely improvising but rather executing a plan ambitious enough to require his authorization. Putin's participation meant that the operation would have been the highest possible priority, and that the WikiLeaks dump might be only the opening salvo.

By law and practice, American intelligence agencies have wide latitude to collect information overseas, whether from human sources, satellites spinning around the globe, or NSA surveillance systems that suck up an astonishing volume of global communications traffic. Such collection methods are considered "passive" forms of espionage, the ingestion of information with the aim of giving American policymakers, including the president, insights into the intentions of other world leaders and early warning about emerging threats or crises. That kind of spying may not be appreciated by its targets, but it is more or less accepted—everyone capable of doing it does it.

When the United States wants to go beyond merely "collecting" and into actively altering the course of world events, that's another matter. Covert action, as it is known, requires the approval of the president in the form of his signature on a top-secret memorandum known as a "finding." In recent years, America's covert operations have included the use of armed drones to carry out strikes on Al-Qaeda targets in Pakistan and computer viruses unleashed to sabotage Iran's nuclear weapons work. But the history of U.S. covert action goes back decades and includes countless cases of clandestine intervention in the affairs of other countries. In some cases that has meant backing favored candidates with cash and propaganda. The more notorious entries in the American record include the orchestration of the 1953 coup in Iran, assassination attempts on Fidel Castro in Cuba, and bloody anticommunist campaigns (often in partnership with brutal dictators) from Asia to Central America. In 1974, amid the Watergate scandal and cascading disclosures of abuses by U.S. spy agencies, Congress imposed new limits on the CIA and covert action, blocking the use of funds for such operations unless the president formally "finds" that each is critical to national security and notifies Congress.[1] There is no equivalent in the Russian system, but given the stakes of mounting a covert operation against the United States, Putin's approval is imperative.

After speaking with McDonough, Brennan also called deputy national security adviser Avril Haines, who had previously served as deputy director of the CIA. Brennan gave both only the broadest outlines of the new intelligence on Russia over the phone, but had a package delivered to the White House by courier later that day with extraordinary handling instructions. It was labeled "eyes only" and addressed to just four recipients: Obama, McDonough, Haines, and national security adviser Susan Rice. Inside the locked pouch was a summary of the intelligence Brennan had only alluded to by phone, describing the Kremlin plan to disrupt the election, the focus on hurting Clinton and helping Trump, and Putin's direct involvement. After reviewing the document, they had to put the pages back in the envelope, which was returned to its pouch and taken back to CIA headquarters. No copy was left in the West Wing.

Brennan was brought into the Oval Office at noon the next day. There were only four others in the room: Obama, Rice, McDonough, and Haines. (Vice President Biden was informed several days later.) The CIA director emphasized that the agency had "two different sources providing the exact same account" about Putin's involvement, a former Obama administration official said. "It was beyond dispute."

The information was "shocking and startling," one official recalled, indicating that the United States was confronting an "organized, sustained effort to influence the election." Obama's reaction was grave. He "was concerned and wanted as much information as fast as possible." Obama declared that he wanted the entire intelligence community "all over this."

Brennan proceeded to lay out how he planned to proceed, clearing each step with the president. He would move quickly to brief leaders of Congress, set up a task force at the CIA with representatives from other agencies to focus full-time on the Russian plot, and use a previously scheduled call with the director of the FSB to issue a blunt warning to the Kremlin. Brennan also urged that all subsequent reporting on the Russian active measures campaign be handled with extraordinary secrecy—U.S. spy agencies' visibility into the Kremlin was limited and precious. They couldn't afford to lose a single source.

As a result, no information on Russia's interference in the election was ever included in the President's Daily Brief, the highly classified intelligence report prepared before dawn each morning for the commander in chief. That digest is typically circulated to senior officials including the vice president, the secretaries of state and defense, top officials at the Justice Department and FBI, and a smattering of high-ranking national security officials in the White House. Brennan worried that even that highly restricted distribution list was far too broad for the agency's explosive information.

Brennan then moved to create a secret "fusion cell" at CIA headquarters. He contacted Comey at the FBI and Admiral Michael Rogers, the director of the National Security Agency, asking them to help assemble a multi-agency team in response to Obama's all-hands-on-deck directive. The group was given unmarked office space in the CIA's old headquarters building, just a few floors down from Brennan. Those joining the cell were required to sign new nondisclosure agreements before they could see any of the highly compartmented intelligence from the three contributing agencies.

The group included not only analysts but operatives expert at cyber intrusions and Russian tradecraft. The cell, comprising about fifteen people at CIA headquarters and a dozen or so others who continued to work from the NSA and FBI, had authority to direct new collection efforts, so among the ranks were also targeters—analysts who are specialists at generating new espionage prey, whether Kremlin officials with personal problems or nodes in computer networks where critical data might cross. Following the team's leads, America's massive espionage apparatus would take aim at critical marks including hacking groups and potential conduits to WikiLeaks. The FBI would also be looking for any sign that the hacking operation was being aided from inside the United States.

On August 4, the CIA communications staff patched Brennan through to Alexander Bortnikov, the head of Russia's FSB, the powerful agency that Putin had once led. The call was scheduled for the purpose of discussing Syria, where the United States and Russia were on opposite sides of an increasingly tense proxy war. The so-called Arab Spring had plunged Syria into chaos, and an Al-Qaeda offshoot took advantage, rebranding itself the Islamic State, vowing war on the West, and declaring the reestablishment of a Muslim empire—a Caliphate—across a vast tract of territory in Iraq and Syria.

Obama had authorized a covert CIA program to arm moderate rebel factions as well as U.S. military air strikes on ISIS strong-holds. To end the civil war, the United States also wanted to oust Syrian president Bashar al-Assad, a ruthless leader who was one of Russia's main allies in the Middle East. Putin had sent Russian forces into Syria to protect Assad's hold on power (though Putin insisted that Russia was simply joining the fight against ISIS). The arrival of Russian troops in 2015 meant the United States and Russia were not only backing opposing Syrian factions but flying armed aircraft, and—covertly or overtly—placing operatives on the ground in the same combustible part of the Middle East.

Brennan and Bortnikov were in some ways mirror images. The two had spent decades on opposite sides of one of history's most intense espionage rivalries—Brennan at the CIA and Bortnikov at the KGB and FSB. They were both born in the 1950s (though Bortnikov was almost four years older) and raised in the anxious apex of the Cold War—a decade-long stretch that included the Cuban Missile Crisis, the spread of communism through Asia, and school drills in which students practiced clambering under their desks in anticipation of a nuclear doomsday.

Brennan had come to see Bortnikov as a hard-line Russian nationalist, but one with influence in the Kremlin, and the Obama administration had discovered that Brennan could not only get messages delivered directly to Putin through the FSB chief but sometimes receive a response from the Russian leader within hours.

Brennan and Bortnikov had visited each other multiple times—each had been in the other's office. There was even a resemblance: both had bald heads and the stern expressions of men who approached their jobs with an all-consuming focus. As they finished talking about Syria, Brennan's voice hardened. He raised the ongoing FSB harassment of U.S. officials in Moscow, including the June 7 beating of the agency officer on the doorstep of the U.S. embassy. Russia's actions were "irresponsible, reckless, intolerable, and needed to stop," Brennan said.[2] Then Brennan turned to Russia's interference in the election. "I told Mr. Bortnikov that if Russia had such a campaign under way, it would be certain to backfire," Brennan later testified. "I said American voters would be outraged by any Russian attempt to interfere. . . . Finally, I warned Mr. Bortnikov that if Russia pursued this course, it would destroy any near-term prospect for improvement in relations between Washington and Moscow."

In hindsight, Brennan overestimated American outrage and resolve if only because it failed to account for the Trump campaign's enthusiasm for Russia's foray into American politics. He didn't know it at the time, but the Trump Tower meeting—in which Trump Jr. welcomed the prospect of damaging material on Clinton from a Russian source—had taken place four weeks before his conversation with Bortnikov. The day after that call, Trump had mocked Clinton for her tough rhetoric toward Moscow and proclaimed, "I'd love to get along with Russia."

Bortnikov denied that Russia was engaged in any election interference—"Mr. Director, we would never do such a thing," he said—and launched into a recitation of Putin's favorite talking points: it was the United States that couldn't keep itself from interfering in other countries' affairs; Moscow was the real victim.

Brennan doubled down. "When I repeated my warning, he again denied the charge," he recalled, "but said that he would inform President Putin of my comments."

The Obama administration had fired its first warning shot. But it went unheeded, the Russian active measures continued, and the Obama team would spend the next five months struggling to respond.

TWO DAYS AFTER OBAMA, BRENNAN, AND THE OTHERS MET IN THE Oval Office, Rice summoned a larger but still limited group of national security officials to the Situation Room in the basement of the West Wing of the White House. A few dozen can fit in the

windowless space, which has a long cherrywood desk, thickly pad-
ded black chairs, and flat-screen monitors mounted on the walls.
Modest seats with armrests line the edges of the room for so-called
"plus-ones," aides allowed to accompany the higher-ranking principals. For this session, the plus-ones were kept out. Some of the
thirteen members of the Principals Committee were not even notified of the meeting. Only eight people were in the room: Obama,
Rice, Haines, Clapper, Brennan, Lynch, Comey, and White House
homeland security adviser Lisa Monaco.[3]

In 2014, returning from a trip to Asia aboard Air Force One,
Obama had wandered toward the back of the plane to meet with
members of the White House press corps. He was agitated, bristling at criticism of his administration's approach to foreign policy,
which was often depicted as timid and trapped in endless cycles
of debate.[4] He told his airborne audience that he did indeed have
very clear ideas about how to advance American interests abroad,
and was aggressive when needed (he had, after all, intensified the
drone campaign against Al-Qaeda), but was also mindful of the
limits of American power to exert its will abroad, exemplified by
the endless bloodshed in Afghanistan and Iraq. Obama had come
into office seeking to end those wars, only to fail on both counts.
He was loath to act without support from allies or to be drawn
into foreign crises, like Syria, with no clear exit. To drive home
the point for the assembled reporters, he distilled his approach to a
single imperative: "Don't do stupid shit."

That meticulous reluctance seemed to capture the administration's mindset toward Russia from the first meeting in the Situation Room. Any impulse to strike back, to send a flare over
the Kremlin in the form of a cyberattack or a retaliatory dump of
compromising material on Putin, was tempered by anxiety over
how the Russian leader might retaliate. Obama, who would depart
the next week for a vacation on Martha's Vineyard, made clear

to McDonough and Rice that his priority was safeguarding the sanctity of the rapidly approaching election. He told his aides to proceed along three main paths: get a high-confidence assessment from the U.S. intelligence community, not just the CIA, on Russia's intentions; brief senior members of Congress and seek a bipartisan statement condemning Moscow's interference campaign; and finally, make sure the country's state-run voting systems were as well defended as possible against the nightmare scenario of rolling outages on election day.

After his early August meeting with Obama in the Oval Office, Brennan began contacting members of the so-called Gang of Eight in Congress—a group that includes party leaders in both chambers as well as the top Republican and Democrat on the House and Senate intelligence committees. The outreach was unusual. Though the CIA director routinely meets with oversight committees, in this case Brennan was arranging urgent, private one-on-one briefings. He wanted to tell the nation's top lawmakers in August what the rest of the country wouldn't learn for months: that Russia was waging an active-measures campaign not only to disrupt the election, but to damage Clinton and improve Trump's chances of winning.

Given that it was summer recess, scheduling the meetings was complicated by the fact that most lawmakers had decamped from Washington. But the bigger problem Brennan encountered was partisan. Democrats rushed to see the intelligence. California representative Adam Schiff, the ranking Democrat on the House Intelligence Committee, drove to CIA headquarters to meet with Brennan in his office. But Republicans reacted with seeming indifference. Schiff's fellow Californian, Republican Devin Nunes, the chairman of the House panel, put off getting his briefing until after Labor Day. And when Brennan finally came face-to-face with key Republicans, their reactions caught him off guard. Nunes seemed dismissive. Mitch McConnell, the Senate majority leader, was openly hostile. As Brennan moved through his talking points, the Kentucky senator expressed no alarm about what Russia might be doing in the U.S. election and instead accused the CIA director of playing politics.

"You're trying to screw the Republican candidate," McConnell said.

McConnell had spared no effort in blocking the agenda of the Obama presidency, and worked to ensure that neither Clinton nor any other Democrat would next occupy the Oval Office. But even in this era of hyperpartisanship, his rejection of the CIA evidence was stunning. Republicans had always cast themselves as the protectors of American security, the champions of its military and intelligence agencies, and yet McConnell seemed to see a greater threat to the election from Brennan than from Russia.

Brennan, who was raised in a strict Irish Catholic family in North Bergen, New Jersey, has a sense of moral rectitude that can border on self-righteousness. His younger brother, Tom, who runs a tavern in New Jersey, was once asked what it was like to have such a straitlaced older sibling. He paused for a moment and said, "It was like having two dads." Brennan flashed with anger at McConnell's accusation, and their conversation devolved into a shouting match.

Other attempts by the Obama administration to enlist congressional help in dealing with Russia's interference also broke down along party lines.

Jeh Johnson, the secretary of homeland security, had been given the job of assessing the nation's voting systems. During a breakfast roundtable with reporters, he raised the idea of designating the election systems as part of the country's critical infrastructure, effectively putting the patchwork of antiquated polling mechanisms on par with defense contractors or banking networks in their eligibility for federal protection. Johnson arranged a conference call with dozens of state officials hoping to convince them of the seriousness of the Russia threat and to get them to accept federal help. He ran into fierce opposition from Republicans who interpreted his critical infrastructure proposal as a sneak attack from Washington. The reaction "ranged from negative to neutral," Johnson said. "There was all this paranoia that it was going to be a federal takeover."[5]

The leader of the resistance was Brian Kemp, the Republican secretary of state in Georgia, who bluntly rejected Johnson's entreaties as "a politically calculated move." Kemp insisted that his state's systems were secure and discouraged others on the call from taking any help from Washington. Johnson was stunned. He was head of a department that was created after 9/11 to protect the country. Now there was a new danger with the potential to cause an election day meltdown (forensics would later show that Russia had probed more than twenty state voting systems). Johnson wasn't trying to seize control of state election systems. Instead, he was going as far as he was allowed in apprising them of the Russian threat. For those who needed it, he was offering help from federal cyber teams with a deeper understanding of Russian tradecraft and a stronger ability than most state offices to detect vulnerabilities that Moscow might exploit. Kemp was not only rejecting that overture, but voicing skepticism that the Russian interference Johnson was warning about was even real. "I don't necessarily believe that," he said.[6]

Ironically, the hodgepodge collection of voting mechanisms in the United States—many of them still reliant on paper—made them, collectively, less vulnerable. It was safety in archaity: no one cyber weapon could cripple so many disperse and incompatible targets. But the resistance from state and national Republicans pointed to a different kind of vulnerability, a distrust of the motives of those who are supposed to protect the public. The level of suspicion was so deep in some pockets that the Kremlin's claims were given more credence than the American government's.

The failed outreach was an early sign of trouble, not only for the Obama administration but the country—a clue that the political fault lines in America had widened to the point that it was no longer safe to assume the two parties could cooperate even against a foreign adversary. And while Trump didn't create this current of hostility and suspicion, he expanded and exploited it, mounting offensives during the campaign to discredit the FBI, CIA, the courts, and other core institutions. In the months ahead, his Republican allies would repeatedly undermine investigations into Russian interference, and turn their attacks on the CIA, FBI, and other core national security institutions. Putin had weaponized intelligence; McConnell and the GOP weaponized denial.

IN EARLY SEPTEMBER—STILL REELING FROM THE REJECTION BY state officials and resistance among the Republican members of the Gang of Eight—Obama decided to appeal directly to Congress. The president invited House and Senate leaders to the White House for a meeting that was presented to the public as a chance to discuss budget issues and his trip to Asia. In reality, as McDonough later revealed, it was "to discuss the alarming news about Russian ambitions to interfere with the election and ask the four leaders to draft a statement of concern." House Speaker Paul Ryan seemed amenable, but McConnell resisted. One participant said he came across as "dismissive, disparaging, disinterested."[7]

Obama followed up with an appeal to a broader group of congressional leaders. He dispatched Johnson, Comey, and Monaco to Capitol Hill on September 8 for an extraordinary, highly classified session with twelve lawmakers, some of whom had been part of earlier Russia-related gatherings. The group included party

leaders from both the House and the Senate, as well as the top
Republican and Democrat from the intelligence and homeland security committees in both chambers. The meeting took place in a
secure underground conference room burrowed under the east side
of the Capitol as part of a vast visitor center that opened in 2008.
The Obama team had been authorized by the president to lay out
the mounting evidence against Russia in the hope that members
would see the gravity of the situation and agree to issue a bipartisan
statement condemning Russia's actions and urging states to secure
their voting systems before it was too late.

From the start of the closed-door session, the Democrats were
calling for a public statement. "The Dems were, 'Hey, we have to
tell the public,'" one participant said.[8] To them, the idea that Putin was working against Clinton had been obvious since the first
dump from WikiLeaks, and here was even more proof of it. Senior
Democrats in Congress were already impatient with the Obama
administration for failing to say a single word to the public about
what it knew Russia was doing, and the Clinton campaign was by
then angry and incredulous. John Podesta had avoided appealing
directly to the White House to call out Russia, reluctant to put
the Obama administration in a political bind. But he was working
through Senate minority leader Harry Reid of Nevada, as well as
other Democrats, to get that point delivered to the White House.

But Republican leaders balked at any notion of a public statement. Instead, they made a somewhat counterintuitive argument
that to call attention to the Russian campaign would only compound its impact, serving Putin's desire to make Moscow appear
powerful enough to cause America to quake, and would sap public
confidence in one of the fundamental mechanisms of democracy.
In short, it would make Moscow look strong and America weak.

McConnell took an even more defiant position. He voiced skepticism of the underlying intelligence, claiming to be unconvinced

that the danger was as dire as Obama officials were depicting it. He went further, suggesting that if the White House were to issue a statement accusing Russia of waging a cyber campaign to hurt Clinton, he would regard that as a political move and say so publicly.

Obama officials were aghast. They saw the accumulating evidence against Russia as irrefutable, and expected Republican leaders to react to the CIA intelligence on Putin with the same sense of alarm that the president and his team had registered in the Oval Office with Brennan. Instead, they were essentially being told by the highest-ranking Republican in Congress that while he wasn't willing to condemn Russia for interfering to hurt Clinton, he was prepared if necessary to accuse Obama of meddling to harm Trump.

Several high-ranking Democrats had had enough—outraged over the Republican objections, and exasperated that the White House seemed unwilling to stand up to McConnell. On September 22, California senator Dianne Feinstein and Schiff, the top Democrats on the Senate and House intelligence panels, did what the White House couldn't bring itself to do. They issued a statement saying that "based on briefings we have received, we have concluded that the Russian intelligence agencies are making a serious and concerted effort to influence the U.S. election."[9] Both had been pressured by McDonough not to issue such a statement, worried it would only worsen partisan frictions. They went ahead anyway but agreed not to explicitly say that the Kremlin's objective was to hurt Clinton, noting only that it "may well be intended to influence the outcomes . . . we can see no other rationale for the behavior of the Russians."

The silence from the White House made Clinton seethe. Long after the election, in her published postmortem, Clinton wrote: "I do wonder sometimes about what would have happened if President Obama had made a televised address to the nation in the fall of 2016 warning that our democracy was under attack. Maybe more Americans would have woken up to the threat in time. We'll never know. But what we do know for sure is that McConnell and other Republican leaders did everything they could to leave Americans in the dark and vulnerable to attack."

McConnell finally acquiesced, to a degree, signing a September 28 letter to state election officials from all four leaders of Congress. The message was remarkable mainly for what it did not say. It warned of unnamed "malefactors that are seeking to use cyberattacks to disrupt the administration of our elections" and urged states to "ensure that their network infrastructure is secure." It made no mention of Russia.

ON OCTOBER 7, THE OBAMA ADMINISTRATION FINALLY BROKE ITS public silence, issuing a single-page statement saying that the U.S. intelligence community was "confident that the Russian Government directed the recent compromises of e-mails" spilled out by WikiLeaks and other sites, and that the "thefts and disclosures are intended to interfere with the U.S. election process." It alluded to Putin, saying that "only Russia's senior-most officials could have authorized these activities," but did not name him or suggest that the Russian leader had a favored candidate.

That statement was sent out with only two signatures, Clapper and Johnson. FBI director Comey had weeks earlier gone to the White House offering to publish a newspaper op-ed about the Russian interference as a way of alerting the public to Moscow's active-measures campaign. But the White House demurred, and when approached about signing the October 7 statement, Comey refused. The reason he cited—that the White House had waited too long and it was now too close to the election for the FBI director to be speaking publicly about anything related to the election—would in hindsight be hard to understand, particularly given the news he was about to make in two weeks' time regarding Clinton's emails.

Obama also kept his name off the statement, again citing his aversion to being accused of politicizing intelligence or intruding in the campaign. As White House officials put it, he didn't want to put his thumb on the scale. But his inaction was itself a political calculation. At that point, virtually every mainstream poll had Clinton on a clear path to victory, and Obama seemed anxious about contaminating that apparent inevitability. He was also influenced, indirectly, by Trump. For months, the GOP nominee had been warning that the election was rigged. Obama, senior aides said, was reluctant to do anything that might play into that conspiratorial narrative. Critics, including some in the administration, thought that Obama's caution was excessive and that Trump, the master of trolling, had succeeded in "working the refs," complaining so loudly and incessantly that he had cowed even the president. Clapper later described his frustration with Obama in biting terms. "I wondered what President Obama was thinking and if he regretted his reticence to 'put his thumb on the scale' of the election," he wrote. Meanwhile, "Putin was effectively *standing* on the other end of that scale." [10]

The White House had hoped that the October 7 statement, tepid as it was, would dominate the news cycle and galvanize the public. Rice secretly summoned Russian ambassador Sergey Kislyak to the White House that same day and handed him a message to relay to Putin, a warning she hoped would be reinforced by a visible public reaction—a show of outrage and unity—to the statement from Clapper and Johnson.

It was an unrealistic, almost quaint expectation in a campaign that more closely resembled a reality show than an exercise in civic deliberation. The statement scolding Russia likely would have sunk from public attention by its own dull weight—three prosaic paragraphs devoid of any actual revelation about the Russian operation or accompanying demonstration of urgency. A visit to the podium or even a statement from Obama would have reinforced the message and helped capture the attention of the public. But the president stayed behind the scenes, and the statement had the misfortune of arriving at another moment of peak Trump chaos.

THE CLAPPER-JOHNSON STATEMENT WAS POSTED ABOUT 3:30 P.M.
Thirty minutes later, *The Washington Post* published a story about sexually explicit comments Trump had made about women that were captured on video—but never aired—by the NBC show *Access Hollywood*.[11] The 2005 recording showed Trump arriving for a cameo appearance on the set of a television soap opera, *Days of Our Lives,* with *Access Hollywood* host Billy Bush. The two are on a bus and not initially in view of the camera, but audio caught a conversation in which Trump bragged about kissing, groping, and propositioning women without remorse or consequence, saying that "when you're a star, they let you do it." The tape was recorded several months after he married his third wife, Melania, and he can be heard recounting his attempt to seduce another woman. "I did try and fuck her. She was married," he said. "I moved on her like a bitch, but I couldn't get there."

As the bus pulled up, the two men appeared to see soap opera actress Arianne Zucker waiting to greet them. "Whoa!" Trump said. "I've got to use some Tic Tacs, just in case I start kissing her." He bragged about forcing himself on women. "I just start kissing them. It's like a magnet. Just kiss. I don't even wait."

"Whatever you want," said another voice, apparently Bush.

"Grab them by the pussy," Trump said. "You can do anything."

The story was the news equivalent of a neutron bomb, vaporizing every other object of media attention. It seemed impossible that the revelation would not be fatal to Trump's candidacy, with potential voters and even with Republican leaders, who recoiled and appeared to be on the brink of abandoning the GOP nominee. Ryan said he was "sickened by what I heard today" and McConnell described the comments as "repugnant . . . unacceptable in any circumstance." Several lawmakers said Trump should withdraw and make way for vice presidential nominee Mike Pence, who issued his own statement saying he was "offended by the words and actions" of the man he was campaigning with.

The news cycle was then further scrambled by another development. Thirty minutes after the *Post*'s *Access Hollywood* story published, WikiLeaks released a new batch of emails that Russia had raided from Podesta's account.

Their exposure had been in the works for months. Roger Stone, the Trump ally and former Nixon hand, had infamously tweeted on August 21, 2016, that "it will soon [be] the Podesta's time in the barrel. #CrookedHillary," then spent the following year deflecting scrutiny about how he had known about the next WikiLeaks dump so far in advance. The contents of Podesta's emails were, like anyone's inbox, tedious and titillating. There were messages about meetings, risotto recipes, and end-of-the-day notices that he was heading home for dinner. There were also excerpts of Clinton's speeches to Wall Street firms that she had refused to release, exchanges that exposed infighting among campaign aides, and cringe-worthy comments about the candidate. In one, a former Clinton campaign adviser lamented that "her instincts can be terrible."

The timing of the release triggered suspicion that WikiLeaks was attempting to come to Trump's aid by diverting attention from the *Access Hollywood* tape. If so, the effort fell far short of that goal.

The dump generated a quick burst of Clinton email headlines but was overshadowed by the crisis over the tape in the Trump campaign. That Friday, Reince Priebus, the chairman of the Republican National Committee, canceled a slate of weekend television appearances and raced to Trump Tower to urge Trump to get out of the race, telling him that if he didn't he would "go down with a worse election loss than Barry Goldwater's." [13]

By then, amid revelations of a ledger of secret payments to him by the Ukrainian government, Manafort had been forced out as chairman of the campaign. (He departed in August.) He was replaced by Steve Bannon, an incendiary political adviser best known as publisher of the right-wing *Breitbart News* and host of a conservative radio show. He looked like he had stumbled out of a bar at dawn, with a thick mat of unkempt hair, stubble on his face, and layers of baggy clothing over his well-fed physique. Temperamentally, he resembled Trump's earlier political guru, Roy Cohn, in sheer abrasiveness and scorched-earth approach to politics.

Bannon fought off Priebus and the GOP establishment, convincing Trump to stay in the race and ratchet up his aggression against Clinton. Late that night, Trump released a video in which he stiffly read a statement, against the backdrop of the nighttime New York skyline, that blended contrition with defiance. "I said it, I was wrong, and I apologize," he said. But he said his "foolish" banter with Bush was nothing compared to the behavior of the Clintons toward the former president's numerous female accusers. Bill had abused women, Trump said, and Hillary "bullied, attacked, shamed, and intimidated his victims." Defying calls for him to leave the race, Trump said, "We will discuss this more in the coming days. See you at the debate on Sunday."

Secretly, Trump and his team were scrambling to suppress even more damaging revelations. The next day, October 8, an editor at the *National Enquirer* learned that a porn actress with the stage name Stormy Daniels was shopping her story about a 2006 tryst with Trump in a hotel room in Lake Tahoe—at a time when Trump's third wife, Melania, was caring for their four-month-old son. The *Enquirer* tabloid had a long-standing symbiotic relationship with the real estate mogul, providing him with a steady stream of mostly positive publicity and secretly taking payoffs from him to kill potentially damaging stories. It was a practice known as "catch and kill" in the world of New York tabloids. David Pecker, the publisher of the *Enquirer*, knew exactly what to do. He contacted Trump's lawyer, Michael Cohen, and put him in touch with Daniels's attorney. The two sides would work out a deal in which Trump would pay $130,000 to keep her quiet. It worked through the election but would erupt less than one year into his presidency.[14]

THE FINAL MONTH OF THE 2016 RACE SEEMED TO COMBINE EVERY combustible element of the campaign in a final decorum-consuming conflagration.

Before taking the stage in St. Louis for that Sunday's debate, Trump arrived accompanied by three women who had accused Bill Clinton of sexual harassment and misconduct, as well as a fourth who had been raped by a man Hillary Clinton defended in a 1975 trial. It was a Bannon-orchestrated spectacle. In the debate itself, Trump at times seemed to stalk Clinton across the blue-carpeted stage. He said Clinton had "hate in her heart" and that as president he would appoint a special prosecutor to investigate her. At one point he snarled at Clinton, calling her "such a nasty woman," and ripped pages from his podium notebook as the event ended.[15]

Trump emerged appearing to have survived the pressure to leave the race, but his performance—in particular, his attacks on the last president to face impeachment and threats to invoke a special prosecutor—would leave a bitterly ironic residue.

Though invisible to the public at the time, the FBI investigation of the Trump campaign and its ties to Russia was intensifying. On October 21, the bureau was granted a warrant from a secret surveillance court giving the FBI permission to begin monitoring the communications of Carter Page, who by then had left the Trump campaign amid mounting press coverage of his travel to Moscow and lavish praise of Putin.

That same day, Trump delivered a performance in the final presidential debate that rattled officials across the U.S. intelligence community for how closely he hewed to the Kremlin's line. He depicted the U.S. intervention in Syria as a lost cause, endorsed Moscow's argument that the country was better off with Assad still in power, and said Russia and Syria were dismantling the Islamic State at a time when the Syrian government was actually shelling civilians in Aleppo. Trump even suggested the United States should switch sides to work with Moscow and Assad, saying that "if Russia and the United States got along well and went after ISIS, that would be good."

Trump also doubled down in disputing that Russia was interfering in the election, saying "our country"—meaning the CIA, FBI, and Obama administration—"has no idea." In one of the most heated exchanges, Clinton said Russia had a clear preference in the race because Putin would "rather have a puppet as president of the United States."

"No puppet. No puppet," Trump shot back. "You're the puppet!"

COMEY AND THE FBI HAD ANOTHER ELECTORAL EXPLOSIVE TO detonate. In late September, FBI agents in New York were investigating former congressman Anthony Weiner for sending sexually explicit texts to a teenage girl. Weiner was at the time married to one of Clinton's most loyal aides, Huma Abedin. As part of their investigation, the agents discovered that Weiner's laptop had thousands of Abedin's work emails. Concerned that the trove might provide material relevant to the already closed Clinton email investigation, the agents alerted headquarters. For reasons that are still debated, FBI officials in Washington waited weeks to act.

Then, on October 31, eight days before the election, Comey sent a letter to congressional leaders telling them that "in connection with an unrelated case, the FBI has learned of the existence of emails that appear to be pertinent to the investigation." Comey, who had yet to say anything publicly about the bureau's investigation of Trump and had pointedly refused to attach his name to the October 7 statement about Russian interference, was again wading into the political fray.

Strzok, the FBI agent who straddled both the Trump and Clinton email probes, led a scrambled effort to examine the Abedin emails. His team finished two days before the election, concluding that the files contained nothing to alter the bureau's previous conclusion that there was no basis to prosecute Clinton. Nevertheless, the final days of the campaign were consumed with stories and headlines featuring the words that the Democratic nominee came to see as fatal: Hillary Clinton and email.

On the eve of the election, major polls were still predicting a Clinton victory. Trump himself seemed to move through his final campaign appearances in an uncharacteristically morose mood. "What a waste of time if we don't pull this off," he said at a rally in North Carolina in late October. "If I lose," he said as the crowd went quiet, "if I lose, I will consider this . . ." He trailed off without finishing.

Russia seemed to be bracing for a Clinton presidency as well. In the campaign's final days, Russian diplomats began publicly berating the American electoral process, as if setting the stage for Trump supporters to question the legitimacy of the result. On the campaign's last night, pro-Kremlin agitators online prepared a sour grapes Twitter campaign to unleash after a Clinton win: #DemocracyRIP.[16] It was to be the culmination of a months-long covert social media effort to damage American democracy, hurt Clinton, and boost Trump—all led by a Kremlin loyalist and his young techies in St. Petersburg.

The next day, Donald Trump was elected president of the United States.

PART
THREE

CHAPTER 8

DEZINFORMATSIYA

O N THE EVENING OF JUNE 23, 2015, A TROLL WORKING AT THE Internet Research Agency in St. Petersburg sent an advertisement[1] to Facebook users thousands of miles away. "Patriotism comes from your heart," it read, "follow its dictates and don't live a false life. Join!" Below the text was a cartoonish sketch of an American Revolutionary War soldier—with a gun in hand and a distinctive three-cornered hat on his head—as he prepared to lead men into battle. The U.S. flag waved in the background as a silhouette of a bald eagle swooped past the banner. It was a stirring vision of America—though its origins were entirely un-American.

Looking back at it now, the ad contained numerous off-key notes, such as its awkward, stilted phrasing, highlighted by the oddly ungrammatical combination of words—*Being Patriot*—that were draped over the image in cursive. And anyone with access to the underlying data for the ad buy also might have wondered why a message aimed at English-speaking American adults was paid for in Russian rubles.

Facebook sold itself to advertisers by being able to specifically target users on the basis of their own self-declared interests. Data

Facebook later turned over to Congress showed that this was the first recorded ad bought by the Being Patriotic group—created, funded, and controlled by the Internet Research Agency. It was viewed 815 times and generated 39 ad clicks. It was the smallest of beginnings, the first minuscule turn of the screw. The cost was 798.92 rubles, or about $15.

The Internet Research Agency enjoyed a broad mandate as it sent messages in multiple languages with the goal of manipulating public opinion across much of the world. But the skilled English speakers working for the Internet Research Agency's Translator Project had the specific task of shaping the political battlefield ahead of the U.S. presidential election.

The Translator Project messaging was mostly soft in its early experimental days. The trolls in St. Petersburg bought sixteen Facebook ads on June 23, 2015—one week after Trump had launched his campaign for president—for the Being Patriotic group. But key was not the number of those ads but that Being Patriotic was one of more than 470 member pages and accounts[2] that the Russians had established to target U.S. voters. Most of the ads that day offered similar montages of flags and eagles alongside uplifting messages, but some began testing the resonance of other themes. One celebrated NFL football[3] with an accompanying motto of "We are proud to live in America!" Another[4] showed the Stars and Stripes next to a Confederate flag over a blood-splattered map of the United States and the words DO NOT BAN AMERICAN HISTORY. A third[5] was sharply anti-immigrant, previewing a theme that would become central to Trump's campaign for president, showing a white outline of the continental United States against a stark black background, along with the words SECURE THE BORDERS DEPORT THE ILLEGALS.

Many of these first Being Patriotic ads were viewed only a handful of times, meaning that the Russian entity had to pay only a few rubles to circulate the messages because Facebook charged advertising customers per click. But one ad[6] that day was an expensive triumph. "United We Stand! Welcome every patriot we can reach. Flag and news!" read the text above the watercolor image of an angry-looking eagle pictured between two U.S. flags. The Translator Project team asked Facebook's advertising platform to single out English-speaking American adults with interests in "Independence or Patriotism"—and the result was a direct hit: Facebook delivered the ad 529,205 times and charged its Russian client 331,676 rubles—more than $6,000.

If the aim was reaching American voters who might be amenable to messages mixing patriotism and politics, the Russian trolls had found their target. By the time Facebook closed Being Patriotic during the U.S. government investigations that followed the 2016 election, the group had amassed more than 219,000 Facebook likes. An independent researcher, Jonathan Albright[7] of Columbia University, would later estimate that Being Patriotic posts, all of them crafted in St. Petersburg, generated shares, reactions, or comments on Facebook more than 4 million times—and potentially reached tens of millions of users.

DISINFORMATION—OR *DEZINFORMATSIYA* IN RUSSIAN, MEANING the spread of information with the goal of deception—has long been a national specialty, dating back to the early days of the Soviet Union. Putin vastly expanded and updated the practice for the twenty-first century, adding round-the-clock information services in multiple languages that closely mimicked the feel of independent newscasts. This state-sponsored information flowed on a range of platforms, including cable and satellite television, YouTube, and other major social media outlets, reaching many millions of people across the world. Putin and his political allies gradually gained control of armies of trolls and automated bot accounts working on Twitter, Instagram, Reddit, Pinterest, and the most potent of them all, Facebook, which soon would have 2 billion users—including most Americans of voting age.

All of these social media companies were American, part of a massively profitable, fast-growing technology industry that was central to the economic might of the United States and, at least potentially, its geopolitical soft power. The global reach of the companies' platforms carried images of America and its influence to every corner of the globe. U.S. intelligence officials for years had exploited the "home court advantage" of having so much world communications traffic flow through American technology by vacuuming up massive volumes of online data flowing to and from American Internet companies. But the United States' dominance in technology also created, incongruously, an asymmetric vulnerability that a country like Russia could exploit. American society's vast migration online, its utter dependence on microprocessors and fiber optics, left it exposed to cyber incursions and attacks. American social media also was open, free, and tuned to the needs of advertisers, which spent billions of dollars trying to persuade users to buy products or support causes on these platforms. As a result, the companies had nearly unfettered access to the eyeballs of Americans, many of whom spent hours a day on their services. Putin and his trolls worked to master them all.

The Internet Research Agency had to study the tone of various American internet communities and learn how to mimic each of them with comments of their own. In retrospect, this mostly seamless immersion into U.S. political conversation was remarkable. The trolls found ready audiences for messages that were strikingly different in style, theme, and political bent while sharing one common quality: they ably exploited underlying tensions among Americans, be they racial, religious, ethnic, sexual, cultural, or ideological. On the left, there were pretend groups for gays and lesbians, politically active Muslims and African Americans upset over police brutality. On the right, there were invented groups for gun-rights enthusiasts, people incensed about illegal immigration, and those worried that efforts to curb police abuses had gone too far. One of the most popular Russian-run groups on Twitter portrayed itself as the voice of the Tennessee Republican Party, complete with the image of a state seal, under the Twitter handle @TEN_GOP. The group[8] attracted 145,000[9] followers, and its stridently political tweets garnered retweets from a wide range of conservatives, among them Michael Flynn, Roger Stone, Ann Coulter, and Eric Trump,[10] as well as celebrities such as Nicki Minaj and James Woods. This vastly expanded the reach of @TEN_GOP. A single retweet from Minaj—regarding the disturbing shooting of an elderly Cleveland man that was streamed on Facebook Live—was potentially displayed to all 21 million of the pop star's followers.

For his part, Flynn retweeted a @TEN_GOP link to a television ad produced by the super PAC supported by Republican financier Robert Mercer. The ad showed an African American actress in what at first appeared to be a pro-Clinton campaign spot. But it abruptly changed tone halfway through when the actress stopped the action and said she couldn't deliver lines that rang so false: "I'm not that good of an actress." Across the screen appeared the words SOME PEOPLE ARE BETTER LIARS THAN OTHERS. STOP HILLARY.

Three days before the election, Flynn tweeted,[11] "Yup, this is a great ad . . . needs to be RT'd frequently." Some 5,300 other Twitter users[12] followed his instructions, retweeting the ad to their followers. This had the effect of amplifying a message key to both Trump's and the Internet Research Agency's campaigns—that Clinton was so repugnant even savvy black voters were abandoning her in droves. Flynn probably only found out about the ad when he did because he was following the bogus @TEN_GOP account.

Actual Tennessee Republican officials, who managed their own @TNGOP Twitter account, repeatedly complained to the company that their online identity had been stolen, but the phony account remained frustratingly active. Yet beyond those Republican officials, it's not clear that anyone else noticed the subterfuge at the time. Researchers later said that the Russians had so thoroughly infiltrated online political conversation that the Internet Research Agency posts and those produced by actual American conservatives were often indistinguishable. And besides, if the ad or post matched up with your opinion, why worry?

On Facebook, the Being Patriotic group mixed bland missives intended to bolster a sense of shared community with occasional bursts of sharp-edged political commentary. But such paid advertisements were a small part of the overall messaging strategy, designed to attract new followers. They were dwarfed in volume by the free posts that trolls could slip into users' Facebook News Feeds and that later got shared onward to their "friends." (Because of Facebook's algorithms, clicking "like" on a paid Being Patriotic post increased the odds that other postings the group hadn't paid for would end up in your feed.) One month after those first advertisements in 2015, Being Patriotic posts were reaching tens of thousands[13] of Americans weekly. The most popular of these posts was an emotionally charged appeal on September 8 about homeless veterans. It featured a grizzled bearded man in a U.S. Navy winter cap and claimed that there were 50,000 more like him that were "starving dying in the streets." The reason was the determination of "liberals" to "invite 620,000 refugees and settle them among us. We have to take care of our own citizens, and it must be the primary goal for our politicians!" Facebook users liked, commented on, or shared this post more than 724,000 times, according to calculations by Albright.[14] Facebook would later disclose that, overall, the Internet Research Agency disinformation campaign conducted on its platform reached 126 million Americans[15]—an astonishing number, given that the total number of Americans who voted for either Hillary Clinton or Donald Trump would turn out to be less than 132 million.

FROM THE BEGINNING OF TRUMP'S CANDIDACY, THE RUSSIAN trolls on Twitter were overwhelmingly supportive of him, and while the homeless veterans post didn't mention any candidates, it managed to hit on two key Trump themes: the perils posed by immigration and the supposed neglect of veterans under Democratic Party rule. Other posts would be far more direct, including tweets showing Trump surrounded by smiling coal miners, soldiers, or police, portraying Putin's favored candidate as uniquely able to protect the nation from threats within and beyond its borders. The Russians working on a variety of internet-managed accounts were equally blunt in attacking Clinton as weak, ailing, corrupt, dishonest, evil, racist, and incompetent. This started during the early days of the Internet Research Agency campaign, when Trump still was regarded by many as a political sideshow, and it continued throughout Clinton's unexpectedly bruising Democratic primary battle with Bernie Sanders,[16] whom the trolls openly touted as the superior choice. The Russian attacks on Clinton continued to intensify throughout 2016, branding her with several derogatory nicknames. In hundreds of Internet Research Agency tweets, Russian trolls referred to her as "Killary"—a moniker that was then retweeted across the internet. One post from the Internet Research Agency's "Army of Jesus"[17] Facebook group pictured Clinton dressed in red

Satanic garb, complete with devil horns, as she faced off in a boxing match with Christ himself. The post implored: LIKE! IF YOU WANT JESUS TO WIN!

As the "actress" clip had demonstrated, the Russians were targeting what for decades had been the most loyal part of the Democratic Party's base: African Americans. Internet Research Agency trolls urged black voters to turn on Clinton in favor of Trump, Sanders, or Green Party candidate Jill Stein—or to not cast ballots at all, a tactic for suppressing votes that otherwise would likely go to Clinton. The fake Facebook group "Woke Blacks"[18] warned that "a particular hype and hatred for Trump is misleading the people and forcing Blacks to vote Killary. We cannot resort to the lesser of two devils. Then we'd surely be better off without voting AT ALL." Another Internet Research Agency account sent a Facebook advertisement on election day to people interested in civil rights, Martin Luther King Jr., and Malcolm X. The background showed Clinton and Trump on a debate stage with a fiery mushroom cloud between them. The foreground showed a young African American man in a gray T-shirt, with dreadlocks pulled back in a ponytail and his arms casually by his sides—as if not sure what to make of the spectacle before him. "We don't have any other choice this time but to boycott the election," the ad said. "This time we choose between two racists. Not one represents Black People. Don't go to vote. Only this way we can change the way of things . . ."

The St. Petersburg trolls also used their social media accounts to pose as grassroots political activists and publicize 129 phony event announcements. Nearly 340,000 Facebook users saw these Russian-crafted fliers, and more than 88,000 indicated online that they were interested in attending or planned to do so. An Internet Research Agency–controlled Facebook group calling itself Heart of Texas organized a rally in Houston on May 21, 2016, around the theme "Stop Islamization of Texas." That same day and place, a second Facebook group run by the Russian group and called United Muslims of America organized its own rally. But this one was dubbed "Save Islamic Knowledge"—with the goal of having two sides of a divisive social issue face off in a major American city. The "Stop Islamization" supporters drew a handful of people who faced a larger group of counterdemonstrators on the opposite side of a street in Houston as police stood in between to keep the peace.

The Being Patriotic group organized two rallies[19] in New York, with the help of American political activists and an Internet Research Agency–controlled Twitter account, @March_for_Trump. The same Russian social media groups organized a series of "Florida Goes Trump" events in that state, including one in which they paid a Republican political activist, retired sales representative Sherrie Hyer, to dress as Clinton.[20] She happily did, donning a blond wig and an orange prison uniform she had bought at Goodwill. "I would have done it for Trump anyway," Hyer said later, after U.S. investigators revealed that the rally had been organized by the Internet Research Agency. "There was still a lot of excitement and Russians had no part of that. This wasn't a trick for me."

The trolls in St. Petersburg were not all business. In the final days of May 2016, they used their burgeoning relationships on social media to convince an unnamed American in Washington, D.C., to stand in front of the White House holding a sign. It said, "Happy 55th Birthday Dear Boss." The "Dear Boss" was Internet Research Agency chief Prigozhin—Putin's "chef"—whose birthday was a few days later, on June 1. Then it was back to work.

CRITICS LONG HAD WARNED ABOUT THE POWER OF SOCIAL MEDIA to distort reality, by creating what amounted to feedback loops as people shared news, commentary, and memes with like-minded friends. Tech company algorithms reinforced this clustering of views, continually pushing content to users based on what they were likely to find appealing, in order to maximize how much time individuals stayed on sites. But conservatives argued something even more nefarious was afoot, alleging that those companies—based in some of the nation's most liberal metropolitan areas—were using their power to bolster the prospects of Democratic candidates and hurt Republicans.

Amid this debate, on May 9, 2016, the tech publication Gizmodo posted a story[21] under the headline "Former Facebook Workers: We Routinely Suppressed Conservative News." The claim in the headline came from anonymous sources asserting that the team managing the "Trending Topics" module on Facebook—a piece of online real estate capable of driving hundreds of thousands of valuable clicks—had a leftward bent. The story quickly went viral, especially among conservative sites portraying it as evidence that their long-standing fears now had been confirmed.

Few outside of Silicon Valley understood that while the private political bent of many of those in the technology industry was liberal, its animating ideology was capitalism. Tech moguls, no matter how they voted, ran their businesses to get rich. And the key to getting rich was massive, apolitical scale. This was especially true for free online services, such as Twitter, Facebook, and Google, that made money by earning a tiny fraction of a cent every time somebody clicked through their ad-filled platforms. Technology companies worked above all to build up their user numbers, since the more people they could reach, the more they could charge for ads. If a significant chunk of users—and especially in a big rich market like the United States—might abandon a platform because they thought it was politically biased, it was a corporate disaster in the making.

Since its founding in Mark Zuckerberg's Harvard dorm room in 2004, Facebook had weathered wave after wave of crises over allegations that it was putting growth—and ultimately profits—ahead of the privacy of its users, sparking investigations among regulators worldwide. The company had responded with apologies, tactical retreats, and the occasional legal settlement, such as the consent decree ending a Federal Trade Commission investigation in the United States in 2011. But the underlying corporate ethos, characterized as "move fast and break things," did not change as the company became among the richest and most powerful in Silicon Valley. Along the way it amassed an unparalleled trove of granular personal data on users worldwide based on how they described their backgrounds, work histories, religious affiliations, and political preferences, as well as what websites they visited and when they hit Facebook's ubiquitous like button while surfing the internet.

Given that most users also were voters in their respective nations, such information was gold to campaigns, as the conservative strategists and financiers who founded the political consultancy Cambridge Analytica would realize. Staked with more than $10 million from hedge-fund billionaire Robert Mercer and with his daughter Rebekah Mercer and then–Breitbart chief executive Steve Bannon serving on the board, the wizards at Cambridge Analytica had collected data on 71 million Americans in 2014. They used this to generate what the consultancy advertised as precise "psychometric" analyses of voters. This was portrayed as a kind of data-driven X-ray that looked beyond stated political preference to glimpse the personality within and, crucially, the kinds of political messaging that might move them to cast a ballot a certain way or to skip an election altogether. This technique and the role of social media data in it were key to Cambridge Analytica's pitch to prospective customers, which would eventually come to include the Trump campaign. And the consultancy, staffed mainly by Britons and other Europeans working out of London, were not alone in seeing this potential for better manipulating voters, and shoppers, based on the innumerable bread crumbs of information they left online. The technique used to collect data for Cambridge Analytica—building a quiz app, then collecting data on its users and all of their friends—was standard practice for years among entrepreneurs seeking to tap into Facebook's valuable data. Its application to electioneering, specifically Cambridge Analytica's improper use of Facebook data for the Trump campaign, led to the firm's demise.

But that scandal would not break for nearly two more years, when a Cambridge Analytica whistleblower began speaking to journalists in 2018. The crisis in 2016 as the presidential campaign loomed seemed both more straightforward and more confined. Facebook needed to convince conservatives that it—not some potential rival—was the natural home for them and their ideas. With this in mind, Zuckerberg invited more than a dozen prominent ones,[22] including Glenn Beck, Heritage Foundation president Jim DeMint, and Fox News commentator Dana Perino[23] to its Silicon Valley campus.

Zuckerberg posted after his meeting with conservatives, "Silicon Valley has a reputation for being liberal. But the Facebook community includes more than 1.6 billion people of every background and ideology—from liberal to conservative and everything in between. We've built Facebook to be a platform for all ideas." The Trending Topics module soon was gone.[24] Additionally, Facebook executives decided that automated formulas would make the decisions about what news stories people would see, and the editors who had managed Trending Topics lost their jobs.[25] Conservatives cheered. At no point did Facebook publicly accept the allegations of bias on Trending Topics, but the company worked hard to convince conservatives that they and their ideas were welcome on the platform.

Concerned with its bottom line, Facebook retreated toward its familiar reliance on algorithms, concluding that the best course was to let complex computations—not potentially biased humans—decide what users would see. This reflex ran deep in the tech world. Engineers ran Silicon Valley, and as a group they tended to favor engineering solutions to dilemmas, often relying on software and the unpaid work of users. Reinforcing this instinct was a key federal law, the Communications Decency Act, that gave technology platforms broad immunity from legal liability for content users uploaded. The more company employees were involved in deciding what content appeared on platforms, the more vulnerable tech companies were to arguments that they should be treated like traditional publishers. Any move in that direction might open Facebook and other tech companies to lawsuits for libelous or defamatory content or even criminal liability for circulating illegal material such as child pornography—a development Silicon Valley and its lawyers were desperate to avoid.

Set against that context, the establishment of Trending Topics editors always had been an experiment. Many would later conclude it was exactly the kind of experiment necessary to combat foreign disinformation, with humans arguably more adept than algorithms at spotting some forms of deception. This is a point that even Facebook officials themselves would later concede. But at this crucial moment, with Trump having seized the Republican nomination and the Internet Research Agency determined to blast disinformation at American voters, Facebook moved away from human judgment and back toward computerized systems that, as would later become clear, were all too easily manipulated.

WHILE RUSSIAN TROLLS WERE POSTING ON SOCIAL MEDIA AND OR-ganizing political events, they also worked to shape what news reports reached Americans. The Internet Research Agency maintained forty-eight Twitter accounts purporting to be from different parts of the country, according to Clemson University researchers Darren Linvill and Patrick Warren. With names such as @TodayPittsburgh or @KansasDailyNews, these Russian-controlled accounts had tweeted more than 531,000 times into 2017, typically a mix of local updates, national news, and sports. But the shaping of the American news agenda went far beyond such posts. The Russia disinformation machinery increasingly sprawled across cyberspace as the American election approached, with fake accounts on every major social media platform working together with dozens of stand-alone websites that the Russians also maintained. The result was a dense tangle of disinformation that was all but invisible as it ensnared U.S. voters. Somebody who saw a Being Patriotic ad might click the Facebook like button or join the group, guaranteeing a diet of its posts for months to come. If users followed links to articles on Russian-controlled news and commentary websites, tracking technology would identify these people for the purpose of delivering ads and Facebook posts to them later. Anyone who entered an email address, as many of the websites requested, would get customized disinformation delivered right to their inboxes.

Each component—Facebook, Twitter, YouTube, Instagram, and the Russian-controlled websites—worked as cogs in churning out content serving the Kremlin's disinformation agenda, including nearly three million Internet Research Agency tweets. In this manner, the Russians figured out a vast, coordinated way to curate the news consumption of Americans by selectively highlighting stories that served Putin's divisive agenda. Such news stories might come from state-funded propaganda organs such as RT or its sister site Sputnik, but they could also come from established newspapers or network news segments. Some stories were outright hoaxes, but often the articles were legitimate news reports focused on themes that bolstered Russian narratives, such as when Clinton stumbled at a September 11 memorial event in New York City. The Internet Research Agency promptly cycled through a variety of related hashtags over the subsequent days: #HillarySickAtGroundZero, #ClintonCollapse, and #ZombieHillary before settling on the favorites #HillarysHealth and #SickHillary. The Russian trolls tweeted these hundreds of times, helping to further amplify a story that already was garnering heavy attention. Trolls also regularly pushed reports about the Benghazi investigation, Clinton's use of a private email server, and the embarrassing dump of hacked Podesta emails. That last story highlighted how Russian efforts worked across realms. Russian government hackers stole the emails, which were provided to WikiLeaks before being posted online by the anti-secrecy group. Russian online sites then helped generate attention about the issues that surfaced in the emails.

Perhaps just as damaging, though, were the news stories that might have struggled to command attention without outside help. The 2016 election will be remembered for the unprecedented gush of phony news reports reaching wide audiences. Among the most infamous was a report in August about Fox News supposedly firing popular host Megyn Kelly "for backing Hillary."[26] That story,[27] though completely false, got a lift from Facebook's Trending Topics module, now freed from human influence or oversight. The Facebook page where it started, "Ending the Fed," also helped push a hoax story about Pope Francis[28] supposedly endorsing Trump.

This was not the first time that Facebook had faced phony news reports. Back in January 2015, two company officials wrote in a blog post,[29] "We've heard from people that they want to see fewer stories that are hoaxes, or misleading news," and asked users to help combat the problem by flagging suspicious stories. But that didn't stop the supposed papal endorsement, the Megyn Kelly story, or many other false reports from going viral on social media. *Buzz-Feed* [30] later calculated that in the final three months of the presidential campaign, phony online news reports generated 8.7 million Facebook interactions—a metric that includes shares, reactions, and comments—reaching more people during this crucial period than stories from such mainstream news organizations as *The Washington Post*, *The New York Times*, and NBC News combined.

Social media companies did not entirely miss the Russian attempts to manipulate Americans over their platforms. But the scale and ambition of the Internet Research Agency's Translator Project caught Silicon Valley unprepared, as did the rampant popularity of fake news. It was not just that the Russians were spreading information that hurt Clinton—it was that the information they were spreading was brilliantly targeted to appeal to partisans. If the first ad from Being Patriotic had been clunky and amateurish, by the last few months of the presidential campaign, Putin's team had mastered their art. First Draft, a Harvard-based site devoted to battling disinformation, asked in June 2016, "Is Facebook Losing Its War on Fake News?" [31] The piece strongly suggested that the answer was yes. Albright, the Columbia researcher, said he was alarmed enough about the flow of suspicious tweets after the second presidential debate, on October 9, that he started collecting posts for later analysis. Even within Facebook itself, some company employees took note of the phony papal endorsement and the Kelly story and grew worried that something was far more awry than the company publicly had acknowledged.

But the corporate instinct to underplay the problem continued for months—despite results on election day that stunned Silicon Valley. Many tech companies let employees take the next day off to grieve. At Facebook there was something of a revolt, with anguished messages flooding an internal message board and many employees wondering aloud what role the company's platform played in Trump's triumph. At a Northern California technology conference two days after the vote, Zuckerberg said,[32] "Personally I think the idea that fake news on Facebook, which is a very small amount of the content, influenced the election in any way—I think is a pretty crazy idea. Voters make decisions based on their lived experience."

But that morning, a troll sitting at a desk at Internet Research Agency headquarters in St. Petersburg appeared to be in a celebratory mood, sending the following message[33] on Facebook's Being Patriotic group: "Good morning, fellow Americans! Trump's victory is a chance given to us by God. It is a chance to rebuild our country and make it great for our children. Long live the United States of America!"

CHAPTER 9

THE RUSSIAN AMBASSADOR

TRUMP ENDED HIS CAMPAIGN WHERE IT BEGAN, AT THE TOWER bearing his name, this time surrounded by members of his family and campaign staff in a war room on the fourteenth floor. The outcome that was regarded as impossible when voters entered the polls seemed to emerge in phases through election night like a waxing moon—becoming improbable, then conceivable, and finally, shockingly, inevitable. Moments after his victory was declared by the Associated Press at 2:29 A.M., Trump adviser Kellyanne Conway saw an incoming call from Huma Abedin, the loyal Clinton aide whose husband's laptop had led to one last round of email woes for the Democratic nominee. Abedin said Clinton wished to speak with Trump "if he's available" for one of the most painful but essential rituals in American politics.[1]

"Donald, it's Hillary," Clinton said. She congratulated him and said she would seek to ensure that the transition was smooth. He complimented her campaign and her family. It was, she later wrote, "one of the strangest moments of my life. . . . It was all perfectly nice and weirdly ordinary, like calling a neighbor to say you can't make it to his barbecue."[2]

There was no replay of the escalator ride. Rather than pack election night supporters into the lobby of Trump Tower, the campaign had booked a ballroom at a nearby Hilton. Trump had run an often savage campaign in an election that was among the most toxic in American history. But for a thirty-minute stretch, in the early morning hours of November 9, he was generous and gracious. He praised Clinton for a hard-fought campaign and said, "We owe her a major debt of gratitude for her service to our country." He described his campaign, incomprehensibly, as one that had championed "all races, religions, backgrounds, and beliefs." His message to "the world community" was "that while we will always put America's interests first, we will deal fairly with everyone. . . . We will seek common ground, not hostility; partnership, not conflict." He then began a long list of thank-yous, beginning with "my parents, who I know are looking down on me right now."

Clinton waited until the next morning to deliver her remarks. The delay enabled her to compose herself and a touching, uplifting speech. She congratulated Trump and said she hoped he would "be a successful president for all Americans." While she couldn't find a credible way to ask her supporters to embrace Trump's vision, she said that "we owe him an open mind and the chance to lead." Clinton spoke of the hurt that she and her backers would feel "for a long time," and then, in the most moving moment of the speech, addressed the demographic that had probably been most wounded by the vitriolic words about women during the campaign, most disappointed by her failure to become the first female president.

"To all the little girls who are watching this," she said, "never doubt that you are valuable and powerful and deserving of every chance and opportunity in the world to pursue and achieve your own dreams."

Putin's dreams had already come true. In Moscow, it was nearing eleven in the morning when news of Trump's victory began to spread. Russia's parliament, the Duma, was in session, and members broke into applause. Vladimir Zhirinovsky, leader of the far-right (and inaptly named) Liberal Democratic Party, dictated a celebratory telegram: "Dear Donald, congratulations on your deserved victory, let the grandma Hillary rest."[3] Putin also sent a message voicing hope that the two men could "work together [to improve] Russian American relations from their crisis state," and that a constructive dialogue would emerge "between Moscow and Washington that is based on principles of equality, mutual respect, and a real accounting of each other's positions."

In the days that followed, U.S. intelligence agencies intercepted communications among senior Russian officials in which they exuberantly congratulated themselves. Their initial aim had been to sow discord in American democracy and damage a candidate reviled by the Kremlin. In the final months, they added another objective: propelling Trump to victory. In all three areas, the operation had exceeded expectations in ways that seemed to astonish its authors.

The White House on the morning after the election "was like a funeral parlor," one official said. Obama sent word asking spokesman Josh Ernest to join him in the Oval Office. When the president learned that his press secretary was in the middle of a meeting with extended staff, he summoned the entire group, more than two dozen people. Obama, who had just finished reviewing that day's PDB, stood in front of a desk that had been given to the United States by Queen Victoria and made from the timbers of a British ship that had explored the Arctic. The desk was named for that vessel, the HMS *Resolute*, and had been used by at least six previous presidents, including Franklin Roosevelt and John F. Kennedy. As Obama stepped in front of the historic piece, he was surrounded by remarkably young faces, many of them in tears.

"The sun is shining," he said, straining to strike a note of optimism, though it was true that overnight rain had given way to sunlight now beaming through the south-facing windows. Obama spoke of the importance of peaceful transitions in American democracy, and instructed his team to deal with the incoming administration with the same professionalism and respect that Obama had gotten from George W. Bush. "We are leaving this country indisputably better off than we found it eight years ago," Obama said, "and that is because of you."[4]

Obama was also leaving behind a political landscape more fractured than it had been when he took office, a party that no longer controlled the White House nor either chamber of Congress, and a country that suddenly seemed, especially to those privy to the intelligence on Moscow's interference, frighteningly vulnerable. Russia had preyed on America's supposed strengths—its openness, technological prowess, and internet dominance—sometimes so brazenly that the Kremlin seemed to be taunting the world's last supposed superpower. And while the American public had yet to learn just how comprehensive Russian interference was on behalf of Donald Trump, those in the inner circles of the executive branch felt a devastating sense of failure.

Ben Rhodes, Obama's deputy national security adviser, felt that the United States had failed to grasp the purpose and dimensions of the Russian attack. "We dealt with this as a cyber threat and focused on protecting our cyber infrastructure," Rhodes said. "Meanwhile, the Russians were playing this much bigger game."

Another senior Obama official was more blunt about the failure to fend off the Russian assault. "It is the hardest thing about my time in government to defend," the official said. "I feel like we sort of choked."[5]

ALMOST IMMEDIATELY AFTER BRENNAN'S EARLY AUGUST TRIP TO the White House, the Obama administration had begun weighing options for retaliating against Moscow. The task of generating ideas was assigned to the Cyber Response Group, an NSC team with representatives from the CIA, NSA, State Department, and Pentagon. They drew up lists of possible punishments—ratcheting up economic sanctions, taking down part of the Moscow power grid with a cyberattack, releasing damaging information about Putin and his offshore accounts. One participant even raised the idea of moving a U.S. naval carrier group into the Baltic Sea to show how seriously the United States regarded election security, a proposal that was never seriously considered. But while dozens of ideas had been passed up to the principals, all seemed to go nowhere. Requests would simply come back for refinements and more options.

After Brennan's brush-back of Bortnikov, the Obama administration had delivered additional pre-election warnings. During a September summit of world leaders in Hangzhou, China, Obama confronted Putin point-blank, telling him that the United States would retaliate—without saying how—if Russia didn't stop. Photos captured the moment, showing the president staring icily down at the Russian leader. Obama then issued a veiled threat in a press conference. "I will tell you that we've had problems with cyber intrusions from Russia in the past," he said. "And look, we're moving into a new era here where a number of countries have significant capacities. And frankly, we've got more capacity than anybody, both offensively and defensively." But as September dragged into October, frustration began to build. Russia's interference was continuing unchecked, with fresh dumps of Podesta emails and waves of propaganda on Twitter and Facebook, and yet there was no sign from the Situation Room that Obama intended to act.

In fact, Obama and his closest advisers—McDonough, Rice, and Haines—had essentially ruled out any pre–election day responses from the start, a decision that chafed even some agency leaders and cabinet members who couldn't understand why the United States would continue to absorb blow after blow from the Kremlin. Obama and his inner circle worried that any moves before November 8 risked triggering a cycle of escalation culminating in a crisis on election day. "We set out from a first order principle that required us to defend the integrity of the vote," McDonough said. In other words, the "don't do stupid shit" edict meant to avoid provoking Putin. But nobody outside the Principals Committee knew that, because their deliberations were sealed off from the rest of the government. Their Situation Room meetings followed the same protocols that the White House had used when planning the Osama bin Laden raid. Meeting notices went out to cabinet secretaries in envelopes that were not allowed to be opened by their aides. Even the principals themselves didn't receive meeting agendas until they sat down. The plus-ones were kept out. The cameras and microphones in the Situation Room remained off.

Among those included in this exclusive arrangement, not all were happy with Obama's restraint. In the final weeks before the election, Secretary of State John Kerry had drafted an "action memo" calling for sweeping new sanctions on Russia. He was an unlikely agitator on the issue. Others in the administration had seen him as too soft on Moscow, strung along during negotiations for a cease-fire in Syria that ultimately collapsed. Knowing Obama didn't want to act before election day, he called for the United States to announce punitive measures as soon as the votes were securely counted. The proposal died without a hearing, along with any prospect of punishing Russia on or immediately after the election.

The final warning to the Kremlin was conveyed on October 31 through a secure channel originally created to prevent miscommunication from leading to a nuclear exchange. The system is known as the "red phone" but has never actually involved placing a call. It began with a teletype connection between the Pentagon and the Kremlin, then turned to fax and finally encrypted email. The late October message alluded, carefully, to war, noting that "international law, including the law for armed conflict, applies to actions in cyberspace."[6] Meddling in the election "would represent serious interference in the fundamentals of U.S. society." Russia confirmed that it got the message but offered no immediate reply.

Obama officials came to believe that these warnings persuaded Putin to abandon any idea of carrying out a cyber offensive on election day. Russia had mounted a final social media barrage to boost Trump, and later forensics work by the FBI and other agencies showed Russian probing of dozens of state voting systems in the final months of the race. But it was true that there were no breakdowns at polling booths, manipulation of vote counts, or other signs of direct Kremlin interference on November 8.

So many pre-election deliberations were built around an assumption that seemed reasonable even into the final hours of the campaign, but proved disastrously wrong: the seeming inevitability of a Clinton victory. It was part of why she failed to campaign in Michigan and Wisconsin, where narrow losses doomed her chances in a race decided by fewer than 80,000 votes. It was why Comey had decided to go public with the FBI's investigation of Clinton's emails, scolding her for "extreme carelessness" in the hopes it would inoculate him against post-election charges by Republicans that the bureau had suppressed or screwed up its investigation of Clinton. (Comey for months denied that politics had played any role in his thinking but acknowledged while promoting his memoir that "it must have because I was operating in a world where Hillary Clinton was going to beat Donald Trump."[7]) Later, Obama officials similarly denied that the expectation of a Clinton triumph had influenced their deliberations. "Our primary interest in August, September, and October was to prevent [Moscow] from doing the max they could do," one senior official said, meaning an election day assault. "We made the judgment that we had ample time after the election, regardless of outcome, for punitive measures."

But those "regardless of outcome" assertions had a ring of retroactive rationalization. Part of Obama's aversion to putting his thumb on the scale was the worry that doing so would taint a Clinton presidency—anything perceived as help during the campaign would be used by the Republicans to undermine her after it was won. There was also a sense among some White House officials that Obama didn't need to be the one to fully mete out Russia's punishment; any sanctions he imposed would only be the first installment. Once she took over, Clinton—the prime target of Putin's ire and attacks—would finish the job.

Instead, the Obama team awoke to an unrecognizable political landscape in which America was about to be led by a president who revered Putin, had praised WikiLeaks, and had prodded Russia to continue hacking his political opponent. Not only was it hard to imagine Trump inflicting penalties on the Kremlin, but it seemed entirely possible that he would roll back whatever sanctions Obama now, after the election, imposed.

In this disorienting climate, the Obama team struggled to regroup. Chastened by the failure of his pre-election proposal, Kerry offered a fallback calling for the creation of an independent commission to investigate Russia's interference and recommend reforms. But that plan was shot down by Obama himself in a National Security Council meeting, dismissed as too partisan with no chance of getting approved by Congress.

"By December, those of us working this for a long time were demoralized," one participant in the White House deliberations said. While Obama continued deliberating, Trump prepared to take power.

FOR THE FIRST TIME IN AMERICAN HISTORY, A BUSINESS EXECUtive with no experience in government service had been elected president. Trump was supposed to bring a corporate acumen to the job, an ability to make decisions and deals that would bog down ordinary politicians. But his true forte, the one that television producers had built an entire show around, was hiring and firing, making instinctual choices about personnel.

The transition period should have played to these strengths, taking Trump out of campaign mode and putting him in charge of building an administration, a task that in theory more closely resembled running a corporation, the government equivalent of launching a start-up with a wide-open opportunity to assemble a peerless staff. The Trump transition wobbled from the outset, however, and within weeks was beset by warring factions, an unwieldy structure, and purges of key players.

Trump had enlisted New Jersey governor Chris Christie to set up a transition staff during the campaign, a group that would lay the groundwork for a Trump presidency by drawing up lists of people who could take key jobs in various agencies and mapping out the decisions and issues that a new cabinet would face.

In fact, the Clinton and Trump campaigns had both set up fledgling teams in the same building on Pennsylvania Avenue, half a block west of the White House. They were on different floors—Clinton on eleven and Trump on seven—but crossed paths in the lobby and on elevators. For months, smirks and eye rolls from the Clinton team made it clear they saw the idea of preparing for a Trump presidency as delusional. But the dynamic changed on

November 9, as Clinton advisers began carrying boxes out of the building, often in tears.

The Trump campaign had been run from Trump Tower. The post-election plan called for decision-making to shift south to Washington, and for Trump himself to meet with a staff of a hundred or more people who had been making preparations for six months, setting up secure rooms for handling classified material, communications equipment for introductory calls with foreign officials, and preliminary meetings with the experts and experienced government officials in line to run the new government.

But Trump himself remained in New York, the transition became split between dueling centers of power, and the job of building an administration became both more complicated and treacherous. Trump called Christie two days after the election to tell him that the Bridgegate scandal in New Jersey—in which Christie's administration was accused of settling political scores by creating traffic jams in the towns of rivals—had become too hot for Trump to keep the governor in the job. Others suspected a shiv from Kushner, who had a deep personal grievance with the New Jersey politician. As the U.S. attorney in New Jersey in the early 2000s, Christie had led the investigation of Kushner's father, the head of the family's real estate empire, for illegal campaign contributions and tax evasion. The case took an ugly turn when Kushner Sr.'s brother-in-law began cooperating with investigators and Kushner—Jared's father—retaliated by hiring a prostitute to seduce his sister's husband, arranging to tape the tryst and then sending the recording to his sibling. Kushner pleaded guilty to eighteen felony counts and spent fourteen months in an Alabama prison. Jared flew to visit him nearly every weekend.

Christie's ouster triggered a broader purge. Former Republican congressman Mike Rogers, who had led the House Intelligence Committee and headed the Trump team's national security planning efforts, was among those pushed out. Subordinates, many of whom had the most familiarity with the workings of Washington, tumbled like dominoes. Establishment figures in Washington foolish enough to think they might be welcomed despite opposing Trump during the campaign faced a venomous reckoning. Eliot Cohen, the George W. Bush official who had drafted the most prominent letter opposing Trump on foreign policy grounds, initially encouraged experienced hands to consider joining the administration.

"After exchange w Trump transition team, changed my recommendation: stay away," he said in a November 15 posting on Twitter. "They're angry, arrogant, screaming 'you LOST!' Will be ugly."

Trump did come to Washington two days after the election and met with Obama for more than an hour at the White House. Obama was cordial to the man who spent years promoting a baseless conspiracy theory that the nation's first African American president had actually been born in Kenya and should not have been eligible for office. The president gently prodded Trump to reconsider some of his campaign vows—including to withdraw from the Paris climate agreement—and offered a single piece of personnel advice: do not give Mike Flynn an important job.

OBAMA HAD NO DIRECT ROLE IN FLYNN'S OUSTER AS HEAD OF THE Defense Intelligence Agency, but he knew that his tenure there had been turbulent. Administration officials were surprised at the truculent way Flynn reacted to his dismissal, repeatedly lashing out and claiming he had been forced out for daring to criticize the administration's approach to fighting terror. None of this was true. After Flynn's trip to Russia and performance at the Republican convention, even many of his former military peers were convinced he was no longer fit to hold high office.

Christie and Rogers had also cautioned against hiring Flynn. Christie had sat through the initial intelligence briefings Trump got upon securing the GOP nomination—those that Trump opted not to skip—and found himself elbowing Flynn, prodding the retired general to stop interrupting and launching into strident expositions of his own views. Through his work on the House intelligence panel, Rogers knew a good deal about Flynn's background—his valiant tours in combat zones as well as his penchant for breaking rules. Flynn had been investigated for sharing classified information without permission to allies and reprimanded for doing the same on a trip to Pakistan. After Flynn arrived at DIA, Rogers had been troubled by Flynn's surprising inability to answer basic questions about the agency's budget during a routine hearing where he should have expected such queries.

Most presidents-elect would have been given pause by so much damning feedback, especially since it came from Republicans and Democrats. But to Trump, reflexively hostile to unwanted direction, all the advice against hiring Flynn amounted to the ultimate endorsement. Flynn had come through for him when virtually no one with any national security stature would publicly back him. Flynn had tirelessly campaigned for the candidate, often serving as a warm-up act during rallies. Flynn had also built up a following among conspiratorially minded conservatives who made up the alt-right, using his social media accounts to spread attacks on Muslims and Clinton in equal measure.

Less than a week after the election, with Christie and Rogers out of the way, Flynn was named Trump's designated national security adviser. It was a job that would make Flynn responsible for coordinating policy and decisions involving the world's most powerful military and intelligence services. He would occupy an office in the West Wing, putting him closer than any other national security official to the novice president.

Within weeks, Flynn was causing problems. One of his first moves after securing a role in the new administration was to bring on his thirty-three-year-old son as an assistant on the transition team. Michael G. Flynn had struggled to live up to the achievements of his three-star father, and their relationship was strained by the elder Flynn's lengthy deployments. For years, Michael G. Flynn had relied on his family for jobs, working for an uncle's printing services company in Orange County, California, and then joining his father's consulting firm after the latter's retirement from the Army. That allowed the two to make up for lost time, and working for the Trump transition team offered an unexpected opportunity.

The two Flynns shared an affinity for the corrosive side of social media, and six days before the election, the father posted a link to a fabricated story claiming that the Clintons were being investigated by New York police for pedophilic crimes—a baseless assertion rooted in preposterous alt-right conspiracy claims that Podesta's hacked emails contained coded messages about human trafficking and a child-sex ring. "U decide—NYPD Blows Whistle on New Hillary Emails: Money Laundering, Sex Crimes w Children, etc. . . . MUST READ!" Flynn wrote about the discredited piece.

The younger Flynn's online antics were even worse. He had tweeted that minorities only voted for Barack Obama in 2012 because Obama was black. In early 2016, he weighed in on an article about whites-only dating sites with a twisted defense of excluding other races: "soooo African Americans can have B.E.T. but whites can't have their own dating site? Hmmm . . ." He spread unfounded claims alleging deviant sexual conduct and drug dependencies by other presidential candidates and was a tireless promoter of conservative conspiracy outlets, including InfoWars, a website run by talk radio host Alex Jones that was among the main backers of the Clinton sex-ring lies.[8]

That insidious rumor ended up having frightening real-life consequences. Part of the supposed conspiracy alleged that the illicit activity was run out of a restaurant, Comet Pizza, in northwest Washington. On December 4, a twenty-eight-year-old North Carolina man who had read about the outlandish claims online drove to Washington and barged into the restaurant armed with a .38-caliber Colt revolver, an AR-15 Colt rifle, and twenty-nine rounds of ammunition strapped to his chest.[9] After workers and customers—including some children—fled, Edgar M. Welch fired several rounds into a locked closet door and took aim at an employee, who turned and ran. No one was harmed, and Welch surrendered after failing to find hidden rooms or evidence of sex trafficking. Dauntless, Michael G. Flynn took to Twitter later that night, refusing to let the conspiracy die. "Until #Pizzagate proven to be false, it'll remain a story. The left seems to forget #PodestaEmails and the many 'coincidences' tied to it," he wrote.

Though Trump had seemed unbothered by previous tweets, this was apparently too much, and young Flynn was forced out of his job on the transition team two days later, making him the rare member of the president-elect's organization to pay such a price for being malicious or mendacious—although his father would soon face trouble of his own.

TRUMP'S ASTONISHING WIN SET OFF A STAMPEDE AMONG FOREIGN leaders desperate to make contact with the president-elect, or if not him, his inner circle of relatives and trusted aides. He spent the day after the election on the phone with a dozen heads of state, including the leaders of Israel, Australia, Egypt, and Japan. Kushner, who had been given a startlingly expansive foreign policy portfolio despite no relevant experience and a variety of possible conflicts due to foreign loans for his real estate holdings, was inundated with

A view of the four-story building allegedly known as the "troll factory" in St. Petersburg, Russia, on February 17, 2018. The U.S. government alleges the Internet Research Agency started interfering as early as 2014 in U.S. politics, extending to the 2016 presidential election, saying the agency was funded by a St. Petersburg businessman, Yevgeny Prigozhin. *AP Photo/Naira Davlashyan*

President Trump and Russian president Vladimir Putin shake hands at the beginning of a meeting at the Presidential Palace in Helsinki, Finland, on July 16, 2018. *AP Photo/ Pablo Martinez Monsivais*

Carter Page, a foreign policy adviser to Donald Trump's 2016 presidential campaign, speaks with reporters following a day of questions from the House Intelligence Committee on November 2, 2017. *AP Photo/J. Scott Applewhite*

Central Intelligence Agency director John Brennan takes questions from reporters during a press conference at CIA headquarters in Langley, Virginia, on December 11, 2014. *Jim Watson/AFP/Getty Images*

A picture taken on September 14, 2015, shows the Kremlin's Spasskaya (Savior) Tower in Moscow. *Kirill Kudryavtsev/AFP/Getty Images*

Retired Lt. Gen. Michael Flynn delivers a speech on the first day of the Republican National Convention on July 18, 2016, at the Quicken Loans Arena in Cleveland, Ohio. *Alex Wong/Getty Images*

Concord Catering general director Yevgeny Prigozhin at a meeting of Russian and Turkish government officials and business leaders in St. Petersburg, Russia, on August 9, 2016. *Mikhail Metzel/TASS via Getty Images*

Russian president Vladimir Putin (left) meets his U.S. counterpart, Barack Obama, on the sidelines of the G20 Leaders Summit in Hangzhou on September 5, 2016. *Alexei Druzhinin/AFP/Getty Images*

The Central Intelligence Agency seal is displayed in the lobby of CIA Headquarters in Langley, Virginia, on August 14, 2008. *Saul Loeb/AFP/Getty Images*

Julian Assange, the founder of WikiLeaks, speaks to the media from the balcony of the embassy of Ecuador on May 19, 2017, in London, where he had sought asylum. *Jack Taylor/Getty Images*

Robert S. Mueller III, the special counsel leading the Russian investigation, leaves Capitol Hill following a meeting with members of the U.S. Senate Judiciary Committee on June 21, 2017. *Saul Loeb/AFP/Getty Images*

A picture taken on November 8, 2016, shows Russian lawyer Natalia Veselnitskaya posing during an interview in Moscow. Veselnitskaya was allegedly among a group of Russians who met with Donald Trump Jr. at Trump Tower on June 9, 2016, a meeting in which Trump Jr. expected to get "dirt" on Hillary Clinton. *Yury Martyanov/AFP/Getty Images*

FBI agent Peter Strzok is sworn in before a joint hearing of the House Judiciary and Oversight and Government Reform committees on July 12, 2018. While involved in the probe into Hillary Clinton's use of a private email server in 2016, Strzok exchanged text messages with FBI attorney Lisa Page that were critical of Trump. After learning about the messages, Mueller removed Strzok from his investigation into whether the Trump campaign colluded with Russia to win the 2016 presidential election. *Chip Somodevilla/Getty Images*

Former FBI lawyer Lisa Page walks to a House Judiciary Committee closed-door meeting on July 13, 2018. *Mark Wilson/Getty Images*

Campaign Chair John Podesta listens backstage to former secretary of state Hillary Clinton at a rally in Cedar Rapids, Iowa, on January 30, 2016. *Melina Mara/*The Washington Post

Michael Cohen, an attorney for President-elect Donald Trump, arrives at Trump Tower in New York on January 12, 2017. *Jabin Botsford*/The Washington Post

A doorman stands at the door of Trump Tower in New York on January 12, 2017. *Jabin Botsford*/The Washington Post

Jared Kushner listens onstage at the Lincoln Memorial during a pre-inaugural "Make America Great Again! Welcome Celebration" in Washington, D.C., on January 19, 2017. *Jabin Botsford*/The Washington Post

Donald Trump Jr. attends the 2018 Easter Egg Roll on the south lawn of the White House on April 2, 2018. *Jabin Botsford*/The Washington Post

Hillary Clinton speaks during a press conference in New York on November 9, 2016, the day after the presidential election. *Matt McClain*/The Washington Post

Former FBI director James B. Comey testifies before the Senate Intelligence Committee on Capitol Hill on June 8, 2017. *Melina Mara*/The Washington Post

James R. Clapper, U.S. Director of National Intelligence, prepares to take part in a Senate Armed Services Committee hearing on January 5, 2017. *Matt McClain*/The Washington Post

Paul Manafort, former Trump campaign chairman, departs U.S. District Court in Washington, D.C., on October 30, 2017. *Bill O'Leary*/The Washington Post

House Intelligence Committee Chairman Devin Nunes (R-Calif.) is pictured on Capitol Hill on March 28, 2017. *Melina Mara*/The Washington Post

Rod Rosenstein is pictured on March 7, 2017, before the Senate Judiciary Committee during his confirmation hearing to be deputy attorney general. *Melina Mara*/The Washington Post

Attorney General Jeff Sessions arrives for a House Oversight Committee hearing on November 14, 2017. *Bill O'Leary*/The Washington Post

calls from countries that didn't make that presidential cut. And while Flynn was on the fringes of Trump's inner circle, his newly designated role established him as a rising power broker and key point of contact for one man in particular: the Russian ambassador to the United States, Sergey Kislyak.

Kislyak had trained to be a Soviet scientist, earning a degree from the Moscow Engineering Physics Institute in the early 1970s. But he joined the Soviet Foreign Ministry in 1977[10] and rose through the organization's ranks even after communism's collapse, serving as Russia's ambassador to NATO in the 1990s and arriving in Washington as Russia's principal envoy in 2008. Flynn had known him since his trip to Russia as DIA director in 2013. Two years later he'd had dinner with Kislyak at the ambassador's lavish Beaux Arts residence four blocks north of the White House, shortly before Flynn left for Moscow to appear at the anniversary gala for the Russian propaganda outlet RT.

With white hair and a fleshy pink face, Kislyak resembled a clean-shaven Santa Claus, and seemed to possess a similar ability to be everywhere at once. A tireless networker, he threw five-course dinners that pulled in hundreds of well-connected guests and turned up routinely at think tank discussions and diplomatic receptions, all while accumulating contacts at an astonishing rate. McFaul, the U.S. ambassador to Moscow, marveled at his counterpart's access, but also at the discipline he brought to the job of advocating for the Kremlin. "Moscow didn't send him to Washington to become friends with U.S. government officials," McFaul wrote. "His writ was to advance Russian national interests, and he remained true to that mission."

Given Trump's admiration for Putin and desire to forge close ties with Russia, managing the Moscow account was a coveted job in the still-forming administration. Flynn positioned himself as Moscow's main point of contact and pursued the relationship with such heedless vigor that others on the transition team more skeptical of Russia became alarmed.

In late November, Flynn flew down from New York to meet with Trump's Washington transition staff for the first time. Surrounded by about a dozen aides and subordinates, Flynn said he was being inundated by requests from diplomats. Most would have to wait until he was in office to exchange more than introductory greetings, but Flynn noted that he'd already set aside time on his schedule for Kislyak. The reference to the Russian ambassador raised eyebrows in the room, particularly given the intense focus on Trump's constant praise of Putin and the mounting evidence that Moscow had meddled in the election. Flynn seemed oblivious not only to the optics of a potential conversation with Kislyak but to the fact that any communication between them would inevitably be intercepted by U.S. intelligence.

Marshall Billingslea, a former senior Pentagon official in the George W. Bush administration and, like most establishment Republicans, a Russia hawk, was managing the Washington-based team, and he spoke up, warning Flynn that Kislyak was surely under constant U.S. surveillance, a fact that should have been obvious to the former director of the DIA. Billingslea didn't feel comfortable telling someone about to hold such a powerful White House job whom he should or shouldn't talk to, but he offered to obtain a copy of the CIA's profile of Kislyak, a document that would likely note that while the ambassador was not technically a spy, he undoubtedly gathered information and passed along whatever he learned to Russian intelligence.[11] Flynn seemed unfazed by Billingslea's comments.

In the last week of November, Billingslea met with lower-level Obama officials in the Situation Room at the White House to discuss transition logistics. At the end of the meeting, he surprised his counterparts by asking for the CIA file. "Can we get material on Kislyak?" one recalled him asking. The Obama team said they would see what they could do.

Days later, on December 1, Flynn and Kushner met with Kislyak at Trump Tower.

The Trump transition kept the meeting secret. In it, Kushner made a bizarre request that caught even Kislyak off guard. Kushner proposed setting up a private communications channel between the Trump team and the Kremlin, perhaps even using encrypted communications gear from inside the Russian embassy. It was an astonishing suggestion. Russia had just waged an unprecedented cyber assault on an American election. The Kremlin's preferred candidate had won against all odds. And here was his son-in-law, who had also secretly taken part in a mid-campaign meeting about acquiring Russian dirt on Clinton, suggesting that the Trump team saunter into the Russian embassy and dial up Kremlin officials with their gear to avoid the eavesdropping powers of U.S. intelligence.

Kislyak, who seemed to recognize the insanity of the idea, demurred. He was later intercepted by U.S. intelligence describing the encounter to his superiors at the Kremlin as if shocked that someone poised for a position of such influence in the United States could be so naive, reckless, or simply determined to befriend Moscow. Trump officials later insisted there was no nefarious intent behind Kushner's proposal, and that he was merely pursuing an offer from Kislyak to arrange a conversation with Russian military officials about prospects for improved cooperation in Syria.

On December 13, Kushner took part in another secret meeting arranged by Kislyak. Kushner sat down with Sergey Gorkov, the top executive at Vnesheconombank, the economic development bank that was supposed to make investments designed to help the Russian economy. In reality, Vnesheconombank was suspected of functioning as "Putin's slush fund," and was hit with U.S. sanctions in 2014 after Russia's annexation of Crimea.[12] Gorkov, who had been in the job for less than a year, had close ties to Putin and was a graduate of the FSB academy. At the time, the Kushner company was desperately seeking an infusion of money to cover rapidly approaching payments due on a $1.2 billion office tower at 666 Fifth Avenue, a property that Kushner had bought in 2008 after his father had gone to prison and before the real estate market crashed.[13] Kushner claimed he did not discuss that debt or sanctions with Gorkov, and that he'd taken the meeting because Gorkov was someone "with a direct line to the Russian president who could give insight into how Putin was viewing the new administration." The bank had a different explanation, saying the meeting was strictly business, a conversation set up to explore investment strategies.

The Trump Tower meeting was the first of a flurry of interactions between Flynn and Kislyak in the final weeks of 2016. As they traded calls and messages, the CIA bio on the Russian envoy was delivered and placed in a secure room of the Trump transition spaces for Flynn to read. It remained untouched.

IN MID-DECEMBER, ELLEN NAKASHIMA WENT TO THE NEWSPAPER'S mailroom on the first floor of its K Street headquarters. The paper had been in the building for just a year, having vacated its historic but architecturally charmless home several blocks away after the sale of the *Post* by the Graham family—which had owned the paper since Katherine Graham's father, Eugene Meyer, acquired it in a 1933 bankruptcy auction for $825,000—to Amazon.com founder Jeff Bezos. The new newsroom was a bright white testament to journalism's digital age with hundreds of computer stations, four television studios streaming video by fiber optics, and a futuristic "hub" where editors worked under giant screens that counted readers' clicks on stories like spinning odometers.

The mailroom, however, was a retreat to the printed word, with slots for press releases, invitations, magazines, and books that still arrived by the bin-load. Old-fashioned letters from readers were increasingly rare, messages from would-be sources delivered by postal service nearly unheard-of.

Nakashima took a small stack of mail back up to her desk on the newsroom's seventh floor. Among the items was a manila envelope with a December 12 postmark from somewhere near Union Station in Washington, D.C. It had a tiny Charlie Brown stamp in the corner but no return address. Inside was a typed single-space letter. As she began to read it, Nakashima was startled.

"Without going into too much detail, I am in a trusted position within the new administration transition," it said. "There are certain elements of this incoming team which concern me tremendously, and about which I feel that I must take some type of action."

The writer proceeded to describe the December 1 meeting at Trump Tower involving Kushner, Flynn, and Kislyak. The meeting was "deliberately kept off the records and off the books," the writer said. Kushner had asked the Russian envoy to arrange "for him to have a direct contact with someone who could convey messages back and forth to Putin." Kushner then said Flynn needed to be able to reach the Kremlin "outside the normal [open] channels of communication." The trio also discussed the possibility of a "secret meeting in another country between Flynn and a Russian contact," an idea that was "deemed impractical as Flynn was now such a public figure." (A meeting matching this description occurred a month later in the Indian Ocean nation of Seychelles, involving Blackwater founder and Trump supporter Erik Prince and a Russian wealth fund manager, Kirill Dmitriev, who had close ties to Putin.)

"I share this with you because of my growing alarm about the ties between this incoming team, and elements of the Russian government," the source said. "It is worth noting that we are aware that the FBI has been running a task force for months now, looking specifically at ties between the incoming team and the Russian government."

There was no signature.

Anonymous tips are treated warily by reporters. Few pan out. Far more fall into the categories of diatribes by disgruntled employees or conspiracy theorists. This letter was not on that easy-to-ignore end of the spectrum. The writer was measured, acknowledging gaps in his or her knowledge. He or she used phrases that had the ring of experience in the government sector. The details seemed to reflect legitimate access, a presence in Trump Tower.

That is not to say that anything in the letter could be used in a story. While it's true that news organizations rely on anonymous sources, what the public often fails to understand is that those sources are not anonymous to the articles' authors. At best, the letter served as an intriguing and incomplete road map on Trump and Russia, marking reporting paths that might lead nowhere but were compelling enough to pursue.

At the same time, several reporters were following leads from Steele. Hamburger and Helderman conducted lengthy interviews with Trump associates including Michael Cohen, the president's personal lawyer identified in the dossier as having traveled to Prague for a clandestine liaison meeting with Russian representatives. "I've never met with a Russian official in my life," Cohen told them, adding that he had been to the city in 2002 but "never actually stepped out of the car." A *Post* reporter spent days in Prague checking with local hotels and could find no evidence of a Cohen visit. Helderman and Hamburger also glimpsed the emotional toll Russia's attacks and Clinton's loss had taken on high-ranking Democrats. In an interview with Brazile, the DNC chairwoman weighed how much to say publicly about the months-long battle against foreign intruders in its networks. Then, in the middle of the conversation, she broke down and sobbed.

There was another reason to take the letter seriously. On December 9, the *Post* published a story revealing that the CIA had concluded in a secret assessment that Russia had interfered in the 2016 election not only to undermine confidence in the American electoral system but also to help Trump. At that point Russia's meddling in the 2016 race was well known, and Democrats had claimed that Moscow was backing Trump. But this was the first time that the public was learning that the CIA believed it to be true, and that the agency had produced a classified report that was shared with the White House and key committees in Congress detailing the proof. The letter was a strong indication that some on the incoming president's team were concerned about interactions with Moscow.

During Obama's final full month in office, the impasse on sanctions finally began to give way. On December 5, he ordered U.S. spy agencies to produce a comprehensive assessment of Russia's interference, assembling all the most compelling intelligence in a single report, with conclusions that would represent the consensus of every agency involved. Obama wanted to understand the totality of what had happened, but he also wanted to create a record that the next administration couldn't erase. He gave his spy chiefs less than a month to finish the job.

Rice then ordered a new round of meetings on punitive measures. The "menu" that came together was a distillation of ideas that had been kicked around for months. Again, for every idea

there was a counterargument. Treasury officials devised plans for
new sanctions that would hit entire segments of Russia's economy,
but opponents warned that damage could spill over into Europe.
Officials revisited the idea of humiliating Putin with leaked intelligence exposing his corruption, but skeptics argued that Putin was
beyond shame, and that embracing those tactics would only erode
America's moral authority—how could Washington scold Moscow
if both were playing the same craven game?

During these final weeks Obama struggled to maintain his com-
posure in the aftermath of an election that threatened to unravel
his legacy. Clinton's loss had led to intense second-guessing within
the party, not only about her failings as a candidate, but Obama's
refusal to confront Russia more forcefully while there was still
time. Publicly he exuded a stoic and calm demeanor, but behind
the scenes, these pressures seemed to build on the president. He
began to worry that he had misjudged the mood of the country
and what it wanted from its leaders. "I don't know," he said during
his last trip abroad as president, standing backstage before a press
conference with German chancellor Angela Merkel, the European
leader who likely had the most to lose with the election of Trump.
"Maybe this is what people want," Obama said about his successor.
"I've got the economy set up well for him. No facts. No consequences. They can just have a cartoon." [14]

Obama mostly kept such frustrations behind the scenes until December 16, when he held one of his final press conferences from the
West Wing. There, his bitterness and disappointment boiled to the
surface and the outgoing president came as close as he ever would to
lashing out—at the public, the press, and Putin. Obama expressed
irritation that American voters had allowed such a consequential
election "to be dominated by a bunch of leaks." He scolded news
organizations for their feeding frenzy coverage of the email dumps,

and for rarely stopping to examine how they were compounding the impact of the Russian attack. (Obama took no blame for his own failure to call out the Kremlin.) Then he unloaded on Russia with a stream of disparaging remarks that seemed aimed at Putin's psychological soft spots—his fixation on Russia's decline from world power status and his obsession with how Moscow was disrespected by the West. "The Russians can't change us or significantly weaken us," Obama said. "They are a smaller country. They are a weaker country. Their economy doesn't produce anything that anybody wants to buy, except oil and gas and arms."

The edge in Obama's voice carried over into deliberations that were again under way in the Situation Room. Among those gathered were Rice, Clapper, Brennan, Kerry, Johnson, defense secretary Ashton B. Carter, and McCabe, subbing for Comey. Rice laid out options along three main fronts. They included plans to aim new economic sanctions at the Russian intelligence services and Kremlin officials behind the DNC hack; to shutter lavish Russian-owned compounds in New York and Maryland that Russian diplomats used for weekend getaways but also served as platforms for espionage; and finally, to expel a collection of Russian spies from the United States.

As participants again began raising concerns and objections, Rice cut them off. "We're not talking anymore," she said. "We're acting." The issue was no longer whether to retaliate, but how severely: Sanction one Russian spy service or two? Close one Russian compound or both? Expel five suspected spies? Or fifteen? More? Rice went around the room, challenging the principals to go to "the max of their comfort zones." One by one, the principals endorsed the most aggressive version of each proposal. When asked how many Russian spies should be expelled, Brennan shot back: "All of them."

It was mid-December, and a plan to take revenge on Russia was finally being sent to the president.

PIONEER POINT LIES AT THE END OF A RURAL TWO-LANE ROAD lined by farms and groves of trees on Maryland's Eastern Shore. The forty-five-acre property occupies a verdant peninsula that juts out into the intersection of the Chester and Corsica Rivers, tidal waterways that spill into the Chesapeake Bay an hour east of Washington. The estate itself was farmland for more than two centuries until it was purchased in 1925 by John J. Raskob, who worked as an executive at DuPont and General Motors. Raskob was turning his attention to real estate at the time in a way that Trump would have appreciated. Five years later he began construction on the Empire State Building, ensuring that it stretched above the Chrysler Building to claim the title of the world's tallest. Raskob was also active in politics, serving as chairman of—of all things—the DNC from 1928 to 1932.

Raskob built a nineteen-room brick mansion at Pioneer Point with ornate painted ironwork and sweeping water views from its north-facing windows. He then added an equally expansive Georgian-style structure next door for his thirteen children. Raskob died in 1950, and the estate changed hands multiple times until it was acquired in 1972 by another buyer with plans to hold on to the property for the long term: the Soviet Union.[15]

The estate became a dacha, or summer home, for Anatoly Dobrynin, who served as the Soviet ambassador to the United States for an astonishingly long tenure, arriving when Kennedy was president and leaving under Reagan in 1986. Over time, fourteen cottages were added to the property—some of them shipped from Finland—as getaways for Soviet embassy staff.

The property became a possession of the Russian government

with the Soviet Union's collapse and continued to serve as a retreat for diplomats. Buses departed from Washington every weekend loaded with Russian families. The gated compound had only expanded in grandeur, with swimming pools added along the waterfront, two sets of tennis courts—one clay and one hard surface—a courtyard with a fountain, and a rustic hunting lodge with a mural depicting a Russian sailor raising a stein of beer. There were two speedboats and a small armada of paddle boats parked near the beach. Kislyak took over the main residence, with its crystal chandeliers, screened-in porch, and walnut-paneled library.

But for years, U.S. intelligence officials had also noticed other, odder architectural additions—a proliferation of chimneys that never released any smoke, as well as antennae and electronic equipment presumably aimed at passing U.S. naval vessels, the Naval Academy in nearby Annapolis, NSA headquarters (also in Maryland), or other U.S. government installations.

The FBI, whose counterintelligence division was responsible for maintaining surveillance on the site, had long lobbied to have the compound closed. Keeping watch over the Russians filing in and out was a considerable burden to the bureau, which already devoted thousands of agent-hours a year to tracking Russian spies around Washington. At the Situation Room meeting in December, Rice pointed to the FBI's McCabe and said, "You guys have been begging to do this for years. Now is your chance."

On the morning of December 29, Kislyak was summoned to the State Department for a meeting with Patrick F. Kennedy, an experienced Foreign Service officer who served as undersecretary for management, essentially making him the department's chief operations officer. When Kislyak arrived, Kennedy ushered him toward a seating area in his seventh-floor office and began reading, verbatim, from a prepared text. He cited the United States' determination that Russia had interfered in the presidential campaign at

Putin's direction and began ticking off a list of sanctions: economic penalties on the GRU, FSB, three Russian intelligence officials, and four companies involved in cyber operations; the expulsion of thirty-five Russian spies; and the closure of the Russian compounds in New York and Maryland. Russia would have twenty-four hours to vacate the properties, seventy-two to get the expelled spies out of the United States.

Kislyak seemed stunned. He interrupted Kennedy to ask whether he would be given a paper detailing these measures. When Kennedy said no, that formal notification would be delivered later to the Russian embassy, Kislyak turned to a wide-eyed aide and said, "Are you getting all this down?"

When Kennedy finished, the two men stood and a flustered Kislyak tried to respond. He denied the allegation that Russia had interfered in the election. "You're wrong," he said. He added that he would be immediately discussing the matter with officials in Moscow, and that "of course, there will be repercussions."

As Kislyak departed, another State Department official who had been in the room for the meeting reached for his phone. Gentry Smith, the director of the Office of Foreign Missions, had broad authority over the operations of foreign missions in the United States—in other words, his office would have to secure the Russian compounds and make sure the expelled spies got out. As he spoke into his cell phone, a pair of unmarked vehicles on the Eastern Shore moved into position in view of the main gate to the Russian compound. State Department special agents had been waiting for that signal to set up a staging area outside the property. They began checking IDs of every Russian entering or leaving the site.

Kislyak had been given less than two hours' notice before the White House announced the sanctions publicly. In a statement, Obama said, "All Americans should be alarmed by Russia's actions. . . . Such activities have consequences."

Obama also said, cryptically, that "these actions are not the sum total of our response to Russia's aggressive activities." Left unsaid was that he had also signed a secret intelligence memorandum, a "finding," authorizing the NSA, CIA, and U.S. Cyber Command to carry out a covert operation involving the deployment of implants in critical Russian networks that in this case could function like bombs, exploding key nodes of Russian infrastructure when detonated. The plan would take more than a year to implement and was aimed at putting the United States in position to inflict immediate damage in the event of a cyber conflict with Moscow. It would be up to Donald Trump to use it—or not.

OBAMA OFFICIALS WERE PUZZLED THAT THEY HAD SO LITTLE IN-teraction with Flynn after he was named Trump's national security adviser. The outgoing team had prepared memos and briefing materials on a range of issues with the expectation of at least a few meetings on transition logistics. Flynn gave the impression he couldn't be bothered, though he did attend one gathering in the Situation Room with Obama officials. Afterward, as he and his aides headed out the West Wing exit, a young White House aide held open the door.

"After you, sir," the aide said. Flynn put his hand on the staffer's shoulder and, as he passed by, said, "I can't wait to take over this place."

Flynn escaped for one last vacation in late December before beginning his new job. He was with his wife at a beach resort in the Dominican Republic when the Obama sanctions were announced. Moscow had reacted with outrage, vowing immediate retaliation. "Of course, we cannot leave such mischievous tricks without a response," Sergei Lavrov, the foreign minister, had said. "Reciprocity is the law of diplomacy and of international relations."

Flynn quickly touched base with the Trump transition team,
reaching his deputy, K. T. McFarland, at Mar-a-Lago to discuss
"what, if anything, to communicate to the Russian ambassador."
Shortly thereafter, Flynn and Kislyak were on the phone. Flynn
urged "that Russia not escalate the situation" and signaled that the
Trump administration would soon be in position to revisit the punitive measures Obama had just imposed.

Flynn had spent much of his life serving his country, including
nearly a decade deployed to war zones. He was about to assume a
job of enormous influence whose main purpose is to protect the
interests of the United States. Russia's election interference was not
the kind of combat that Flynn knew firsthand, but it was nevertheless an attack. The penalties that Flynn's own government was imposing had not yet even been implemented. And yet here he was,
on a beach in the Caribbean, telling the Kremlin not to worry, that
it would all be taken care of once Trump was in power.

WITHIN HOURS, BUSES BEGAN ARRIVING AT THE PIONEER POINT
complex loaded with Russian personnel to begin evacuating the
property, hauling off its equipment, protecting its secrets. "There
was a smell of burning paper in the air," said a U.S. official who
witnessed the operation. By midday on December 30, U.S. agents
seized control of the main gate and the eerily empty compound.
FBI and State Department agents swept the site in the ensuing
days and found it stripped of antennae, electronics, computers, file
cabinets, and other gear—their absence made obvious by visible
markings on the floors, tables, and walls. Left behind was a Christmas tree still standing in the main residence, the ornaments left in
place, but little else of note.

Two days later, State Department security escorted buses bearing diplomatic plates from the Russian embassy in Washington to Dulles International Airport. Thirty-five suspected spies had been declared "personae non gratae," but with their families, the total number of departing Russians was about 115. They were taken to a private gate at Dulles, away from the main passenger terminal, a section typically reserved for high-ranking U.S. officials and foreign dignitaries. The thirty-five departing Russians were checked against an FBI-assembled list, then boarded a plane that had been sent by their government to take them home.

Obama officials waited for the inevitable, certain that Russia would soon take revenge. But the reaction from Moscow took a strange turn. "We regard the recent unfriendly steps taken by the outgoing U.S. administration as provocative and aimed at further weakening the Russia–U.S. relationship," Putin declared. "Although we have the right to retaliate," he added, they would not, "but will plan our further steps to restore Russian–U.S. relations based on the policies of the Trump administration."

Putin wasn't finished trolling the outgoing president. He said Russia would "not create any problems for U.S. diplomats. We will not expel anyone. . . . Moreover, I invite all children of U.S. diplomats accredited in Russia to the New Year and Christmas children's parties in the Kremlin." He offered "New Year greetings to President Obama and his family" and also "to President-elect Donald Trump and the American people." [16]

It was as if Putin had been abducted and replaced by a writer of cloying greeting cards.

The Trump campaign made no acknowledgment of its communications with the Kremlin, and Flynn would later deny that he had conveyed anything to Kislyak beyond holiday wishes and a desire to set up a preliminary conversation between the two countries' leaders. Rice and other national security officials were baffled. What could account for this reaction? In their waning days they would pore over intelligence searching for clues to a secret Putin-Trump deal.

Trump provided the first clue himself, tweeting on December 30, "Great move on delay (by V. Putin)—I always knew he was very smart!"

CHAPTER 10

BRIEFING THE PRESIDENT

O N JANUARY 6, WITH TEMPERATURES HOVERING AROUND freezing in Washington, four armored sport utility vehicles streamed across the Anacostia River toward Andrews Air Force Base on the outskirts of the city. Each carried one select passenger: Clapper, Brennan, Comey, and NSA director Michael Rogers. All had just departed Capitol Hill after delivering an 8:30 A.M. briefing to the Gang of Eight and were about to board a pair of government jets to New York and their next stop—Trump Tower.

The quartet was heading toward potentially hostile territory. Their agencies had completed work on the assignment Obama gave them in early December, and their conclusions affirmed what by then was increasingly clear even to the public: Russia had waged a far-reaching campaign to undermine the 2016 election that involved cyber operations against multiple targets, the use of cutouts and the eager complicity of WikiLeaks to dump large volumes of material online, the dissemination of fake news, and a massive manipulation of social media platforms—all as part of an attack authorized by Putin himself.

The most striking aspect of the report was how it characterized the operation's magnitude and motives. While Russia had been meddling in American affairs for decades, the 2016 operation represented "a significant escalation in directness, level of activity, and scope of effort" beyond anything the U.S. intelligence agencies had ever seen. Then came the first bullet point: "We also assess Putin and the Russian Government aspired to help President-elect Trump's election chances when possible by discrediting Secretary Clinton and publicly contrasting her unfavorably to him."

All four U.S. officials knew that this judgment had the potential to enrage the thin-skinned future president, and they braced for an ugly confrontation in New York. "We were prepared to get thrown out," Clapper said.[1]

At Andrews, Clapper, Brennan, and Rogers boarded a 737 with the signature sky-blue belly of the U.S. Air Force wing that handles air transportation for the president and the upper ranks of government. On board they took their seats in a front section equipped with a conference table, secure phones, internet connections, and video screens for encrypted communications with their agencies back in Washington. Comey, who planned to stay longer in New York for meetings with bureau officials, flew separately on a smaller Gulfstream.

Comey was becoming isolated from his traveling companions in other ways. Unlike Clapper and Brennan, he expected to stay on with the Trump administration, not because of any special rapport with the new president, but because FBI directors are given ten-year terms that are supposed to insulate them from the cycles and pressures of politics. (As it turned out, Rogers would also stay in his position at NSA.) Comey also had a solo task on this trip and it involved the infamous "dossier."

Weeks earlier, Christopher Steele had submitted his final installment for the compendium of Trump-Russia memos, though he continued to pursue leads even after Trump was sworn in as president. Steele's sense of alarm had grown more acute with each new file he'd submitted to Fusion GPS. He had gone repeatedly to the FBI and in early October went to Rome for a meeting with an agent he'd first contacted in July and three others, reiterating that the Kremlin had compromising information on Trump and warning that Moscow had launched a full-scale operation to help him win the election.

The former British spy's dispatches were written in the syntax and format of a MI6 report, terse and bureaucratic. The final memo, "Company Intelligence Report 2016/166," alleged that Russia had been using "botnets and porn traffic to transmit viruses, plant bugs, steal data, and conduct 'altering operations' against the Democratic Party Leadership"—claims that were never publicly substantiated. It said that Trump's personal lawyer, Michael Cohen, had functioned as the campaign's secret conduit to the Kremlin, taking part in a meeting in Prague to make sure all the necessary cash changed hands immediately after the election and that the cyber teams involved could "go effectively to ground to cover their traces."

Steele had secretly gone to *The Washington Post* in late September with the hope that the paper would pursue the allegations, which were then uncorroborated by American intelligence. There he spent two hours with a pair of reporters in a glass-walled conference room, expounding on the material outlined in his dossier. The reporters remained in intermittent touch with him afterward.

Discouraged by the lack of any sign of an active U.S. investigation before election day, Steele sought to enlist more high-powered help. In November, Andrew Wood, a retired British diplomat with close ties to Steele, met with Senator John McCain, the Arizona Republican, on the sidelines of a security conference in Halifax, Canada. Wood told McCain about the dossier that Steele had compiled on Trump and the former British spy's adamant belief that his findings should be investigated. McCain said their meeting "felt charged with a strange intensity. No one wisecracked to lighten the mood. We spoke in lowered voices." Ten days later, Steele met with a McCain associate at Heathrow Airport in a scene straight out of a spy novel. David Kramer, a former State Department official close to McCain who had also taken part in the meeting at Halifax, was instructed to look for a man in a blue raincoat carrying a copy of the *Financial Times*.[2]

After that encounter, Kramer reported back to McCain, who agreed to accept a copy of the dossier and "did what any American who cares about our nation's security should have done. I put the dossier in my office safe, called the office of the director of the FBI, Jim Comey, and asked for a meeting." On December 9, McCain quietly delivered a copy to the FBI chief though the bureau for months had been aware of Steele's research.

As Clapper, Comey, Brennan, and Rogers began discussing their plans to brief Trump on the findings of the report on Russia, Comey kept wondering how they could avoid mentioning the existence of the dossier. The main intelligence report did not rely on any material from Steele, but a two-page summary of the dossier's contents was included at the back of the report as an appendix. The arrangement allowed intelligence chiefs to have it both ways—calling attention to Steele's research without vouching for its allegations and keeping the salacious elements at arm's length.

In their planning sessions, the four explored the possibility of having Clapper and Comey discuss the dossier with Trump together, after the main Russia briefing had ended. But the claims about prostitutes and "kompromat" were so lewd and intimate that Comey argued that it might be better if only one person had that conversation with the president-elect. Brennan, who had been more reluctant than the others to include the Steele material, saw no reason to give the document additional credence by sending an intelligence official in to talk about it with Trump. At one point, he pulled Clapper aside, telling him, "You don't want to go any-where near it."

Assigning Comey this task, however, created other risks. With seven years left on his term, Comey had more at stake in forging a relationship with the incoming president than any other participant—and more to lose if Trump came to associate him with the dossier and came to doubt the FBI director was someone he could trust.

On his wooden desk at FBI headquarters, Comey kept a smudged document under glass. It was a memo from J. Edgar Hoover to Attorney General Robert F. Kennedy seeking authority to put civil rights leader Martin Luther King Jr.'s organization under "technical surveillance." The document was dated October 7, 1963, just six weeks after King had delivered his "I have a dream" speech from the steps of the Lincoln Memorial. Kennedy signed Hoover's request three days after it landed on his desk.

Comey kept the page on display as a reminder of the bureau's power and how it had been abused. Hoover had maintained extensive "dossiers" of his own on politicians, religious leaders, and even movie stars and musicians. He documented marital transgressions, homosexuality, drug habits—anything that the FBI leader saw as troubling or a potential tool of influence. His arguable blackmail of presidents (he informed John F. Kennedy that the bureau knew of his affairs) was believed by some to account for his longevity in the job.

"There was a real chance that Donald Trump, politician and hardball dealmaker, would assume I was dangling the prostitute thing over him to jam him, to gain leverage," Comey later reflected. "He might well assume I was pulling a J. Edgar Hoover, because that's what Hoover would do in my shoes."[3]

The planes carrying Clapper, Brennan, Comey, and Rogers arrived at Newark International Airport around 11:30. They climbed into another fleet of SUVs for the trip to Trump Tower. To avoid news organizations staking out the main lobby, they were led through the residential entrance on 56th Street into elevators that took them to the fourteenth floor. They crossed back over to the business side of the building and gathered in a small conference room with eight chairs around a table and several more placed against a wall. A heavy curtain stretching across a window into an adjoining hallway was the only visible security precaution. This was the makeshift SCIF (sensitive compartmented information facility) where they would discuss highly classified intelligence with the president-elect, who, after a ten-minute wait, arrived with his entourage.

Many targets of Trump's long-range attacks found him oddly obsequious in person. As he strode into the conference room, he was in magnanimous, back-slapping mode, going so far as to tell Clapper that he "looked good on TV" during a congressional hearing in which the intelligence director had chastised Trump for disparaging comments about U.S. spy agencies. Trump either hadn't absorbed what Clapper said or, ever consumed with appearances, was more focused on how the spy chief carried himself on camera.

Trump and Pence took seats at the ends of the table. Clapper, Brennan, Comey, and Rogers were joined by Flynn and Priebus in the remaining spaces. Three others settled into chairs along the wall: CIA director nominee Mike Pompeo, Flynn's deputy K. T. McFarland, and Trump spokesman Sean Spicer. Clapper led the briefing and outlined the report's conclusions before turning to his three colleagues for sections they had agreed to handle. They in turn dove into the classified material that formed the basis of their individual assessments. The evidence was "overwhelming," Clapper said, and support for the conclusions was unanimous. (The NSA differed from the other agencies on one narrow point, agreeing that Russia "aspired to help President-elect Trump's election chances" with "moderate" confidence rather than the "high" confidence reached by analysts at the CIA and the FBI.)

Trump raised questions about some of the evidence and conclusions, but he registered no significant objections to a case that he had repeatedly denounced as fraudulent. In fact, Trump didn't seem particularly interested in any aspect of the report, with one glaring exception: whether Russia had succeeded in altering the outcome. "You found there was no impact on the result, right?" Trump interjected.[4] Clapper replied that the government saw no evidence that Russian hackers had tampered with *voting systems* but that U.S. intelligence agencies had "neither the authority nor capabilities to assess what impact—if any—the Russian operation had."

Clapper's answer was less than satisfying for the president-elect, but it seemed to bring a sigh of relief from his team, whose main concern seemed to be ensuring that no part of the report suggested that any factor other than the candidate's own strategic vision and charisma had accounted for his triumph. Comey later marveled at their myopic focus. The core of a new American administration had just been told, in extraordinary detail, about an assault on the United States by a powerful adversary, and yet no one in the room posed a single question about what Russia might do next, or what the incoming administration could do to guard the country against another attack.

Instead, Comey recalled, "with the four of us still in our seats—including two outgoing Obama appointees—the president-elect and his team shifted immediately into a strategy session about messaging on Russia. About how they could spin what we'd just told them." They began composing a press release highlighting the supposed finding that Russia's interference ultimately had no bearing on the outcome. Clapper pushed back, reminding them that the report didn't look at that question. (For many obvious reasons, U.S. spies are supposed to stay out of domestic politics.) They were "speaking as if we weren't there," Comey said.[5] Nor were they apparently able to hear Clapper's protest.

As the group began to stand up around the table, Priebus asked whether there was anything else to discuss. Clapper said there was "some additional sensitive material" that Comey would stay behind to address with a small group. "How small?" Trump asked. Priebus suggested that he and Pence participate, but Trump waved them off and motioned to Comey, saying, "Just the two of us."

As the others filed out, Trump engaged in his close-quarters bonding ritual of flattery and feigned camaraderie. Trump told Comey that he'd had "one heck of a year" but acquitted himself well under the difficult circumstances of the Clinton probe. "You saved her and then they hated you for what you did later, but what choice did you have?" Trump said. He said he hoped Comey would stay in his job, the first of many times that he would raise the issue in ways that hinted that the matter should not be considered settled.

Comey then eased into the subject of the dossier, explaining in broad terms the origin of the material and how it came to be in the bureau's possession. The FBI director braced Trump for what would come next, telling him he "didn't want him caught cold by some of the detail." One of the memos said Trump had been with prostitutes at the Ritz-Carlton hotel in Moscow in 2013, Comey said, and that Russia had tapes. Before Comey could even get to the caveats of how the bureau wasn't interested in these allegations or investigating them, Trump jumped in and said, "There were no prostitutes. There were never prostitutes."[6]

Trump became stuck on the issue, asking with a snicker whether he seemed like the kind of guy who needed to "go there." He muttered, "Two thousand thirteen," to himself as if searching his memory of that year's trip to Moscow, and said he always assumed any hotel room he stayed in was bugged. Comey tried to explain that he was bringing this to the president-elect's attention in the interest of protecting him—making sure he knew this material existed and that some news organizations already had it, so that he was prepared for the possibility that it would be released. Trump then veered into other uncomfortable subjects, grousing about the women who had accused him of groping them, referring derisively to the claims of a "stripper," as if trying to lump the dossier and these other allegations into a single discredited category.

Comey then took a risk. He had been so worried about a blowup over the dossier that he had thought of things he might say to soothe the president-elect. As Trump became agitated about the prostitute claim, Comey told him, "We are not investigating you, sir." The FBI director's statement was accurate, but Comey's top aides had warned him that it might not be accurate for long. In fact, James Baker, the FBI's general counsel, had argued forcefully against giving such an assurance to the president. The counterintelligence probe had only expanded since it opened in late July, and it certainly seemed possible, if not inevitable, that it would turn its attention to Trump himself. When that happened, wouldn't Comey be on the hook to tell Trump? Wouldn't he face another "speak or conceal" dilemma, as he put it with the reopening of the Clinton email probe? Comey, however, opted for the short-term gain of placating the president-elect. Whatever comity it achieved didn't last.

Hours after their extraordinary session ended, the Trump transition team released a statement saying that "while Russia, China, other countries, other groups and people are constantly trying to break through the cyber infrastructure" of the United States, "there was absolutely no effect on the outcome of the election." It was a brazen perversion of what four of the nation's highest officials had said. Trump doubled down on Twitter later that night, blaming "gross negligence" by the DNC for allowing the hack, and saying that the RNC had been untouched because it "had strong defense."

In fact, the RNC had also been penetrated by Russian hackers, along with dozens of other political organizations and think tanks in Washington. Russia even extracted piles of material from these systems, fuel that could easily have been thrown onto the WikiLeaks fire. But Moscow didn't do that. There was no corresponding dump of GOP secrets, and that curious asymmetric act of restraint had further bolstered the conclusion that Moscow aimed to hurt Clinton and help Trump.

ONE OF COMEY'S PRINCIPAL RATIONALES FOR DISCUSSING THE dossier was that he didn't want Trump to be blindsided—and angry at the bureau—if it became public. Comey testified later that the bureau had "been told by the media that it was about to launch." In reality, dozens of reporters had been digging into the Steele allegations for months without being able to substantiate them or cross the publication threshold. Now, because of Comey's conversation at Trump Tower, news organizations had reason to reconsider. Salacious memos circulating in Washington were one thing; the director of the FBI briefing the incoming president on those allegations was news and word leaked swiftly. Comey had in effect triggered the launch.

On January 10, the BuzzFeed website went first. "A dossier making explosive—but unverified—allegations" about Trump and Russia "has been circulating among elected officials, intelligence agents, and journalists for weeks," the article began, quickly getting to its "allegations of contact between Trump aides and Russian operatives, and graphic claims of sexual acts documented by the Russians."

Trump erupted at 7:48 the next morning with his infamous "Are we living in Nazi Germany?" tweet.

That night, Comey was in his seventh-floor office at FBI headquarters when Trump called. Looking out at the nighttime traffic on Pennsylvania Avenue, Comey listened to the president-elect perseverate. Trump wanted to discuss the dossier again. He said he had gone back and spoken to others who accompanied him to Moscow, and that he now remembered that he had not even stayed overnight in the Russian capital—a supposed recollection that was untrue. Besides, he said, "I'm a germophobe. There's no way I would let people pee on each other around me. No way."

Comey had intentionally not mentioned that lewdest of the dossier's allegations—that Trump had hired prostitutes to urinate on a bed where Obama had slept in the Moscow Ritz-Carlton—in the FBI director's private meeting with the president. Trump had clearly taken a closer look at Steele's report. For a man about to assume the weight of the most powerful office in the world, and who had cursorily denied scores of allegations and lawsuits that had hounded him on the campaign trail, Comey thought that Trump was oddly preoccupied with what he insisted was a baseless claim.

AS SPIES ASSEMBLED THE REPORT THAT OBAMA HAD ORDERED ON Russia, the process of pulling material from deep in the classified databases of disparate agencies had brought dozens of new fragments of information to the surface—forensic details about the hack, Russian ties to WikiLeaks that went beyond the DNC dump, and the Kremlin's connection to the bots, trolls, and torrents of fake news that inundated voters. And since the project required work on a much bigger scale than Brennan's fusion cell, dozens of high-level officials were finally coming to terms with what the CIA had first grasped in August: that Putin had assigned his intelligence services the task of helping to elect Trump.

Suddenly Trump's behavior throughout the campaign could be perceived in a troubling new light. His hiring of Manafort, Page, and Flynn had been puzzling from the beginning, but perhaps there were hidden reasons for him to prefer advisers in good standing with the Kremlin. His praise of Putin, his penchant for reciting Moscow's talking points, his dismissive attitude about Kremlin brutality toward dissidents and refusal to accept that Russia was responsible for the DNC hack—it all seemed more ominous given the apparent investment Russia had made in his candidacy.

When Obama hit Russia with steep sanctions in late December and Putin responded with an olive branch, it rattled officials at the NSC, including Rice. Since when had Russia responded to American retaliation with a bemused shrug?

That bizarre reaction—combined with other information only beginning to emerge—resulted in a deep sense of unease among national security officials in the early days of 2017, a gnawing sensation that after failing to grasp the magnitude of Russia's attack before the election, America's spies were still seeing only portions of a plot that hadn't ended on November 8.

IT WAS ONLY A MATTER OF TIME BEFORE KISLYAK'S DECEMBER 29 call with Flynn showed up in the torrent of digital traffic ingested daily by the NSA.

The United States and Russia had always viewed each other's diplomatic compounds as high-priority targets for espionage. In 1980, Soviet officials declared that they had discovered eavesdropping devices in the living quarters for their embassy employees that could pick up "every sound, from a word spoken in the drawing room to a whisper in the bedroom or a splash of water in the toilet."[7] Soon thereafter they would learn—through the betrayal of FBI agent Robert Hanssen—that the United States had embarked on an even more audacious eavesdropping plan, constructing a secret tunnel under the entire Soviet embassy complex in the Glover Park neighborhood of Washington.

By the time Kislyak arrived to begin his tenure as Russian ambassador, American spies did most of their tunneling via computer. He knew that his communications were being monitored, and his embassy was equipped with encrypted systems that he could use to avoid American ears when a message to Moscow had to be secure. Even so, his everyday conversations were picked up routinely by U.S. spies, and analysts came to believe that Kislyak rarely bothered to transmit intentionally false messages to the foreign ministry to confuse any Americans listening. His tendency was to be honest and reliable, which—to those who pored over his communications—made him a source of valuable insight into the Kremlin.

Because Flynn was an American citizen, the NSA had initially struck his name out of the reports it generated from its surveillance of Kislyak, a practice in keeping with strictures designed to protect Americans whose communications are captured "inadvertently" while monitoring foreign targets. But high-level officials have the authority to request that names of U.S. citizens be revealed in cases when knowing that identity is critical to understanding the underlying intelligence. It was under these circumstances that Flynn's name was "unmasked" for a small group of senior officials at the White House, the FBI, and intelligence agencies desperate to understand why Putin had pulled his punches after being hit with the Obama sanctions.

At the *Post*, reporters had been focused on the Trump team's interactions with Kislyak ever since the arrival of the anonymous letter in Nakashima's mailbox, but it had seemed like a dead end. On its face, there was nothing wrong with a newly designated national security adviser speaking with foreign diplomats. (Whether it was wise was another matter. McFaul and others in the Obama administration had avoided such interactions with Russia during the 2008–2009 transition partly to avoid the appearance of jumping the gun diplomatically.) But while word began to leak that Flynn and Kislyak had spoken, determining what they had said to each other and whether the two had explicitly discussed sanctions was a far more difficult reporting target. Those who knew the answer were part of a tiny circle in government, and as much as the public may think of Washington as a leaking sieve, officials cleared to see such narrow slices of sigint take their obligations of secrecy seriously. (Employees at CIA and NSA also face polygraph tests.)

On January 12, a crack formed. *Post* columnist David Ignatius reported that Flynn had phoned Kislyak "several times on December 29, the day the Obama administration announced the expulsion of 35 Russian officials as well as other measures in retaliation for the hacking." He attributed this information to a senior U.S. government official, then posed the central question: "What did Flynn say, and did it undercut the U.S. sanctions?"

Ignatius raised the issue deep into a column that explored other questions about the election and Russia, but it was the detail about Flynn that seized Washington's attention and altered the reporting dynamic: the pressure had been on the press to figure out what was said; now it was shifting to the incoming administration to explain.

WASHINGTON SCANDALS FOLLOW THEIR OWN LAWS OF NATURE. They reach a point where they can either expand or contract depending on a collection of variables: the severity of the transgression, the number and motivations of those in position to expose it, and the transgressor's impulse when faced with the inevitable decision of whether to come clean. Trump has upended this natural order, avoiding consequence for offenses that were long considered politically fatal often by lying in the face of overwhelming evidence. Flynn, however, had no such immunity.

The day after the Ignatius column, Trump transition team spokesman Sean Spicer fielded questions about Flynn in a call with reporters. He laid out a supposed timeline of the Flynn-Kislyak interactions during the final week of December and strenuously denied any discussion of sanctions. The exchange started on Christmas Day, Spicer said, with Flynn sending the Russian envoy a holiday greeting by text and saying, "I wish you all the best." Flynn followed up with additional texts and a December 28 call "centered around the logistics of setting up a call with the president of Russia and the president-elect after he was sworn in."

"That was it," Spicer said. "Plain and simple."

That wasn't it. On January 15, five days before Trump took the oath of office, Mike Pence appeared on the CBS Sunday morning show *Face the Nation*. It was inevitable, given the news of the week, that he, too, would face questions about Flynn and Kislyak.

"It was strictly coincidental that they had a conversation" on the same day that sanctions were announced, Pence said. "They did not discuss anything having to do with the United States's decision to expel diplomats or impose censure on Russia." Pence made clear he was relaying the facts straight from Flynn, "having spoken to him about it," and repeated that the conversations Flynn had with Kislyak "had nothing whatsoever to do with those sanctions."[8]

Flynn's deceit was, in hindsight, hard to understand. The legal jeopardy that he faced bordered on nonexistent. The only applicable law was an archaic measure, the Logan Act, which was passed in 1799 after a Philadelphia-area physician and politician, George Logan, traveled to Paris—without the authority of the administration of President John Adams—hoping to seal a pact with France to stop harassing U.S. merchant ships. He got an agreement but came back to accusations of treason, and the law that bears his name was adopted to prevent such diplomatic freelancing. The measure has mainly served as a caution for incoming administrations to abide by the principle that there is only one president in office at a time. In more than two hundred years, no violation of the Logan Act has ever been prosecuted.

The false statements Flynn made, however, created problems that only escalated every time they were repeated. Transcripts or summaries of the Kislyak call had already been disseminated to a handful of officials in Washington. That meant that leaders at the NSC, the Justice Department, and the FBI were already aware, or soon would be, that the statements by Spicer and Pence were untrue. They knew that Flynn not only had urged Russia not to retaliate but had taken a subsequent call from Kislyak two days later, on December 31, with the ambassador explaining that Putin had held off at Flynn's request. If, as they claimed, Spicer and Pence had truly relied on Flynn's accounts, then the next national security adviser had lied to the future vice president, the future White House spokesman, and by extension, the American public.

There was another entity, of course, that also knew immediately how inaccurate those statements from Spicer and Pence were. Russia now had extraordinary leverage over America's next national security adviser. If Flynn was lying to his peers, his job hinged on his ability to prevent them from learning that he had done so. Russia knew his secret and was in position to reveal the truth—a prospect that Moscow wouldn't necessarily even have to mention to induce cooperation from Flynn.

AFTER COMEY AND OTHERS BECAME AWARE OF THE CALLS WITH Kislyak, the bureau's counterintelligence division began looking into whether Flynn had violated the disused Logan Act. He was already under FBI scrutiny because of his failure to register with the Department of Justice as a foreign agent after taking hundreds of thousands of dollars in payments from overseas interests and working as a paid lobbyist on behalf of the Turkish government.[9]

The false statements coming from Trump's inner circle created a dilemma for law enforcement officials. Should the Justice Department warn the White House that Flynn was vulnerable to Russian blackmail and risk alerting the retired general to the nascent FBI probe? Or should the Justice Department put the bureau investigation first, wait for a chance to question Flynn, and allow a compromised national security adviser to be sworn in? Justice opted to let the FBI make the first move, but gave it only a few days.

Flynn moved through inauguration weekend with oblivious elation. Under cloudy skies on the west-facing stairs of the Capitol, he sat in the stands behind Trump as the Republican took the oath of office. The next day Flynn accompanied Trump to the CIA for the speech that dismayed so many of the agency's rank and file. Flynn himself was sworn in a day later as part of a group of White House officials. Wearing a bright blue tie and raising his right hand, he vowed that he would "support and defend the Constitution of the United States against all enemies, foreign and domestic; that I will bear true faith and allegiance to the same. . . ."

Two days later, McCabe, Comey's deputy, called Flynn at the White House. McCabe said the bureau needed to speak with him, proposed sending a pair of agents over, and asked whether Flynn wished to have an attorney present. Flynn knew this was about Kislyak and must have assumed that the bureau had a transcript, but the retired general also had a misplaced confidence in his ability—whether in combat zones or in Washington—to navigate perilous situations.

"No," Flynn said about needing a lawyer, "send them over."

Several of Flynn's senior aides came looking for him at his office in the West Wing a few hours later. As the staffers approached, they could see that Flynn's door was closed. The Coast Guard captain who served as Flynn's executive assistant said that the national security adviser was with a pair of FBI agents. At first the staffers thought there had been a scheduling mix-up. Flynn was supposed to meet with FBI officials the next day for a counterintelligence briefing. The Coast Guard captain said this was something else, added to the schedule at the last minute, and that Flynn had gone into the meeting saying something about how "he just wants to get this settled. Wants this over with."

That set off an alarm. With speculation about Flynn's call with Kislyak still swirling, it didn't require any flash of insight to figure out why the FBI was in the West Wing. One of the NSC staffers grabbed a secure phone and called the NSC legal office across the street in the Eisenhower Building, where he reached John Eisenberg, the deputy counsel for national security affairs.

"You need to get over here," the aide said. "Flynn is meeting two FBI agents."

Inside, Flynn's legal problems were mounting by the minute. He flatly denied that he had made any suggestion during his call that Russia refrain from retaliating. He said he did not recall the follow-up conversation in which Kislyak reported that Moscow had indeed put off its planned response. But the agents had even more ammunition, asking Flynn about a December 22 call in which he asked Russia to vote against a United Nations Security Council resolution on Israeli settlements. That, too, would be a violation of the Logan Act. Flynn said he'd only asked Kislyak what Russia's position would be and made no request.

Eisenberg raced to Flynn's office, but by the time he got there the meeting was wrapping up and the national security adviser was smiling and shaking hands with the two agents—Joe Pientka and Peter Strzok—as if they were all old friends. When Eisenberg pressed for an explanation, Flynn shrugged. "I brought these guys over," he said. "I don't have anything to hide." [10]

The FBI interview was part of a sequence that had been choreographed in advance by Comey and the acting attorney general, Sally Yates. Yates had agreed to hold off on notifying the White House about Flynn's exposure to Russian blackmail until the FBI could lock down his account. The interview had taken place on Tuesday. Yates was briefed about it on Wednesday. On Thursday, she went to the West Wing, accompanied by Mary McCord, the acting head of the department's national security division. Yates knew that her time in the job would be brief, ending as soon as Sessions was confirmed, so she wanted someone who would remain behind at Justice to be a witness to this encounter. They were led to the upstairs corner office of White House counsel Don McGahn.

A former chief counsel of the Republican National Committee, McGahn had served as the top lawyer on Trump's campaign before settling into the White House job. He was an expert on laws dealing with elections, not criminal or national security—a credential that put him at a disadvantage in the gathering legal maelstrom around Trump.

Yates, a Georgia native with a syrupy drawl, laid out the problem in detail, retracing Flynn's calls with Kislyak and then reading verbatim language from the transcripts. She then reviewed the public statements by Pence and Spicer, making it clear there was no way to reconcile what Flynn had said to the Russian ambassador and what he had told officials in the White House.

Yates told McGahn that Flynn had already been interviewed by the FBI. When he pressed on "how he did," she refused to answer (information that, in her mind, belonged to the investigators).

Yates laid out three overlapping reasons for her visit: the White House needed to know that Flynn was compromised; the vice president needed to know he'd been lied to; and finally, the administration had made a series of innacurate statements, creating a situation in which the American public had been misled while the Kremlin knew the truth. When McGahn asked whether Flynn should be fired, Yates demurred, though to her the answer seemed obvious. "That was up to them," she said later, but "we were giving them this information so that they could take action."[11]

Action wasn't what the White House had in mind. McGahn asked for a follow-up meeting the next day, and when Yates returned, he spent much of it asking questions that suggested he was searching for a rationale not to remove Flynn. Wouldn't doing so interfere with the FBI investigation? he asked. Yates assured him that the probe already had what it needed from Flynn. McGahn tried another tack. "Why does it matter to DOJ if one White House official lies to another White House official?" he asked. Yates found herself repeating points she'd made the previous day. "To state the obvious," she later testified, "you don't want your national security adviser compromised with the Russians."

McGahn then said he wanted to see the underlying evidence against Flynn—the transcripts of his calls with Kislyak. Yates said she would make arrangements for McGahn to view the material at the Justice Department. She called him the following Monday to let him know it was ready and waiting.

"The defining moments in our lives often don't come with advance warning," Yates said months later about the final days of her twenty-seven years at the Department of Justice. She was in a car on the way to the airport on January 27—the same day as her second meeting with McGahn—when she saw the first flurry of news reports that President Trump had signed an executive order banning people from seven predominantly Muslim countries from entering the United States. The order created chaos at the nation's airports, where thousands of travelers already en route faced immediate deportation upon arrival. Protests began to form around the country, and the order came under immediate legal challenge.

Yates was stunned. She had expected an uneventful, brief tenure as acting attorney general. Now, under her leadership, the department was facing a legal crisis unleashed on a late Friday afternoon to achieve maximum chaos. The White House cast the order as a security measure that had nothing to do with religion, a position that Justice Department lawyers would have to defend if the order were to survive inevitable legal attacks that it was unconstitutionally discriminatory. That would be hard, given how often Trump had described Islam as a religion that "hates us," and because his campaign had issued a statement after deadly attacks in San Bernardino, California, "calling for a total and complete shutdown of Muslims entering the United States."

The following Monday, Yates used her fleeting authority as acting attorney general to declare that the department would not defend the travel ban order. Four hours later, around 9:00 P.M., an aide delivered a letter of termination from McGahn. Yates had been fired. Flynn remained in place.

ON JANUARY 27, THE SAME DAY AS YATES'S LAST TRIP TO THE WHITE House, Comey had been eating lunch when his assistant put through a call. A woman's voice said to hold for the president. Trump got on the line and asked whether the FBI director "wanted to come over for dinner." They settled on a time, 6:30 P.M., and after hanging up, Comey called his wife, Patrice, to break their own plans for a date. The thought of dining alone with Trump made Comey nervous—speaking privately with the president was a fraught endeavor for an FBI director under normal circumstances, let alone when the bureau is actively investigating the president's associates. Comey, who had been so critical of others (including Lynch and her meeting with Clinton on the tarmac) for their missteps in comparable circumstances, wrote in his memoir that he "felt like I had no choice." Attending the dinner would be one in a series of instances where he set aside supposed misgivings to accommodate the new president.

That evening, Comey arrived at the White House and was ushered into the Green Room. The cluttered space, with a pair of windows looking out over the South Lawn, had seen historic moments. It was where President Madison had signed the nation's first declaration of war, and where President Lincoln's eleven-year-old son, Willie, lay for viewing after he died of typhoid fever in 1862. In recent decades, it had served mainly as a parlor, a place where White House guests were served drinks before state dinners. When Comey arrived, he was seated with Trump at an oval table in the center of the room.

The conversation with Trump was jumbled, skipping across seemingly unrelated subjects. Trump spoke (inevitably) about the size of his inauguration crowd, the height of his youngest son, Barron, and the accommodations at the White House and how they compared to his Mar-a-Lago compound.

At one point, Trump made an odd reference to Flynn, saying that he had reservations about his national security adviser's abilities. Trump was livid after learning earlier that day that Putin had called almost immediately after the inauguration to congratulate him, and that Flynn had failed to tell him or schedule a return call for nearly a week.[12]

"The guy has serious judgment issues," Trump declared. Comey, presumably more aware than Trump at that point of the seriousness of the national security adviser's issues, stayed silent.

After cycling through complaints about all the unfair accusations he'd faced—for mocking a disabled reporter and groping women—Trump finally came around to the true purpose of this choreographed meal.

"So what do you want to do?" Trump asked.

It was a question that had only one purpose. Trump wasn't asking Comey about how he intended to use the remaining seven years on his tenure or the ideas he might have for the bureau's ever-evolving mission. He wanted only one thing in that moment, to take something that Comey already possessed—his job—and reclaim it as an object of leverage. To drive the point home, Trump implied that there was a long line of would-be applicants for the position, "about twenty people" just waiting for the signal to submit their résumés, a clunky attempt to pressure Comey into bidding for the job as if it were an overpriced oceanfront condo.

As he continued, Trump tacked between not-so-subtle threats and blandishment, saying that he "had heard great things" about Comey and hoped he didn't depart just yet, because it would look so bad for him personally. But Trump also made clear that he had the power to make a change if he wanted with no acknowledgment that he and Comey had previously discussed—and presumably settled—this matter.

Comey acknowledged "that he could fire me any time he wished but that I wanted to stay and do a job I love and think I am doing well."[13] He told Trump that while he could be counted on to tell the truth and to not leak secrets to the press—two qualities he assumed were central to Trump's approval—he wouldn't be "reliable" in the political sense of unwavering devotion to the president. Trump replied that "he needed loyalty and expected loyalty."

Comey let the remark go without responding, but their verbal wrestling was only beginning.

Trump then wandered through another thicket of subjects, reprising his denials of what he called the "golden showers thing." He suggested that perhaps the FBI should look into the matter so that he would be exonerated. Comey cautioned that doing so would have major downsides, most notably that no matter the merits of the allegation, what the public would take away was that the FBI was investigating him.

Then Trump circled back to his quest for a pledge from Comey, saying, "I need loyalty."

Comey replied that he would always provide honesty.

That's what I want, Trump said back, "honest loyalty."

Finally hearing terms that sounded acceptable, Comey said, "You will get that from me."

Trump and Comey had utterly conflicting views on the issues they had spent nearly an hour and a half sparring over obliquely: the merits of FBI independence, the boundaries of presidential power, the conditions of loyalty. The extent to which their positions were irreconcilable would become clear in the ensuing months. And yet, as they shook hands and parted ways after their private dinner, each believed he had achieved what he needed to in that face-off; each thought he had prevailed.

THE ISSUES THAT HAD CAUSED SO MUCH TROUBLE FOR FLYNN AT DIA—confusion about direction, infighting in the upper ranks—resurfaced as he took the reins at the NSC. He often seemed overwhelmed by the sheer expanse of issues that needed attention, and the bureaucracy he now led. He had made puzzling personnel choices, doling out assignments to candidates who couldn't get security clearances they needed for the jobs, and hiring McFarland, a Fox News commentator who hadn't been in government since Reagan was president. NSC employees waited for days to get even an introductory all-staff email from the new boss. And it wasn't until his second week on the job that Flynn convened an all-hands meeting, sending out a notice that warned employees not to bring their phones.

It was a rambling session in which Flynn tried to lighten the mood by telling the three hundred or so employees on hand not to believe what they saw about him on television. The NSC relies heavily on career officials detailed from other agencies, including the Pentagon, State Department, and CIA, for one- or two-year assignments. Many had served in the same positions under Obama and there were raised eyebrows when McFarland told the group they were there to "make America great again."

It quickly became clear that despite his title Flynn was not in control. He was routinely blindsided by foreign policy pronouncements that Trump made in early morning blasts on Twitter. He worried that he was losing West Wing influence battles to other players including Bannon, who stunned experts by taking a seat on the NSC. Flynn's grip on the job was also weakened by the persistent questions about his conversations with Kislyak. An atmosphere of intense distrust also set in, and some staffers—particularly those who had held jobs under Obama—began using encrypted communications, fearful that Flynn deputies were making lists of supposed "insider threats."

On February 1, Flynn sought to reassert himself with an attack on two of the Trump team's favorite targets: Obama and Iran. After Tehran conducted a ballistic missile test, Flynn issued a bellicose statement that accused the Islamic Republic of violating United Nations restrictions and the previous administration of failing to respond to "Iran's malign actions." Then, in one of the most bizarre scenes of his brief tenure, Flynn appeared at that day's White

House press briefing, replacing Spicer at the podium for a two-minute diatribe, saying that the Trump administration was "officially putting Iran on notice" but providing no clue to what that vaguely menacing statement meant. Flynn then slapped shut the folder he'd been reading from and rushed offstage before reporters could bombard him with questions about Kislyak.[14]

But while Flynn could dart from the stage, the questions were catching up to him. His false accounts, and the White House's exposure in those lies, dismayed those who knew otherwise. Each day that the White House failed to correct those misstatements, continuing to allow someone so compromised with the Kremlin to have access to classified secrets, added to the level of concern among those in position to expose the mounting dishonesty.

At the *Post*, reporters Adam Entous, Ellen Nakashima, and I had for weeks been getting signals from sources that there were problems with the White House's statements about Flynn and Kislyak. But the accounts were cryptic and finding someone willing to say specifically what was problematic, even on deep background, proved daunting. (In journalism, deep background is the most protective form of attribution. It means that the source won't be identified or even quoted anonymously, but has agreed to permit the information to be included in an article.)

In late January, I took a taxi to the Marriott Wardman Park hotel in Northwest D.C. on a reporting excursion that seemed certain to be a waste of time. The American Physical Society, an organization of physicists, was holding a conference on an array of mind-numbing topics including gravitational-wave detection and the spin structure of the nucleon. But one session on the January 31 schedule stood out: at 10:45 A.M., Kislyak was slated to deliver a speech on the prospects that cooperation on science and technology could improve relations between Russia and the United

States.[15] The Russian embassy had been stonewalling requests to speak with Kislyak. Now he was going to be appearing in public. It was worth a shot.

The crowd resembled a convention of retired college professors, and when I arrived, Kislyak was sitting in the front row. As the envoy was called up to the stage, I slipped into the seat adjacent to the one he had just vacated. Whatever the state of scientific collaboration, his speech wasn't going to improve relations between Moscow and Washington. He accused America of meddling in the 2014 election in Ukraine, foisting Edward Snowden on Russia as an unwelcome "guest," and pushing NATO to mass troops on Poland's border with Russia. Kislyak tried to dismiss U.S. sanctions against Russia as a minor nuisance, saying, "We can live with them." With no irony, he said cyberspace could "be an area of interaction, rather than confrontation."

I had hoped, at best, to be able to approach Kislyak at the edge of the stage when he was finished or follow him out the hotel exits asking questions. Instead, after speaking for more than an hour, Kislyak stepped down from the stage and went right back to his seat—next to me.

As the next speaker began, I leaned over to the Russian envoy and whispered a wary introduction. Trapped by the circumstances—the glaring lights and proximity to the stage made it too conspicuous to stand up and leave—Kislyak reluctantly but politely engaged. He said he had known Flynn for many years, and that he had communicated with him frequently in the months both before and after the election. "It's something all diplomats do," he declared. He refused to address the central question—whether the two had discussed sanctions—but I came away with something. Any story we developed on Flynn and Kislyak would inevitably rely heavily on unnamed sources. I now had firsthand on-the-record confirmation from one of the two participants in the calls that he and Flynn had communicated more extensively than the White House had acknowledged.

Back in the newsroom, Entous, Nakashima, and I weighed the idea of writing a story about the unusual frequency of the interactions between Flynn and Kislyak. Entous, who had been at the paper for only a few months, wanted to keep pushing, and days later achieved a breakthrough.

A seemingly inexhaustible well of reporting energy, Entous seemed to spend hours each day pacing the newsroom, his left hand propping up his right elbow, his right hand pressing a phone to his ear. When meeting sources in person, he liked to bring a typewritten list of facts to lay on the table and work through point by point, probing for feedback and reading facial reactions for clues. Sitting across from a source at a coffee shop in early February, he began going through his fact sheet on the Flynn-Kislyak call. He brought a copy of the Logan Act, so they could go through it line by line. The source kept referring to Pence's statements on television, encouraging Entous to review them closely. The Logan Act was key to understanding what had occurred on the call, the source said, and Pence's claim that "they did not discuss anything having to do with the United States's decision to expel diplomats" was flatly untrue. He would say no more, but Entous grasped the implication—that Kislyak was under surveillance and Flynn's words had been captured, incidentally, as a result.

With that source nailed down, others began to fall into place. Within days, the three reporters had confirmed key facts with other individuals and gathered more detail about the intercepted call. They began drafting a story that would say the national security adviser had in fact discussed sanctions with Kislyak and that the White House denials were untrue. There was a final reporting step to complete: giving Flynn a chance to respond.

It was not yet five in the evening but already dark when Karen

DeYoung left the *Washington Post* building for the five-block walk to the White House. DeYoung had worked for the *Post* since the 1970s, serving multiple tours as a foreign correspondent before coming back to D.C. to work as an editor and reporter covering national security issues with a focus on the White House. She had done most of the paper's sit-down interviews with national security advisers dating back to the George W. Bush administration, and she had requested a meeting with Flynn weeks earlier for a story that would focus on the administration's priorities and how the retired Army general planned to approach the job.

Before she'd departed the building, DeYoung had huddled with her three colleagues to plan a second set of questions regarding Flynn's conversations with the Russian ambassador. The paper was confident enough in its sourcing that a draft of the team's story was already in the *Post*'s system when DeYoung entered the West Wing on February 8. Flynn's spacious corner office had large windows on the north and west walls, with a large desk, a couch seating area on one side, and a conference table with chairs on the other. DeYoung and Flynn spoke for the better part of an hour on foreign policy issues until NSC spokesman Michael Anton interrupted to say the interview would need to wind down. DeYoung took that as a cue.

"My colleagues at the *Post* are preparing to publish a story which says that you did in fact discuss sanctions with Ambassador Kislyak," she said. "This is from current and former officials, people who have listened to the intercepts. . . ."

Flynn's eyes narrowed. "How can they listen to the intercepts? How can they do that? Imagine that you're listening to . . ." He trailed off, shaking his head. A career intelligence officer, he seemed preoccupied by the idea that such a recording was in circulation. (In fact, the recording itself wasn't shared as widely as a report summarizing the contents.) Flynn, who had been characteristically voluble to that point, suddenly became monosyllabic.

"No."

"Never?" DeYoung asked.

"No."

"Was there any signaling to the ambassador that if they would wait in terms of their response . . ."

"No."

"It was about phone calls with the president of the United States and [a global conference] coming up immediately after the inauguration," he said, finally elaborating. The two talked briefly about how Flynn knew Kislyak from a prior trip to Russia, but DeYoung had gotten what she came for.

The bulk of the interview had been on background, but as she walked back across Lafayette Square in the dark, she spoke to Anton by phone, who said that Flynn's denials about the call with Kislyak could be used on the record. When DeYoung got back to the newsroom, her waiting colleagues were huddled in the office of national security editor Peter Finn. The group had expected a denial from Flynn, but not necessarily such an emphatic one. DeYoung had told him a story was coming with multiple sources confirming the discussion of sanctions, but Flynn hadn't flinched—if anything, he punched back.

There is a scene in *All the President's Men*, the movie about Watergate, in which *Post* executive editor Ben Bradlee, played by Jason Robards, pulls the reins on a pending story implicating Nixon chief of staff H. R. Haldeman in the cover-up. "Now hold it," Bradlee says, "we're about to accuse Mr. Haldeman, who only happens to be the second most important man in America, of conducting a criminal conspiracy from inside the White House. It would be nice if we were right."

The stakes weren't exactly analogous, but accusing the national security adviser of undermining American interests and lying about it to the vice president was at least in a similar neighborhood. A lot was riding on this story, including the reputation of the paper at the start of a new presidency and the career of a decorated war general. Flynn's flat denial was thus disconcerting. Could we have gotten something wrong? We agreed to hold off for a night and regroup in the morning.

On February 9, I walked into a meeting in *Post* editor Marty Baron's office determined to make the case that the story was solid and should be published no matter what Flynn said. The three of us had gone over our sourcing that morning and counted nine current or former officials who had confirmed the account. To Baron and the assembled editors I emphasized that number in the meeting, and described the caliber of those sources. The reaction of those in the room made it clear they were convinced. Baron ordered that the story go forward, but said Flynn should be informed of the plan and given one more chance to respond.

I called Anton and relayed this message. Anton went back to Flynn and informed him that the paper was planning to publish despite his denials. By that point, the ground had already shifted for Flynn inside the White House. After Flynn's interview with DeYoung, word spread that a *Post* story was coming. Priebus, McGahn, and Eisenberg gathered with Flynn and pressed him on his conversations with Kislyak. They told him what DeYoung has also said—that there were transcripts. Flynn was cornered and his story crumbled. Now he "either was not sure whether he discussed sanctions or did not remember doing so," according to a timeline that McGahn put together.[16]

Anton called the *Post* to say that Flynn now wanted to withdraw his denials to DeYoung and replace them with a statement saying that "while he had no recollection of discussing sanctions, he couldn't be certain that the topic never came up." It was an amazing reversal, an acquiescence to the facts that the *Post* had painstakingly assembled over a period of weeks. The paper refused

Flynn's request to withdraw his on-the-record denials to DeYoung (the apparent attempt to mislead the paper was, on its own, newsworthy and mentioned in the ensuing story).

The article, initially posted online, said that Flynn had discussed sanctions with Kislyak despite his denials, and that his words to the Russian ambassador were interpreted by some U.S. officials "as an inappropriate and potentially illegal signal to the Kremlin that it could expect a reprieve from sanctions that were being imposed by the Obama administration." The story spread rapidly, carried by cable news channels, picked up by wire services, and matched by rival news organizations. Trump, who got most of his news from TV, could not possibly ignore it.

Flynn staggered through several more days in office. He apologized to Pence and traveled to Mar-a-Lago for the weekend, where Trump was hosting Japanese prime minister Shinzo Abe. On the February 10 flight to Florida, Trump claimed to the gathered reporters to be unaware of the *Post*'s report about Flynn but said that he planned to "look into" it. Things got even more surreal at Mar-a-Lago that evening when word reached the president that North Korea had launched a ballistic missile test. National security officials huddled around Trump to brief him on the development, discussing classified information in an outdoor eating area surrounded by dozens of other diners.

Administration officials sent conflicting signals about Flynn's fate. Asked whether Trump still had confidence in Flynn, adviser Stephen Miller said on a Sunday talk show, "That's a question for the president." White House adviser Kellyanne Conway stepped forward to say that Flynn had Trump's "full confidence," only to watch Spicer take the podium less than an hour later to say that the president was "evaluating the situation."

Flynn tried to create the appearance that it was business as usual, taking his seat alongside other White House officials for a Trump-

Abe press conference at the White House on Monday, February 13, but the tightened muscles in his face and dazed look in his eyes betrayed the strain he was under. The *Post* was already working on a follow-up story that sealed his fate, revealing that Yates had weeks earlier warned McGahn that Flynn had lied to Pence, was under FBI investigation, and was vulnerable to blackmail by the Russians. The story was published online around eight P.M. By eleven, Flynn had submitted his resignation. In his letter, Flynn refused to admit his falsehoods were intentional. He said he had "inadvertently briefed the Vice President Elect and others with incomplete information regarding my phone calls with the Russian ambassador," and that he had "sincerely apologized to the president and the vice president." Again, White House officials presented conflicting versions of events, with some saying Flynn had stepped down voluntarily and others insisting Trump had demanded his departure.

In the following days, Trump spoke with fondness about the man he'd fired and anger toward those who he seemed to blame for forcing him to do so. "General Flynn is a wonderful man," he said in a press conference with the Israeli prime minister Benjamin Netanyahu. "I think he's been treated very, very unfairly by the media—as I call it, the fake media, in many cases. And I think it's really a sad thing that he was treated so badly."

Flynn had survived thirty-three years in the Army, but only twenty-four days in the White House. He left the West Wing around 11:30 that night alone and drove to his house, across the Potomac River, in Old Town Alexandria. Failed military missions are followed by after-action reports, autopsies of what went wrong. Flynn spent the next several days sequestered with his wife, taking walks and taking stock. The truth fears no questions, Flynn had said during his trip to Moscow. But sometimes the truth has consequences.

On Valentine's Day, the day after Flynn's resignation, Trump had lunch at the White House with former New Jersey governor Chris Christie. Trump had beaten Christie for the Republican nomination, denied him a position in the Trump administration, and rejected his advice against hiring Flynn. But if Trump always had the upper hand in the relationship, it was Christie who had the more reliable instincts.

"Now that we fired Flynn, the Russia thing is over," Trump said.

Christie just laughed. "No way," he said. "This Russia thing is far from over. . . . We'll be here on Valentine's Day 2018 talking about this." The former federal prosecutor tried to give the president some sobering advice, telling him that in his experience there were no ways to make investigations shorter but many ways to make them longer. He told Trump not to talk about it publicly, even if he became frustrated. He also said that he would never be able to get rid of Flynn, that the ousted national security adviser would become "like gum on the bottom of your shoe."[17]

UNTIL THAT POINT, THE TRUMP ADMINISTRATION HAD LARGELY succeeded in deflecting the Russia story, depicting it as a phony scandal conjured by the press and his political opponents. Trump's specious attempts to dispute Russia's role in the DNC hack had failed to persuade even senior officials in his own administration. But the idea that there might be hidden, nefarious ties between the Trump team and the Kremlin was still in the realm of the unproven, even farfetched—until Flynn was fired.

The exposure of Flynn's secret communications with Kislyak created a cascade of further questions: Why had the White House failed to act on Yates's warnings about Flynn until his vulnerability was exposed publicly? Which other members of Trump's inner circle had secretly engaged with Kislyak or the Kremlin? How much did Trump and others on his team know about Russia's interference in the election, and what, if anything, did Putin expect from the president he had sought to install in the Oval Office? What did Trump officials know about Flynn's calls with Kislyak when he made them? These lines of inquiry would consume reporters and congressional investigators for the rest of 2017 and beyond, but the search for answers would largely depend on the course of the investigation that the FBI had begun in July 2016.

Three days after firing Flynn, Trump held the only press conference he would conduct during his first nineteen months in office, aside from intermittent appearances alongside other world leaders. The atmosphere was charged because of Flynn's firing, and the president's exchanges with reporters bordered on belligerent. The first question was whether he had fired Flynn. Trump was defiant. "What he did wasn't wrong," Trump said. "What was wrong was the way that other people, including yourselves in this room, were given that information [about Flynn's call with Kislyak] because that was classified information that was given illegally. That's the real problem. And you can talk all you want about Russia, which was all a fake news, fabricated deal to try and make up for the loss of the Democrats, and the press plays right into it."

The rest of the press conference continued along that combative, convoluted path. He claimed to have never spoken to the campaign aides who had contacts with Russia, despite the photos of his meeting with Page and Papadopoulos. He said he himself had "nothing to do with Russia . . . no deals there. I have no anything," ignoring the letters of intent to pursue Trump Tower developments in Moscow, his son Eric's 2014 statement to a reporter that Trump golf courses got "all the funding we need out of Russia," and the mysteriously massive overpayments for Trump condos by Russian oligarchs. He bristled at a series of pointed questions on whether he would ever respond to Russian provocations against American interests, arguing that "it would be much easier for me to be tough on Russia, but then we're not going to make a deal."

One of the overlooked lines in the press conference was among the most ominous. It came in the midst of an extended rant about how the Russia story was "fake news" propagated by his enemies in the Obama administration. "We have our new people going in place right now," he said. "As you know, Mike Pompeo is taking control of the CIA. James Comey at FBI. Dan Coats is waiting to be approved" as director of DNI. "Our new people are going in."

The line suggested that Trump thought of Comey, at least in that moment, as one of his people. More than that, he thought that having his "people" in place meant that the bad stories, the perceived disloyalty among national security agencies—perhaps even the investigations—were about to end.

TRUMP'S ADMIRATION FOR PUTIN WAS GROUNDED IN ENVY OF THE way he ruled. Putin faced none of the annoyances that Trump complained about most, including the recalcitrant press, haranguing political opposition, and the disloyal ranks of the "deep state." Putin's authority was, or at least appeared to be, absolute. He could spread falsehoods at will, order investigations of adversaries, and never worry about sagging poll numbers (because elections were reliably rigged).

Most important, Putin was immune to the kind of investigations that were beginning to encircle and enrage Trump. The American president couldn't replicate that arrangement, but Trump seemed to anticipate something approximating it once he had installed subordinates he could count on in key positions. The emerging tensions between Trump and Comey—the gap between "loyalty" and "honest loyalty"—reflected a conflicting vision of government and accountability that could never be reconciled. Which would prevail?

PART
FOUR

CHAPTER 11

YOU'RE FIRED

O N FEBRUARY 8, FIVE DAYS BEFORE MICHAEL FLYNN WAS fired, Comey was at the White House for a conversation with chief of staff Reince Priebus. They talked briefly about the Steele dossier and the proper channels for White House communications with the bureau before Priebus asked to discuss something "private."

"Do you have a FISA order on Mike Flynn?" he asked.

Comey explained that was the kind of question that should go through the Justice Department, but answered anyway, saying no (the warrant was for surveillance of Kislyak). Priebus then proposed they walk to the Oval Office.

There, Trump again brought up the "golden showers thing" and again denied hiring prostitutes but also said to Comey that Putin had told him that Russia had "some of the most beautiful hookers in the world."

Trump then mentioned a television interview he'd done with Bill O'Reilly that aired on Fox News before the Super Bowl. O'Reilly pressed Trump on how he could have such admiration for a ruthless killer like Putin. "There are a lot of killers. We've got a lot of killers," Trump replied. "What do you think? Our country's so innocent?" Replaying the exchange in his head, Trump looked to Comey for affirmation, saying, "You think my answer was good, right?"

"The first part of your answer was fine, Mr. President," Comey said. "But not the second part. We aren't the kind of killers that Putin is." Trump seemed stunned by the criticism and looked at the FBI director without speaking for a moment. Comey went back to the bureau and told aides that he "had probably ended any personal relationship with the president."

DAYS LATER, ON FEBRUARY 14, A DOZEN SENIOR OFFICIALS ASSEMbled in the Oval Office for a counterterrorism briefing with Trump. Unlike other presidents, who tended to take a seat near the fireplace and gather advisers around, Trump stayed parked behind his imposing desk. The lead briefer, Nick Rasmussen, director of the National Counterterrorism Center, sat with his knees pressed against the wood. Next to him was Comey, back in the Oval Office for the second time in less than a week. Absent was Flynn, who that day was surrendering his badges and phones, a final severing of his government service.

Trump seemed disengaged during the session, then ended the meeting with a loud "Thanks, everybody." As he stood up to walk people out, he motioned for the FBI chief to stay behind, saying, "I just want to talk to Jim." Attorney General Jeff Sessions seemed to hesitate, hanging on as others filed out, but Trump moved him toward the exit. Kushner lingered as well, approaching Comey and making comments about the Clinton email investigation. It was as if both Sessions and Kushner sensed that Trump was about to do something regrettable but didn't know how to prevent it. "Okay, Jared, thank you," Trump said, ushering his son-in-law out.

As the door by the grandfather clock in the Oval Office closed, Trump turned to Comey. "I want to talk about Mike Flynn," he said.[1] The president declared that his national security adviser "hadn't done anything wrong" in his call with the Russian ambassador but had to be fired because he misled the vice president. Trump alluded to other concerns about Flynn but didn't elaborate.

Trump tried to argue that the more serious problem deserving the FBI director's attention was how Flynn's interactions with Kislyak had surfaced in the press. "It is really about the leaks," he said. He voiced irritation with a February 2 story in the *Post* about his belligerent calls with Australian prime minister Malcolm Turnbull and Mexican president Enrique Peña Nieto, pointing to "this beautiful phone" on his desk and asking why the words he said into that secure device had so quickly spilled out before the public. Comey finally found an area of agreement with the president, saying he was "eager to find leakers" and that there was value in "putting a head on a pike as a message." Trump seemed to relish the tough talk, and said that he favored putting reporters in jail. "They spend a couple days in jail, make a new friend, and they are ready to talk." (Reading this many months later, I cringed when I saw the references to Trump's calls and realized that I was the reporter they were discussing.)

Priebus poked his head in through the door by the clock, a portal curved and painted to blend almost invisibly into the Oval Office walls. Outside, in an area used by the president's assistant, Comey could see the vice president and others waiting behind Priebus. But Trump waved them away and returned to the discussion of Flynn. "He is a good guy and has been through a lot," Trump said. "I hope you can see your way to letting this go, to letting Flynn go. He is a good guy. I hope you can let this go."

Comey, who was perfecting the art of silently registering reservation while outwardly signaling concurrence, replied: "I agree he is a good guy." With that exchange, Trump ventured into a domain somewhere between inappropriate and illegal.

It was forty-five years earlier, in that same setting, that a president's attempt to impede the FBI ensured his removal from office. The 2017 encounter was different in important respects from the 1972 exchange between Nixon and his chief of staff, H. R. Haldeman. Trump and Comey—who left the Oval Office alarmed, wrote a private memo to record what had transpired, and complained to Sessions about being left alone with the president—were not like-minded conspirators and their words were not captured on tape (although Trump would later make empty threats that they had been). But after the Watergate scandal and Nixon's resignation, even casual students of American politics knew that it was illegal for a president to attempt to block or subvert an investigation. It is a basic tenet of the American legal system, grounded in the idea that no individual is above the law. The attempt put Trump in the Nixon-like position of facing an investigation that expanded from alleged campaign crimes to obstruction of justice.

PROSECUTORS LOOK FOR THREE CORE ELEMENTS IN AN OBSTRUC-tion charge: the existence of an active investigation, a defendant aware such a probe is under way, and a corrupt attempt to "influence, obstruct, or impede the due and proper administration of the law." Comey was troubled by what he perceived as direction from the president to abandon its investigation of Flynn, to forget about what he had told Kislyak and what he had told the FBI agents who came to see him at the White House. Trump's defenders would later attribute his actions to inexperience, and argue that "hoping" the FBI would back off was very different from instructing it to do so. But if Trump were merely unfamiliar with the boundaries of conduct for presidents, if his motives were innocent, why had he sent Sessions and others out of the room? Why was it so important to isolate Comey?

More than most presidents, Trump had extensive firsthand experience with the legal system (though not with constitutional law). He had hired lawyers to help him with his business deals, lawyers to go after those he felt had cheated him, lawyers to intimidate those he was angry with, lawyers to take care of his multiple bankruptcies and divorces, lawyers to push back against those who challenged him in civil and criminal court, and even lawyers such as Michael Cohen, who arranged payoffs to mistresses in exchange for their silence. The law was something he had almost always used to his advantage in life, and he seemed oblivious to the risks of acting as if he were above it as president.

That arrogance had surfaced throughout the 2016 campaign when he threatened to jail opponents. It had been central to presenting himself as a populist wrecking ball that would not wait for permission from Washington or be held up by traditional legal regulation. And it was fully in line with the worldview of a man he regarded as a model: Vladimir Putin.

TRUMP HAD ALLIES IN POSITION TO MONITOR THE MOUNTING INvestigations of Russia. Sessions, Trump's earliest and most prominent supporter in the Senate, was Comey's boss. Devin Nunes, who had served on the transition team (and reportedly turned down the chance to be CIA director), was the chairman of the House Intelligence Committee, one of the panels in Congress that had launched probes of Russia's campaign interference. The Senate investigation was led by Senator Richard Burr, a North Carolina Republican lukewarm toward Trump. But Sessions and Nunes could try to steer the probes in their domains toward other targets and protect the president's interests.

Sessions was Trump's first announced cabinet pick, nominated to serve as attorney general ten days after the election. The four-term senator from Alabama, then sixty-nine, wasn't without controversy, most famously when his chance at a federal judgeship under President Reagan was derailed by allegations of racism.

Trump brushed that aside, heaping praise on Sessions as "a world-class legal mind" who was "greatly admired by legal scholars and virtually everyone who knows him." While Sessions seemed to benefit from the deference the Senate shows other members of that exclusive club, his two-day confirmation hearing on January 10 and 11 had included several contentious moments. There were tough questions about his views on race and on Trump's conduct. The most problematic exchange, however, had to do with Russia.

Senators probed Sessions on whether he would allow the federal investigation of Moscow's campaign interference to proceed (he said he would) and whether he shared the president's skepticism that the Kremlin had attacked the DNC (hedging, he said he had "done no research into that" but had no reason to doubt it). Then Senator Al Franken of Minnesota cited a story published by CNN reporting that the nation's intelligence leaders had briefed Trump on the Steele dossier, including its allegation that "there was a continuing exchange of information during the campaign between Trump surrogates and intermediaries for the Russian government."

If that is true, Franken asked, what will you, as attorney general, do about it?

"Senator Franken, I'm not aware of any of those activities," Sessions replied. "I have been called a surrogate at a time or two in that campaign and I did not have communications with the Russians."

That was far from honest. On March 1, several weeks after exposing Flynn's misleading statements, the *Post* reported that Sessions had spoken at least twice in 2016 with the Russian ambassador, including once on September 8 in Sessions's Senate office. Kislyak had relayed information about this meeting back to the Kremlin, communication that was snatched by U.S. intelligence.

Scrambling to contain the damage, Sessions issued a statement later that night saying that, yes, he had met with Kislyak, but in his capacity as a member of the Senate Armed Services Committee, not as a Trump proxy. The claim defied credulity. At that point in the campaign, Sessions's profile among diplomats and lobbyists was rising precisely because of his role as a Trump adviser, and as Entous learned after conducting an exhaustive poll of Sessions's colleagues, he had been the only one of all twenty-seven members of the Senate Armed Services Committee to meet with the Russian ambassador. The timing of his meeting with Moscow's representative was also problematic. Russia's meddling in the campaign was such a front-burner issue in Washington by September—after the DNC hack and WikiLeaks dump—that most lawmakers would have rejected an approach from Kislyak. And yet Sessions had opened his door eagerly.

Other members of the committee seemed bewildered by Sessions's explanation, and within hours, numerous Democrats and even some Republican lawmakers were calling for him to recuse himself from the Russia investigation. Coming so closely on the heels of Flynn's ouster, Democrats smelled blood, and some demanded that Sessions resign.

What Trump didn't know was that Sessions, mindful of the obvious conflict of presiding over a probe of the campaign, had already been meeting with ethics officials at the Justice Department. On March 2, a seemingly rattled attorney general stepped forward at a hastily scheduled news conference to announce that he would remove himself from any involvement in the Russia probe, citing those internal consultations. "They said that since I had involvement with the campaign," Sessions said, "I should not be involved in any campaign investigation."

Trump's reaction in public was muted. He issued a statement saying Sessions "is an honest man. He did not say anything wrong. He could have stated his response (during the confirmation hearing) more accurately but it was clearly not intentional."[2] He added that Democrats were "overplaying their hand" in criticizing Sessions and called their attacks a "total witch hunt!"

Behind the scenes, the president seethed, furious that he had been abandoned by someone he had counted on being one of his "people." The perceived betrayal was all the more acute because it went against the president's explicit wishes—earlier that day he had instructed McGahn to convince Sessions not to step aside. In his mind, attorneys general were not holders of an office sworn to serve the public, but legal attack dogs there to protect the president and do his bidding. He was convinced that his predecessors had that arrangement—John F. Kennedy and his younger brother, Robert; Barack Obama and Eric Holder. "Where's my Roy Cohn?" he asked.[3]

Trump's relationship with Sessions never recovered. In the ensuing months, it got to the point where Trump could hardly bring himself to look at the attorney general, subjecting him to withering treatment in private and castigating him mercilessly in public. Sessions hung on despite the humiliation, protected by the intervention of White House aides concerned about the optics of firing an attorney general and the support of Senate Republicans who would have to serve as Trump's firewall if the probe ever led to impeachment.

Early in the morning on March 4—two days after Sessions stepped aside—Trump picked up the weapon he so frequently turned to when embattled. Clutching his phone, he composed a tweet whose purpose was to retake the initiative and force his pursuers into a confused retreat. The tweet he sent had no basis in fact, but in some ways that was the point. The Justice Department was an entity of law and order that pursued its quarry across a landscape of probable evidence. Trump was the opposite, an agent of disorder whose preferred climate for conflict was a sandstorm of falsehoods. That is what he set out to create with his 6:35 A.M. tweet.

"Terrible!" he wrote. "Just found out that Obama had my 'wires tapped' in Trump Tower just before the victory. Nothing found. This is McCarthyism!" In seconds, the phony allegations scattered across the internet.

DEVIN NUNES MIGHT AS WELL HAVE COME FROM A DIFFERENT planet than Donald Trump. The Republican congressman was raised on a flat stretch of farmland in California's Central Valley that has more in common with Kansas than with the soaring sky-line of Manhattan. Trump was obsessed with fame and building his brand from the time he set out in business, while Nunes was relatively anonymous to all but the closest observers of House politics until Trump was elected president.

Nunes and Trump had some similarities, including ambition to rise beyond their families' stations and an early entrepreneurial focus. While Trump was staked at least a million dollars by his father to get started in real estate, Nunes spent his teen years on dairy and cattle farms that his family had worked for decades, pooling money with a brother to buy more acreage. Trump and Nunes relied on the force of their personalities to gain power and shared a disdain for details. (During his early years on the House Intelligence Committee, Nunes's aversion to reading briefing materials was so notorious that the chairman at the time, Michigan Republican Mike Rogers, cut off the Californian's travel budget until he had at least scanned relevant reports.) Most important, Trump and Nunes shared a fondness for conspiracies and a view of politics as a blood sport in which rules and facts should never impede the greater imperative of vanquishing opponents.

Well before Trump was sworn in, Nunes was working to deflect damaging claims about Russia. In December 2016, when the *Post* reported on the CIA's conclusions that Moscow had sought to help elect Trump, Nunes attempted to muddy the issue by insisting he was unaware of any such finding—even though he had been among the first to hear it directly from Brennan. In late February, after Flynn's resignation had triggered a wave of new stories about suspicious contacts between the Trump campaign and Russia, the White House turned to Nunes to knock down the reports.

In a phone interview at the time, Nunes said something that stayed with me, that in hindsight could only be seen as deliberate disinformation. The FBI and other authorities had been investigating Trump-Russia allegations for months, Nunes said, and turned up no evidence of a single interaction. "They've looked, and it's all a dead trail that leads me to believe no contact, not even pizza-delivery-guy contact," he said. Investigators, Nunes said, "don't even have a lead."[4] That was, of course, completely untrue.

Nunes at first seemed eager to charge ahead with the committee's investigation of Russia, at least in part as a platform for carrying out attacks on the president's critics and accusers. It was an approach that closely tracked the Republican strategy on Benghazi, but it backfired almost immediately. On March 20, Nunes's committee became the first to hold a public hearing on Russian interference in the 2016 presidential election. On the witness stand were two of those who had briefed Trump in January: Comey and the NSA director Rogers.

In his opening remarks, Nunes laid out priorities for the hearing that notably skipped the question of Trump-Russia contacts. Instead, he planned to focus on questions about leaks and improper surveillance of the Trump campaign. "We know there was not a physical wiretap of Trump Tower," Nunes said. "However, it's still possible that other surveillance activities were used against President Trump and his associates."

Though it wasn't clear at the time, Nunes's opening was part of what would become an ongoing siege by Trump and his allies to discredit the FBI and those who might provide evidence against the president.

Schiff, a cerebral politician and former federal prosecutor, used his time at the start of the hearing to deliver a blistering monologue that resembled a lawyer's opening statement. Schiff spent half an hour walking through the mounting evidence about Russia and Trump and posed a series of questions: "Is it a coincidence," he asked, "that Jeff Sessions failed to tell the Senate about his meetings with a Russian ambassador . . . Is it a coincidence that Michael Flynn would lie about a conversation he had with the same Russian ambassador . . ." Schiff continued the refrain, citing suspicious transactions by a Russian gas company with ties to Trump advisers, and Trump ally Roger Stone's mysterious foreknowledge that hacked DNC and Clinton material would be exposed by WikiLeaks.

"Is it possible," he concluded, that all of these developments are "nothing more than an entirely unhappy coincidence?" Perhaps, he concluded, "but it is also possible, maybe more than possible, that they are not coincidental, not disconnected, and not unrelated."

Moments later it was Comey's turn to speak, and he delivered a bombshell. The FBI was not only investigating Russia's interference in the election, but "the nature of any links between individuals associated with the Trump campaign and the Russian government and whether there was any coordination between the campaign and Russia's efforts," Comey said. "This will also include an assessment of whether any crimes were committed."

The FBI director, who had so notoriously talked about the probe of Clinton while staying silent on Trump throughout the campaign, had finally corrected that inequity. With that, Nunes's agenda for the hearing had effectively been obliterated. The Trump campaign was officially, publicly, in the FBI's crosshairs.

Asked about the president's claim to have been wiretapped, the FBI director said that Justice Department officials now working for Sessions had looked into the matter extensively. "The department has no information that supports those tweets," he said.

As Comey's testimony continued, Republicans clawed out small concessions, forcing the FBI director to repeat Trump's only acceptable talking point from the spy agencies' assessment—that they had no evidence that Moscow had altered votes on election day. Even so, the headlines battered the president. ("FBI Director Comey Confirms Probe of Possible Coordination Between Kremlin and Trump Campaign," was the *Post*'s version.) And the hearing had gone so badly that Nunes abruptly canceled others already on the committee's schedule. Clapper, Brennan, and Yates were all lined up to testify on Russian interference. The president's closest ally in Congress no longer wanted to hear from them, though all would eventually appear before multiple committees. In May 2017, Brennan uttered one of the more memorable lines of the Russia scandal. "Frequently," Brennan said, "people who go along a treasonous path do not know they are on a treasonous path until it is too late."

IN LATE JANUARY, AN AMBITIOUS YOUNG NSC OFFICIAL EMBARKED on a seemingly legitimate project: a review of the White House rules on "unmaskings," the revealing of the names of U.S. citizens in intelligence reports at the request of senior officials in government. The citizens in question were often U.S. officials whose conversations were inadvertently collected as part of routine surveillance of foreign nationals like Kislyak. To guard against abuse, the Americans' identities are typically "masked," meaning their names are deleted from any reports or transcripts circulated in government, designated only in generic terms as Individual A or B. (The issue was of little consequence to most Americans, whose calls to relatives or friends overseas were of little interest to U.S. spies and legally protected.)

Ezra Cohen-Watnick, the NSC aide who set out to overhaul the White House rules, had never held a high-level job in America's spy services before landing in the Trump administration as the White House's senior director for intelligence. Cohen-Watnick had gone to work for the Defense Intelligence Agency after he finished college, training at the CIA's espionage academy known as "The Farm" in Southern Virginia and serving in intelligence posts in places including Afghanistan. (Though always in the CIA's shadow, the DIA has its own overseas spies, focused on gathering information for the military.) Through a series of connections, he met Flynn in 2016 and was offered the NSC's intelligence director position, a job that gave him extraordinary visibility into the sensitive operations of American spy agencies and influence over their interactions with the White House. It was a stunning leap in station for the then thirty-year-old.

Cohen-Watnick noticed that unmasking requests weren't being reviewed by lawyers before they were submitted, nor was anyone keeping detailed records at the White House of who was asking for names of Americans and why. Requests were approved seemingly routinely, almost never denied, under long-standing policies that seemed surprisingly lax.

Planning to write updated guidelines, Cohen-Watnick asked his deputy to help generate a list of categories of unmasking requests that could be checked off on a new form that officials would be required to fill out. What came back was a log of all the requests made during the prior year by White House officials under Obama. The size of the file surprised Cohen-Watnick—it was an inch thick, with entries for between 400 and 500 requests.

Cohen-Watnick shared the material with White House staff working with him on the review, and then with John Eisenberg. A few days later, Eisenberg came back with two entries highlighted. He wanted to see the full text of the intelligence reports—the summaries of intercepted emails or conversations—linked to those requests.

He took the copies from Cohen-Watnick's printer, then came back several days later with a bigger order. The NSC legal office now wanted to see details on every single intelligence report tracked in the log. These were documents that often ran ten or more pages, meaning the full stack would run into the thousands. Worried that it would look suspicious and possibly trip security systems put in place to detect unusual handling of classified material, Cohen-Watnick insisted that an NSC lawyer sit with him in his office as a witness while pages spilled out of a special printer for classified documents.

Among them were intelligence reports reviewed by the Obama administration's ambassador to the United Nations, Samantha Power, at a time when she was trying to figure out how UN Security Council members were going to vote on a December 2016 resolution regarding Israeli settlements. (It had been these reports that showed Flynn on December 22 urging Kislyak to push his government to "vote against or delay the resolution," and the Obama administration position.)[5]

The reports were put in binders and hauled back to the NSC legal offices. Eisenberg and the other lawyers now had a pile of documents showing virtually all the instances during the election year in which Obama White House officials had asked to see the names of Americans talking with foreign targets of U.S. surveillance, or mentioned in communications between foreigners. It was not long after the binders arrived at the NSC lawyers' offices that Trump claimed, seemingly out of the blue, to have discovered his wires had been tapped. It defied the odds of coincidence.

A few weeks later, Nunes fielded a call while in a car in downtown Washington with one of his staffers. He abruptly asked the driver to stop, jumped out, and switched into another car—a sequence of events that remains murky. Without telling the subordinate he'd just deserted, Nunes headed to the White House.

That evening, March 21, Cohen-Watnick came looking for Eisenberg on a different matter and saw the light on in his office. Cohen-Watnick asked a White House attorney when Eisenberg might be free. The attorney said it wasn't Eisenberg behind the door; it was Michael Ellis, his deputy. Ellis had joined the NSC legal office after serving as general counsel on the House Intelligence Committee—in other words, he came to the White House directly after working for Nunes. When the attorney said he didn't know who Ellis was meeting with, Cohen-Watnick pressed him to peek inside. The attorney came back to report that Ellis was with Nunes. The intelligence committee chairman and his committee's former lawyer were having a private reunion at the White House.

Nunes announced the next day that he had discovered alarming new information that he urgently needed to share with the president (without mentioning that this information had been furnished to him by White House lawyers). The matter wasn't so urgent, however, that Nunes couldn't set aside time for an impromptu press conference on Capitol Hill before departing for the White House.

"I recently confirmed that on numerous occasions the intelligence community incidentally collected information about U.S.

citizens involved in the Trump transition," Nunes said from Capitol Hill. His face was fixed in a look of grim concern, though what he had just said was, at least to those familiar with the rules of intelligence gathering, unremarkable. Any American who interacts with a foreign official important enough to be monitored by U.S. intelligence is liable to show up in the reports. Claiming that what he had discovered would trouble ordinary Americans, Nunes said that he had "confirmed that additional names of Trump transition team members were unmasked."[6]

It was a head-scratching performance. Nunes refused to explain where or how he had obtained this allegedly troubling new material. He said that Trump's surveillance claim was wrong in the most literal reading of his tweet, but implied that he had discovered new information substantiating the president's concerns. Finally, Nunes came perilously close to exposing classified information himself. Asked by a reporter whether the reports he'd seen were from surveillance conducted on the orders of the special FISA court—whose proceedings are highly classified—Nunes blurted out: "It appears so."

After a high-visibility visit to the White House, the situation for Nunes deteriorated. The press quickly figured out that Nunes's supposed breakthrough had been gift-wrapped for him by the president's subordinates. Democrats on the House Intelligence Committee attacked him for the stunt, with some calling for his resignation. A collection of activist groups filed complaints with the House Ethics Committee to investigate Nunes's possible violation of FISA secrecy. When the panel announced on April 6 that it would do so, Nunes was ensnared by his own scheme and forced to give up control of the Russia probe (though he would continue to wield influence behind the scenes).

Flynn had been forced to resign, Sessions had recused himself, and now Nunes—who presumably would have had tremendous value to Trump by remaining in charge of the Russia investigation—was forced to the sidelines.

TRUMP'S IRRITATIONS AND INSECURITIES TENDED TO REVEAL themselves early in the day. Too early to be stifled by aides or derailed by the day's events, he would brood in the White House residence surrounded by stacks of newspapers and staring at a droning television. Morning was when he was most likely to lash out on Twitter or pick up the phone to vent.

As Trump entered his third month in office, he made a pair of morning calls to Comey. The first, on March 30, came into the bureau through the Royal Crown switchboard, the code name for the secure routing capability in the White House. Trump joked that Comey was getting more publicity than he was, a barb that anyone who knew the president would understand reflected true annoyance.

The "cloud of this Russia business," he said, was making it difficult for him to do his job as president.[7] He ran through the usual reasons for why the allegations against him shouldn't be believed ("can you imagine me, hookers?"). He said the investigation was damaging his effectiveness with Congress, undermining his influence with European allies, and becoming a "very painful" issue for his wife, Melania.

What can be done to lift the cloud? Trump asked. Comey again tried to placate the president by saying that the FBI was not investigating him and that he had said so in his private meetings with congressional leaders. That reassurance was no longer enough for Trump. He wanted the world to know what the FBI chief kept saying in closed quarters. "It would be great to get that out," Trump said.

The conversation fell into a familiar rut, with Trump pressing

Comey for something the FBI chief would neither give nor explicitly refuse. Groping for leverage, Trump noted that he "hadn't brought up the McCabe thing" as a way of doing exactly that. Trump had voiced concern about Comey's FBI deputy in earlier encounters, questioning McCabe's loyalties and political leanings. The issue traced back to one of Trump's lines of attack on Clinton in 2016. McCabe's wife, a pediatrician, had lost a race for a Virginia state senate seat in 2015 running as a Democrat. She'd had extensive political and financial backing from Virginia's then governor, Terry McAuliffe, who in turn had close ties to the Clintons. On the campaign trail, Trump had hammered away at the issue, repeatedly implying that Clinton money (through McAuliffe to McCabe's wife) was influencing the FBI's handling of the email probe. The claim was full of holes, among them the fact that McCabe's wife had lost her race by the time the FBI email probe started.[8] But Trump kept up the attacks, and in raising the matter with Comey suggested that he had done the FBI director a favor in allowing him to keep a deputy compromised by connections to the Clintons. On the phone, Comey defended McCabe as "an honorable person" and Trump seemed to stand down. But the president had outlined a murky quid pro quo—get the word out that the FBI wasn't investigating Trump, and the president would continue to tolerate McCabe.

Twelve days later, Comey again found himself on a morning call with the president. This time, there were no preliminary pleasantries. Trump wanted to know if Comey had done what he'd been asked to do, to "get that out." Comey said he had relayed the request to Dana Boente, a Justice Department official who briefly had authority over the Russia probe after Sessions's recusal. Comey explained that this was the appropriate path for such a request from the White House, but had not heard back. "I perceived him to be slightly annoyed by my reply," Comey recalled.

Again, Trump began negotiating with the FBI director and making vague assertions of an unstated contract between them. The president made clear that he was bothered that the cloud was still hovering "because I have been very loyal to you, very loyal." Then, in a cryptic reference to their tense dinner in the Green Room, Trump said, "We had that thing, you know."

Comey didn't know, but the president's meaning seemed obvious. Trump was remembering his demand for loyalty and Comey's counteroffer of "honest loyalty." The gap in their understandings of that Green Room compromise was about to have serious consequences.

It was the last time the two men would speak.

SHORTLY AFTER THE NOVEMBER ELECTION, JEFF SESSIONS WAS VISited in his Senate office by a veteran prosecutor who seemed to have the right credentials for a job in the Trump administration. Rod Rosenstein was a graduate of the Wharton School at the University of Pennsylvania, Trump's alma mater. He was a lifelong Republican who had spent more than a decade as a U.S. attorney in Baltimore racking up victories in cases involving violent crime and—as part of a special assignment that the president-elect might appreciate—national security leaks. He had also been a part of the Whitewater investigation in the 1990s, a multiyear probe of an Arkansas land deal that veered into the Monica Lewinsky scandal and led to the impeachment trial of Bill Clinton.

Sessions and Rosenstein did not know each other before their November conversation on Capitol Hill, but they quickly hit it off. Rosenstein had a far more impressive legal résumé than the attorney general nominee, but a mild-mannered personality and reputation for collegiality. As the two men talked, they realized that they shared a view that Comey had severely mishandled the

Clinton email probe, overstepping his role in announcing there would be no prosecution and seizing the spotlight in ways that both men abhorred. (In a farewell email to the U.S. attorney's office in Baltimore, Rosenstein urged employees to "stay humble and kind," the lyrics of a Tim McGraw song.)

At Sessions's urging, Trump nominated Rosenstein to be deputy attorney general in early February. He was confirmed in April, just as the president's relationship with Comey was turning toxic. The FBI director's standing deteriorated further on May 3, when Comey vigorously defended his handling of the Clinton email investigation in an appearance before the Senate Judiciary Committee. While Comey was always seen as somewhat sanctimonious, his refusal to accept the possibility that he had made a grievous mistake infuriated Democrats and vexed his new Justice Department bosses, Sessions and Rosenstein. His failure during the hearing to declare that the bureau was not investigating Trump himself, and his statement that it made him "mildly nauseous" to think that his handling of the email probe had possibly cost Clinton the race, incensed the president.

The fallout was swift. A White House official returned from a meeting with Rosenstein to inform McGahn that the deputy attorney general had been troubled by Comey's performance and wished to discuss how to address his refusal to acknowledge—let alone correct—his errors in judgment. Trump stewed about Comey all weekend during a trip to his golf club in Bedminster, New Jersey, and returned to Washington clutching the draft of a letter firing his FBI director—something he had begun composing numerous times only to be talked down by Priebus and others who feared that dismissing Comey would unleash a legal and political maelstrom.

On Monday, May 8, five days after Comey's testimony, Trump

summoned Pence, Priebus, McGahn, Sessions, and Rosenstein to the Oval Office. It was a Comey-bashing session in which nearly everyone—including Rosenstein—participated with enthusiasm. The president declared that he had decided to get rid of the FBI director, and mentioned the letter he'd written. It faulted Comey for his handling of the Clinton email investigation—something Trump had praised in his personal meetings with the FBI chief—and expressed his continued irritation that Comey had failed to tell the public what he had said several times in private, that Trump was not a target of the FBI probe.

The president was the only one in the room who seemed to fail to see the problem of drawing such a clear line between his frustration with the Russia probe and his firing of the FBI director. Priebus and others convinced Trump to abandon the text he'd drafted. Instead, as Trump listened to Sessions and Rosenstein voice their criticism of Comey over the emails case, Trump settled on an alternate plan, instructing his Justice Department team to produce memos documenting their concerns with their FBI subordinate. Rosenstein agreed to go along, believing, as he would put it later, that he was simply providing "advice and input." But there was no mistaking the dynamic—the president had reached his conclusion and wanted to be able to pin the decision on others.

THE DIRECTORS GUILD OF AMERICA BUILDING IN SOUTHERN CALIfornia resembles a stack of film canisters rising from the southern edge of the most iconic street in Hollywood, Sunset Boulevard. Posters and red-velvet rope lines were already in place at the building's entrance on Tuesday, May 9, directing would-be FBI agents to a minority recruiting job fair inside a theater normally reserved for movie screenings and appearances by prominent directors. The event—aimed at diversifying the ranks of a federal law enforcement agency whose 13,000 agents are 83 percent white—was scheduled to get under way at 4:00 P.M., with a keynote speech by Comey.

He never made it.

The FBI director had arrived in Los Angeles early to visit the FBI's field office, an equally imposing if less architecturally redeeming structure on Wilshire Boulevard. He was speaking to a group of assembled agents in a room at the bureau's command center about a seemingly trivial issue—the recent revision of the FBI's mission statement—when television screens at the back of the room flashed a startling headline: COMEY RESIGNS.

Comey thought it was a practical joke. "That's pretty funny," he said. "Somebody put a lot of work into that one." Then the screens, tuned to three separate newscasts, displayed a revised banner: COMEY FIRED. A nervous energy spread through the room. "Look, I'm going to go figure out what's happening," Comey said. "But whether that's true or not, my message won't change, so let me finish it and then shake your hands." He insisted on completing his remarks to a crowd that was still watching but had stopped listening. The head of the nation's most powerful law enforcement agency was being stripped of his command before their eyes.

Only one other FBI director in the bureau's 109-year history had ever been fired. William Sessions (no relation to Jeff) had been terminated by Bill Clinton in 1993 amid allegations of serious ethical lapses documented in a scathing government report. The FBI's Sessions had set up flimsy official appointments to charge the government for otherwise personal travel, billed the government for a $10,000 fence around his home, and refused to turn over records related to a $375,000 mortgage that investigators viewed with suspicion.[9] Those all seemed like reasonable grounds for termination and, notably, had nothing to do with Clinton.

Trump's letter to Comey went out of his way to put the firing on Sessions and Rosenstein: "While I greatly appreciate you informing me, on three separate occasions, that I am not under investigation, I nevertheless concur with the judgment of the Department of Justice that you are not effectively able to lead the Bureau." In emphasizing the supposed reassurances from Comey, Trump was again calling attention to the Russia probe, which, in theory, should have had nothing to do with the FBI director's termination.

The White House promptly released the letters from Sessions and Rosenstein as the main exhibits in the case against Comey. Sessions's was a single paragraph recommending Comey's removal but leaving it to his deputy to list the reasons. Rosenstein's memo spilled over three pages. He said Comey "deserves our appreciation for his public service," but that he could "not understand his refusal to accept the nearly universal judgment that he was mistaken" in his handling of the Clinton probe. The FBI chief had been "wrong to usurp the attorney general's authority" in announcing there would be no prosecution. He chastised Comey for blasting Clinton in a press conference, his defiant testimony before Congress, and his maddening "speak or conceal" explanation for his public reopening of the Clinton investigation in the final weeks of the election. Rosenstein listed seven former top Justice Department officials who had similarly denounced Comey and closed with a devastating assessment: "The FBI is unlikely to regain public and congressional trust until it has a director who understands the gravity of the mistakes and pledges never to repeat them."

In a chaotic scene at the White House grounds that night, spokesman Sean Spicer ducked behind some bushes to huddle with other aides out of earshot from reporters clamoring for answers about Comey's termination, then reemerged to claim that Trump hadn't even been thinking of firing the FBI chief until he saw the letter from Rosenstein. "It was all him," Spicer said.

Trump had somehow convinced himself that he would be praised for removing Clinton's tormentor. His claim to be acting out of concern over the email case was not particularly persuasive from a president who had never seemed troubled with how others—especially his 2016 opponent—were treated by the legal system but was consumed with the "witch hunt" pursuit of himself.

But Trump badly miscalculated the reaction, not only from Democrats but from members of his own party. As much as Comey had become a target of bipartisan anger in Washington, his firing brought immediate comparisons to the Saturday Night Massacre in 1973, when the attorney general and deputy attorney general both resigned rather than carry out Nixon's order to fire the Watergate special prosecutor.

A sense of panic began to spread in Washington, a fear that the president was steering the country into a constitutional crisis. Burr, chairman of the Senate Intelligence Committee, said he was "troubled by the timing and reasoning of Director Comey's termination," describing the FBI director as a "public servant of the highest order."

Rosenstein, an Ichabod Crane–like figure who smiles nervously under stress, seemed shaken by the sequence of events. For a man accustomed to navigating some of the most complicated legal and bureaucratic terrain in federal law enforcement, his political naiveté was surprising. He had delivered a detailed indictment of the FBI director and failed to anticipate how it—how *he*—would be used. After twenty-seven years of cultivating a reputation for rectitude, Rosenstein was being accused of betraying both Comey and the department, as well as being manipulated by the president—in short, of being a stooge.

Reporters began staking out his brick ranch-style home in Bethesda, Maryland. Colleagues began whispering in the hallways at Justice, "What happened to Rod?" Rosenstein called McGahn at the White House in a state of extreme agitation the day after Comey's firing, threatening to resign if the White House continued to be misleading about his role in the decision. (Rosenstein would publicly deny he had done so.) He began sending late-night text messages to friends in which he seemed to be consumed with agony and anger. Some worried about his emotional state.

The damage worsened as Trump inevitably began undermining his own subordinates' claims that this was all about the emails. He first did so in private. The day after Comey's firing, Trump welcomed Kislyak and Foreign Minister Sergei Lavrov to the White House, then bragged that he had "just fired the head of the FBI. He was crazy, a real nut job."[10] Heedlessly, he declared his troubles over. "I faced great pressure because of Russia," he said. "That's taken off."

But even before those words leaked, Trump had demolished his explanation for firing Comey in public.

Trump's penchant for claiming credit and settling scores—even when against his own interests—undercut the White House script pointing blame at Sessions and Rosenstein. During a May 11 interview with NBC News anchor Lester Holt, Trump was pressed on whether the Russia probe was a factor in Comey's firing. He replied: "When I decided to just do it, I said to myself, I said, 'You know, this Russia thing with Trump and Russia is a made-up story. It's an excuse by the Democrats for having lost an election they should have won.'"

Amid the fallout, the Justice Department and White House were forced to get on with the search for a new FBI director. Potential candidates began passing through the Justice Department's Art Deco and Greek Revival building a few blocks east of the White House. Among them was someone Rosenstein had known for decades, one of his first supervisors at the department. Rosen-

stein had joined Justice in 1990 through an honors program for
promising recent law graduates and went to work prosecuting public corruption cases as a trial attorney for the Criminal Division.
The unit was led in those days by an anvil-jawed assistant attorney
general named Robert S. Mueller III.

MUELLER HAD GONE ON TO SERVE AS FBI CHIEF LONGER THAN
anyone except J. Edgar Hoover. He was originally appointed by
George W. Bush, and Obama had taken the extraordinary step
of securing congressional approval to extend Mueller's ten-year
tenure rather than replace someone no one particularly wanted
to leave. After the crisis of the Comey firing, Rosenstein probed
Mueller on whether he might be willing to come back to restore
confidence and order. The two met in Rosenstein's fourth-floor
office during the tumultuous week after Comey's termination, and
while Mueller didn't appear particularly eager to return to his old
job at age seventy-two, he understood the gravity of the situation
for his beloved bureau. The conversation went well enough that
arrangements were made for the retired FBI director to meet with
Trump at the White House on May 16.

The Mueller who arrived at the White House seemed not to
have lost a step. On his way to the Oval Office, he bumped into
political adviser Stephen Bannon, who had been an officer in the
Navy, as had Mueller's own father. Mueller chided Bannon, a Navy
man, for allowing his daughter to go to West Point. He wasn't even
supposed to see Bannon that day, but had clearly done his homework. Mueller and Trump talked for about thirty minutes. Trump
found him "smart and tough," a type he instinctively admires. But
Mueller had signaled from the start of the conversation that he was
not certain that it made sense for him to return to the job he'd held

for twelve years. As Mueller demurred, the president didn't know that another job offer was coming for the former FBI director.

THE SAME DAY AS MUELLER'S VISIT TO THE WHITE HOUSE, *THE NEW York Times* reported that Comey had secretly kept memos documenting his interactions with the president, including one that described Trump's effort to convince Comey not to pursue charges against Flynn.[11] Comey months later admitted that he had orchestrated the story, instructing a friend, a professor at Columbia Law School, to reveal the memo's contents to the *Times*. In testimony before the Senate Intelligence Committee, he said that he had done so in the hopes that it would spur the appointment of a special counsel. The fired FBI director, who over dinner with Trump had gone to such lengths to say that he didn't "do sneaky things, I don't leak, I don't do weasel moves," had just orchestrated a leak of major proportions.

The next day, Wednesday, Rosenstein and Sessions were scheduled to meet with Trump themselves to talk about the candidates for the FBI job. Instead, Rosenstein stayed behind at Justice, sending Sessions ahead without him, saying something pressing had come up. As Sessions and Trump began talking in the Oval Office late that afternoon, an alert went out to reporters who cover the Justice Department, summoning them to a first-floor conference room. As they assembled, Rosenstein called McGahn to tell him that as acting attorney general on the Russia investigation— because of Sessions's recusal—he was appointing a special counsel to take over the probe. He had already signed the paperwork.

It was a devastating development for the White House. Special prosecutors have been used since the Ulysses S. Grant administration to handle investigations where a conflict of interest (such as a president's sway over the attorney general) threatens to influence the outcome. It's not just their broad investigative powers that presidents find so unnerving, but the tendency of an entity that is specially created to look for a crime to keep going until it finds one.

McGahn pulled Sessions out of the meeting with Trump and forced Rosenstein to tell the attorney general himself. Sessions's recusal meant he was no longer making decisions related to the Russia probe, but he didn't expect to be blindsided. Sessions, staggered by the news, went back in to inform the president. Trump, so certain that he had turned a corner on the Russia probe by getting rid of Comey, went ballistic, screaming obscenities that rattled the walls of the White House.

Moments later, Rosenstein issued a statement. "The public interest requires me to place this investigation under the authority of a person who exercises a degree of independence from the normal chain of command," it said. He had already signed an order, No. 3915-2017, appointing Mueller special counsel with sweeping investigative authority and resources. Rosenstein, who had been so thoroughly played by the president just eight days earlier, had ambushed the commander in chief and the attorney general.

Mueller, arguably the nation's most experienced and respected law enforcement official, was taking on the case of his life.

CHAPTER 12

THE SPECIAL COUNSEL STRIKES

IT IS HARD TO OVERSTATE THE SIZE OF THE SELF-INFLICTED wound that Trump sustained in firing Comey. The move was so predictably damaging to the president's self-interest that his own adviser, Bannon, later called it the biggest mistake in modern political history.[1]

Trump's decision was driven by his own deep-rooted traits, including his impulsiveness and excessive confidence in his own instincts, as well as his tendency to personalize problems—equating impediments to individuals. Comey had come to embody all of the frustrations of the Russia probe for Trump, but firing Comey only made the situation worse. At the same time, Trump's preoccupation with his own grievances impaired his ability to sense others' shifting moods and motivations. He failed to anticipate how Rosenstein would react to being manipulated, or grasp how a provoked deputy attorney general could complicate life for a president. For someone who built his entire persona on a supposed talent for firing people, Trump had botched this one spectacularly.

THE SITUATION THAT TRUMP FACED WITH COMEY WASN'T GREAT. Their relationship was increasingly dysfunctional, and the FBI chief was never going to offer the unqualified loyalty that Trump kept demanding. But in retrospect, that strained status quo was eminently preferable. At least then the investigation would be proceeding under the control of someone who worked for, and regularly interacted with, the president, and anchored in an organization that was constantly being pulled in a thousand different directions—criminal cases, terror threats, cyberattacks, surveillance assignments—not just Russia and Trump.

All of that changed with the creation of the Special Counsel's Office, an entity with a single, all-consuming mission—the investigative equivalent of a shark.

The SCO, as some called it, was given considerable authority and latitude. Rosenstein's order created an organization with all the power of a U.S. attorney's office to issue subpoenas, compel testimony, and access records. It could also count on a continuing flow of information from the CIA and NSA. The order identified a clear target for investigators: the relationship between Russia and the Trump campaign. But it also contained a seemingly innocuous line that dramatically broadened the inquiry's potential scope: the special counsel was free to pursue "any matters that arose or may arise directly from the investigation." For years leading up to the 2016 election, Trump had toiled to shield large swaths of his life and business empire from public view. Suspicious financial dealings, secret legal settlements, hush payments to mistresses, tax records—all those areas were now arguably fair game for investigators as long as they were following paths that might be traced back to the Russia probe. Mueller's budget was substantial but not unlimited—adding up to about $17 million as of May 2018.

The line that mattered more than any other in Rosenstein's order, however, had nothing to do with prosecutorial boundaries or resources. It ensured that the investigation would be as disciplined as it was unrelenting. It said, "Robert S. Mueller III is appointed to serve as Special Counsel for the United States Department of Justice."

THERE ARE SUPERFICIAL SIMILARITIES BETWEEN TRUMP AND Mueller. Both were born in New York City into families of considerable wealth (Mueller's father was a long-serving executive at DuPont) in the 1940s at a time when the United States was emerging from World War II as one of the globe's dominant powers. The two are both of German-Scottish descent and just twenty-two months apart in age (Mueller, born in 1944, is older). They attended all-male private schools, were distinguished high school athletes, and went on to earn Ivy League degrees (Mueller from Princeton). Both were known for spending an inordinate number of hours at the office, but also taking breaks for rounds of golf. They are similar in stature—though Trump is slightly taller—and perpetually wear the same work uniform: dark suit, white shirt, cinched tie. Each exudes the self-confidence of someone convinced by life's experiences that he was put on earth to lead. But there could not be a greater chasm between Trump and Mueller when it comes to their values, views of public service, and decisions that shaped their destinies.

At St. Paul's School in New Hampshire, Mueller stood out even among the East Coast elite at an academy that had taken the scions of the Astor, Mellon, and Vanderbilt families. He was captain of the soccer, lacrosse, and hockey teams (where one of his teammates was future secretary of state John Kerry). The traditional impressions of a New England prep school often include blazers, Gothic arches, and elaborate hazing rituals. But classmates depict Mueller as a student who wouldn't tolerate the abuse of others, even when they weren't present. Once, as boys gathered at a campus snack shop, someone in Mueller's group began making derisive comments about another student who hadn't joined them. It wasn't particularly vicious—seemingly routine banter among teenagers—but Mueller refused to let it slide. "We all said disparaging things about each other face-to-face," recalled Maxwell King, a St. Paul's classmate who went on to become editor of *The Philadelphia Inquirer*. "But saying something about someone who wasn't there was something that Bob was uncomfortable with, and he let it be known and just walked out."[2] It was a glimpse of a personal code that would guide Mueller for decades.

MUELLER GREW UP IN PRINCETON, NEW JERSEY, AND HAD thoughts of pursuing a career in medicine when he entered his hometown Ivy. But he couldn't get past organic chemistry and graduated in 1966 with a degree in politics. That same year, he married Ann Cabell Standish, whose ancestors had arrived on the *Mayflower*. The two had met when they were seventeen at a high school party and were into their sixth decade of marriage (Anne was a special education teacher and together they raised two daughters) when he was appointed special counsel.

Trump had spent his high school years at the New York Military Academy in Cornwall, New York, where his father had sent him over concerns about his conduct. His record there was mixed. Trump was known for being neat and possessing leadership skills, but also for setting up a tanning booth in his dorm room and terrorizing cadets who refused to obey him.

The Vietnam War had escalated dramatically during Mueller's time at Princeton, from a distant conflict to which the United States had sent 11,300 troops in 1962 to a terrifying war zone with 385,000 troops by 1966. It had also become a polarizing issue for almost everyone of Mueller's and Trump's generation, forcing many young Americans to make a difficult decision about how to serve their country.

Despite attending a military academy, Trump did not serve in Vietnam. It was something he shared with many of his age, though there is no evidence that his reluctance was tied to any moral stand. Through a series of deferments—four for being a student and one for medical disqualification—he avoided being drafted. Trump later said the medical disqualification was for bone spurs in his foot, though during the campaign he could not recall which foot.[3]

In contrast, Mueller enlisted in the U.S. Marine Corps within weeks of completing college. In some ways he was following in the footsteps of his father, who served in the Atlantic and Mediterranean theaters during World War II. But Mueller cited a different reason for signing up—the enlistment of a Princeton lacrosse teammate. David Hackett had graduated a year before Mueller and volunteered for Vietnam. Mueller was already in the Marines, undergoing training at the service's officer school, when Hackett was shot in the back of the head while leading a platoon in an effort to evacuate fallen Marines from a Vietnam battleground. "A number of his friends and teammates joined the Marine Corps because of him—as did I," Mueller said in a 2017 graduation speech at a private boarding school in Massachusetts where his granddaughter was among the 133 graduates.[4]

Mueller excelled at the Marines' officer school in Quantico, Virginia, though—perhaps tellingly—he received a D in delegation before deploying to Vietnam. He also completed the Army Ranger and Airborne schools. On December 11, 1968, Mueller's rifle platoon came under heavy fire on a ridge in Quang Tri province. As one after another Marine fell, Mueller "fearlessly moved from one position to another, directing the accurate counterfire of his men and shouting words of encouragement," according to an account by the Marine Corps. "With complete disregard for his own safety, he then skillfully supervised the evacuation of casualties." He earned a Bronze Star with a distinction for valor, and was subsequently promoted to first lieutenant. A picture of him from that period shows a gaunt figure whose eyes were nearly hollow. Four months later, Mueller was shot in the thigh while leading an effort to rescue Marines who had been ambushed. "Although seriously wounded," according to the citation on the medal he subsequently received, he "maintained his position and, ably directing the fire of his platoon, was instrumental in defeating" the North Vietnamese attackers. He left active duty service in 1970 and returned to civilian life not only with a collection of medals including a Purple Heart, but with a deep sense of obligation. "I consider myself exceptionally lucky to have made it out of Vietnam," he said later. "There were many—many—who did not. And perhaps because I did survive Vietnam, I have always felt compelled to contribute."[5]

In 1976, three years out of law school, Mueller began working as a prosecutor for the U.S. attorney's office in San Francisco. It was the beginning of nearly four decades in federal law enforcement. He headed the Justice Department's criminal division under President George H. W. Bush, handling cases including the prosecution of Panamanian dictator Manuel Noriega and the bombing of Pan Am Flight 103 over Lockerbie, Scotland. He left government briefly, taking a $400,000-a-year job with a Boston-based law firm in 1993, but was deeply unhappy and two years later called U.S. attorney Eric H. Holder Jr., who later became attorney general under President Obama, and asked for an assignment he found far more gratifying—prosecuting Washington, D.C., homicides. "I love everything about investigations," he said years later. "I love the forensics. I love the fingerprints and the bullet casings and all the rest that comes along with doing that kind of work."[6]

Mueller was named FBI director on September 4, 2001—seven days before Al-Qaeda terrorists stormed the cockpits of four aircraft and plunged the country into an era of hypervigilance in domestic security and seemingly endless foreign conflicts. Mueller was charged with one of the most daunting post-9/11 tasks: transforming the FBI from an entity focused on crime and convictions—the investigations and forensics that Mueller so loved—into a counterterrorism apparatus expected to stop attacks before they happened. Mueller struggled at times to turn the massive organization toward this new mission, as well as to master the charismatic elements required of leadership. Unlike his successor, Comey, who frequently chatted up special agents in the cafeteria, Mueller was often painfully stiff with subordinates. (Some in the bureau quietly referred to Mueller as "Bobby Three Sticks," a way of mocking his patrician bearing and the trio of Roman numerals denoting his inheritance of the Robert Swan Mueller name. They never said it to his face.) His former counsel Chuck Rosenberg recounted an excruciatingly awkward attempt by Mueller to seem more personable, calling Rosenberg at his FBI desk around six in the morning.

"Yes, sir," Rosenberg said.

"How are you?" Mueller asked.

"Fine."

"Everything okay?"

"Yes, sir." Having established that Rosenberg didn't need anything at that hour and being unable to muster any small talk, Mueller hung up.[7]

Accounts of his aloofness were abundant. A senior aide recalled Mueller refusing to write a job recommendation, explaining that he had a blanket policy against granting such requests. (It was, in part, a reflection of a broader reluctance to lend his endorsement. He had never signed any letter opposing Trump, either.) But whatever he lacked in warmth was made up for by the indefatigable example he set. There was a reason Rosenberg was at his desk at dawn to take that awkward call.

Mueller retired on September 4, 2013, twelve years to the day after he started. He joined the WilmerHale law firm as a partner in Washington but continued to handle high-profile (though now private) investigations, including the NFL's probe of running back Ray Rice's assault of his fiancée in an elevator. But once again his life in the private sector didn't last, though this time it wasn't Mueller searching for a new perch but an old colleague, Rosenstein, who came looking for him.

Mueller, often described by those who worked for him as a stern and press-averse disciplinarian, issued a characteristically terse statement upon taking the special counsel position, saying, "I accept this responsibility and will discharge it to the best of my ability."

The only public remarks he's made since came at his granddaughter's graduation—an event he'd committed to before accepting the special counsel job. He didn't mention Trump by name, but his advice to teenagers about integrity and honesty must have echoed through the White House: "You can be smart, aggressive, articulate, and indeed persuasive," he said. "But if you are not honest, your reputation will suffer, and once lost, a good reputation can never, ever be regained."

WHEN SESSIONS RETURNED TO THE OVAL OFFICE TO TELL TRUMP that a special counsel had been appointed, the president exploded. "Oh my god. This is terrible!" he said. "This is the end of my presidency. I'm fucked." He railed at the attorney general—"You were supposed to protect me!"—and demanded that Sessions resign.[8]

Afterward, the attorney general rode back to his office and

drafted a letter of resignation. Advisers pleaded with the president not to accept it—the departure of the nation's top law enforcement official on the heels of Comey's firing would have further intensified comparisons to Nixon and the Watergate scandal and, given Sessions's decades in the Senate, increased the odds of congressional revolt. Aides convinced Trump not to even open the letter at first, worried that once he read Sessions's words, he wouldn't be able to resist the offer. But he eventually ripped it open and returned it with a curt handwritten note: "Not accepted."

In typical Trump fashion, that didn't mean the matter was resolved: the president would continue to discuss the idea of ousting Sessions for months with Priebus and others. Even a year later, Trump was still publicly voicing regret that he had ever hired one of his first and most loyal supporters. "The Russian Witch Hunt Hoax continues, all because Jeff Sessions didn't tell me he was going to recuse himself," he said on Twitter in June 2018. "I would have quickly picked someone else. So much time and money wasted, so many lives ruined." In another tweet two months later, Trump described Sessions as "scared stiff and missing in action." Notably, there was never any acknowledgment by the president of the damage caused by his own hand.

With the White House in disarray, Mueller began assembling a legal team with characteristic efficiency and stealth. From WilmerHale, he took with him two longtime loyalists: Aaron Zebley, who had been his chief of staff at the FBI, and James Quarles, who as a young graduate of Harvard Law School in the early 1970s had served on the Watergate special prosecution force. They became Mueller's inner circle, with Zebley essentially reprising his role as chief of staff, managing the day-to-day operations of the probe, while Quarles served as a sort of senior litigation counsel. The two had eyes on virtually every aspect of the expanding investigation.

In the ensuing weeks, Mueller added more legal firepower. He brought in Jeannie Rhee, a former Justice Department official with expertise in cyber cases, and Andrew Weissmann, who had served as Mueller's general counsel at the FBI and later as head of the fraud section of the criminal division. Weissmann had a reputation for being ruthless. He had spent years as a prosecutor at the Eastern District in New York, known for its dogged pursuit of organized crime—charging, squeezing, and flipping witnesses like a coil of cascading dominoes snaking toward the organization's core.

Weissmann brought these mob takedown tactics to other targets, most notably Enron, the energy-trading giant exposed as a massive fraud—to get the company's chief financial officer to flip, Weissmann went after his wife, charging her with tax violations. The approach was effective but had enormous costs. Arthur Andersen, a Big Five accounting firm with thousands of clients, essentially ceased to exist after being convicted of shredding evidence to hide its audits of Enron—a conviction that was later overturned. By then, Weissmann had moved on to his next target.

Convinced that the special counsel was on an historic mission that might end with the downfall of a president, high-end law firms and individual attorneys lobbied for slots on Mueller's team even though for some it meant massive salary cuts. By mid-June, Mueller had thirteen lawyers on staff, and he added another four by August. Their political leanings later became an issue when it was revealed that thirteen had previously registered as Democrats, and nine had made political donations to Democratic candidates including Clinton. That may not have been the ideal composition for Mueller, a Republican, but he saw himself as bound by policies that forbid asking federal employees about their political positions.

Mueller also had his pick of FBI investigators, and because he was absorbing cases that the bureau had been pursuing for nearly a year against Flynn, Manafort, and Papadopoulos, he brought in several agents who had done much of that spadework. In building what some were calling a "dream team," Mueller also inadvertently took on a potential nightmare. On its face, the inclusion of Peter Strzok and Lisa Page made perfect sense. Strzok had been there at the formation of Crossfire Hurricane, opening the Papadopoulos case and hopping on a flight to London for the first interview in the FBI's probe of a Trump-Russia conspiracy. Page was legal counsel to FBI deputy director Andrew McCabe, who was running the bureau after Comey's departure, and had been read into the rapidly expanding probe from the outset.

The two were torn about being part of the Mueller team at a time when their personal relationship was unraveling. They were both drawn to its mission and historical significance, but also anxious about being marginalized in such a high-powered operation and weighing other career prospects. (Strzok was hoping to become special agent in charge of an FBI field office.) Page seemed apprehensive about the potential toll on their personal lives and careers, the risk of bringing their secret into a high-pressure situation, sealed off from the rest of the bureau, that was certain to face more scrutiny than anything they had ever been a part of.

"You shouldn't take this on," she wrote Strzok after midnight on May 19, less than two days after Mueller had been appointed. "We can't work closely on another case again, though obviously, I want you to do what is right for you."

Strzok, who at times seemed more invested in the relationship, tried to gauge whether her guidance was being driven by professional or personal interests. "But god we're a good team," he wrote, trying to calm her misgivings. Probing for reassurance, he asked: "Is that playing into yur [sic] decision/your advice to me?"

"No," she replied. "Not at all. I just think we are both ready for a change. . . . Let's talk about this tomorrow."

In terms of their then-thriving careers, there weren't many tomorrows left. In January, the Justice Department inspector general had launched its internal review of the bureau's handling of the Clinton email investigation. The IG probe was wide-ranging in scope, encompassing Lynch's meeting with Bill Clinton on the airport tarmac, Comey's public pronouncements about the case, and the questions of bias swirling around McCabe and his wife's political campaign. The inspector general, Michael Horowitz, also wanted to look into a bout of troubling leaks that coincided with the campaign. There was suspicion among senior officials that disgruntled anti-Clinton agents at the FBI's field office in New York were—via surreptitiously shared information and innuendo—behind stories and public statements (including some by former prosecutor, ex–New York City mayor, and current Trump lawyer Rudy Giuliani) implying that investigators were sitting on explosive material uncovered in the Clinton emails. The claims made in those suspected leaks were either exaggerated or untrue but found purchase in conservative circles. There was also internal heartburn at the FBI and Justice Department over anonymous sources defending McCabe in stories about his role in the Clinton probe.

As part of his inquiry, Horowitz began compiling the emails and phone records of FBI officials involved in the Clinton case—a path that led straight to Page and Strzok. There he found evidence that Page had been in contact with a *Wall Street Journal* reporter shortly before publication of a piece about tensions inside the bureau over the reopening of the Clinton probe. The *Journal* story included language defending McCabe's decisions and disputing that he had taken any steps to favor Clinton. McCabe denied to Comey, the bureau's Office of Professional Responsibility, and the inspector general any involvement in those leaks. But when confronted, Page said she had spoken with the reporter at the instruction of McCabe. Under pressure from Trump, McCabe was fired just hours before he would have become eligible for a higher-paying retirement.

From their extensive involvement in the Clinton, Russia, and Trump probes, Strzok and Page should have been as attuned as anyone to the explosive potential of unguarded correspondence. Yet they had continued texting, bringing that baggage with them as they set aside their hesitation and took positions in the special counsel's office. Once the inspector general began plowing through the traffic on bureau cell phones, it was inevitable he would find the mountain of texts between them capturing their affair and all of their politically charged comments.

COMEY HAD REPEATEDLY TOLD TRUMP THAT HE WAS NOT A TAR-get of the investigation. But when Trump fired him, the investigation trained its sights on the conduct of the president.

Mueller had set up his team in temporary space a block and a half west of FBI headquarters. The group divided their work preliminarily along three investigative fronts: Manafort, Flynn, and, essentially, everything else. The latter was telling, reflecting the extent to which Mueller and his investigators at that point were still surveying what must have seemed a vast landscape of potential crimes connected to Russia's interference in the election. It included the core question of whether the Trump campaign had conspired with Moscow, as well as the prospect of criminal financial connections between Trump and his associates and oligarchs close to the Kremlin.

From the outset, however, Mueller and his investigators also focused on whether the president had sought to obstruct justice. He gathered Comey's memos documenting the FBI chief's interactions with Trump—including the president's appeal to drop the Flynn investigation—even as the special counsel's office was still setting up its furniture and computers. Within weeks, Mueller and his investigators were tracking down other evidence and arranging interviews with witnesses who had also had troubling encounters with the president.

In mid-June, Mueller's team contacted three senior intelligence officials who were serving or had served in the Trump administration: Coats, now in place as Clapper's successor; Michael Rogers, the head of the NSA; and Rogers's deputy, Richard Ledgett. Doing so hinted that Mueller was zeroing in on Trump's actions surrounding a March 22 briefing that had taken place at the White House, at a time when Trump was still fuming about Comey's testimony two days earlier, when he confirmed that the FBI was investigating the Trump campaign's ties to Russia but didn't say that Trump was not a target.

As the briefing broke up, Trump asked Coats and CIA director Mike Pompeo to stay behind. The president then asked Coats whether he could intervene with Comey to get the bureau to abandon its criminal investigation of Flynn. The request and circumstances under which Trump made it—after ushering others out of the Oval Office—closely tracked his approach to Comey.

A few days later, Trump followed up with separate calls to Coats and Rogers, asking them to issue public statements that their agencies had no evidence of any coordination between the Trump campaign and Russia. The spy chiefs refused Trump's entreaties and were troubled enough by the request to report it to colleagues. When Rogers told his deputy about the call, Ledgett wrote an internal memo documenting the NSA director's interaction with the president, generating a contemporaneous record much as Comey had done.

It is almost inconceivable that Trump wouldn't have made a similar request to Pompeo, who from very early on was more effective than any other member of the national security team at ingratiating himself with the president. The CIA director had previously shown he was willing to do the president's bidding. In mid-February, after *The New York Times* published a story saying that there had been extensive interactions between Trump campaign associates and Russian individuals, the White House enlisted Pompeo, Nunes, and Senator Richard Burr, the North Carolina Republican and chairman of the Intelligence Committee, to call other news organizations (including the *Post*) to convince them the *Times* story was wrong, and dissuade them from writing similar accounts. While it's not unusual for an administration to contest critical stories in background calls with reporters, the lineup used by the White House in this instance was problematic. Nunes and Burr were supposed to be heading independent Russia investigations and here they were secretly spreading talking points on behalf of the White House. (Burr seemed chastened when asked about his role in this matter by the *Post*, acknowledging on the record that he had done so. Nunes was unapologetic.)[9]

Pompeo was another matter. By tradition, the CIA director is also supposed to present facts to policymakers but stay out of politics. Pompeo, who had been a stridently conservative congressman from Kansas, never embraced that vision of the job. The CIA was at that point relaying intelligence to the FBI as part of its burgeoning probe of Russia and ties to the Trump campaign. The agency had been the first to sound the alarm about Russia's intent to help Trump, and largely responsible for the January intelligence report. Yet throughout his tenure, Pompeo downplayed the significance of Russia's interference in ways that denigrated the work of his own agency. Unlike Burr and Nunes, he never acknowledged making calls to discredit the *New York Times* report. And though he was in the Oval Office when Trump asked Coats to intervene with Comey, Pompeo never broke his silence about that moment, nor was he known to have ever drafted a memo or turned to a subordinate about a troubling encounter with the president.

In mid-June, Coats and Rogers sat down for interviews with

Mueller's team, and while Coats maintained that he never felt "pressured" to take any steps to interfere in the investigation, his testimony was seen as important, reinforcing Comey's accounts of the president's attempts to impede the probe. Ledgett's memo also made its way into the special counsel's files. Mueller had barely settled into his role and already his staff had a pile of potential evidence of the president's intent to obstruct. More was coming.

On June 14, 2017, *The Washington Post*, having learned of the special counsel's interviews with Coats and others, published a story stating that the president of the United States was under investigation for possible obstruction of justice. Trump responded with a series of ranting "witch hunt" tweets and secret efforts to have Mueller removed. Two days after the story ran, Trump called White House counsel Don McGahn at home to push him to orchestrate the ouster of the special counsel over specious conflicts. "You gotta do this," Trump said. "You gotta call Rod."[10] McGahn and others thought that Trump's grievances—including a long-dormant effort by Mueller to get money out of a Trump golf course membership—were petty and pointless. But Trump wouldn't let the issue go.

After a second call from Trump, in which he was more explicit, saying, "Mueller has to go," and "Call me back when you do it," McGahn felt he might have no option but to resign. He drove to the White House that weekend to pack his things and called both Priebus and Bannon to tell them he was done. They talked him down, and McGahn returned to work on Monday having made no call to Rosenstein and proceeding as if Trump's request had occurred.[11]

By then, Trump had turned to another would-be accomplice. On January 19, Trump met in the Oval Office with Corey Lewandowski, his former campaign manager, and drafted a message he wanted delivered to Sessions. "Write this down," Trump said, dictating the outlines of a speech he wanted Sessions to give saying that the president was "being treated very unfairly" and "didn't do anything wrong except he ran the greatest campaign in American history." Sessions was then to say that he was instructing Mueller to drop the probe of the president and focus on vulnerabilities in future elections. Lewandowski tried to arrange a meeting with Sessions, but they failed to connect. The dictated note ended up sitting in Lewandowski's personal safe.[12]

Of course, the efforts to derail Mueller would ultimately be uncovered by the special counsel himself. McGahn's testimony about Trump's calls in mid-June would be central to a catalog of improper interference by the president. But his subsequent interactions with the president would only make it worse. When news reports in January 2018 revealed that Trump had ordered McGahn to have Mueller fired, Trump tried to get McGahn to deny the story—effectively engaging in a second act of obstruction to conceal the first. For weeks, Trump stewed about McGahn's refusal to dispute articles that the White House counsel knew were correct. The friction over the issue culminated in a face-to-face meeting in the Oval Office on February 6.

"This story does not look good, you need to correct this," Trump said.

McGahn refused, saying the stories were accurate.

"Did I say the word 'fire'?" Trump said.

Consulting his notes, McGahn responded with precision: "What you said is, 'Call Rod, tell Rod that Mueller has conflicts and can't be the Special Counsel.'"

Trump denied having said so and turned his ire to McGahn's record of the disputed call. "Why do you take notes?" Trump said. "Lawyers don't take notes. I never had a lawyer who took notes."

McGahn shot back that he kept notes because he was a "real lawyer" and that, in most settings, accurate records were to a client's advantage. That only riled Trump up further. "I've had a lot of great lawyers, like Roy Cohn," Trump said. "He did not take notes."[13]

AS THE FBI INVESTIGATION GAINED SPEED DURING THE SPRING OF 2017, and an array of congressional investigations began seeking testimony from witnesses, senior administration officials began hiring lawyers, assessing their exposure and—inevitably—turning on one another. The maneuvering reached into the inner circle of the president.

As lawyers for Trump's son-in-law and adviser Jared Kushner began combing through his campaign calendar and communications for investigative vulnerabilities, they came across a potentially explosive chain of emails. The messages showed that Kushner had taken part in the meeting with a Russian lawyer at Trump Tower in June 2016, along with Donald Trump Jr. and Paul Manafort (who had turned over his notes on this session to investigators in Congress). Sitting through a meeting wasn't necessarily a crime, but this one made Kushner's attorneys nervous, particularly because he had failed to disclose the encounter despite repeated demands in the preceding months from bureau and congressional investigators for information relevant to their inquiries. More important, scrutiny of that meeting led to the discovery of the fateful exchange in which Goldstone, the music promoter, told Trump Jr. that allies in Moscow had potentially damaging information on Clinton and the president's eldest son responded by saying, "I love it."

Having stumbled onto this buried munition, the Trump team was divided about what to do. Some, including White House communications official Hope Hicks, urged disclosing it preemptively to minimize its destructive impact. After reading the exchange, Hicks recalled thinking it looked "really bad" and warned the president that it would be "massive" when it inevitably leaked.[14]

But candor, even when out of cornered self-interest, went against every Trump impulse. In a series of meetings with Hicks, Kushner, and others, Trump refused to read the incriminating emails, hear details about what had transpired at Trump Tower, or believe that the messages would ever be exposed to the public. Overruling subordinates, he sought to keep the emails buried under denials and falsehoods.

Inconveniently, *The New York Times* began asking about the Trump Tower meeting. The paper seemed to have limited details about the session, including the name of the Russian lawyer and the involvement of the trio of Trump advisers, though not the offer of dirt or the effusive Trump Jr. response.

As the paper moved closer to publishing, the president was attending a G20 summit in Hamburg, Germany. The July 2017 gathering of the world's economic powers had produced a series of headlines and images contrasting Trump's hostility toward European allies with the warm greeting he gave Putin. The president's advisers were secretly scrambling to head off even more damaging news, and spent the final day of the summit huddling to sort out how to respond to the *Times*' inquiries.

The issue was still unresolved as they began boarding Air Force One for the evening flight back to Washington. By then Trump Jr. and his lawyer, Alan Futerfas, were involved in the discussions, although neither was in Hamburg. There was an emerging consensus that Trump Jr. should issue a "fulsome statement," in Futerfas's words, getting most of the bad news out in hopes that doing so would at least prevent a protracted scandal. But before the plane was even in the air, the president, just catching up to the deliberations about the planned statement from his son, overruled his aides and assorted lawyers. Instead, Trump personally dictated a statement in Trump Jr.'s name, saying that the participants in the Trump Tower meeting "discussed a program about the adoption of Russian children." Hicks relayed the dictated statement to Trump Jr. by text. He responded with a single modification, saying the participants had "primarily" discussed adoption. Otherwise, he said to Hicks, "it appears as though I'm lying later when they inevitably leak something."[15] The statement depicted the meeting as utterly inconsequential, emphasizing that Kremlin restrictions on Americans' ability to adopt Russian children was "not a campaign issue." There was no mention of the offer of dirt, Veselnitskaya's ties to the Kremlin, the material supposedly being relayed from Russia's "crown prosecutor," not even a glancing acknowledgment that Trump Jr. had agreed to a meeting in which he expected to be getting illicit campaign assistance from a hostile government. It was a gross misrepresentation of the facts, as the president would himself tacitly admit a year later.

THE "TRUMP JR." STATEMENT FAILED TO DIMINISH CURIOSITY about the mysterious gathering at the Trump's campaign headquarters, and the scenario that administration advisers had feared quickly unfolded. The initial *Times* story, published July 8, led with the revelation that the president's son had met with a Russian lawyer at Trump Tower two weeks after his father had clinched the Republican presidential nomination. The article was missing the most incendiary aspects of the email exchange, but at a time when the Trump administration was still reeling from the disclosures of the secret meetings with Russian officials by Flynn, Kushner, and Sessions, the news sent fresh shock waves through Washington. The next day, following further leaks, the *Times* posted a follow-up story saying that Trump Jr. had been "promised damaging information about Hillary Clinton before agreeing to meet with a Kremlin-connected lawyer."

The FBI, and later the special counsel's office, had quietly been ahead of the press and the public on almost every major development in the Trump Russia story, but this time the dynamic was reversed. The Trump Tower meeting appeared to be one of the most potentially incriminating interactions between Russia and the Trump campaign, but federal investigators had no inkling about it until reading it in the press. And as details surfaced about Trump's role in drafting the highly misleading statement attributed to his son, Mueller had another piece of obstruction evidence.

Trump Jr. belatedly embraced the "fulsome" disclosure strategy his father had overruled, posting the entire email chain on his Twitter account. He emphasized that the campaign got no damaging information out of the meeting and excused his receptivity to Russian help as the mistake of a political novice. In subsequent appearances, he was defiant, suggesting that it was practically his patriotic duty to hear out the lawyer's offer in case the Russians truly had relevant information about Clinton's fitness to be president. But in the immediate aftermath, he seemed stunned. In an appearance on Fox News he came as close as he ever would to a mea culpa, saying, "In retrospect I would have done things differently."

Trump Jr.'s relationship with his father had always been troubled. After watching his parents' marriage disintegrate amid a barrage of tabloid headlines about Trump's affair with the actress Marla Maples, Trump Jr. refused to speak to his father for a year. Not that there was much father-son bonding time to begin with—Ivana, Trump's first wife, said that her husband was uncomfortable interacting with his children until they were grown. Trump Jr.'s Wharton classmates recalled him as a sullen, heavy-drinking student who got into ugly showdowns with his father in the rare moments when the elder Trump came to visit his son on campus. After the Trump Tower meeting was exposed, Trump spoke of his son with rare empathy, but also as if the thirty-nine-year-old were still a wayward adolescent. "He's a good boy. He's a good kid," Trump said. "And he had a meeting. Nothing happened."

In reality, bad things were happening with distressing frequency for Trump on the Russia front. Explosive disclosures and bungled responses hit the headlines with such regularity that some in Washington—even within the administration—began to wonder whether the chaos was sustainable, whether the Trump presidency could survive a single year. In case after case, the damage had either been caused or been compounded by decisions Trump had made, usually against the admonitions of attorneys and advisers. The intervention in the deliberations over the Trump Tower statement was only the latest example. "Now someone can claim he's the one who attempted to mislead," one of his aides said. "Somebody can argue the president is saying he doesn't want you to say the whole truth."[16]

MUELLER'S APPOINTMENT RAISED THE STAKES IN WAYS THAT LED Trump to slowly, reluctantly, recognize that he needed legal help. Marc Kasowitz, one of Trump's longtime lawyers, had asserted himself as Trump's main defender in the Russia case but seemed ill suited for the job in legal expertise and temperament. In their fifteen-year association, Kasowitz had mostly been used by Trump to handle lawsuits about failed ventures—including a $25 million settlement of fraud claims over "Trump University"—and handle defamation suits against reporters who dared to question Trump's inflated net worth. Kasowitz had scant experience in criminal cases or legal battles with the Justice Department, let alone a team of prosecutorial predators like Mueller's. It was possible that high-pressure situations might also prove problematic in other ways. Kasowitz had struggled with repeated bouts of alcoholism and entered a rehabilitation clinic in 2014, according to ProPublica, the nonprofit news organization, citing interviews with more than two dozen employees of his law firm. When someone who had seen coverage of the story on television emailed Kasowitz to tell him to resign, the combustible attorney wrote a scathing response, saying, "I'm on you now. . . . Watch your back, bitch." If he could be thrown off-balance by a random emailer, how would he fare against the likes of Mueller?

IN MAY, AS MUELLER'S APPOINTMENT WAS ANNOUNCED, THE WELL-known Washington attorney John Dowd was on a train to New York, traveling to take part in an event honoring John Kelly, who had retired after forty-five years in the Marine Corps the previous year and been appointed head of the Department of Homeland Security. Dowd was also a former Marine, and after graduating from Emory Law School rose to the rank of captain in the Judge Advocate Division. Post-military service, he embarked on what became a high-profile legal career. Dowd spent nearly a decade as a prosecutor in the Justice Department before leaving for private practice and a series of attention-grabbing assignments. He had represented an up-and-coming congressman named John McCain in the Keating Five scandal in the early 1990s. Prior to that he had served as a special counsel for Major League Baseball and its gambling investigation of Pete Rose. The "Dowd Report," as the 1989 document came to be known, was so damning that Rose was banned for life from baseball.

As the train wended its way northward, Dowd got a call from Kasowitz's partner, Michael Bowe, asking if he would be willing to meet to discuss joining Trump's legal team. Days later, in early June, Dowd was in the White House having lunch with the president. Dowd, who was seventy-six at the time, is an avuncular presence who speaks in plain, direct terms and has the drooping facial features of a bulldog. The two men hit it off, with Trump making clear that his priority was "how can we get this done, get it over with."[17] Dowd urged a firm but cooperative approach, in contrast to the combative theatrics of Kasowitz. A week after their lunch in the Oval Office, Trump asked Dowd to take over as lead lawyer in dealing with the Mueller probe.

Dowd promptly encouraged Trump to make another hire: Ty Cobb, a former federal prosecutor who had experience working as a trial lawyer for an independent counsel as well as a defense attorney for officials in the Clinton White House. He specialized in corruption and campaign finance cases. The oldest of eight children, Cobb grew up in western Kansas and was a distant relative of the baseball player whose career in the early twentieth century had parallels to Rose's—setting the career record for hits and being implicated in a gambling scandal. Cobb the lawyer wore a handlebar mustache that seemed a throwback to that era, and embraced the idea of careful but cooperative engagement with Mueller to bring the investigation to the swiftest possible end.

Dowd and Cobb took on complementary roles inside and outside the White House. Dowd worked as a private attorney for the president to protect his interests, while Cobb was named a White House lawyer, putting him in charge of organizing the administration's response to the Mueller investigation, including negotiations over access to witnesses and documents. Given the emphasis on speed, Cobb proposed a deal with Mueller in which the White House would turn over thousands of files at a rapid rate without preemptively engaging in document-by-document brawling. In turn, Mueller would agree that the provision of those files didn't constitute a waiving of executive privilege. In other words, Mueller got to review the files turned over and identify the ones he truly wanted as prosecutor. Then the two sides could negotiate terms over those.

But first they had to find Mueller, and that wasn't easy. It took four days for Dowd to track down a phone number for the special counsel, let alone the office's physical coordinates. When Dowd finally caught up with Mueller, the two former Marines bonded with stories about their military and Justice Department days—though it was implicitly clear that such connections were strictly personal. Mueller said he would always be ready to engage with Trump's legal team, that he hoped to develop a relationship of mutual trust, and that he understood the president's desire for swift resolution. For his part, Dowd tried to emphasize that delays were not just personally frustrating to Trump, but also damaging to the country.

During their early interactions, Dowd shared examples he had been authorized to relay to the special counsel by the president, telling Mueller about negotiations with foreign leaders in which Trump's counterparts supposedly questioned whether the U.S. leader would be in position to deliver. Trump would be "in the middle of meeting with a foreign leader" on a trade deal or talks about a hostage, when the leader would say, "Donald, are you going to be around?" It was, Dowd explained, "a kick in the nuts."

Mueller said that he understood, and that he "wouldn't let grass grow under him." In time, Dowd and Cobb both came to question the sincerity of Mueller's assurances. Their signals to Trump that the investigation would soon be over proved time and again to be hopelessly premature.

THE STRUGGLE TO LOCATE MUELLER WAS A SIGN OF THINGS TO come. He had always given the press a wide berth, but as special counsel he made himself nearly invisible. He made no public appearances upon taking the position and never uttered so much as a word to the outside world during his first year in the job aside from his remarks at his granddaughter's graduation. Once staffed, he moved the special counsel's office from its temporary quarters near Union Station to a building pinned between railroad tracks and a freeway on the south side of the Capitol, an isolated pocket of the city far removed from the bustling corridors of tourists, lobbyists, and lawyers. The office took up an entire floor, but there was no way to find it—no marker in the lobby—and no way to get past security without being escorted into an elevator by one of Mueller's hires. Those who did make it that far arrived on a floor with no receptionist, no sign, just doors with electronic locks. Inside was a warren of offices, cubicles, and conference rooms. Much of the space was a SCIF—cordoned to handle highly classified information. Visitors including Dowd were brought into a charmless conference room near the entrance but taken no farther. Dowd and others became convinced that Mueller often slept in the space, and that his isolation affected his perspective. "He lives there," Dowd said with dismay. "How about some fresh air?"

There were psychological aspects to all the stealth. Mueller and his team would disappear for long, unnerving stretches punctuated by sudden legal strikes. His targets were left to scan the seemingly placid horizon for a dorsal fin—then, out of nowhere, jaws.

Mueller's approach had its advantages against the combative president, who loved to draw his adversaries into public scuffles, probing for their deepest insecurities and then preying on them mercilessly. His adolescent habit of assigning nicknames—"Little Marco," "Lyin' Ted," "Cheatin' Hillary"—was part of a relentless baiting of his enemies with taunts and insults until they felt compelled to defend themselves. Once they made the mistake of engaging, they were usually bloodied by an unremitting Trump barrage saturated with falsehoods. It had happened to his rivals in the campaign. After trying desperately to remain above the fray only to see their poll numbers plunge, Jeb Bush and Rubio tried to embrace Trump's insult-hurling tactics only to realize there was no way to prevail in such an exchange.

Mueller seemed impervious to such tactics. He never stepped out into the open, never presented any surface for Trump to make contact with. The nature of his assignment afforded some of that protection. Unlike Comey, Mueller was under no obligation to interact with the president, and therefore wasn't subjected to the pressure that the FBI director had faced. But Mueller's disposition was also very different from that of his former Justice Department colleague. Comey, Clapper, Brennan, and others all found themselves behaving in ways after leaving government that they never would have imagined—firing off tweets laced with venom, hurling insults at the commander in chief. (In his memoir, Comey even zeroed in on Trump's insecurities about his hair, skin, and the size of his hands.) No one who knew Mueller ever expected him to write a memoir, much less trade insults on Twitter.

Mueller's discipline didn't extend to all of his subordinates, however, and couldn't completely protect the special counsel's office.

Page and Strzok continued texting at a torrid pace into June 2017. Page had gone ahead and joined Mueller's office but seemed frustrated with her assignment. Surrounded by high-powered prosecutors, she was relegated to staff and support work. She wrote to Strzok about conversations she was having with one of Mueller's deputies about landing a job closer to the high-stakes casework. "We talked for about an hour on Friday night," she texted, pleased that the lawyer she met with had used the word *partner* in describing the role she might take, "with a plan to give the grunt work to two of the younger attorneys."

Strzok was drawn to the adrenaline-fueled mission at Mueller's office but still deliberating about the best course for his career and whether to return to headquarters. Besides his hopes that he might be promoted to special agent in charge at one of the bureau's field offices, he may also have been hesitating because Page was pushing to put more distance between them. "I deeply sincerely meant it earlier when I said I simply want you happy," Strzok wrote on June 20 around nine P.M. "Then don't join the team," she snapped back, referring to an arrangement that might have them working more closely together.

Days later, Page said she was "thinking I might leave the SC." Perhaps she had a clue to what was coming. Page managed to escape the special counsel's before the ticking time bomb of their texts detonated. On June 25, a Sunday, about two thirty in the afternoon, Page hit send on the last of their thousands of messages. To Strzok, she wrote: "Please don't ever text me again."

Their affair had been discovered by their spouses well before the appointment of the special counsel, but the history of their relationship and their incendiary comments about Trump were unknown to Mueller until he was contacted in late July by the Justice Department inspector general.

Strzok was fired by Mueller and went back to the FBI, where he was given a holding job in human resources. Page had returned to the FBI after leaving Mueller's team but soon gave up on her government career. Mueller would never be able to completely repair the political damage that Page and Strzok did to his team. Their texts about Trump cast continuing doubts about the impartiality of the bureau, providing ammunition to Trump's defenders that the Mueller probe was grounded in the investigative work of an FBI agent who had vowed months before the election that Trump would never become president: "No. No he won't," Strzok wrote. "We'll stop it."

ALMOST A MONTH AFTER DEALING WITH THE PAGE-STRZOK PROBlem, Mueller and his team carried out a pair of surprise attacks that provided the first indication of the aggression he would bring to the Russia investigation.

In late July, a team of FBI agents arrived before dawn outside a posh condominium complex overlooking the Potomac River waterfront in Old Town Alexandria, Virginia. The agents quietly made their way into the building, its residents still slumbering, and to the doorway of a unit that had sold for $2.7 million in 2015. The agents pounded on the portal, jolting Paul Manafort awake from the last night of sleep he would know before understanding just how directly he was in Mueller's sights. The agents waved a warrant and spent much of the day rifling through the political consultant's files, computers, phones, and personal effects. Manafort's lawyers voiced shock at the tactics, saying their client had already turned over a substantial volume of material to congressional investigators and would have been willing to comply with a special counsel request. Mueller, it seemed, wanted to send a message.

Two days later, on July 27, as George Papadopoulos stepped off a Lufthansa flight from Germany around seven P.M. at Dulles International Airport in Virginia, he was intercepted by FBI agents who diverted him from the winding path leading other passengers toward customs and immigration checks.[18] Papadopoulos was arrested, taken to a jail in Alexandria, and booked at 1:45 A.M. on charges of lying to the FBI in a January 27 interview. His mug shot showed him with stubble on his face, his eyelids drooping. After calling his lawyer in Chicago, Papadopoulos was placed in a cell for a few hours and then turned over to U.S. marshals around 8:30 A.M. when he was taken to court for his arraignment.

There was no doubt that Papadopoulos had repeatedly lied to the bureau in January. Among other falsehoods, he had claimed that he had learned about the "dirt" Russia had on Clinton before he joined the Trump campaign, though it had happened after he had been named an adviser. He tried to tell the agents that the source of the information, Joseph Mifsud, was "a nothing," when the bureau had emails showing that Papadopoulos knew the professor had ties with the Kremlin and had corresponded with him for months hoping to set up meetings with top Russian officials.

If the airport scene was intended to scare Papadopoulos and persuade him to cooperate, it worked. Later that morning, Mueller's lawyers told a judge that Papadopoulos was confidentially "willing to cooperate with the government in its ongoing investigation into Russian efforts to interfere in the 2016 presidential election."

In a span of two days, Mueller had seized troves of material from Trump's campaign chairman, boxes that contained tax documents and banking records that would culminate in the charges the special counsel would level at Manafort months later. He also had extracted a guilty plea from a Trump campaign insider. Papadopoulos's agreement to cooperate would remain secret for months, enabling the special counsel to employ him to gather evidence from other unwitting witnesses and suspects.

After months of stalking, Mueller had struck.

PART
FIVE

CHAPTER 13

"I CAN'T PUT ON THE CHARM"

IN MARCH 2018, A DOCUMENTARY ABOUT PUTIN AIRED ON ROS-
siya 1, one of Russia's main state-run television channels. The
four-hour program opens with the image of Putin in a dark wood-
paneled room, his face lit dramatically from an angle that leaves his
left eye in shadow under a furrowed brow. He grasps his armchair
intently with his left hand and gestures with his right as he de-
scribes his recollection of a Soviet comedy classic called *Gentlemen
of Fortune.*

"There's a scene in which the main character turns up in the jail
cell and a second character—some kind of ogre—tells him: Your
place is by the piss bucket!" Putin says. "Well, in essence, as crude
as it may sound, this, in fact, was how Russia was treated after the
disintegration of the Soviet Union. They keep trying to show us
our place. Well, we don't like this place."

THE WEEKS IMMEDIATELY AFTER TRUMP'S WIN WERE HEADY DAYS
in Moscow. Russia's foreign policy establishment had long spoken
of the need for a "new Yalta," an agreement akin to the conference

toward the end of World War II in which Stalin, Churchill, and Roosevelt gathered on the Black Sea and divided up postwar Europe into spheres of influence. A grandiose Trump–Putin summit seemed like the first order of business. Putin sent Trump a congratulatory letter expressing a desire to "bring our level of collaboration on the international scene to a qualitatively new level."

"A very nice letter from Vladimir Putin," Trump said in a statement released by his transition team. "His thoughts are so correct."

As the end of 2016 approached, the evidence of Russian interference had begun to intrude on the good feelings. News of the secret CIA assessment that Russia had sought to help elect Trump and damage the American brand of democracy was ridiculed in Russia as ludicrous and sour grapes among Democrats (another point on which Trump agreed with Putin).

At Putin's end-of-year press conference—a marathon four-hour event held before 1,400 journalists at Moscow's world trade center, with one Russian journalist holding up a photo of Putin as superman—state TV reporter Yevgeny Primakov had said that his Western colleagues described the Russian president as an all-powerful figure who "can manipulate the whole world, plant presidents, and interfere in elections all over the place."

"How does it feel to be the most powerful person on earth?" Primakov asked.

"The Democrats didn't just lose the presidency, they also lost the Senate and the House," Putin responded. "Did we—did I—do that, too?

"They are losing on all fronts and are looking elsewhere for people to blame," Putin continued. "In my view, this, how shall I say it, degrades their own dignity. You have to know how to lose with dignity." This was rich coming from someone who blamed Clinton for the protests in Moscow that had challenged him, who rigged elections and refused to get over decades-old slights against the post-Soviet state.

WITH HIS VICTORY, THE NEW YORK REAL ESTATE MAGNATE WHO had schemed his way into magazine rankings and craved the acceptance of Manhattan elites now belonged to an infinitely more exclusive club—one that was convening in the northern German city of Hamburg in July 2017. The presidents and prime ministers of the G20 nations command an overwhelming share of global influence. Their countries account for 85 percent of the world's gross domestic product, 75 percent of its population, and half of its land. Here were the world's most powerful leaders, all in one room, seated at a banquet table so long that it was hard to make out who was sitting at either end. Donald Trump was given a seat of prestige, toward the center of the table and the action.

The "social dinner" for the July 2017 summit in Hamburg had been a chance for heads of state and their spouses to take a break from discussing the weighty topics on that year's agenda—global migration, women's empowerment, and development aid. Trump had little interest in these issues or many of the faces he saw across the centerpieces of chrysanthemums and calla lilies. There was one exception. Looking down the table to his left, Trump sought eye contact with Vladimir Putin and raised his fist in a gesture of solidarity. As waiters began clearing plates, he stood up and walked past some of America's closest allies, largest trading partners, and geographic neighbors toward a dour figure who shared his disdain for the assembled forces of globalism.

Trump had been pursuing an introduction to Putin since before his 2013 trip to Moscow, and the two had traded words of praise across the Atlantic since the U.S. presidential campaign. The G20 summit marked the first time Trump and the Russian leader had ever met face-to-face, and the encounter took place at a moment of growing peril for the U.S. president: not only would the first stories about his son's meeting with a Russian lawyer at Trump Tower break only days later, but Congress was already moving toward passage of new sanctions against Russia in defiance of Trump's opposition. And while Trump didn't know it yet, by the end of the month, Mueller's team would execute its first arrests and raids. But Trump and Putin were undaunted, and their conversations at the summit—through interpreters, though Putin speaks passable English—heightened anxiety about the ties between the Russian and the American presidents.

News crews brought in for a staged photo op earlier that day had captured images of Trump extending his hand to Putin with the palm facing straight up as if balancing an object. It was an unusually submissive gesture for someone known for violent handshakes in which he deliberately tried to pull his victim off-balance. As the reporters and photographers filed out, Putin pointed at them with his thumb and said in English, "These are the ones who insulted you?" Trump laughed appreciatively at the joke by the leader of a country where journalists have been killed for their coverage of politics and corruption.

The two then proceeded with a meeting under unusual circumstances. Trump was accompanied only by Secretary of State Rex Tillerson, who had met Putin years earlier while serving as chief executive of ExxonMobil. (Tillerson had even been awarded Russia's Order of Friendship by Putin in 2012.) Leaders routinely have "pull-asides" in global gatherings, but the often tense encounters between the presidents of the United States and Russia are usually carefully scripted to avoid diplomatic misunderstandings or missteps. (A year earlier, Obama had glowered at Putin and warned against further election interference.) A U.S. president would normally be accompanied by his national security adviser, a senior Russia aide, and an interpreter, a reflection of the presumed importance of having multiple witnesses. Trump dispensed with that decades-old practice, even excluding his then national security adviser, H. R. McMaster, and the National Security Council's expert on Russia.

The meeting was supposed to last about thirty minutes, but it went on for more than two hours. Tillerson later testified that Putin "had come very prepared to talk," contrasting the Russian leader's preparation with that of the president. The only discussion of election interference came when Putin denied that Russia had done so, and Trump replied, "I believe you." Their warm exchanges were translated by a pair of interpreters, each scribbling notes to keep up. Afterward, Trump approached the U.S. interpreter, a longtime State Department employee, and demanded that he surrender the notes. As he seized the pages, Trump told the interpreter never to discuss what had transpired in the meeting, even with officials of the U.S. government.[1]

Trump emerged and announced that he and Putin had agreed on the outlines of a cooperative cybersecurity plan, including the creation of a joint unit against election hacking. For reasons that seemed obvious to everyone but Trump, the plan was poorly received in Washington. Republican senator Lindsey Graham described the proposed pact as "pretty close" to "the dumbest idea I've ever heard" and promptly introduced additional provisions to a Russia sanctions bill that was working its way through Congress— language that would strip Trump of his ability to avoid enforcing congressionally mandated sanctions or lift penalties already in place against Moscow.

Nevertheless, prospects for the sanctions legislation still seemed uncertain until two weeks after the Hamburg meeting, when news reports revealed that Trump had had a second conversation with

Putin at the conclusion of the banquet—this time with no witnesses, not even Tillerson, only an interpreter who worked for Putin. The White House had not disclosed the encounter, and once word was out, refused to provide any detail about the secret discussion, except to insist that Trump had only wandered in Putin's direction because the Russian leader was seated next to the first lady, Melania Trump. Whatever hesitation Republicans in Congress had about forcing Trump's hand on sanctions evaporated. Little over a week later, both chambers passed the punitive measure with overwhelming margins that would withstand any veto.

Trump was "apoplectic" as the bill was delivered to his desk, one adviser recalled. The president saw the legislation as an attack on multiple fronts—diminishing the grandeur of his election win (by validating claims of Russian interference), encroaching on his executive authority, and delivering a potentially fatal blow to his aspirations for kinship with Putin. It took four days for aides to persuade him to sign it. "If you veto it, they'll override you," one Trump adviser said, "and then you're fucked and you look like you're weak."

Telling Trump he would appear inadequate was, as his staff was learning, always an effective argument. He signed, but made his displeasure known: a White House statement asserted that the measure included "clearly unconstitutional provisions," and Trump, who had turned even mundane bill-signing ceremonies into spectacles, blocked the media from covering this one. No cameras were to capture his moment of capitulation.

THE REACTION FROM RUSSIA WAS WITHERING. PUTIN RESPONDED by ordering the United States to slash the size of its embassy and consular staff in Russia by 755 positions, an edict that would decimate America's diplomatic ranks, force the CIA to reduce its

Moscow presence, and throw hundreds of Russian nationals who worked as support staff at U.S. facilities out of jobs. Prime Minister Dmitry Medvedev taunted Trump in Facebook and Twitter posts that echoed the president's style, saying that he had shown "complete impotence, in the most humiliating manner, transferring executive power to Congress."

Medvedev's tirade reflected the Kremlin's rising frustration with its inability to get specific returns on its investment in the American president. Time and again, Trump's attempts to act on his pro-Kremlin impulses had been thwarted by forces he seemed unable to understand or control. It was certainly useful to Putin to have an American leader so willing to turn a blind eye to human rights abuses and eager to support the Russian leader's worldview. But on the most transactional aspects of the relationship, Trump faced resistance from Congress, the senior ranks of national security agencies, and even members of his own cabinet. At the same time, he proved unable or unwilling to do what was politically necessary—taking an occasional hawkish position toward Russia—to advance his desire for close ties with Putin. Nixon's trip to China in 1972 was accepted by American voters in large measure because his long-standing hardline positions on communism inoculated him against most suspicion that he would sell American interests short. Trump faced an even higher burden of proof to skeptics of his approach with the Kremlin, and his actions—insisting that there had been no Russian interference, echoing so many of Putin's talking points—compounded their concerns.

Nor could Trump seem to avoid blunders that deepened suspicion of his motives. Among them had been his decision to welcome Lavrov and Kislyak to the White House the day after Comey was fired.

Trump's advisers took pains to keep word of the gathering from leaking to reporters early; it wasn't until late into the evening of

May 9 that the meeting was added to the president's public schedule for the following morning. This would be Trump's highest level in-person contact with the Russian government since taking office. Because of his involvement in the meetings that felled Flynn and forced Sessions's recusal, Kislyak seemed a particularly toxic person to put in the same room as the president. When the Russian delegation's motorcade arrived at the White House grounds, it bypassed the main driveway and rolled down West Executive Avenue, a narrow strip of blacktop between the West Wing and the Eisenhower building, to prevent television cameras from capturing their arrival.

McMaster and other aides would typically have taken an hour before such a sensitive meeting to brief the president and supply him with talking points. But Trump's aversion to such sessions, and the fallout from the Comey mess, left aides little chance to prepare him. Ostensibly, Trump and Lavrov were in town to discuss Syria. A month earlier, Syria's President Bashar al-Assad, who depended on Russian military support for his survival, launched a chemical weapons attack on a rebel stronghold, killing at least 70 and sickening scores of others in a toxic fog. The Kremlin was furious when Trump chose to retaliate on April 7 with a volley of cruise missiles that tore up the runway at one of Assad's air bases. The blast craters were promptly filled in, and Syrian planes were soon back in the air, and on May 2, Putin called Trump for some further patching up. The Russian leader said he had some "new ideas" on Syria and mentioned that Lavrov was going to be in the United States for meetings.

"Will you see him?" Putin asked.

"Yes," Trump replied.

In fact Lavrov hadn't been planning on being anywhere near Washington. He was scheduled to fly to Fairbanks, Alaska, for a meeting of the Arctic Council, an intergovernmental partnership intended to further cooperation among the countries and indigenous communities whose lives are touched by proximity to the northern oceans' reaches. Lavrov promptly reworked his itinerary by four thousand miles.

For the Kremlin, the meeting was about much more than Syria. An audience with Trump was a chance to show the world that U.S.-Russian relations were shifting positively after years of recriminations. Putin may also have relished the sight of his loyal aides being welcomed into the Oval Office, an accommodation that would have been unlikely if Clinton had won.

On the president's official schedule, the meeting was marked "closed press," meaning that the pool of White House reporters would not be allowed into the Oval Office for a quick photo, known as a press spray—routine access that usually lasted no more than a minute or two. But for all their focus on blocking American media, White House staffers failed to catch a Russian journalist from the Moscow-controlled news agency, TASS, accompanying the Kremlin delegation. The photographer made his way into the Oval Office carrying technical gear that was probably legitimate photo equipment but represented a worrisome breach of security to counterintelligence experts.

Fresh off firing his FBI chief, Trump was in a backslapping, loquacious mood. The TASS photographer captured him resting an arm on Lavrov's shoulder as the portly ambassador stifled a laugh. In another shot, the president pointed at a grinning Kislyak. Trump even joked that he seemed to be the only person who had not met the ambassador—a reference to Kislyak's disturbing ubiquity among Trump campaign officials. This was the meeting during which Trump made his "nut job" remark about Comey and said that firing the FBI chief had eased pressure on his relationship with Russia. But that disclosure came only after a separate part of Trump's conversation with Lavrov and Kislyak triggered internal alarms.

Trying to impress his guests and show them that Russia would have much to gain from a close partnership on counterterrorism, Trump began bragging about the extraordinary secrets presented to him each morning by U.S. spy agencies. "I get great intel," Trump boasted. "I have people brief me on great intel every day." To prove his point, Trump began describing an Islamic State threat emanating from Raqqa, the group's de facto capital in Syria, to take down passenger aircraft with explosives-rigged laptops. Such information was of keen interest to the Russians. Nearly two years earlier, terrorists linked to the Islamic State brought down a Russian airliner in Egypt's Sinai, killing 224 people on board.

Trump didn't disclose the specific source of intelligence that had uncovered the plot or name the country that had collected it. But he had made it clear that there was an ongoing stream of information about Islamic State plans stemming from a penetration of the group's operations center. This was enough to arouse Russian curiosity—high-level intimate intelligence being gathered in a country where Putin wanted to exert maximum influence, at the expense of the United States.

In fact, details about the threat were being relayed to the United States by Israel, under restrictions so tight that everything about the program was "code-word information," the highest classification level used by American spy agencies. NSC discussions of the plot were accompanied by stern warnings that only three governments knew about this stream of intelligence: the United States, Britain, and Israel. And yet Trump couldn't help bringing it up.

"Can you believe the world we live in today?" Trump told the Russians. "Isn't it crazy?"

Soon after the meeting broke, summaries of the discussion were being disseminated throughout the White House (which at that point in the Trump presidency was still adhering to the long-standing practice of having a note taker produce transcripts of important meetings so that the president's national security team could keep up with developments). As those memos spread, White House officials became worried that Trump had committed a serious breach and moved to contain the fallout. White House counterterrorism official Tom Bossert placed calls to the CIA and the NSA to warn them of what had been disclosed. U.S. intelligence officials were concerned that Russia could use details that Trump had provided to identify how Israel had gathered the intelligence. And they feared that Trump's decision to share the information without Israel's permission could endanger cooperation from a key ally.

TRUMP'S MEETING WITH LAVROV AND KISLYAK CAME AT A TIME OF exhilaration and anxiety in the *Post*'s newsroom. The blockbuster stories that the paper had produced since December had created an atmosphere unlike any the lead reporters on the Russia story could remember. Many were finding their mailboxes full of letters and postcards from readers praising the paper's work. It was the closest thing to fan mail any of us had ever gotten, and while appreciated, it could be a little unsettling. Most seemed to be coming from readers who were dismayed by Trump's election, were outraged by his attacks on the press, and hoped that stories by the *Post* and others would lead to the end of his presidency. We were disturbed by Trump's attacks on the press as well, but, sanctimonious as it sounds, getting at the truth was the paramount objective.

At the same time, we were also seeing a spike in angry calls and emails embracing Trump's description of us as enemies of the people. In the spring of 2017 we got seemingly credible warnings from sources that *Post* journalists might be under surveillance—not necessarily by the government, though that didn't seem out of the question, but by private investigators bankrolled by Trump supporters. At one point, we even had an internal meeting with security consultants who spent an hour telling us about the dangers of leaving unshredded documents in our trash and educating us about how to tell if we were being followed. It all seemed a little hysterical, and we never saw any hard evidence that the warnings were warranted, but we adopted greater discipline in how we spoke with sources, communicated with colleagues, and wrote stories. Reporters began using encrypted communications apps on their phones almost all the time—a practice that wasn't confined to journalists. An app called Signal showed how many of your existing contacts had also installed the software, and it was remarkable how many Washington officials were also downloading a product designed to protect against the prying of the government they worked for.

Finally, and most important, information was flowing in from all directions. The anonymous letter that Ellen Nakashima received in December had been the start of a groundswell of outreach from sources across numerous government agencies. The approaches came by phone, email, encrypted apps, and in some cases, human intermediaries. The *Post*, like other news organizations, devoted a page on its website to providing instructions on how to contact reporters securely. Among the options was a function called SecureDrop that enabled sources to provide information without leaving a trace. Only a small percentage of the dozens of messages and documents that ended up in such inboxes panned out as both reliable and newsworthy, but even that small percentage meant a volume of information was flowing into the newsroom that few of us had ever experienced.

It was through one of these means that someone came forward with information about Trump's meeting with Kislyak and Lavrov. I was skeptical and struggled to understand the source's initially cryptic account of what had transpired but was struck by the person's concern and persistence. We devised a plan to communicate under the guise of a mundane commercial transaction, and I ended up spending several hours with the source in an isolated location going over aspects of Trump's meeting in detail. The individual seemed profoundly worried that Trump had jeopardized a critical intelligence capability in what he had told his Russian visitors, and the source believed that only if the president's actions were exposed would it lead anyone to take steps preventing Trump from causing further damage. (The source withheld details about the intelligence capability in question, including the country responsible for it.)

To confirm the information, I enlisted the help of Greg Jaffe, a colleague with deep experience covering the Pentagon and national security. Within days, we had confirmed the initial source's claims and began drafting a story. When we notified the White House that we were preparing an article about what Trump had revealed, officials reacted with alarm, angrily warning that even publishing the name of the Syrian city from which the intelligence emanated could jeopardize important intelligence capabilities or jeopardize lives (even though Trump had done so with his Russian guests). One White House official went further and, in a conference call with reporters and editors at the *Post*, flew into a rage. He questioned the paper's patriotism and vowed to begin a merciless hunt for leakers. He then said something that seemed both odd and troubling, urging us to call our sources back to ensure we weren't misunderstanding any information. It was as if he were inviting us to light up the phones of our sources so the White House could pinpoint them for retribution.

The story that was published later that evening on May 15—"Trump Revealed Highly Classified Information to Russian Foreign Minister and Ambassador"—set off a firestorm at the White

House, a new Russia-related breach to reignite the election-related concerns about the president. As news organizations raced to confirm the details, White House aides rushed to contain the damage.

Shortly after the article appeared, McMaster ran into a gaggle of reporters waiting outside the White House press secretary's office. "This is the last place in the world I wanted to be," McMaster said as the reporters closed in around him.

McMaster had been planning to retire from the U.S. military and take a university teaching job when he was plucked from a relatively sleepy three-star command at Fort Eustis, Virginia, to replace Flynn as national security adviser. Jim Mattis had urged him to join the Trump administration as a civilian, so he could advocate forcefully for the president without worrying about playing a political role. But McMaster believed that remaining in uniform would allow him to best serve the nation and restore a degree of nonpartisanship to foreign policy debates.

McMaster had been on his way to a dinner party with his wife when his top press adviser urged him to step out publicly and deny the *Post*'s reporting. McMaster, who first met Trump when he flew to Mar-a-Lago to interview for the national security adviser job, was struggling to build a rapport with the president. "He was stressed every time he had to go into the Oval Office," recalled one White House official. Trump was a boss unlike any McMaster had served under during his accomplished thirty-three-year military career. As had been made clear to Comey, among others, the president demanded absolute loyalty from his subordinates and expected them to fight and, if necessary, mislead the public on his behalf. Defending Trump publicly was deemed essential if McMaster wanted to earn Trump's trust. McMaster had been in the room with Trump, Lavrov, and Kislyak. In this instance, at least, he believed that Trump had not disclosed any information that the Russians couldn't have figured out from what was already known publicly.

Other news outlets were posting their own versions of the *Post*'s scoop when McMaster strode out of the West Wing, passing the Marine guard who stands a ceremonial watch in a dark blue dress uniform and white pants whenever the president is at work. McMaster fumbled with a piece of paper on which he had written some remarks. He looked uncomfortable and upset. "I just have a brief statement for the record," he said, pulling on his glasses. "The story as reported tonight is false . . . I was in the room, and it didn't happen."

The next morning Trump undercut his national security adviser's denials, tweeting that he wanted to share the intelligence "with Russia (at an openly scheduled W.H. meeting) which I have the absolute right to do." The tweet forced McMaster to make a second appearance in front of the White House press corps. This time he refused to say whether Trump had revealed classified information, but insisted that the president had not given away damaging secrets by discussing the plot or Syrian city where it originated. (McMaster himself did not name Raqqa.)

A week later, on a trip to Jerusalem, Trump went even further. He was standing next to Prime Minister Benjamin Netanyahu when a reporter asked the Israeli leader if he was concerned about Trump's Oval Office meeting with Lavrov and Kislyak.

"The intelligence cooperation is terrific," Netanyahu punted.

Trump hushed the room so that he could respond as well. "Just so you understand, I never mentioned the word or the name Israel," Trump told reporters. "Never mentioned it during that conversation. They're all saying I did, so you have another story wrong. Never mentioned the word Israel."

At the White House's request, the *Post* had not named Israel as the source of the sensitive intelligence. The White House then sent McMaster out to denounce the article and claim that its version of what transpired in the Oval Office had "never happened." Now core elements of that account—as well as the connection to Israel—had essentially been confirmed by the president.

It was one in a series of challenges and indignities for McMaster, whose formal bearing around the president, penchant for highly detailed briefings, and ingrained skepticism of Russia created endless friction with Trump. "The president thinks he can be really good friends with Putin," McMaster sometimes complained. "I don't know why or why he would want to be."

McMaster had recruited an internal ally on Russia in March with the hiring of Fiona Hill as the senior Russia adviser on the NSC. Hill shared McMaster's distrust of the Kremlin and had even written a critical biography of Putin. Her relationship with Trump couldn't have gotten off to a worse start. In one of her first visits with the president in the Oval Office—a planning session for a call with Putin on Syria—Trump appeared to mistake Hill for a member of the White House clerical staff and handed her an edited document to type up. When she responded with an arched brow, Trump lashed out at what he perceived to be insubordination. "What's the matter with this one?" he shouted, motioning for McMaster to intervene. McMaster followed Hill out the door and scolded her. Later, he and others explored ways to repair her damaged relationship with the president. As it turned out, she was still in the White House long after McMaster had been fired.

McMaster's interactions with Trump on Russia were also strained because it was often left to the national security adviser to deliver bad news that the president's intelligence briefers tended to skip over. The President's Daily Brief, or PDB, often seemed more structured to avoid upsetting the president than to inform him. The written version—which Trump never took time to read—was full of Russia-related intelligence that might draw the president's ire, including new developments on Russian election interference and cyber intrusions. But the verbal presentation often seemed to elide these sensitive subjects.

"Why don't you ever raise this with the president?" a senior White House official said at one point, confronting the CIA briefer. The agency analyst responded that the intelligence community was waiting for smoking gun evidence strong enough to overcome Trump's resistance. The approach created a "really bad cycle," the official said, in which Trump didn't see intelligence documenting Russia's aggressive behavior and therefore became increasingly convinced that the concerns about Russia were overblown.

The president's personal insecurities added to the problem. To Trump, charges of Russian interference in the election were mostly, if not entirely, the product of a conspiracy by his political enemies to undermine his legitimacy. "If you say 'Russian interference' to him, it's all about him," said a senior Republican strategist. "He judges everything about him."

As a result, White House officials began gaming the internal policymaking system to improve the odds of implementing more forceful action against Russia. On sensitive matters likely to trigger Trump's aversion to upsetting Putin, senior advisers at times adopted what one official described as a policy of "don't walk that last five and a half feet"—meaning to avoid entering the Oval Office and giving Trump a chance to erupt or overrule. The result was an almost unfathomable situation for the country's national security apparatus: a belief that working around the president might be the only way to confront Putin—and thus protect the United States.

It was an arrangement contrary to McMaster's professed beliefs. As a young Army officer he had written a well-regarded book in 1997, *Dereliction of Duty*, that harshly criticized military leaders for acceding to President Lyndon Johnson's doomed strategy in Vietnam and failing to stand up to the lies being told in Washington

about the war. McMaster had often raised the issue of Russian interference in ways that worked to the detriment of his own relationship
with the president. But he found himself in a White House where
shielding Trump from unpleasant news or backing his false assertions appeared to be a price of admission others were willing to pay.

FOR ORDINARY RUSSIANS, THE DEVELOPMENTS IN WASHINGTON
were a source of increasing confusion and disappointment. Initially
elated by Trump's win, they mistakenly assumed that the U.S.
president was as politically powerful as the one in the Kremlin, and
that Trump could direct U.S.-Russian relations without constraint.

Inauguration day had brought a burst of Trumpomania to Moscow. On state TV, Vladimir Zhirinovsky, the nationalist firebrand,
had predicted that Trump would serve two full terms, followed by
eight years of an Ivanka Trump presidency and eight more of Jared
Kushner. A food company had released special-edition sugar cubes
featuring Trump's likeness. A military surplus store across from
the U.S. embassy in Moscow offered a 10 percent discount for all
American citizens. And the same nationalist group that had held an
election night watch party in a Moscow bar had thrown an encore,
the venue upgraded to the historic Central Telegraph building near
the Kremlin. Some partygoers wore sweat shirts that said, "You've
been hacked."

By midway through 2017, the joke was starting to get old. The
Trump administration had been buffeted by one revelation after another, U.S.-Russia relations seemed in free fall, and there were few
indications that life for ordinary Russians was about to improve.
U.S. sanctions were still taking their toll, and the congressional
threat of new ones kept many investors out. Economic growth was
still sluggish—averaging about 1 percent a year since 2008, on a
gross domestic product smaller than that of Texas. The ruble stood

at half its value from when the first Western sanctions hit in 2014. Trump, objectively, still looked like a major disappointment to his investors in the Kremlin.

From March to July, the share of Russians who viewed the American president positively—never very high—dropped from 38 percent to 18 percent, pollster VTsIOM found. Even the July meeting between Trump and Putin in Hamburg didn't stop the slide. "I thought that if Trump won, there would be a revolution, the world would be different," Zhirinovsky later reflected. "Not our October Revolution but an American revolution—a Trump Revolution." Instead, he said, the American establishment had crippled Trump. "Your president is weak," Zhirinovsky told the *Post*. "We thought he would be powerful. But he is weak. He is afraid of everything."

Yet even as Trump failed to deliver in ways that ordinary Russians could measure, Putin realized gains that to him were just as substantial. The impact of the Kremlin's interference added to his domestic aura as a master manipulator of world events to Russia's advantage. America's brand of democracy suddenly looked vulnerable and damaged, its ability to lecture the authoritarians of the world—Putin among them—degraded. The Russian leader got two things he prized most dearly in his long struggle with Washington: power and payback.

Still, Putin's patience with the American president had been abraded, and he was pulled into the downward spiral. His order to evict American diplomats in July 2017 was an unmistakable sign that the uncharacteristic restraint he'd shown the previous December—when Obama announced sanctions and Flynn secretly appealed to Kislyak—was now over.

This time it was Trump who reacted with bizarre magnanimity. Rather than voice any support for the dozens of State Department and CIA employees being forced back to Washington, he expressed gratitude to Putin. "I want to thank him because we're trying to cut down on payroll," Trump told reporters during an outing at his golf club in Bedminster—remarks his aides later said were meant as a joke. "We'll save a lot of money."

Such comments were one reason that Trump was starting to lose the battle on Russia even inside his own administration. A month after Trump thanked Putin for the expulsions, the State Department announced its response to the Kremlin's action, ordering the Russian government to close its consulate in San Francisco, a chancery annex in Washington, D.C., and a consular annex in New York City. Tillerson, whose background had raised concern that he would be soft on the Kremlin, given ExxonMobil's joint ventures with the Russian oil company Rosneft, had become increasingly defiant. It was even reported that in a meeting at the Pentagon over the summer, he had referred to Trump as a moron.[2]

It was a remarkable pivot for Tillerson, who just months earlier had been secretly exploring options for returning the two Russian compounds seized by the Obama administration. The loss of the two country estates had become a major grievance for Moscow, and Lavrov had raised the issue in nearly every meeting with his American counterparts. Tillerson was then still searching for ways to deliver a breakthrough with Russia—and improve his standing with the president. But after a report in the *Post* revealed that the administration was considering the return of the "dachas," hardliners in the White House mobilized the FBI to hold an elaborate briefing for Trump in the Oval Office. Edward Priestap, the assistant director of the counterintelligence division at the FBI, brought in three-dimensional models of the compounds as well as satellite photos showing their proximity to sensitive U.S. military and intelligence installations. Priestap explained that the Russians were using the facilities to steal U.S. secrets, and Trump seemed inclined to keep them. Then, as he eyed the 3-D renderings, his inner developer marveled at the potential of the parcels and he asked, "Should we sell this off and keep the money?"[3]

THE SANCTIONS BILL AND SHUTTERING OF MORE RUSSIAN DIPLO-matic sites were victories for Moscow skeptics in the White House and State Department. But the moves grated on Trump, who repeatedly complained that pressure from Congress, the media, and the Mueller probe was preventing him from building the bond with Putin that he needed to manage a dangerous world. "I can't be president. This is not good for me or the country," he complained to aides. "I can't develop my relationship with Putin. I can't put on the charm . . . because of this witch hunt."

In November, Trump was on a twelve-day swing through Asia when he and Putin met again, this time on the sidelines of an economic summit in Da Nang, Vietnam. Afterward, on the flight from Da Nang to Hanoi, a high-spirited Trump wandered back to the press cabin to talk about the trip. Reporters quickly asked about Russia's meddling in the 2016 election.

"Every time he sees me, he says, 'I didn't do that,'" Trump said. "And I believe, I really believe, that when he tells me that, he means it. . . . I think he is very insulted by it."

Though Trump appeared to be losing some of the internal battles over Russia policy, he was still the president, and his refusal to accept the objective reality of Russia's interference in 2016 was impairing the government's ability to respond to a continuing threat. Respected U.S. national security officials had described Russia's hack of the 2016 election in catastrophic terms. Former CIA deputy director Michael Morell, who was George W. Bush's personal briefer on the day airplanes plunged into New York's twin towers and the Pentagon, said the Kremlin assault was "the political equivalent of 9/11." Al-qaeda's attack was followed by a massive

U.S. mobilization—intelligence agencies were restructured, border security measures adopted, and wars launched. There was no higher priority for Bush, or even Obama, as president, than ensuring the United States was not attacked again.

Trump, by contrast, failed to convene a single cabinet-level meeting on Russian interference until well into his second year in office, and even then—in July 2018—it had the appearance of a perfunctory exercise to deprive his critics of a talking point. He gave the matter less than an hour, issued no orders or instructions, and departed soon thereafter to his golf course in Bedminster. Before that meeting, the subject had been discussed only at the lower levels of the NSC. One former high-ranking Trump official said there was an unspoken understanding within senior levels of government that to raise the matter would be to acknowledge its validity, which the president saw as an affront.

As the months went on, White House officials continued to pick their shots when it came to Russia policy. McMaster oversaw the drafting of the country's National Security Strategy, which named China and Russia as competitors who were "attempting to erode American security and prosperity." The document is supposed to serve as an overarching guide for the entire government on foreign policy and was especially hard on Russia, describing it as a "revisionist power" that is "using information tools to undermine the legitimacy of democracies" in the United States and Europe. McMaster and Nadia Schadlow, who was the document's lead author, briefed Trump several times. McMaster told staffers that it had to be plainly written and clearly argued—Trump had to see it as *his* strategy.

He did not. Although the president took the document to Mar-a-Lago, it is not clear that Trump ever read it. His speech in December 2017 introducing the new strategy almost entirely ignored Russia. Schadlow had worked to draft the speech with White House aide Stephen Miller, who warned that it would need to walk a fine line to include any reference to Russia without triggering the president's aversion to damaging his relationship with Putin. "Our argument [to Miller] was that we can't be this hard on Russia in the strategy and not have a single mention of Russia in the speech," one White House official said. Miller responded that they could put it in the prepared text, but he couldn't promise the president would read it. As a result, the thirty-minute speech included just one sentence on the threat posed by Russia and China.

Foreign policy analysts quickly homed in on the vast gulf between Trump's view and those of his advisers. "The National Security Strategy is a stunning repudiation of Trump," wrote Thomas Wright, a scholar at the Brookings Institution, "and Trump's speech was a stunning repudiation of the National Security Strategy."

The split was a further sign that Trump's relationship with McMaster, never strong, was fast deteriorating. McMaster's allies in the White House said that he was one of the few advisers who were willing to challenge the president. "He got a lot of what he and the NSC wanted, but it was a painful process," one official said. As the months passed, his struggles with Trump became personal. In February 2018, one day after a federal grand jury indicted thirteen Russians and three Russian entities with conspiracy, McMaster told an audience of government officials and foreign policy wonks at the Munich Security Conference in Germany that the evidence of Russian meddling in the U.S. election was "incontrovertible." The general's remarks drew a swift Twitter rebuke from Trump, who wrote that "McMaster forgot to say that the results of the 2016 elections were not impacted or changed by the Russians and the only Collusion was between Russia and Crooked H."

It was perhaps inevitable that the final breaking point between Trump and McMaster would come in the middle of a new showdown with Moscow. On March 4, 2018, Sergei Skripal, a former Russian spy, and his adult daughter, Yulia, were discovered unconscious on a park bench in Salisbury, England. The two had been poisoned with a nerve agent developed by Soviet scientists, and within days, British officials had determined that it was "highly likely" that the Kremlin was behind the attack.

The poisoning and Putin's reelection on March 18 were the prelude to Trump's next outreach to the Russian leader, a phone call scheduled for two days later. McMaster urged Trump to postpone it, and when that failed, warned that Putin's victory had been marred by his suppressive actions to prevent any serious opposition. "Whatever you do," McMaster told the president, "don't congratulate the guy." When McMaster's aides typed up talking points for Trump's conversation, at the top of the list was the warning: "DO NOT CONGRATULATE."

Because the call was scheduled for the morning and Trump typically does not leave his residence for the Oval Office until after ten A.M., McMaster was able to do some final preparations with the president via phone.

Hours later, the *Post* published a story that incensed Trump. "President Trump did not follow specific warnings from his national security advisers when he congratulated Russian president Vladimir Putin on his reelection," it began. Trump had also ignored talking points instructing him to condemn the Salisbury poisoning, according to the report. The president blamed McMaster and his team for the leak.

McMaster had another problem, too. In his call with Putin, Trump had invited the Russian leader to visit Washington. McMaster had persuaded the president not to include mention of the invitation in the White House readout of the call. Such invites, the national security adviser insisted, were best handled through official channels. Trump reluctantly agreed but made it clear that he wanted McMaster to get to work at once on the visit.

"Invite him," he ordered.

Two days later, on March 22, McMaster was at Fort McNair when his staff spotted John Bolton, the conservative firebrand and former UN ambassador, walking up the White House driveway and into the West Wing. Bolton's meeting with the president wasn't on Trump's schedule, and McMaster's aides quickly surmised that the president was going to replace their boss with Bolton.

The aides rushed to track down Ivanka Trump and Hope Hicks, often sought at moments of crisis in the White House because of their perceived ability to reason with the president. McMaster's aides pleaded with them to intervene and ensure that Trump didn't fire the general via tweet. Around four P.M. as Bolton walked out of the Oval Office, Hicks and the president's daughter hurried in. They prevailed on Trump to pull McMaster out of his meeting at Fort McNair and tell him over the phone that he was being replaced, which he did.

McMaster negotiated to stay in the job for two more weeks, after which Bolton would take the chair. During those final days, McMaster continued to work with European officials to coordinate an international response to the Russian poisoning. The chasm between Trump and his aides over Russia was reaching its widest point. Outraged British officials described the attempt to kill the Skripals as the first use of a nerve agent on European soil since World War II. Initially (and by now unsurprisingly), the president was hesitant to believe the intelligence that Russia was behind the attack—a fact that some aides attributed to his tendency to look for deeper conspiracies, as well as his reluctance to confront Putin.

Prime Minister Theresa May, who had a prickly relationship with Trump, told him by phone that British authorities were 95 percent sure that Moscow was responsible.

"Maybe we should get to 98 percent," Trump countered.

Trump argued that the poisoning was largely a European problem and that the allies should take the lead in moving against Russia. "Why are you asking me to do this?" he asked May. He was

especially worried that if he went along with Europe's plan to punish Russia, German chancellor Angela Merkel, whose economy
was dependent on Russian natural gas, might back down at the last
second, leaving Trump looking like the aggressor in a new confrontation with the Kremlin. "Putin has got her by the balls with
that gas pipe," Trump told aides and allies.

When May failed to get a commitment from Trump, it fell to the
advisers who had traveled with him to his Florida retreat to convince the president to sign off on new sanctions. At Mar-a-Lago,
just thirty feet away from club members, deputy national security
adviser Ricky L. Waddell briefed him on proposed plans to retaliate for the attempted Skripal assassinations by expelling sixty
Russian diplomats and suspected spies. The United States, Waddell
explained, would be ousting roughly the same number of Russians
as its European allies.

"We'll match their numbers," Trump instructed, referring to
the targets set by the other countries protesting Russia's actions.
"We're not taking the lead. We're matching."

Trump's uneasiness was apparent on the trip home to Washington. "Maybe we shouldn't do this?" he said to Waddell as he
boarded the presidential helicopter for the short flight from Andrews Air Force Base to the White House. That evening, Waddell
scrambled to pull together a Situation Room meeting to confer
with key players on how to proceed. John Kelly, Trump's chief
of staff, called in to the meeting on a secure phone line. The expulsions were going to be announced early the next morning on
March 26, and everyone in the room realized the political outcry
that would ensue if the allies moved forward without the United
States. "I'll convince him," said Kelly, who phoned Trump at his
residence.

WHEN THE EXPULSIONS WERE ANNOUNCED PUBLICLY, TRUMP erupted. To his shock and dismay, France and Germany were each expelling only four Russian officials—far fewer than the sixty that his administration had decided on. The president, who seemed to believe that other individual countries would match the United States, was furious that his administration was being portrayed in the media as taking by far the toughest stance on Russia.

His briefers tried to reassure him that the sum total of European expulsions was roughly the same as the U.S. number. "I don't care about the total!" the administration official recalled Trump screaming. Growing angrier, Trump insisted that his aides had misled him. "There were curse words," the official recalled, "a lot of curse words."

The mixed signals regarding Putin continued. "Nobody has been tougher on Russia, but getting along with Russia would be a good thing, not a bad thing. And just about everybody agrees to that except very stupid people," Trump said in a meeting with the leaders of Estonia, Latvia, and Lithuania shortly after the expulsions.

A reporter asked if he considered Putin a friend or foe.

"We'll find out," Trump replied. "I'll let you know."

Days later, on April 6, the administration announced sanctions targeting seven of Russia's wealthiest men and seventeen senior Russian officials—essentially severing their access to Western financial institutions. Among them were Kirill Shamalov, Putin's son-in-law, and Igor Rotenberg, an oil executive whose father was a former judo partner of Putin and whose companies had been enriched by state contracts on construction projects including a bridge connecting the Russian mainland to Crimea. Treasury secretary Steven Mnuchin said the reason for the sanctions was Russia's engagement in "a range of malign activity around the globe." Even the administration's critics described the new penalties as serious and biting. The ruble suffered its worst day in three years, and shares in Sberbank, Russia's biggest bank, plunged 17 percent. One of the sanctioned individuals was Manafort's former business partner, Oleg Deripaska. The company Deripaska ran, aluminum giant Rusal, employed tens of thousands of people across Russia and was pushed to the brink of collapse by the targeting of its top executive—righting itself only when the oligarch left the company.

The measures were touted in a White House fact sheet released that same day. It carried no new statement from the president.

PUTIN ADOPTED A MORE AMBIVALENT STANCE TOWARD THE AMERican president as well, at least in public. In the fall of 2017, he mocked the notion of a Trump-Putin alliance in terms that nonetheless made misogynistically clear that if there could have been such an attachment, it was Putin who was the dominant male. Trump "is not my bride," Putin said, "and I am not his groom." In phone conversations with Trump, however, he would whisper conspiratorially, telling the U.S. president that it wasn't their fault that they could not consummate the relationship that each sought. Instead, Putin sought to reinforce Trump's belief that he was being undermined by a secret government cabal, a bureaucratic "deep state."

"It's not us. We get it," Putin would tell Trump, according to White House aides. "It's the subordinates fighting against our friendship."

The Russian president was still cultivating the candidate he had backed. When Kremlin spokesman Dmitry Peskov—one of Putin's closest confidants, having worked for him since 2000—spoke to the *Post* in June 2018, he had one key takeaway from a year-and-a-half of Trump: the American-led international order was in shambles. Now it was up to Putin—and like-minded leaders around the world—to build a new global system out of the ruins.

"If you take only purely economic indicators, then Russia greatly lags behind America," Peskov explained. "If you take issues of strategic stability in the world, then these are two equal partners."

Trump was bringing them closer into parity. He was a disrupter, ripping at old alliances and tearing up multilateral agreements, punishing democratic friends and embracing dictatorial adversaries.

"On the one hand, we've got this drawn-out pause in our dialogue with Washington," Peskov said. "But on the other hand, this all changes the political landscape even more quickly and allows us to already start building out the structures of the future."

And Russia, he said, had not given up on Trump, viewing him as caged by his own establishment, but a leader who could yet break out. Putin was a new modern "strongman," Peskov said, an archetype who was spawning imitations across the globe. "People around the world are tired of leaders that are all similar to each other. There's a demand in the world for special sovereign leaders, for decisive ones who do not fit into general frameworks," the Kremlin spokesman explained. "Putin's Russia was the starting point." Others that fit the mold included Viktor Orban in Hungary, Xi Jinping in China, Rodrigo Duterte in the Philippines, and Recep Tayyip Erdoğan in Turkey.

"There's getting to be more of them all over the world," Peskov predicted. "Trump in America, too."

AS HE EXITED THE WHITE HOUSE, MCMASTER HAD TOLD FRIENDS that he was confident that history would judge him as someone who didn't hold back in the Oval Office. "Some people think the way to preserve your influence is not to tell the president what [you] really think," he often said while still in the national security adviser job. "Well, what good is your influence?"

Bolton, who had started work on April 9, was less inclined to try to manage Trump. He cut back on the big Situation Room meetings and instead relied on smaller, more ad hoc sessions with Trump and a few key aides in the Oval Office that were a better match to the president's short attention span and freewheeling style. Bolton also shared both Trump's disdain for diplomatic niceties and his penchant for denigrating the Washington foreign policy establishment.

The resulting change was clear in early June as Trump stopped to answer questions from the press before leaving for the G7 summit in La Malbaie, Canada. Shouting to be heard over Marine One's engines, the president complained about "Comey and his band of thieves," and insisted that he had the "absolute right" to pardon himself.

"I'll never do it because I didn't do anything wrong," he continued. "Everybody knows it. There's been no collusion. No obstruction. It's all a made-up fantasy."

He then broached an idea that he knew would both alarm America's closest European allies and appeal to the Kremlin. Obama and those allies had punished Russia for its annexation of Crimea in 2014 by expelling it from what was then the G8 group of leading industrial democracies. Trump insisted it was time to end Putin's isolation.

"You know whether you like it or not—and it may not be politically correct—but we have a world to run," Trump said. "They should let Russia come back in, because we should have Russia at the negotiating table."

With McMaster gone, Trump also finally got what he had wanted from the outset. In late June, the White House and the Kremlin, in synchronized statements, announced that Trump and Putin would meet in Helsinki on July 16. The meeting, Trump said, "would be good for the world."

CHAPTER 14

HELSINKI

A FTER BEING SWORN IN AS PRESIDENT, BEHIND BULLETPROOF glass streaked with rain, Trump delivered an inaugural address depicting the country he had been elected to lead as a blighted land. He spoke of the rusted factories and failing schools that politicians almost always lament and vow to restore. But his was a nation ravaged beyond recognition—afflicted with "pain," exploited by allies, infested with "crime and gangs and drugs." As he rendered this dystopia, Trump delivered one of the most chilling lines ever uttered in an inaugural: "This American carnage stops right here and stops right now."

By the end of his first year in office, there seemed no end to the carnage that could be traced back to Trump himself. He laid waste to longstanding norms of presidential conduct—expectations of civility, avoidance of conflicts of interest, restraint in the exercise of power and at least a passable commitment to honesty. Every president bends the truth, but under Trump it had been shattered. He made false or misleading statements a staggering 2,140 times during the first twelve months of his term—nearly six per day—according to a tally maintained by a team at the *Post*. There was harm (much of it intended) to historic alliances, to the country's international reputation and its standing on rankings of countries by their records on human rights, press freedom, judicial independence and other measures of democratic function.[1] Racial tensions surged with his intermittent refusal to denounce white supremacists, his references to "shithole" countries and his angry condemnations of African-American protests.

The fallout related to Russia was in a category all to itself. Campaign and administration officials had been fired, forced to recuse and subjected to raids and arrests. Senior officials at the FBI, the Justice Department and spy agencies had been dismissed, pressured and repeatedly attacked by the president. Congressional oversight was subverted, particularly in the House, where the intelligence committee's Russia probe morphed into a Republican-led project to discredit the FBI and its sources—all to provide cover for the president. The public's understanding of what happened in 2016 was obscured by clouds of misinformation, largely emitted by Trump. And then there was the damage that he had done to himself, giving investigators every reason to suspect he had sought to obstruct justice, prompting Congress to strip him of presidential authority on sanctions because of his pro-Russia impulses, sowing confusion and concern within his own administration through his unrelenting pursuit of a bond with Putin.

As Trump approached his second year in office, there was more carnage to come. The year would be eventful for the two men who seemed to loom over Trump's presidency. Mueller would also begin his second year on the job, entering what appeared to be the final stretch of his investigation. Putin would be elected to his fourth term as Russia's president. Both men would pursue meetings with Trump in 2018. The president's advisers and attorneys—many of whom would be pushed aside before the year was out—saw peril in allowing Trump to sit down with either the ex-KGB agent he saw as an ally or the former FBI chief he treated as an enemy.

THAT ADVERSARY WAS CLOSING IN.

On October 30, 2017, Mueller announced criminal charges against former Trump campaign chairman Manafort and his deputy Rick Gates. It had been just three months since agents raided Manafort's home in Alexandria, but in that time the special counsel had assembled an astonishingly detailed blueprint of the political insider's finances. He was accused of money laundering, failing to register as a foreign agent and hiding from U.S. tax collectors tens of millions of dollars in payments from a political party in Ukraine with close ties to the Kremlin. He and Gates both faced twelve criminal counts, including taking part in a conspiracy against the United States. But the power of the document was in the details. The special counsel had diagrammed Manafort's alleged use of hidden accounts overseas to wire money to dozens of merchants in the United States to hide his incoming flow of cash from the American government—a massive, illicit bounty. The special counsel had emails, retrieved from the computers FBI agents had seized, that purportedly showed Manafort involved in falsifying financial records so that he could qualify for bank loans he used to convert illicit funds abroad into cash and hard assets in the United States.

There was a message to Trump and his associates beyond the words in the 31-page indictment. The special counsel was not hesitating to take advantage of the wide latitude he'd been given in his charter from Rosenstein. He had scoured parts of Manafort's and Gates's lives that they had endeavored to keep hidden. If he'd done that for Trump's campaign chairman, what was to prevent him from scouring the hidden accounts of the president?

The charges Mueller brought were not directly tied to the 2016 election, though he had undoubtedly also seized the defendants' emails and cell phone records from their work for Trump. This was a Mueller move meant to compel Manafort to scan his future and see two paths—one leading to growing old in prison, the other to cooperating with investigators. Mueller, who had once cut a deal with mafia hitman "Sammy the Bull" Gravano to take down the Gambino crime family, was using a similar playbook for the Russia probe, putting pressure on subordinates to get at the boss.

That same day, the special counsel disclosed that Papadopoulos had pleaded guilty to lying to the FBI, admitting that he had misled agents back in January about his knowledge that Russia had damaging material on Clinton. Again, there was meaning not explicit in the plea. Papadopoulos had surrendered after his brief stint in a Virginia jail cell in late July, which meant he'd been cooperating with prosecutors for three months before his deal with the special counsel was revealed. What he'd gathered in that stretch was for Trump and his legal team to guess.

Mueller wasn't done. Four weeks later, on November 30, Flynn pleaded guilty to lying to the FBI and agreed to cooperate with investigators. Flynn's falsehoods about his conversations with Kislyak had been known since the *Post*'s story in February, but the charging materials revealed damning new details, including that Flynn had consulted with senior Trump transition officials before and after his conversation with the Russian ambassador—in other words, that his request that Russia not retaliate (and implied signal that Trump would soon be in position to lift the Obama sanctions) wasn't a case of the future national security adviser freelancing but undermining existing American policy in consultation with others close to Trump.

The leniency of the deal was remarkable and telling. Flynn

averted a long list of additional possible charges Mueller could have brought including Flynn's failure, like Manafort, to register as a foreign agent. Instead, the former national security adviser was allowed to plead guilty to a single criminal count. His son's close involvement in his foreign consulting work also likely rendered him vulnerable if the special counsel wanted to apply maximum pressure, but Mueller left him unscathed as part of an agreement in which prosecutors expressed their support for a reduced sentence for the older Flynn because of his acceptance of responsibility. Those were major concessions by Mueller, suggesting Flynn had something valuable to provide prosecutors in return.

The indictments and guilty pleas offered the first glimpse of Mueller's course, but were also powerful markers that afforded the special counsel new protection. His investigation was delivering results. Any Trump attempt to fire Mueller now carried additional risks—of bolstering the obstruction case against the president, of causing rebellion within his own party and, perhaps, of inviting a backlash by the public.

On November 21, just two days before Thanksgiving, Mueller met with Dowd and raised the prospect of questioning Trump directly. He was moving onto delicate legal terrain—no sitting president had ever been forced to testify as part of a criminal probe. The question of whether a special counsel or any prosecutor can compel a president to testify is not entirely resolved, though presidents Clinton and Nixon had surrendered in their efforts to avoid providing testimony or evidence when faced with a subpoena. There were important distinctions in those cases—Clinton succumbed to political pressure and agreed to testify voluntarily (though only after the independent counsel had issued, and then agreed to withdraw, a subpoena), while Nixon was compelled to turn over records, not testify. The issue is one of constitutional complexity: the executive and judicial branches of government are co-equal, and some legal experts believe a subpoena of a president can be considered an intrusion on his powers and duties. Others see no conflict.

Mueller appears not to have raised the threat of subpoena in this initial, exploratory conversation with Dowd, but months later he would when negotiations over the president's testimony broke down. Dowd's aversion to allowing Trump to testify in part hinged on his assessment of the Mueller probe: he didn't believe that the special counsel had compelling evidence of any criminal conspiracy involving Trump and, therefore, was far from meeting any legal threshold to expect sworn testimony from the president. But of course there was a more fundamental concern about putting Trump in any situation where he faced legal sanction for failing to be truthful. Trump's performance during the 2006 deposition he faced as part of his lawsuit against the author of a book claiming Trump's net worth was a fraction of what he claimed it was had caught him in dozens of falsehoods. (The lawsuit was thrown out.) How could someone who racked up untruths as rapidly as Trump survive even an hour-long grilling by Mueller and his small army of veteran federal prosecutors, an encounter in which anything deemed a lie could be charged as a crime.

In early January, Mueller raised the issue again, this time in a conversation that included another of the president's lawyers, Jay Sekulow. A frequent pro-Trump voice on Fox News and Christian radio broadcasts, Sekulow had emerged in some ways as the public face of the president's legal team. He served as counsel for the American Center for Law and Justice, an organization founded by televangelist Pat Robertson that sought to advance Christian causes in court. The role led to several appearances by Sekulow in cases before the Supreme Court, and he was credited by some with helping to convince the Trump administration to nominate Neil Gorsuch to the court in 2017.

The meeting with Mueller on January 8 was meant to serve as

a more detailed discussion of the special counsel's interest in questioning the president. Dowd had asked for a run-down of subjects that Mueller wanted to raise, and the special counsel responded with sixteen areas of interest.[2] Prosecutors wanted to take Trump through the timeline of Flynn's conversations with Kislyak and subsequent statements once inside the White House. They wanted to see what Trump knew and when about the signal that Flynn had conveyed to Kislyak as well as the warning from Sally Yates about his vulnerability to Kremlin blackmail. There were questions about Trump's reaction to Sessions's recusal, to Comey's testimony revealing the investigation of the Trump campaign's contacts with Russia. They wanted to ask the president about his efforts to enlist Coats, Rogers, and others to help contain the expanding probe or issue misleading public statements about the evidence. There were numerous questions about Comey's firing and Trump's contradictory explanations. Finally, there were questions about Trump's involvement in drafting the highly misleading statement about his son's meeting with a Russian lawyer at Trump tower seeking damaging material on Clinton.

The questions were deliberately vague, designed to delineate broad subject areas without revealing Mueller's hand or spooking the president in a way that might discourage him from cooperating. The special counsel and his team went out of their way to depict the request to speak to Trump as pro forma, as if it were merely a step needed to tie up loose ends before wrapping up a probe that they knew the president was desperate to conclude. Mueller even used Marine jargon with Dowd, saying he merely wanted to "square his corners"—a reference to the taut sheets on a bed ready for military inspection—before winding down the Russia probe.

But the thrust of the questions Mueller and his team laid out was unmistakable: The special counsel was digging into decisions and actions by the president that could form the basis for a case that Trump had sought to obstruct justice.

By then, investigators had amassed a wealth of material and testimony from dozens of sources. Mueller's team had already interviewed Sessions, Comey, Kushner, Flynn, Priebus, Yates, Coats, Rogers, Pompeo, Hicks, Spicer, Stephen Miller and other senior figures who were serving or had served—some very briefly—in the Trump administration. Mueller had been ushering witnesses before a grand jury impaneled in August at the federal courthouse in downtown Washington. The probe was also ingesting classified reports from the Treasury Department, the NSA, CIA and other spy services. It had transcripts of Carter Page's conversations gathered under a repeatedly renewed FISA wiretap. It was sitting on a small mountain of emails, phone records, bank filings and other documents obtained about individuals associated with the Trump campaign, the administration and the president's business empire. The White House alone had turned over 20,000 pages of material, including 5,000 pages relating to Flynn and Russia, and another 8,000 about the firing of Comey.

When word of the Mueller request to meet with Trump leaked to the media later that month, the president reacted with characteristic bravado. "I would love to do it, and I would like to do it as soon as possible," he said to reporters at the White House.[3] He dismissed allegations that he had sought to obstruct justice, saying that he had merely been "fighting back" and that there was "no collusion." Then he took a dig at Clinton, noting that she had not been under oath when she was interviewed by the FBI in the email case. "I would do it under oath," he said, "absolutely."

In public, Trump's lawyers stepped on the brakes. Later that night, Cobb said to a reporter that the president had only meant to signal that he was *willing* to meet with Mueller, not that any agreement was in place. The next day, Dowd went a step further, saying that he—and not Trump—would be the one to decide.[4]

Behind the scenes, however, the president and his attorneys had already embraced a plan for Trump to sit down with the special counsel, a tentative deal that was rapidly unraveling. Weeks earlier, Dowd had come to Trump with a proposal that would have had the president speaking under oath to the special counsel on subjects worked out in advance by Dowd and Mueller by the end of January. The negotiations were still under way, but Dowd treated the development as a breakthrough and Trump seemed enthusiastic. The planning had progressed to the point that Trump's lawyers and Mueller had set a date and location: January 27 at Camp David, the wooded White House retreat in the Maryland mountains. Cobb, White House Chief of Staff Kelly, and assorted aides were even beginning to work out logistics—helicopter transport, room assignments, and the delicate choreography of the actual interview. Trump's impulsive remarks had accurately reflected his own eagerness and hidden progress.

Then, seemingly out of nowhere, Dowd pulled the plug. With little more than a week to go, the president's lawyer went to his client to say he had changed his mind and now adamantly opposed any sit-down with the special counsel. The risks of doing so had been obvious from the outset, but it was as if the magnitude of that decision had not fully registered with Dowd until the Camp David date got closer. He couldn't turn on a television without seeing a panel of legal experts warning that putting Trump in a room with Mueller verged on malpractice. And while Dowd still believed Mueller was playing a weak hand, the rapid timeline gave him and his team almost no time to prepare a president who had a notoriously short attention span and refused to engage in anything that resembled homework. Trump, Sekulow, and Cobb—

now keyed up by the promise of a deal and largely kept in the dark about Dowd's growing doubts—were stunned by the collapse of the interview plan.

"Dowd had presented it to the president as a great achievement and was very enthusiastic about it," one participant in the discussions said. "And then, stunningly, he did a backflip."

In fact, Dowd had secretly begun drafting an extraordinary letter to Mueller, a 20-page "Confidential Memo" responding to the special counsel's areas of interest and rejecting his request to speak with the president. Investigators already had all the evidence and testimony they needed from other witnesses and documents, Dowd wrote. "All of which clearly show that there was no collusion with Russia, and that no FBI investigation was or even could have been obstructed."

The document went far beyond the interview question, delivering blistering attacks on the special counsel, the credibility of his witnesses, and the foundations of the conspiracy and obstruction charges he seemed to be contemplating. It read as an angry, pre-emptive refutation of the report Mueller was expected to deliver.

The letter provided a roadmap for Republican efforts to discredit the investigation—efforts that were to intensify in the ensuing months. Dowd's missive cast the entire probe as compromised by "the astounding public revelations about the corruption within the FBI and Department of Justice." It made a series of esoteric legal arguments for why Mueller failed to reach certain thresholds to reasonably expect testimony from Trump, and (in a passage that was widely panned as outdated legal thinking) why FBI investigations were not covered by the obstruction statute.

The memo devoted pages to an elaborate defense of one of the most seemingly incriminating actions by the president, his alleged attempt to pressure Comey to back off any investigation of Flynn and "let this go." Dowd noted that Trump denied saying those words, then proceeded to argue that even if he had they didn't amount to obstruction—an odd hedge if it were true he hadn't made the comment. Finally, the president's lawyer turned the whole Flynn episode on its head, and implied that, if anything, Trump should be praised for firing his national security adviser. "Far, far from obstructing justice," Dowd wrote, "the only individual in the entire Flynn story that ensured swift justice was the president."

There was a similarly elaborate explication of Trump's firing of Comey. Dowd attacked Comey's credibility, said that he had been "fired in disgrace," and was such a disastrous director of the FBI that Sessions and Rosenstein had eagerly concurred with the need to remove him. It was in this lengthy Comey section that the letter made its most sweeping and controversial assertion.

"As you know," Dowd wrote, "a president can fire an FBI director at any time for any reason . . . no president has ever faced charges of obstruction merely for exercising his constitutional authority." Dowd then went a step farther, saying that "a president can also order the termination of an investigation by the Justice Department or FBI at any time and for any reason"—a staggering, and legally questionable, assertion of presidential power. By Dowd's logic, a president could fire prosecutors and shut down probes without obstructing justice even if his actions were *intended* to do so. Congress could impeach, but short of that scenario, Dowd seemed to be saying, one of the core concepts of American jurisprudence—that no one is above the law—had one glaring exception: the president.

Around one in the afternoon on Saturday, January 27—the very day that Trump was to have sat down with Mueller—Dowd arrived at the White House to go over the memo with the president. Trump was dressed informally in a white shirt with no tie or jacket. Dowd had dispensed with a tie as well, wearing slacks and a blazer. The duo sat at a table in the living room on the second floor of the residential quarters of the White House, a space with expansive views of the Mall and monuments. Trump (somewhat uncharacteristically) took his time reviewing the lengthy document. He asked a few questions, but made no markings and proposed no changes. Then he leaned back in his chair.

"Now I see what you're doing," he said in a way that made it seem his spirits had been lifted.

The two septuagenarians talked for a while about the strategy outlined in the memo and the challenges ahead. Dowd remained convinced that Mueller's case for conspiracy and obstruction was flimsy, and that the special counsel was playing a dishonorable game of "gotcha," racking up charges of lying to investigators and individual financial fraud without getting any closer to proving campaign or Russia-related crimes. Suddenly Trump was looking past the short-term legal obstacles and at the eventual lifting of his cursed "cloud." His elation provided a rare glimpse of his sense of vulnerability, the relief he expressed revealing the weight he had been carrying because of the probe. "This," he said to Dowd, "is one of the best days I've had." Trump's good mood was still intact when he called Dowd the next morning. "I slept so well," Trump said, and "feel so good about what we're doing."

Emboldened, Dowd delivered the memo (by then also signed by Sekulow) to Mueller by hand two days later, expecting it to serve as the final word on the special counsel's request to meet with the president. It wasn't. Mueller was undaunted by any aspect of Dowd's letter—its broadside attacks on the integrity of the probe, its novel interpretations of the Flynn and Comey firings, its distended Constitutional arguments. Instead, Mueller would respond with further indictments, pass leads to other prosecutors regarding the president's longtime lawyer and fixer, and soon signal that he was prepared to subpoena the president.

THE FALLOUT FROM RUSSIA'S ELECTION INTERFERENCE HAD played out mainly in Washington and Moscow. In the final months of 2017, the repercussions reached another capital that rivaled those others in global influence: Silicon Valley.

Facebook founder Mark Zuckerberg had been notoriously dismissive of the network's responsibility for the deluge of manipulative and misleading information leading up to the 2016 vote, saying days afterward that "to think it influenced the election in any way is a pretty crazy idea," and that it demonstrated a "profound lack of empathy" to suggest "the only reason someone could have voted the way they did is they saw some fake news."

By September 2017, the company faced a painful reckoning. In a blog post that month, Alex Stamos, the company's chief security officer, said that an internal review had uncovered evidence that Russian operatives had purchased about 3,000 geographically-targeted Facebook ads during the campaign on divisive issues ranging from gun rights to immigration to race to LGBTQ. The payments for those ads totaled $100,000.

Independent researchers suspected that Facebook was wildly understating the scope of the problem. Albright, the data journalism professor who had focused his research on social media, saw the Stamos blog post as a variant of the very scourge Facebook was vowing to stamp out, calling it "selective framing, a partial truth." For example, Stamos had written in his blog that the Russian ads were connected to 470 different Facebook "pages"—the online repositories for all the postings by an individual or organization—but hadn't said anything else about them in his post.

Companies, clubs, nonprofits, news organizations and other groups and individuals buy Facebook ads not only to directly sell or solicit, but to promote specific posts and attract more followers to their pages. Attracting a larger audience ensures that subsequent posts (including those that aren't promoted through ad payments) have a bigger and bigger reach. Albright wondered why Facebook hadn't disclosed the number of *free* posts put out by those 470 pages, or the number of followers they had. That was precisely the type of information Facebook routinely shared with advertisers, literally at the company's data-compiling fingertips, yet now it went unrevealed.

He suspected that the company was hiding something. The reach of free content, he presumed, would likely be orders of magnitude larger than the minimal reach of those 3,000 ads.

In the weeks following Facebook's initial blog post, the names of some of the Russian-backed pages trickled out. A fake Black Lives Matter page was called Blacktivist. A fake LGBTQ page was called LGBT United. Other names included Heart of Texas, Being Patriotic, Secured Borders. (One group, it later emerged, even tried to pit pro-Beyoncé fans against Beyoncé haters.) Facebook has an analytics tool called CrowdTangle that advertisers can use to assess the effectiveness of their campaigns. Anyone with access to CrowdTangle can see the number of followers for a given Facebook page, along with the number of interactions, such as likes, comments, and shares. Albright began looking at the performance of six known Russian pages on CrowdTangle. What he found was astounding: free content from those pages alone had been "shared"—Facebook's technical term for the number of times they surface in people's newsfeeds—340 million times. And Facebook had said there were 464 more pages linked to Russian ads. Albright estimated that the number of times content from all the Russian pages showed up in people's feeds could reach into the billions.

Albright's revelation put enormous political pressure on Facebook.[5] At the same time, Facebook's Silicon Valley rivals also unearthed evidence of Russian meddling in their own digital stables: Google found ads across its YouTube, Gmail, and search properties. The Russian campaign was so successful on Twitter that the company's own founder and CEO, Jack Dorsey, was among hundreds of thousands of Americans who had been duped into retweeting Internet Research Agency content, sharing it with tens of millions of followers.[6]

In late October, Silicon Valley's most powerful companies were summoned to Washington. For months, Facebook, Google, and Twitter had been doling out information about Russian activity on their networks on their own, self-serving terms. Now their lawyers would be under oath, forced to answer to Congress. In a preemptive move, Facebook put out a press release the night before the hearings began acknowledging the magnitude of Russian meddling through its network. In contrast to their earlier estimates, Facebook now said some 126 million Americans—nearly half the U.S. population—had been exposed to content strewn across Facebook by Russian operatives.[7] It no longer seemed "pretty crazy" to imagine the impact.

It was also increasingly difficult to believe that Russia's interference had not been a factor in Trump's win.

U.S. intelligence agencies had pointedly not rendered any judgment on the actual impact of the Kremlin's cyber-assault. But Trump and his top officials and Congressional allies distorted that position repeatedly, twisting the agencies' refusal to tackle that question into a supposed determination that Moscow's meddling had no impact. Vice President Pence, spokeswoman Sarah Huckabee Sanders, House Majority Leader Paul Ryan all asserted publicly that the Kremlin's schemes hadn't mattered. Refusing to concede that possibility had become a firewall for nearly everyone who worked for the president. In perhaps the most egregious instance of such devotion, Pompeo, while serving as CIA director, misrepresented his own agency's position during an appearance at a 2017 security conference in Washington.

"The intelligence community's assessment is that the Russian meddling that took place did not affect the outcome of the election," he said. It was an assertion so demonstrably false that his own press office had to issue a statement saying that nothing about the agency's conclusions on Russia had changed and that "the director did not intend to suggest that it had." Even that struck a false note. Pompeo, in fact, had a consistent pattern of erring in his public statements on this issue, always in line with Trump.

As Facebook, Twitter, and Google began to take measure of the Russian incursions into their networks, the math became overwhelming. Besides the 126 million people fed Russian propaganda on Facebook, tens of thousands of Russian bots had pumped out pro-Trump messages to roughly 1.4 million users on Twitter—a seemingly modest number until retweeting (including by Trump) massively increased the reach of those bogus and manipulative snippets. A BuzzFeed analysis concluded that in the final months of the campaign fake stories—mostly favoring Trump—spread farther and faster online than legitimate news. This was not even counting the impact of the thousands of emails stolen from Democratic party computers by Russian intelligence agencies and dumped online via WikiLeaks.[8] That some Trump loyalists dismissed the power of Twitter to shape public opinion was especially ironic given the president's unwavering embrace of the medium.

Clearly there were other critical—and probably more important—factors in the 2016 race, including Comey's handling of the email investigation and Clinton's own undeniable failings as a candidate. Even so, Russia's pro-Trump propaganda flooded into the Facebook and Twitter feeds of tens of millions of voters in an election decided by fewer than 80,000 ballots across just three states. To believe that Russian interference was immaterial required a willful ignorance of the power of such pervasive messaging—or an aversion to an uncomfortable truth.

As much as the tech companies tried to downplay their culpability, the image of the three general counsels of Facebook, Google, and Twitter in the Senate chamber showed that the ground had shifted for America's internet aristocracy. The scandal of Russian interference had cracked the grandiose illusions Silicon Valley had about itself—that its products only made people better informed, spread enlightenment, strengthened democracy. The industry would not be the same.

And Russia would not relent. In July 2018, Facebook said it had uncovered a new deluge of disinformation on its platform, dozens of false pages and profiles that had exposed nearly 300,000 users to divisive postings on race, feminism, and fascism—all of it material that had flooded into the network long after the 2016 race. The company did not finger Russia, but one of the main pages it identified was tied to the Internet Research Agency in St. Petersburg. Experts said the latest outbreak was a sign that Kremlin operatives were still active leading up to mid-term elections in the United States, but better at covering their tracks.

AS TRUMP'S ADVISERS AND ASSOCIATES WERE SWEPT UP INTO THE special counsel probe, he regained an important congressional ally in the early days of 2018. Nunes, the chairman of the House Intelligence Committee, had been cleared by the GOP-controlled House Ethics Committee of charges that he had revealed classified information after his surreptitious trip to the White House. That probe had forced him to step aside from the committee's Russia investigation, but now he was free to retake the reins. He wasted no time redirecting the committee's energies to Trump's advantage. On January 4, Nunes sent a letter to Rosenstein, the deputy attorney general, reiterating the committee's demands to see sensitive files related to the origin of the Russia investigation and revealing that the committee had embarked on "investigations into matters involving DOJ and FBI." Nunes demanded access to files and individuals at the heart of an active investigation. His committee wanted to question senior bureau and Justice officials, to see thousands of text messages between Strzok and Page that the bureau had yet to locate or turn over, and to review dozens of internal records tracing nearly every consequential development in the early stages of the probe. It was a massive fishing expedition aimed at uncovering material that could undermine the credibility of the inquiry. Rosenstein and FBI director Wray were aghast, but trapped between two powerful entities—the White House and the Republican-controlled Congress—with a shared interest in forcing them to comply.

Nunes zeroed in on one document in particular—the FBI's application for a FISA warrant to put Carter Page under surveillance. Republicans, who had been able to review the document in a classified setting, knew that the bureau had included references to the Steele dossier in its request for wiretapping authority, and saw the reliance on the work of the former British spy—bankrolled by the DNC—as a way to depict the application as tainted by politics. It was, Nunes and his supporters believed, their cleanest shot at obliterating public confidence in the Russia probe.

Days after the letter to Rosenstein, Nunes's aides began drafting a memo that plucked carefully selected passages of the classified FISA application. The Nunes memo served its disruptive purpose before it was ever glimpsed by the public. Republican backers of the president began depicting it as a bombshell proving that the whole probe had been shaped by political corruption. Fox News host Sean Hannity, who regularly spoke with Trump and appeared to coordinate on lines of attack against the special counsel, devoted his January 18 broadcast to breathless denunciations of the investigation. Alluding to the supposed revelations in the memo, Hannity stared into the camera with a message to Mueller: "Your witch hunt is now over."

Nunes's campaign to release the memo was cynical but effective. The document drew upon such highly classified material (at that point, no FISA application had ever been made public) that the bureau had no choice but to object to its release. And when it did, Trump's supporters insinuated that officials were covering up their own hostility to the president. But the document was in some ways more valuable to Trump and his allies when it could be cited as a frightening indictment of FBI corruption without having to defend its actual contents. At first, Nunes refused to let Wray or Justice Department officials see the memo he was vowing to release to the public. On January 24, the Justice Department fired off a letter to the House chairman saying that it "would be extraordinarily reckless for the committee to disclose such information" without giving officials the chance to review it and assess "the risk of harm to national security and to ongoing investigations that could come from public release." When Nunes relented and allowed Wray to examine the document the FBI director emerged even more alarmed. Wray found Nunes's creation packed with misleading assertions and worried that its release would set a dangerous precedent, inviting future presidents and lawmakers to troll through sensitive files for material to derail probes targeting political allies. More broadly, federal law enforcement officials were deeply troubled by what they saw as an attack on their ability to maintain control of evidence in the middle of an active investigation. They feared that Nunes was taking steps that could expose sources and even endanger lives.

The House Intelligence Committee voted along party lines Jan-

uary 29 to release the Nunes memo and rejected a plan by the committee's Democrats to issue a rebuttal. (The minority's response,
"Correcting the Record," was finally released nearly a month later).

The Nunes memo covered four pages but came down to one
core claim: that the FBI's application to wiretap Page had relied on
material from the Steele dossier but failed to "disclose or reference
the role of the DNC, Clinton campaign, or any party/campaign
in funding Steele's efforts, even though the political origins of the
Steele dossier were then known to senior DOJ and FBI officials." If
true, it would have gone a long way toward bolstering Republican
claims that the Russia probe was, as Trump so often asserted, a
politically tainted operation orchestrated by Democrats.

Trump was exultant. "This memo totally vindicates 'Trump' in
probe," he said on Twitter. "But the Russian Witch Hunt goes on
and on. Their [sic] was no Collusion and there was no Obstruction
(the word now used because, after one year of looking endlessly
and finding NOTHING, collusion is dead). This is an American
disgrace!"

But it wasn't true. The Nunes memo's false assertions were allowed to circulate for months before the public finally glimpsed
the FISA application itself and could see how it had been distorted.
Much of the 412-page record was smeared with black lines redact-
ing material still deemed too sensitive to release, but there was
more than enough intact to expose Nunes's efforts. Rather than
hide Steele's ties to the DNC, the FBI had devoted a nearly full-
page footnote to disclosing his political entanglements and potentially problematic motivations. The note said Steele—identified as
"Source #1"—had served as an FBI source and was considered
credible, but that the bureau had terminated its relationship with
him after learning that he'd shared his findings with the press.
Steele, the document noted, had been hired by someone who
"was likely looking for information that could be used to discredit

[Trump's] campaign." These details were not buried in an appendix but spelled out in bold type.[9]

The full application also contained startling language about Trump's campaign adviser, saying that the "FBI believes that Page has been collaborating and conspiring with the Russian government" and was likely serving as "an agent of a foreign power." The application was filed in late October 2016 (months after the "Crossfire Hurricane" investigation had begun with its initial focus on Papadopoulous—a fact rarely mentioned by Republicans) and renewed three separate times for additional 90-day increments. That meant the application had been scrutinized by four separate judges, all of them appointed by Republican presidents.

Nunes had charged the bureau with burying salient facts to advance a politically-driven attack on the president. It was hard to look at his memo and not conclude that what he had done was similar to what he had falsely accused the bureau of—seeking to deceive the public by deliberately hiding essential information as part of a politically-driven campaign against the FBI and Mueller investigations.

The fight over the memo was the opening of a months-long battle between Trump's congressional allies and the Justice Department. The House Intelligence and Judiciary Committees issued subpoena after subpoena, demanding document after document in the search for vulnerabilities to exploit. Justice turned over more than 800,000 documents, but Republican lawmakers kept moving the goal line, issuing new demands with shorter deadlines and accusing the department of stiff-arming Congress.[10] They wanted to see more FISA materials, internal records on the eternally-resurrected Clinton email probe, and details about a secret FBI informant—Stefan Halper, the professor at Cambridge—who had arranged meetings with Page and Papadopoulos. All of this was accompanied by a steady drumbeat of Trump tweets. "They don't want to turn over Documents to Congress. What are they afraid of?" he said May 2. "If the FBI or DOJ was infiltrating a campaign for the benefit of another campaign, that is a really big deal," he tweeted two weeks later about Halper, dubbing the informant's involvement "Spygate."

Republicans insisted they were just conducting vigorous oversight. Democrats saw the campaign as a political smear, and an attempt to give Trump cover to fire yet another DOJ employee—in this case, Rosenstein, who had provided the rationale for pushing out Comey but was by now seen by the president as yet another part of a "Deep State" anti-Trump conspiracy. In June, the House passed a resolution insisting that Justice comply with the subpoenas, a largely symbolic rebuke, but it was accompanied by a threat from one of the GOP members leading the attack, Republican Mark Meadows of North Carolina, who said that "contempt and impeachment" of Rosenstein could soon be "in order." (Meadows would eventually introduce just such articles, but they never reached the House floor.)

The effectiveness of the attacks on the FBI's reputation, particularly among Republican voters who had for decades seen themselves as the law and order party, was evident. In January 2017, before Trump took office, favorable views of the FBI among Republicans outnumbered unfavorable opinions by a nearly three-to-one ratio, according to a study by the Pew Research Center. By mid-2018, Republicans were nearly equally divided on the bureau—with the percentage holding a favorable opinion having plunged twenty-six percentage points.

Russia had set out with its interference campaign to discredit American democracy. The president was succeeding in doing much the same, damaging the reputations of institutions that are supposed to enforce America's laws and protect its citizens.

THE TRUMP-JUSTICE DEPARTMENT BATTLES PLAYED OUT AMID A flurry of developments on the Russia front. On March 12, Nunes shut down the House investigation of Russian interference, a month later issuing a report—endorsed only by Republicans—that concluded there had been no collusion between Russia and the Trump campaign.

On March 13, Trump fired Secretary of State Rex Tillerson, who had supposedly been in charge of managing relations with the Kremlin. Tillerson's language toward Moscow had become particularly strident after Putin presided over a video simulation of a new Russian nuclear tipped missile streaking toward the coast of Florida. The poisoning of the Skripals further incensed him; reacting to that attack, Tillerson said that Russia was "an irresponsible force of instability in the world, acting with open disregard for the sovereignty of other states and the life of their citizens."

Hours later, he was fired.

The termination had been rumored for months. Tillerson and Trump had clashed on other issues besides Russia, including the Iran nuclear deal and how to approach diplomacy with North Korea. But the firing was executed in typically haphazard fashion by the president in contrast to his choreographed reality-show dismissals. Tillerson was on an extended trip to Africa when he took a middle-of-the-night call from White House Chief of Staff John Kelly urging him to return to Washington before Trump announced his ouster on Twitter. Tillerson was on the toilet, afflicted with a stomach bug, when Kelly reached him. Tillerson made a beeline back to Washington, arriving around 4 A.M., and saw confirmation of his firing when it was reported in the *Post* followed by a Trump tweet. It took hours for Tillerson to get a call from the president.

In a farewell to State Department employees, where morale had plummeted during his tenure, Tillerson thanked diplomats for their "honesty and integrity" and the American people for their "acts of kindness." He made no mention of the president. Trump moved his ardent loyalist Pompeo from CIA into Tillerson's former spot, eliminating the chance of having another incompliant Secretary of State.

DOWD WAS THE NEXT TO DEPART.

Months after the placid meeting with Trump at the White House and the delivery of his memo to Mueller, Dowd found himself facing another attempt by the special counsel to secure a sit-down with the president. In a heated encounter in early March, Mueller had suggested for the first time that he was prepared to issue a subpoena for the president to appear before a grand jury. "This isn't some game," Dowd exploded. "You are screwing with the work of the president of the United States."

Mueller had by then provided a more detailed list of subjects he wanted to raise with the president. The new read-out was presented by his deputy, Quarles, at a meeting in late February in the special counsel's office. Mueller stopped in briefly, but left the session to his deputy. Dowd listened intently while Sekulow scribbled furiously onto a legal pad—notes that he would later distill into 49 separate questions. The queries built on the broad subjects Mueller had raised months earlier, but also pushed into some new areas. Now investigators wanted to know whether the president was aware of outreach by campaign advisers to Moscow about election assistance, as well as how had the president reacted when he learned that the special counsel was meeting with senior intelligence officials including Rogers, Pompeo, and Coats. Some of Mueller's questions centered on Mueller himself—he wanted to know how

Trump responded to the appointment of the special counsel, and whether he had considered having him terminated.

By this point, the question of whether Trump should meet with Mueller had become one of the most difficult and divisive matters for his attorneys to manage. Dowd had intended for his January memo to serve as a final answer. Sekulow, Cobb and others held more flexible views—understanding the concerns but seeing no reason to sever discussions and raise the hostility level with the special counsel. Trump continued to want a face-to-face showdown.

Dowd's relationship with the president during this period had turned volatile. Dowd, and other attorneys, were increasingly vexed by their inability to rein in the president's self-destructive behavior, including his intemperate "witch hunt" tweets that only complicated his legal position and needlessly provoked the special counsel. Almost all of his lawyers at one point or another had urged Trump to go silent on the Russia probe, at least on Twitter, but every intervention was futile. Trump, for his part, had grown frustrated with perceived inconsistencies in Dowd's legal recommendations. He and Dowd were heard having screaming matches as the strain of the situation intensified. "At that stage of the game they weren't having friendly conversations," one participant said. "And the president gets tired of people who say no to him."

Dowd, who increasingly operated without consulting the other lawyers, quietly began planning another attempt to shut down Mueller's effort to secure an interview with Trump. Through a variation of the approach he had tried in January, Dowd again began mapping out a lengthy memo providing answers to all 49 questions. In some cases it would point to answers given in others' testimony, or available from existing evidence. But Dowd was also composing new responses that would have the weight of sworn statements from the president. Dowd's plan was to deliver this document to Mueller with the intent that it would serve as Trump's only response to the special counsel's questions—in effect, the interview.

Other lawyers on Trump's team began to pick up on Dowd's plan in part because he was turning to junior members of the legal team for research help on portions of the draft. As the full scope of Dowd's endeavors came into view, the reaction among the other attorneys was overwhelmingly negative. Sekulow and others (including one brought onto the team by Dowd himself) raised immediate objections, saying that Mueller hadn't asked for such a document or given any indication that he would accept one in lieu of an interview. Turning over these answers and all of the underlying material to support them—without any clear language on the terms under which it was all to be delivered—would amount to handing the special counsel a massive piece of new evidence, one with detailed assertions and statements that the president would be accountable for. Any errant tweet or subsequent statement that wasn't consistent with the memo would compound his legal problems. And what if Mueller came forward with a subpoena anyway and Trump were compelled to testify? He would have to ensure that his answers were not at odds with this complicated, lengthy document.

"John was insisting on a written submission—a proffer," a person familiar with the matter said. "There was a group of lawyers who didn't want to send it." Others were more emphatic. "It would have been a reckless, unprecedented move that I think most serious criminal defense attorneys would be hard pressed to explain," a second person familiar with the discussions said. "Everybody would contend it was malpractice."

Ultimately, Trump sided with Sekulow and other lawyers against the new memo plan. Dowd, who had come out of retirement to take on the job of serving as the president's attorney, had lost a critical showdown. He resigned almost immediately thereafter, on

March 22, telling Trump that he couldn't continue if the president wasn't willing to accept his advice definitively on a matter as crucial as whether to sit down for an interview with Mueller. "I cannot sit next to you knowing this is not good for you," Dowd said. "This is like a doctor watching you medicate yourself."

Dowd's departure was followed by more turmoil in the Trump legal team, including the addition of Rudy Giuliani. But in the end, a version of Dowd's plan prevailed.

In November 2018, Trump's legal team submitted written answers to the special counsel, remarkable mainly for how comprehensively unresponsive they were. The president who had once claimed to have "one of the great memories of all time" became foggy about all things Russia. He couldn't recall whether he had learned about the Trump Tower meeting before it happened. He couldn't recall ever being told that Russia supported his candidacy, that campaign associates had been in contact with WikiLeaks, that members of his team were discussing a potential trip for him to Moscow, or that Russia-friendly alterations were being made to the Republican platform at the convention. In twenty-two answers, Trump used variations of "I don't recall" thirty-six times.

Mueller had also submitted questions about obstruction of justice—queries that attempted to get at Trump's intent when he prodded Comey to drop the Flynn probe, for example, or directed McGahn to have the special counsel fired. Trump and his lawyers ignored the obstruction questions entirely, refusing to reply. The gambit succeeded in large measure because Mueller, near the end of his probe, balked at subpoenaing the president.

Testifying in 2019, Mueller said that the special counsel had battled for a year to get Trump to testify but in the end feared that issuing a subpoena would lead to a protracted court fight—one likely to drag deep into the upcoming election year. Mueller's team believed it had the right to subpoena the president but decided it "did not want to exercise" that power "because of the necessity of expediting the end."[11] As a result, Mueller said, his team was left with answers that were "generally" neither truthful nor helpful. And Trump had avoided a legal showdown that his lawyers regarded with dread.

TRUMP TENDS TO EXPOSE HIS WEAK SPOTS AND WORRIES THROUGH the vigor of his attempts to deflect attention from them. In July 2017, Trump sat down with reporters from *The New York Times* for a wide-ranging interview and was asked how he would view any attempt by Mueller to scrutinize his finances. Would that be a breach of Mueller's authority, would that cross a red line? Would that mean that Mueller would "have to go"?

Trump took the bait. "I think that's a violation," he said. "My finances are extremely good, my company is an unbelievably successful company. And actually, when I do my filings, people say, 'Man.' People have no idea how successful this is." Stammering along, he claimed that he derived no income from Russia, and that even when he held the Miss Universe pageant there "it wasn't Moscow, it was outside of Moscow"—a bizarre distinction because it was just outside the city. Pressed on whether he would fire Mueller if the special counsel began digging into the Trump organization's financial records, Trump said, "I can't. I can't answer that question because I don't think it's going to happen."

On Monday, April 9, FBI agents raided the offices of Michael Cohen, Trump's longtime lawyer, personal fixer, and prospector of development deals—including the Trump Tower in Moscow proposed to Kremlin officials during the campaign. Michael Cohen had for years been a guardian of Trump's secrets, a trusted conduit of payouts to mistresses and others who might complicate the president's life—including a $130,000 payment to porn star Stormy

Daniels in the final months of the 2016 race that, beyond evidence of yet another Trump scandal involving women, might be construed as an illegal campaign donation. (A payment that Trump said he hadn't known about when confronted by reporters weeks earlier aboard Air Force One.) Agents seized piles of documents, computer records, and a vault of audiotapes kept by Cohen, who had a practice of recording his conversations with reporters he was badgering on behalf of Trump, women he was paying for their silence, and even, as it turned out, Trump himself. One tape appeared to show that Trump was aware that a *Playboy* model had made a deal with American Media Inc., the parent company of the *National Enquirer*, to sell the rights to her story of an alleged affair with him. The story was never published by the *Enquirer*, which was controlled by an ardent backer of Trump.

Trump spent much of the day staring at television screens as cable news channels aired coverage of the raids on Cohen's office, home, and hotel room in Manhattan. The agents were not operating under the orders of the special counsel, but the operation had Mueller's fingerprints all over it—it seemed clear that his investigators had come across evidence implicating Cohen that he regarded as beyond his purview (including alleged fraud related to New York City taxi medallions), and so passed it along to prosecutors of the Southern District in New York.

The raid of Cohen's office meant that the probe of Russian interference and possible collusion had spun off into another inquiry targeting one of the keepers of the president's personal and financial secrets. It was, one former U.S. attorney said, "like dropping a bomb on Trump's front porch." [12]

Trump spent the morning huddled with advisers, and much of the rest of the day venting to subordinates. He railed about Sessions for recusing and allowing all of this to unfold, and about Rosenstein, whom he blamed for approving the Cohen raids. In the late afternoon, as he prepared to meet with senior military officials on Syria, Trump let loose to reporters at the White House.

"They broke into the office of one of my personal attorneys, a good man, and it's a disgraceful situation," he said. He said again that he would have chosen a different attorney general, and that "many people" had urged him to fire Mueller. "It's a real disgrace. It's an attack on our country in a true sense," he said. "It's an attack on what we all stand for, so when I saw this and when I heard it, I heard it like you did, I said that is really now in a whole new level of unfairness."

Trump had never used the words "attack on our country" in reference to Russia, or spoken of "what we all stand for" in relation to that intrusion on American democracy, but he employed those phrases now in his furious indignation with the special counsel.

HELSINKI HAS FOR CENTURIES BEEN DEFINED BY ITS UNEASY PROX-imity to Russia. It was founded as a Baltic Sea port by Swedes who began building an island fortress, just off the city's coast, to guard against Russian aggression in the eighteenth century. But the star-shaped garrison walls were breached in 1808 by Russian forces that consolidated their control of the tiny citadel and seized control of all of Finland within a year. A merchant began building a lavish residence on the city's waterfront several years later, a neoclassical structure soon coveted by Tsar Nicholas I and converted to his imperial palace.

After agreeing on Helsinki as the setting for a summit with Putin, Trump's advisers made clear to Finnish officials that the palace—the most gilded structure in the Nordic capital—was the location that most appealed to a president who, like the Tsar, also collected extravagant properties and built his brand on gold-plated opulence.

Trump headed toward Helsinki after a weeklong trip through Europe in which he had again shown contempt for traditional allies. At a meeting of NATO leaders in Brussels, he berated his European counterparts, accusing them of being freeloaders on American-provided security, demanding they double their military spending and saying Germany was "captive" to Russia because of its natural gas imports. He then traveled to Britain where he took pointed jabs at Prime Minister Theresa May in an interview that was published one day before he appeared alongside her in a press conference. British officials kept him away from London, where a blimp of Trump's likeness clad in a diaper floated over gathering protests. At Windsor Castle he took tea with Queen Elizabeth then, during a ceremonial inspection of her guards, impatiently strolled in front of the 92-year-old monarch, briefly blocking her path in a minor faux pas.

Events in the United States leading up to Helsinki had also been turbulent.

In mid-June, Manafort became the first of Trump's former advisers to be taken off to jail for an extended period. The former Republican powerbroker was accused of witness tampering after contacting former associates in an apparent effort to coach them on testimony before his upcoming trial. His incarceration added to the pressure that the special counsel had been putting on Manafort for months, having secured a guilty plea and testimony from Gates, his former deputy, and bringing more charges against Trump's former campaign chairman with a new indictment. Manafort's refusal to turn on the president prompted speculation that he was counting on a pardon (perhaps with good reason—Trump's pardon of former Bush administration official Lewis "Scooter" Libby in April was seen as a signal that he might reward loyalists). Around noon on June 15, the political mercenary with multiple homes was led through the backdoor of the courtroom—turning around briefly to lift his hand in a reassuring wave toward his wife, who nodded in reply—to a jail in Warsaw, Virginia, as prisoner number 45343.[13]

On July 12, embattled FBI agent Strzok came into public view for the first time as a person with a voice rather than the collection of disembodied texts that had led to his bureau downfall. Testifying before the House Oversight and Judiciary committees, Strzok was excoriated by Republicans and threatened with contempt for refusing to answer questions about the inner workings of what became the Mueller probe. He was shamed for his conduct and perceived arrogance—at one point Texas congressman Louie Gohmert said, "When I see you looking with a little smirk, I wonder how many times did you look so innocently into your wife's eyes and lie to her about Lisa Page." South Carolina's Trey Gowdy accused the FBI agent of "an unprecedented level of animus," and grilled him on his intent behind the text in which he said "We'll stop" the election of Trump. Strzok's reputation would likely never recover from his conduct, but he insisted that he had not allowed his personal beliefs to affect the course of the Russia probe—noting that word of the investigation never leaked while the campaign was under way. After a bristling exchange with Gowdy, Strzok asked for a chance to respond uninterrupted. He delivered a three-minute monologue in which he said that he had sent his text about stopping Trump after watching the then-candidate mock the Khans, the Muslim parents of a soldier who had been killed in Iraq fighting for the United States.

"My presumption was . . . that the American population would not elect somebody demonstrating that behavior to be president of the United States," he said. "It was in no way, unequivocally, any suggestion by me the FBI would take any action whatsoever to improperly impact the electoral process." He had quieted his tormentors, if only for a moment. On August 10, Strzok was fired.

The final prelude to Helsinki was delivered by Mueller. On Friday, July 13, three days before Trump and Putin were to convene their summit, the special counsel unveiled an indictment that provided seemingly incontrovertible proof that Russia had hacked the American election. The details in the document were compelling and astonishing—the special counsel charged twelve specific Russian intelligence operatives with direct involvement in the plot, provided the addresses of their GRU workplace, described the "X-agent" malware they used to penetrate the DNC networks, listed the search terms they employed to scour Democratic databases and traced the bitcoin payments they used to lease computer servers in Arizona and Illinois (of all places) to serve as repositories for their loot. Mueller had the Russian agents' real names, but also the phony American identities they adopted—Jason Scott, Richard Gingrey—to promote the leaks of their purloined files when they were posted online. The special counsel had uncovered WikiLeaks' approach to the GRU (operating under the guise of Guccifer 2.0) to ask for the trove, promising a "much higher impact than what you are doing."

The granularity of the information was so striking that CIA veterans were astonished, saying they could not recall any Russia-related disclosure ever providing so much current insight into American espionage capabilities. (Russia House, among others, had clearly been working overtime.) It was also not only an indictment of Kremlin spies but of Trump's countless attempts to discredit and disparage a case that Mueller had now made virtually ironclad.

Rosenstein, who had survived Trump's repeated impulses to have him fired, had the unenviable duty of delivering the indictment personally to Trump at the White House, just days before he departed for Europe. While the president was away, Rosenstein issued a statement in Washington. Some of his words seemed aimed at the ears of the traveling commander-in-chief. "When we confront foreign interference in American elections, it is important for us to avoid thinking politically as Republicans or Democrats and instead to think patriotically as Americans," he said. "Our response must not depend on which side was victimized." [14]

An ocean away, Trump conveyed his apparent disagreement and displeasure via Twitter days later: "Our relationship with Russia has NEVER been worse thanks to many year of U.S. foolishness and stupidity and now, the Rigged Witch Hunt!"

Trump arrived in Helsinki at 8:55 P.M. on Sunday, with the city still bathed in abundant daylight at a northern latitude where the sun would not set until 10:30 P.M. He arose the next day for breakfast with Finland's president, then waited for Putin's plane to touch down. Helsinki was in some ways home turf for the Russian leader, a Baltic neighbor of St. Petersburg where he had started his career in politics as an adviser to the mayor.

Demonstrations of dominance were inevitable between two leaders given to masculine posturing. Putin arrived in Helsinki an hour behind schedule and seemed to be employing the same tactic he often used with guests at the Kremlin to establish that it was his timetable that mattered, no one else's. He then climbed into a Russian-made limousine—a model noticeably larger than the so-called "beast," the armored Cadillac in which the American president traveled—that Putin had brought to Helsinki to make its debut. And while Trump's car may have been shorter, his motorcade was longer, with 33 vehicles, compared to just 23 in the Russian convoy.

The two men made their way toward the center of Helsinki past a smattering of protests. One of Finland's leading news outlets, *Helsingin Sanomat*, had placed ads on electronic billboards along the presidents' route taunting them with the same message in both Russian and English: "Welcome to the Land of Free Press." They arrived at the palace in the early afternoon, and posed for pictures seated in a room decorated with columns, historic shields of

Finnish provinces and a chandelier hanging from a domed recess, their countries' flags displayed as a backdrop. Trump leaned forward at the edge of his seat, Putin slouched, gripping the arm of his chair firmly with his left hand.

The camera crews were escorted out, as were the leaders' entourages, save two interpreters who would be the only witnesses to this closed-door encounter. Trump and Putin spoke privately for nearly two hours. Once done, they shook hands and moved into an adjoining room, the Hall of Mirrors, for a lunch with their staffs. On Trump's side of the table were John Kelly, Fiona Hill, Mike Pompeo, U.S. ambassador Jon Huntsman Jr., and John Bolton, who had traveled to Moscow weeks earlier to make final arrangements for the summit.

Trump's aides had spent the days leading up to the event coaching and coaxing him to maintain a tough posture toward Putin— especially in front of the press or public. For a time, he seemed to comply. After lunch and their private conversation, the two leaders gathered for a press conference in a palace ballroom packed with American, Russian, and international reporters. They stood on a riser, five Russian and five United States flags behind them, and read statements scripted for this high-pressure moment.

"Our relationship has never been worse than it is now," Trump bluntly said. He then made his first apparent ad-lib, declaring "that changed as of about four hours ago." He claimed that he had brought up Russia's interference in the U.S. election and "addressed it directly with President Putin. I felt it was a message best delivered in person. Spent a great deal of time talking about it." He then moved on to say they had conversed about nuclear proliferation, negotiations with North Korea, the crisis in Syria, and prospects for improved ties between their two countries. "I would rather take a political risk in pursuit of peace," he said with a Kennedy-esque cadence, "than to risk peace in pursuit of politics."

Even before Trump had stepped onto the riser, Trump's aides—indeed, the entire room—had seemed on edge, as if waiting for an eruption that was inevitable. It came as Trump faced his first question from an American reporter who reminded him of his tweet earlier that morning about U.S. foolishness. He was asked whether he held Russia accountable for anything at all.

"Yes I do," he said. "I hold both countries accountable. I think we've all been foolish . . . And I think we're all to blame." Then, unable to resist any longer, he took aim at Mueller. "The probe is a disaster for our country. I think it's kept us apart . . . There was no collusion at all. Everybody knows it."

That was the moment of no return in Helsinki. Trump plunged into all his deepest insecurities about 2016 and its aftermath. Utterly unprompted, he said he had "beat Hillary Clinton easily . . . We won that race. And it's a shame that there could even be a little bit of a cloud over it." He recited his margin in the Electoral College and said there had been "no lying" to the FBI by Flynn, his fired national security adviser. He bragged he had run a "brilliant campaign, and that's why I'm president," then lashed out at U.S. intelligence agencies, political opponents, and investigations that were designed, in his mind, solely to deprive him of the glory of that victory.

Putin, who seeks control in all settings, seemed alternately bemused and unnerved by the unhinged display three steps to his right. When it was his turn, he repeated his ritual denials of meddling in the American election. He also outlined an extraordinary, cynical offer to help Mueller. U.S. prosecutors could travel to Moscow, Putin said, and working through Russian authorities question the accused GRU operatives. There would, of course, be a condition that the United States in turn grant Russian authorities access to perceived Kremlin enemies in America. Trump leaped at the proposal, oblivious to its implications, calling it "an incredible offer."

Putin's most telling moment came in response to a question aimed at him about Russia's actions. He replied with a line that distilled his world view and captured the disdain both men on the stage have toward truth and reality. "Who is to be believed and who is not to be believed," Putin said. "You can trust no one."

TRUMP'S PERFORMANCE WAS MET WITH SHOCK AND DISBELIEF IN the United States. Brennan, the former CIA director turned Trump nemesis, said that the American president's statements had exceeded "the threshold of 'high crimes and misdemeanors,'" a reference to conduct deemed impeachable. "It was nothing short of treasonous." Coats, Trump's own intelligence director, issued a statement saying that the nation's spy services had not wavered from their conclusion that Russia was engaged in "ongoing, pervasive efforts to undermine our democracy." It was a message of repudiation from inside Trump's own administration. Senator John McCain, wheelchair bound by brain cancer, said that "no prior president has ever abased himself more abjectly before a tyrant."

The final question Trump faced in Helsinki was from an American reporter who challenged him, "with the whole world watching," to denounce what Russia had done in 2016 and warn Putin in person not to repeat it. It was an opening that might have transformed his presidency, a chance to alter, in a moment, how he will be regarded by history. Even a tepid endorsement of his intelligence agencies, or a tame upbraiding of Putin, would likely have brought the accolades and respect he so desperately seems to crave. But he couldn't bring himself to do it. Instead, Trump launched into a disjointed discussion of conspiracy theories about a DNC server and the missing Clinton emails. He equated the credibility of U.S. intelligence officials sworn to defend the Constitution with that of the former KGB agent standing next to him.

"I have great confidence in my intelligence people," he said. "But I will tell you that President Putin was extremely strong and powerful in his denial today." In Trump's vocabulary, there are no words of higher praise than "strong and powerful." They are adjectives he applies constantly to himself, regardless of circumstance, and among the attributes he admires most in others—particularly Putin.

The Russian leader appeared to be knocked off balance by the sustained election-related questions. Asked whether he had wanted Trump to win and had ordered his spy services to work to that end, Putin seemed exasperated and blurted out—before it was clear that he had fully heard the second half of the question—"Yes, I did. I did. Because he talked about bringing the U.S.-Russia relationship back to normal." Putin summarized his view of the American preoccupation with the election allegations by saying he had never seen "nonsense of a bigger scale than this."

Putin had fielded the final question, but it was Trump who took the last word. Unplugging the earpiece through which he could listen to a translation of the Russian leader's statements, Trump leaned into his microphone and took a parting shot against the FBI agent who had sat down at a bureau keyboard two years earlier to open the Russia probe, and whose private texts were now a weapon to discredit it. "If anybody watched Peter Strzok testify over the last couple of days—and I was in Brussels watching it—it was a disgrace to the FBI, it was a disgrace to our country," Trump said. "You would say that was a total witch hunt."

The two leaders, entangled forever by the 2016 election, shook hands, clasped shoulders, and walked past their countries' flags off stage. Their separate motorcades carried them from the former palace of the tsar to the airport in Helsinki, along miles of road cordoned off by Finnish police. Trump boarded Air Force One at 8:19 P.M. for the eight-plus-hour flight back to Washington—to the White House, to the witch hunt, to the awaiting American carnage.

EPILOGUE

ON THE THIRD DAY OF SPRING IN 2019, A WALL OF FRIGID WIND and water gathered north of Washington. By late afternoon, the squall line began sweeping across the capital, unleashing an incongruous, concentrated blast: hail, lightning, rain, thunder, and snow. Wind gusts reached nearly sixty miles per hour. Temperatures plunged twenty degrees. Then, minutes after it began, the freakish front was gone, giving way to a dull sky of mammatus clouds.

Under these precarious conditions, a car from the FBI fleet departed Patriots Plaza in southwest Washington, heading north across the National Mall toward the Department of Justice. Inside, a security officer clutched 448 pages of portentous material, the results of an investigation that had cast its own pall over the city— one the president had often referred to as a cloud.

The Mueller Report was burdened with expectations that it would not only reveal the reasons for Trump's inexplicable behavior toward Russia but also go far in determining the country's course. Had the president conspired with Russia to win office? Was he acting under the coercive leverage of *kompromat*? Was impeachment, with the prospect of a constitutional crisis, in store? Here, many thought, would be the answers.

But the document, like the vehicle it traveled in, was arriving at a time of profound turbulence in the nation's capital, a period in which facts, evidence, and the rule of law—the raw material of the special counsel—were no longer reliably prevailing currents in American democracy. Trump and his allies (not only almost every Republican politician but right-leaning media figures who fostered a conspiratorial echo chamber) had devoted the better part of two years to denigrating Mueller and his team, seeking to ensure that the report was greeted with deep skepticism and derision by the president's political base. The report would be entrusted to a newly sworn attorney general, who approached the assignment with the mindset of a defense lawyer. The document would then be presented to Congress and the public, both of whom would be baffled by its contradictions and equivocations, incapable of divining any clear direction.

And then there was Mueller, whose restraint and rectitude had seemed such ideal attributes throughout the investigation but quickly became liabilities. When pulled against his will onto the public stage one last time, the visibly enervated special counsel suddenly seemed to embody the frailties of the nation's virtues.

IN THE EARLY MONTHS OF 2019, WHEN MUELLER'S TEAM WAS PUT-ting the finishing touches on the final report, the White House was in the throes of a fresh round of upheaval as a pair of attorneys from opposite ends of their profession's spectrum crossed into and out of Trump's orbit.

Michael Cohen, Trump's bottom-feeding "fixer," had spent nearly a dozen years demonstrating ferocious fealty to his client, only to turn on him venomously when he felt abandoned by the president. William Barr was, by contrast, a highly pedigreed Washington attorney with an agile mind and unflappable manner.

Barr's deep association with the Republican establishment (he had contributed $55,000 to support Jeb Bush in 2016[1]) seemed more likely to place him in the ranks of "never-Trumpers." Instead, Barr auditioned masterfully for a role in Trump's cabinet and almost immediately became the president's most powerful defender.

Cohen's break from Trump was breathtaking in its drama and execution. The Coney Island native had been critical to Trump's efforts to contain two potentially devastating disclosures in the final months of the election: the truth about Trump's pursuit of business in Moscow well past the Republican primaries, as well as his hush-money payments to an adult film actress and model.

But the stakes for Cohen in smothering those stories had changed radically after the April 2018 raid of his home and office. By then, he was already aggrieved by his exclusion from the Trump administration. He felt so mistreated by Trump that he alternated between pleading with his former patron on the phone—"Boss, I miss you!"[2]—and meeting conspicuously with the president's adversaries, including Dallas Mavericks owner Mark Cuban.

In the days after the raids, Trump posted a series of tweets describing Cohen as "a fine person" with a "wonderful family" who had made his own impressive mark in the world of business. "Most people will flip if the government lets them out of trouble, even if it means lying or making up stories," Trump said. "Sorry, I don't see Michael doing that."

Cohen did exactly that just four months later, pleading guilty to eight fraud and campaign finance violations, including two in which he implicated Trump—referenced anonymously as "Individual 1" in court filings.

On August 22, the day after Cohen pleaded guilty and began cooperating with Mueller, Trump lashed out on Twitter: "If anyone is looking for a good lawyer, I would strongly suggest that you don't retain the services of Michael Cohen!" In ensuing attacks, he accused Cohen of doing "TERRIBLE" things, including "fraud, big loans, taxis, etc."—a reference to Cohen's ownership of New York City taxi medallions. He called Cohen a "weak person" and turned on Cohen's previously "wonderful family," suggesting that his father-in-law should be investigated for corruption.

Unlike many of Trump's targets, Cohen was accustomed to such brawling. On February 27, 2019, shortly before he was scheduled to begin serving a three-year prison sentence, he appeared before the House Oversight Committee.

"I am ashamed of my weakness and misplaced loyalty—of the things I did for Mr. Trump in an effort to protect and promote him," he said as the hearing opened, later adding, "He is a racist. He is a conman. He is a cheat."[3]

It was fair to treat Cohen's new display of conscience with skepticism, and there were moments of hypocrisy. (At one point, the attorney who had once threatened a reporter investigating Trump to "tread very fucking lightly because what I'm going to do to you is going to be fucking disgusting"[4] chastised lawmakers for their lack of decorum.) But many of his words rang true. The documents he brought, including a copy of the check Trump had written to cover payment to Stormy Daniels, were damning. And before it was over, Cohen managed to deliver one of the most moving admonitions yet to those who would compromise their principles for the president.

When GOP lawmakers hoisted a sign calling Cohen a liar, the witness responded with pained understanding. "I'm responsible for your silliness because I did the same thing that you're doing now for ten years," Cohen said. "I protected Mr. Trump for ten years. Look at what's happened to me. I had a wonderful life . . . And I've lost it all."[5] But, as had been true so many times during Trump's ascent, the accomplice's contrition came too late.

AS COHEN TESTIFIED, AN EAGER NEW PROTECTOR WAS ARRIVING.

Two weeks earlier, the Senate had voted to confirm Barr as attorney general. At sixty-nine, he was covered in the East Coast credentials supposedly despised by Trump's base. Both parents had taught at Columbia University, though his father left to become headmaster of the Dalton School, an elite prep academy in Manhattan. Barr earned his bachelor's degree and master's degrees, in Chinese and government, at Columbia.

In the early 1970s, as the counterculture wars raged, Barr went to work for one of its favorite targets. During his tenure as a CIA analyst, he showed none of the misgivings he would express years later when he all but accused the agency of spying on a Republican presidential candidate.

Barr seemed to be on a promising but unexceptional trajectory—earning a law degree at night—until 1989, when he was appointed by President George H. W. Bush to head the Justice Department's Office of Legal Counsel. Under Barr, the office became a bulwark of presidential power. He provided legal cover for the U.S. invasion of Panama and the "rendition" of its leader, Manuel Noriega, to the United States to stand trial.

Barr's assertive posture so impressed the first Bush White House that, in 1991, he was nominated to serve as attorney general. His two years in that position were marked by a massive mobilization against gangs, drugs, and violent crime.[6] Federal prisons expanded and their populations exploded. His signature work was a 1992 report, *The Case for More Incarceration,* which argued that "the benefits of increased incarceration would be enjoyed disproportionately by black Americans."[7]

In one of his final actions, after Bush lost the 1992 presidential race to Bill Clinton, Barr advised the outgoing president to pardon a half dozen officials who had been convicted for their roles in the Iran-Contra scandal—a move that signaled his willingness more than a generation ago to thwart an independent prosecutor.

Barr would spend the next twenty-six years earning millions of dollars as a corporate lawyer while mostly remaining on the political sidelines. But in 2018, as a new Republican president faced another special counsel, Barr saw an opening.

In June, he wrote an unsolicited memo to the Justice Department, addressed to Deputy Attorney General Rod Rosenstein, in which he argued that the entire Mueller probe was founded on a "fatally misconceived" legal theory.[8] At its core, his paper made the case that presidents could not be accused of obstructing justice through the exercise of their authority—in other words, that firing an FBI director, suggesting a case be dropped, or issuing pardons to influence possibly hostile testimony should be beyond criminal scrutiny. Only when a president stepped beyond his powers—by, say, indisputably destroying evidence—could he legitimately face sanction.

The memo was full of incendiary language. It said that Mueller's approach was "grossly irresponsible" with "potentially disastrous implications." At a time when investigators were desperately seeking access to Trump, Barr said, "Mueller should not be permitted to demand that the President submit to interrogation."

The memo arrived just as Sessions was entering the final humiliating stretch of his tenure. "Attorney General Jeff Sessions should stop this Rigged Witch Hunt right now," Trump tweeted on August 1. Weeks later, he complained in an interview that he had "put in an Attorney General that never took control of the Justice Department."[9]

On November 7, the day after Democrats took control of the House, Trump finally put Sessions out of his misery.

BARR RETURNED TO THE NATION'S TOP LAW ENFORCEMENT JOB
having substantially more in common with Mueller than with the
president. He and Mueller had known each other for three decades
and owed their most prestigious appointments to Bush presidents.
Mueller was a guest at the weddings of two of Barr's daughters,
and their wives attended the same Bible study. In his confirmation
hearing, Barr said that he had told the president that the Barr and
Mueller families "were good friends and would be good friends
when this was all over." [10] He described Mueller as a "straight
shooter" and maintained that the probe should be allowed to finish
unimpeded—none of which prevented Barr from plotting ways to
contain the looming threat his "good friend" posed to the president.

A lifetime of bureaucratic maneuvering had given him exquisite
political instincts. He understood in ways the president could never
grasp that a frontal assault on the report—an attempt, for instance,
to prevent it from being released to the public—was not only un-
tenable but also probably unnecessary. Doing so would have extended the Russia scandal, putting enormous political pressure on
Trump, and Barr never gave any indication that he contemplated
such a step. Instead, Barr would take advantage of his keen aware-
ness of Mueller's tendencies, especially the special counsel's deep
aversion to publicity or violating the chain of command. Instead
of seeking to bury the report, Barr would use the discretion of his
office to delay, distort, and distract.

Five weeks after Barr was sworn in, on March 22, the first sealed
copy of the special counsel's final report was delivered to Barr's
desk with a cover letter bearing Mueller's signature. There were
no elaborate handling instructions—Mueller would never give the
attorney general direction—but the report contained executive

summaries that seemed drafted specifically so that something of substance, and scrubbed of any sensitive material, could be shared immediately with the public.

Barr ignored them. Instead, he spent the next two days composing a four-page letter to Congress that would serve as his highly subjective substitute. He couched the move as an act of apolitical consideration, saying that he had determined it was "in the public interest to describe the report and summarize the principal conclusions." Before disclosing the bottom line, he emphasized his sober deliberations, his consultations with other Justice Department officials, and their many months of interaction with Mueller.

Then, on the second page, he revealed that the special counsel "did not find that the Trump campaign or anyone associated with it conspired or coordinated with Russia."

Nearly three years after the FBI had opened the Russia probe, it was remarkable to see those words and that conclusion. Trump supporters inevitably pounced, seeing vindication in their howls about the merciless, meritless "witch hunt." Many of the president's political opponents and most ardent public critics, on the other hand, reacted with a combination of disappointment, skepticism, and confusion.

The outcome would inevitably lead to introspection, and even second-guessing, within many of the nation's newsrooms. But the reality was that many of the reporters most immersed in the story had long seen reasons to doubt the case for direct "collusion." As they'd investigated the story, and observed the presidency in action, it became nearly impossible to imagine the chaotic and often inept Trump campaign executing such an elaborate conspiracy. There were also holes in logic—for example, the campaign's clumsy efforts to figure out what WikiLeaks had would have been unnecessary if Trump operatives were working hand in glove with Russia. And then, counterintuitively, there was also Trump's behavior. A politician under actual control of the Kremlin would be coached to act tough toward Russia while quietly easing sanctions, not publicly fawn over Putin. And while Trump's immense ego might have left him confident enough to believe he didn't have to hide his fidelity to the Russian leader, the consistency of his bonding with autocrats throughout the world was more indicative of aspiration than allegiance.

It was always possible, and apparently assumed by a large part of the American public, that Mueller would find evidence of secret collaboration. But by spring of 2019, the more pressing question about the probe—and the area of greatest perceived vulnerability to the president—was obstruction of justice.

This was where Barr did his most deftly suffocating work. The attorney general noted, with almost parental disappointment, that when it came to the seemingly binary question of whether Trump had illegally impeded the investigation, Mueller had "ultimately determined not to make a traditional prosecutorial judgment." Providing no clues to Mueller's reasoning, Barr leaped into this vacuum. Mueller's indecision, Barr wrote, "leaves it to the attorney general to determine whether the conduct described in the report constitutes a crime." His unsurprising verdict: it did not.

To bolster the legitimacy of this conclusion, Barr noted that he had consulted other officials in the Justice Department. He emphasized the lack of evidence "of an underlying crime" whose investigation the president would have intent to obstruct. Barr also enlisted the endorsement of Rosenstein. It was a final act of ethical contortion for the deputy attorney general, who had gone from abetting the firing of Comey to plotting the removal of the president,[11] from protecting the special counsel from the president's attacks to eviscerating his work on obstruction.

Mueller had left no indication that he had intended to defer judgment to Barr or Rosenstein. But the impact was substantial and permanent. "Mueller Finds No Conspiracy" was splashed across the front page of *The Washington Post* the next day. Variants of that headline raced across television screens, erupted in email alerts, and spread virulently across Twitter and Facebook. Deeper in their coverage, news organizations noted that Mueller had not exonerated the president. But without the full text of the report, and predictable silence from the special counsel, the public's perception began to harden.

"No Collusion, No Obstruction, Complete and Total EXONERATION," Trump tweeted triumphantly. "KEEP AMERICA GREAT!"

On the same Sunday that Barr dispatched his letter, Mueller made a rare public appearance, attending services at St. John's Episcopal Church across Lafayette Square from the White House, a historic chapel where every president since the early 1800s has prayed.

Over the next three days, as members of Mueller's team grew restive with how the report was being depicted in news coverage, the special counsel sent a pair of pointed letters to the attorney general. The first, on Monday, asked Barr to release the executive summaries. The second, on Wednesday, was more sharply worded: Mueller complained that Barr's depiction "did not fully capture the context, nature, and substance" of the investigation. Moreover, it had fostered "public confusion about critical aspects" of the special counsel's findings.

Barr later testified that he had found the second letter "kind of snitty" and had called the special counsel. "I said, 'Bob, what's with the letter? Why don't you just pick up the phone and call me if there's an issue?'" The American public, which had also yet to hear from Mueller, could probably relate to the sentiment.

Had Mueller's letters been revealed at the time, they might have triggered public outrage, calls for Barr to resign, and urgent congressional hearings. All three of those things would occur eventually, but only after Barr had taken additional cracks at distorting the special counsel's findings.

On April 9, he falsely testified that he was unaware of any dissatisfaction on the special counsel team. At the same time, Barr declared that he believed spying on the Trump campaign "did occur" and that he was mounting an investigation into the origin of the Russia probe—how and why the FBI had decided to launch an investigation and if it was prompted by political bias.

Nine days later, as the Department of Justice finally prepared to release the full report, Barr staged a preemptive press conference where he proclaimed that Trump's anger toward the special counsel and attempts to end the probe were understandable because he "faced an unprecedented situation." Trump, Barr added, was being hounded by investigators, pilloried in the press, and denounced as a traitor in public, and "yet, as he said from the beginning, there was no collusion." It was a clever and disingenuous defense from the leader of a law enforcement agency that routinely sent ordinary citizens to prison for obstructing justice, no matter how righteous or well founded their indignation.

Visually abetted by his droopy features and tortoiseshell-framed glasses, Barr fended off questions about his handling of the Mueller Report with an expression of bemused boredom. Pressed on whether it might be improper for him to comment so extensively on a report he had yet to allow the public to see, Barr said no and walked away from the podium.

WHEN IT WAS FINALLY MADE PUBLIC ON MARCH 22, 2019, THE *REport on the Investigation into Russian Interference in the 2016 Presidential Election* proved to be a remarkably comprehensive and compelling— yet flawed—document.

A *Washington Post* critic judged it the "best book on the Trump

White House so far," with depictions of conduct so venal and dialogue so vivid—"I'm fucked!"—that it would have strained credulity in any fictionalized account of the White House.

The report was divided into two volumes. The first, on Russia's
wide-ranging election assault and innumerable interactions with
Trump associates, was largely familiar to anyone who had followed
coverage of the story or skimmed Mueller's earlier indictments.
The DNC hack, the meeting at Trump Tower, Flynn's calls to
Kislyak, and all that followed had transpired almost exactly as news
reports had indicated—a near total exoneration for the media.

The second, and in many ways more revelatory, volume documented eleven episodes in which the president had arguably
acted in ways that impeded or attempted to obstruct investigators.
Among them were Trump's:

- refusal to acknowledge Russian meddling and false denials of
  his pursuit of a Moscow real estate deal;
- appeals to Comey to drop the Flynn investigation;
- prodding of Pompeo, Coats, and others to declare him innocent;
- termination of Comey;
- scheming to fire or constrain the special counsel;
- efforts to conceal the purpose of the Trump Tower meeting;
- pressure on Sessions to un-recuse and take control of the
  Russia probe;
- haranguing of McGahn to have Mueller removed (and then
  falsify records to suggest otherwise);
- and attempts to discourage Flynn, Manafort, and Cohen from
  cooperating with prosecutors.

Cumulatively, the case seemed overwhelming. The report noted
that in many instances Trump's orders were thwarted only by his

subordinates' refusal to execute them. McGahn, the White House counsel, had helped investigators reconstruct such episodes over days of testimony bolstered by the notes he kept over the strenuous objections of the president.

Even the footnotes on the pages of this volume served as damning miniature portraits of the president's enablers. ("I'll get the president to send out a positive tweet about you later," Kushner told Flynn after his forced resignation.[12])

Mueller's lawyers dissected the episodes and the president's probable motivations in blocks of text that checked off the statutory components of obstruction (intent, nexus to legal proceeding, etc.).

And then . . .

And then . . .

Nothing.

No determination, caveated or otherwise, of how Trump's conduct might be considered in a court of law. No clear view into the professional interpretations of the members of Mueller's team, among them some of the nation's most experienced prosecutors. Not so much as a suggestive note on what Congress, the Justice Department, or the American people were now supposed to do. Instead, there were sentences entangled in double negatives and tortured conditionals. Indeed, the signature line of the Mueller Report was a muddled declaration of what the special counsel could *not* conclude: "If we had confidence that the president did not commit a crime, we would have said so."

The rationale that Mueller cited for refusing to reach a conclusion was a nineteen-year-old opinion by the Office of Legal Counsel that stated: "the indictment or criminal prosecution of a sitting president would impermissibly undermine the capacity of the executive branch to perform its constitutionally assigned functions." Mueller, however, found reason to hesitate well short of this legitimate barrier to prosecuting the president. Even saying that a president committed a crime was problematic, Mueller decided, because the fact that a president couldn't be tried for that crime deprived him of a venue to contest the charges. (Why Mueller didn't think that such a conclusion could be rendered in private, or why he did not see impeachment as a viable process for litigating such charges, was left unexplained.) In fact, there is no language in the law delineating this constraint that Mueller felt he could not surmount. Instead, he described it as a matter of decency, a fundamental issue of "fairness."

Barr mocked Mueller for this show of restraint. During a Senate hearing, he marveled at Mueller's logic, saying that if he was not going to "go down the path of making a traditional prosecutive decision, then he shouldn't have investigated" Trump in the first place. In a television interview, Barr said that Mueller "could've reached a decision as to whether it was criminal activity." [13]

Hundreds of other legal experts tried to fill in the space that the report had left empty. In early May, a group of more than 450 former federal prosecutors—who had served in Republican and Democratic administrations—signed a public statement declaring the evidence so overwhelming that Trump would have been charged were it not for his office. "Each of us believes," the statement said, that the president's conduct in any other context would have resulted "in multiple felony charges for obstruction of justice." [14] But none of them was named Robert Mueller.

AMONG THOSE MOST EMOTIONALLY AND POLITICALLY INVESTED IN the prospect of impeachment—the president's impassioned critics and a large faction of Democrats in Congress—there was a palpable let-down after the report's release. In some, that manifested as denial and a refusal to let go of the idea of Mueller as savior. For others, there was frustration and confusion.

In the House, where an impeachment proceeding would have to begin, the issue divided Democrats. Speaker Nancy Pelosi was adamantly opposed to an exercise that she believed would only animate the Republican base, ultimately be repelled by Senate Republicans, and possibly spell electoral doom for her party's new but fragile majority. Others believed that directing sustained public attention to the president's conduct could only turn voters against him, and they saw impeachment—whatever its political ramifications—as an unshirkable duty. Among them was Congressman Jerry Nadler, the chairman of the House Judiciary Committee, which would have jurisdiction over any impeachment proceeding.

The one point of agreement for both factions was they wanted to hear from Mueller.

His reluctance to testify was predictable for someone who had avoided the spotlight throughout his career and regarded even the intermittent public testimony required of an FBI director as a senseless chore. At the same time, it was unrealistic, if not selfish, for someone engaged in government service of such gravity to expect to be excused from any public accounting.

The House Judiciary and Intelligence Committees opened negotiations with Mueller within days of the release of the report. The talks were laborious and ground on for nearly four months. All the while, Barr's version of the report's findings remained virtually unchallenged in public.

The special counsel's opening position, according to an official involved, was "we would like you to drop the idea of having him testify." Mueller's representatives gradually, grudgingly, gave ground. They proposed a closed hearing, then a hybrid with a brief appearance followed by a closed session. In the end, Mueller capitulated to nearly a full day of testimony, split into two sessions—but insisted that he be subpoenaed (and was) to formalize that he had been compelled to attend.

Such obstinacy revived rumors about Mueller's health that had surfaced months earlier, whispers that the former workaholic was mysteriously absent at times and had delegated much of his decision-making. But when reporters raised these delicate questions, the special counsel's office pushed back strenuously. Allies dismissed the rumors as smears designed to reduce confidence in Mueller and imply that the probe was really being run by, as Trump alleged, a staff of "hardened Democrats." And while members of the committees had heard similar concerns about Mueller's health, they would have no direct interactions with him until he arrived at the Rayburn House Office Building on the morning of his long-awaited testimony. There had been one faint hint of concern, but it seemed significant only in hindsight.

Members of both committees went to extraordinary lengths to prepare for Mueller, reviewing videos of his prior appearances before Congress dating back more than a decade. They were struck anew by how evasive and obstinate he could be. Democrats on the House Intelligence Committee even staged mock hearings in which a former prosecutor was cast as Mueller and played him as a hostile, monosyllabic witness.

Two days before Mueller was to appear, a member of the special counsel team registered a last-minute objection. News reports had suggested that the House Intelligence Committee was considering altering the previously agreed upon five-minutes-per-member format to bundle questions in fifteen-minute rounds. Andrew Goldstein, one of the senior prosecutors, called Daniel Goldman, a former federal prosecutor who had been hired by Congressman Adam Schiff to run the Intelligence Committee's Russia investigation.

"It's a really bad idea" to change the format, Goldstein said, adding cryptically that Mueller would do better with more frequent opportunities to "reset" and that the special counsel was "almost 75 years old."

THE SILVER-HAIRED FIGURE WHO SETTLED INTO THE WITNESS chair before the House Judiciary Committee at 8:30 A.M. appeared virtually unchanged from his years as FBI director—his slightly forward lean as he stood, the set jaw, the deep part, and the dark brows all instantly familiar.

He opened with much the same statement he had recited on camera weeks earlier in one last attempt to satisfy the public's need to hear his voice and avoid further testimony. He then laid down a terse marker, warning that he would not stray from the language of a document on which he saw no need to elaborate. "The report is my testimony," he said, "and I will stay within that text."[15]

But from the moment Mueller set aside that prepared script, it was clear that something was amiss. In his opening exchange with Nadler, he stammered, searched for words, and seemed uncertain about the answers to such basic questions as whether any White House official had refused to testify.

On the inevitably central question of whether Trump had truly been exonerated, Mueller responded with what sounded like mush: "Well, the finding indicates that the president was not—that the president was not exculpated for the acts that he allegedly committed."

Some would later say that poor acoustics made it hard for Mueller to hear members' questions. His aversion to uttering anything provocative also undoubtedly contributed to his stilted performance. But it was impossible over the course of that day not to wonder whether the former FBI chief, once known for being deeper in the weeds on the bureau's cases than most of its agents, had lost some cognitive function.

Democrats seemed determined to squander the moment they had sought for so long, asking long, meandering questions even when it became clear that Mueller was struggling to keep up. Belatedly, some tried prompting Mueller simply to recite damning passages from the report, only to have him refuse. Congressman Ted Lieu briefly seemed to score a startling concession from Mueller—that only Justice Department guidelines had kept him from indicting Trump for obstruction of justice. But then, after a midday break, Mueller took it back, essentially saying he had misspoke.

Mueller seemed more comfortable in the afternoon session, before House Intelligence, where the focus turned to Russia's interference and away from the potential crimes of the president. The most compelling exchange of the day was orchestrated by Schiff, himself a former prosecutor, who led Mueller through rapid-fire questions requiring only a few words to answer.

Russia interfered in sweeping and systemic fashion, right?

"That is correct."

Trump campaign officials welcomed the Russian help, did they not?

"That occurred, yes."

Trump campaign officials built their messaging strategy around the stolen DNC documents?

"Generally that's true."

And then they lied to cover it up?

"Generally that's true."

The staccato exchange covered the entire damning chronology and seemed to help Mueller recover his footing. And yet, by the end of the day, the hearings were widely regarded as a disaster for the Democrats who staged them and a victory-sealing outcome for the president.

Mueller's shaky performance (he asked lawmakers to repeat themselves at least forty-eight times) undoubtedly contributed to this perception. But his willful refusal to see a broader role for himself in a moment of national crisis was equally important.

Millions of Americans tuned in to his testimony—many of

them undoubtedly bewildered by the events of the past three years, lost in a forest of fragmentary media accounts, combative cable television segments, and the stream of falsehoods from the president. Here, finally, was a chance to have the two-year probe, the 448-page report, distilled to its most salient elements by a voice of knowledge, experience, and authority. Instead, Mueller retreated deeper into the myth of his own reticence.

Many had expected the outcome of the Russia probe to turn on the characters of its two main protagonists. And in a perverse way, it did. Throughout his life, Trump has exploited the advantage that often falls to someone who fights dirty over someone who fights fair. It is a mindset that is almost a matter of pride for the president, and he used the power of his office to impede the investigation at every turn. But in the end, Trump prevailed more in spite of his efforts than because of them. The most significant obstruction on the path to impeachment was not the president or his actions, but Mueller's rigid code and the constraints that he alone imposed on the Office of the Special Counsel.

THE FINAL TALLY OF THE RUSSIA PROBE IS A TESTAMENT TO THE resilience of the rule of law. The special counsel indicted or secured guilty pleas from three companies and thirty-four individuals. Among them were six former advisers or close associates of the president. The cases against Flynn, Manafort, Gates, and others exposed a level of corruption and venality in American politics—money laundering, payoffs, profound betrayals of the public—that would likely have gone undetected and unpunished were it not for Mueller's team as well as Trump's incriminating conduct. It was Trump, after all, who drew attention to these crimes. He was the reason for the special counsel.

For all its flaws, the investigation did help the country achieve a measure of closure. Because of Mueller, the country can be reasonably confident that an American president did not gain office by conspiring with an enemy state, an outcome that should be reassuring, though it is also disorienting. So much of Trump's apprentice-like behavior toward Putin seemed to make sense only in the context of criminal conspiracy. What we are left with is the profile of a president who is a sincere admirer, and covets the power, of one of the world's most malignant tyrants. The Mueller Report's final pages include the obligatory line, drawn from an 1882 Supreme Court case, that in the United States no person "is so high that he is above the law." The post–Russia probe reality, however, raises new questions about that aspect of the national legend. The report catalogs abuses of power and potential criminality on a scale beyond anything the country has seen since Nixon. But that same document concludes with a line of near-meaningless equivocation: "While this report does not conclude that the president committed a crime, it also does not exonerate him."

Perhaps Mueller and his team intended for that line to signal to the country that the case was not yet closed and to serve as an invitation to Congress. But without even reading the report, Trump understood its elemental implications. Mueller was trying to say the Russia cloud was still there, but Trump knew that it had lifted.

MUELLER'S MOST COHERENT AND IMPASSIONED HEARING MOMENT came late in the day, when asked whether the Russia threat had been a one-off assault on American democracy. He bristled. "It wasn't a single attempt," he said. "They're doing it as we sit here, and they expect to do it during the next campaign."

In June, three months after the report's release, Trump arrived at yet another global summit and again sought a private audience with Putin. In what has become a ritual opening to their encounters, the two leaders sat before a spray of cameras and Trump was pressed on whether he would finally warn the Russian leader to stay out of American politics.

"Yes, of course I will," Trump said, a smirk spreading across his face. "Don't meddle in the election please," he told Putin, raising his right finger in a mock scolding gesture. "Don't meddle in the election."

The smirk remained and spread to Putin's face.

ON THE MORNING AFTER ROBERT MUELLER'S HALTING TESTIMONY removed whatever threat the Russia probe had ever posed—seemingly ending any prospect of impeachment—Donald Trump single-handedly put his presidency in its gravest peril yet with a thirty-minute call. The conversation with the leader of Ukraine was supposed to be pro forma, a few words of congratulations after the country's parliamentary elections, perhaps a brief message of encouragement for the president of a country besieged by Russia and beset by corruption. Instead, Trump turned the call into a shakedown, an attempt to use the power of his office to coerce cooperation from Ukraine on investigations that would benefit Trump personally and politically—and had no meaningful relation to the national security priorities of the United States.

A former state of the Soviet Union still fighting decades later for its sovereign life, Ukraine was a particularly needy—and, to most U.S. foreign policy experts, worthy—recipient of American support and aid. Ukraine counted on steady, $400-million installments of security assistance to help it withstand Russian-backed military groups seeking to carve up the eastern half of the country. Perhaps most of all, Ukraine's reform-minded new leader, Volodymyr Zelensky, wanted a meeting with the American president, a photographed handshake from inside the White House that would serve as a potent symbol and deterrent to Moscow.

For years, the U.S. foreign policy establishment, Republican and Democrat, had seen supporting Ukraine—and countering Russia—as unambiguously in American interests. Trump seemed to size up Ukraine's vulnerabilities and see something else that attracted his interest in almost any context: a mark.

Trump spent much of the call emphasizing how generous the United States had long been toward Ukraine, and complaining that America hadn't gotten enough in return. "We do a lot for Ukraine," Trump said.[16] "I wouldn't say that it's reciprocal necessarily because things are happening that are not good but the United States has been very good to Ukraine." Zelensky all but prostrated himself to assuage Trump's concerns, telling the American president that the United States was Ukraine's biggest partner, expressing the country's deep gratitude, and, in a gesture he no doubt thought would speak more compellingly to the cash-minded president, vowed that Ukraine was ready to spend tens of millions of dollars on U.S. military hardware, including Javelin missiles, to survive a conflict that had already claimed more than 13,000 lives.

Trump cut him off.

"I would like you to do us a favor though," Trump said, "because our country has been through a lot and Ukraine knows a lot about it." In typical Trump fashion, the train of thought meandered in ways that were difficult to follow. But he made the favor he was asking explicitly clear. It was Ukraine, Trump said, that was behind the interference in the 2016 election, and it was Ukraine that was not hiding the supposed evidence that the whole episode had always been what Trump said it was: a hoax. "That whole nonsense ended with a very poor performance by a man named Robert Mueller, an incompetent performance," Trump said, barely sixteen hours after Mueller had finished testifying on Capitol Hill. "But they say a lot of it started with Ukraine. Whatever you can do, it's very important that you do it, if that's possible."

Trump's claims were beyond baseless, veering into areas of conspiracy so far-fetched that even his allies refused to entertain them. Among the most egregious was that the computer equipment Russia hacked in 2016—the scene of a crime documented in extraordinary depth by the FBI and Mueller's team—actually hadn't been targeted by Russia at all but were props in a plot launched from Ukraine to discredit the Trump campaign and entangle it with Russia. In his mind, Trump had turned that collection of exploited computer servers into a single device. "The server, they say Ukraine has it," he said, suggesting that the evidence that could finally prove his fantastic conspiracy theories had been smuggled to Ukraine and hidden from the world.

Trump went on to list more demands. He wanted Zelensky to meet with his personal lawyer, Rudolph Giuliani, for direction on how to pursue an investigation of this plot, but also to coordinate on another probe that Trump hoped would deliver dirt on Democratic presidential nominee, and former vice president, Joe Biden. Trump urged Zelensky to revive a dormant Ukrainian anti-corruption investigation of an energy company, Burisma, that had once employed Hunter Biden, the son of the vice president. To get all this right, Trump wanted Zelensky to coordinate with Giuliani as well as Attorney General William Barr. "There's a lot of talk about Biden's son," Trump said. "A lot of people want to find out about that so whatever you can do with the attorney general would be great."

The magnitude of this abuse of the institution of the presidency is hard to overstate. On a White House phone, on a call witnessed by as many as a dozen others in the executive branch, an American president was commissioning a political hit job from a foreign government, and using hundreds of millions of dollars in taxpayer money, as well as that very status of the Oval Office itself, as leverage of coercion on a vulnerable American ally. A president who had spent much of his tenure seeking to fend off allegations that he had colluded with a foreign government to win the presidency followed his miraculous political victory over that threat by seeking to collude with a different country—though a neighbor of Russia—as the election of 2020 approached.

In time, the broader breadth of this scheme came into view after a CIA employee—someone familiar with the inner workings of Russia House—filed a whistleblower complaint against the president on August 12 after learning from White House counterparts about the call. Within weeks, after a *Washington Post* story disclosing that the whistleblower complaint centered on a troubling Trump phone call, an impeachment inquiry was under way in the House of Representatives. The testimony and revelations came in waves, revealing other disturbing events. The July 25 Trump-Zelensky call had been preceded months earlier by the removal of a U.S. ambassador who had sought to prevent Ukraine from becoming a political pawn; by cable television appearances by Giuliani all but proclaiming his determination to commandeer the U.S.-Ukraine relationship to help the president; and the secret text exchanges of American diplomats deputized by Trump to close the deal with Zelensky before any White House meeting, or further military aid, would be allowed. But in the end the most damning evidence was the call itself, Trump in his own words, laying out his own scheme, consumed by his own destructive impulses.

In many ways, the scandal over Trump's attempts to produce damaging information on Joe Biden was inextricably linked to the scandal that Mueller had investigated. There was overlapping geography and there were recurring characters, including Giuliani and Barr. There was of course the familiar outline of foreign interference and a president who not only welcomed it—"Russia, if you're listening"—but actively sought it. As the scandal grew, there were the well-rehearsed attacks on those who testified against the president, with tirades on Twitter and demands that the whistleblower be unmasked.

But there were deeper interscandal connections relating to 2016 and Trump's lingering grievances about that race. Trump harbored resentment toward Ukraine because he believed that Manafort's financial crimes—many of them grounded in his lucrative work in Kyiv—had been exposed in the middle of the 2016 race to damage Trump's candidacy. Other connections touched on the psychology of the president. Trump's inability to accept the reality of 2016, that Russia had interfered on his behalf, may be the most compelling reason he placed his presidency at risk. He appears to have seen in Ukraine a chance to rewrite that history, and replace it with wild conspiracy theories that were easier for him to accept: it was Ukraine all along, not Russia, that had sought to undermine him.

No matter when Trump leaves the White House, it seems unlikely that history will treat him kindly. The wreckage of his attacks on democratic norms and institutions, the damage to America's reputation in the world, will outlast his tenure. For Vladimir Putin, who had authored the 2016 campaign to destabilize the United States through the instrument of the Trump presidency, the payoff continued deep into the impeachment proceedings on Ukraine. That was another connection between the two scandals: losses for America, gains for the Kremlin.

ACKNOWLEDGMENTS

THIS BOOK IS A MEASURE OF MY GREAT FORTUNE TO BE A MEMber of the *Washington Post* staff, working alongside some of the most talented editors and reporters in journalism at a time of historic purpose—and challenge—for our profession. Our ability to navigate this daunting terrain is a testament to the leadership of a collection of editors who set an unfailing example of integrity, determination, and excellence.

Among them are Executive Editor Martin Baron, Managing Editors Cameron Barr, Emilio Garcia-Ruiz and Tracy Grant, National Editor Steven Ginsberg, Deputy National Editor Lori Montgomery, Senior Politics Editor Peter Wallsten, and Political Investigations Editor Matea Gold.

I am particularly indebted to National Security Editor Peter Finn, a graceful and generous colleague and friend, who made this book possible with his leadership, ideas, encouragement, and patient attention to every word written on these pages—and by the national security staff for the past five years.

That staff is remarkable for its skill, resourcefulness, and camaraderie. I wish to honor the exceptional talents of Adam Entous and Ellen Nakashima, who generously collaborated with me on stories that were among the most complex and consequential in our careers. I am grateful to Greg Jaffe and Julie Tate for their friendship, encouragement, and expertise.

I owe thanks to reporters across the newsroom whose contributions were critical. Among them are Devlin Barrett, Robert Costa, Josh Dawsey, Karoun Demirjian, Karen DeYoung, Elizabeth Dwoskin, Marc Fisher, Tom Hamburger, Shane Harris, Rosalind S. Helderman, David Hoffman, Sari Horwitz, Spencer S. Hsu, David Ignatius, Carol D. Leonnig, Ashley Parker, Philip Rucker, Craig Timberg, Anton Troianovski, Julie Vitkovskaya, Scott Wilson, Dan Zak, and Matt Zapotosky. Thanks also to photo editors MaryAnne Golon, Robert Miller, Olivier Laurent, and Chloe Coleman for pulling the photo insert together. Brooke Lorenz and Shani George worked tirelessly to draw attention to our reporting.

Geoff Shandler, the editor of this book, provided unwavering encouragement and took painstaking care with every page. Andrea Molitor went to extraordinary lengths in production editorial to incorporate every possible development yet get the book out on time. And Raphael Sagalyn, literary agent extraordinaire, helped shepherd the project to life.

The Apprentice builds on stories *by The Washington Post* that won the Pulitzer Prize for national reporting in 2018 with new material from hundreds of interviews with senior officials in both the Obama and Trump administrations, as well as in Moscow. We are indebted to our sources. The book benefits from the important work done by dozens of other news organizations. With that in mind, I wish to extend my sincere compliments to the staffs of *The New York Times, Los Angeles Times, The Wall Street Journal,* CNN, and NBC for their work. We are rivals who share a common commitment to journalistic principles that are as important to uphold now as at any time in history.

Most of all, I thank my wife, Rebecca, for the love and support that sustain me.

NOTES

A note on sources: This book is largely based on reporting by the staff of *The Washington Post* and includes interviews with hundreds of U.S. and foreign officials, most of whom requested anonymity to speak frankly. The book also draws on the work of numerous other news organizations and authors. Dialogue in the book is based on interviews with people who participated or were briefed on the exchange.

PROLOGUE

1. https://www.nytimes.com/interactive/2017/01/22/us/politics/womens-march-trump-crowd-estimates.html.
2. CIA World Factbook 2017 https://www.cia.gov/library/publications/the-world-factbook/rankorder/2066rank.html#rs.

CHAPTER 1: **THE HACK**

1. http://video.foxnews.com/v/4519442873001/?#sp=show-clips.
2. Hillary Clinton, *What Happened* (New York: Simon & Schuster, 2017), p. 300.

CHAPTER 2: **PUTIN'S TROLLS**

1. *Moscow Times*, October 16, 2017.
2. https://www.politico.com/story/2016/07/dnc-by-the-numbers-226037.
3. "Russian government hackers penetrated DNC opposition research on Trump," *Washington Post*, June 14, 2016, https://www.washingtonpost.com/world/national-security/russian-government-hackers-penetrated-dnc-stole-opposition-research-on-trump/2016/06/14/cf006cb4-316e

-11e6-8ff7-7b6c1998b7a0_story.html?noredirect=on&utm_term=.d34
8db25f213.

4. Raffi Khatchadourian, "Julian Assange, a Man Without a Country,"
New Yorker, August 21, 2017.

CHAPTER 3: **MOTHS TO THE FLAME**

1. https://www.theguardian.com/world/2017/dec/22/trump-carter-page
-phd-thesis-trump.

2. Those agencies are the Office of the Director of National Intelligence,
Central Intelligence Agency, National Security Agency, Defense In-
telligence Agency, Federal Bureau of Investigation, Department of
State—Bureau of Intelligence and Research, Department of Homeland
Security—Office of Intelligence and Analysis, Drug Enforcement Administration—Office of National Security Intelligence, Department
of the Treasury—Office of Intelligence and Analysis, Department of
Energy—Office of Intelligence and Counterintelligence, National
Geospatial-Intelligence Agency, Air Force Intelligence, Surveillance
and Reconnaissance, Army Military Intelligence, Office of Naval Intelligence, Marine Corps Intelligence, and Coast Guard Intelligence.

3. https://www.theguardian.com/uk/1999/may/13/richardnortontaylor1.

4. House Intel interview with Page, p. 19. Carter Page interview with
U.S. House of Representatives, Permanent Select Committee on Intelligence, November 2, 2017, p. 19. https://www.lawfareblog.com/docu
ment-carter-page-house-intelligence-committee-hearing-transcript.

5. https://www.apnews.com/122ae0b5848345faa88108a03de40c5a.

CHAPTER 4: **"I BELIEVE YOU HAVE SOME INFORMATION FOR US"**

1. Erin Carlyle, "Trump Exaggerating His Net Worth (by 100%) in
Presidential Bid," *Forbes,* June 16, 2015, https://www.forbes.com/sites
/erincarlyle/2015/06/16/trump-exaggerating-his-net-worth-by-100
-in-presidential-bid/#23adf98c2a97.

2. Jonathan Greenberg, "Trump Lied to Me About His Wealth to Get onto
the Forbes 400. Here Are the Tapes," *Washington Post,* April 20, 2018,
https://www.washingtonpost.com/outlook/trump-lied-to-me-about
-his-wealth-to-get-onto-the-forbes-400-here-are-the-tapes/2018/04
/20/ac762b08-4287-11e8-8569-26fda6b404c7_story.html?utm_term
=.c2fa0404193f.

3. Michael Kranish and Marc Fisher, *Trump Revealed* (New York: Scribner,
2017), p. 32.

4. https://www.justice.gov/opa/pr/deutsche-bank-agrees-pay-72-billion
-misleading-investors-its-sale-residential-mortgage-backed.

5. Jonathan O'Connell, David A. Fahrenthold, and Jack Gillum, "As the 'King of Debt,' Trump Borrowed to Build His Empire. Then He Began Spending Hundreds of Millions in Cash," *Washington Post,* May 5, 2018, https://www.washingtonpost.com/politics/as-the-king-of-debt
-trump-borrowed-to-build-his-empire-then-he-began-spending-hun
dreds-of-millions-in-cash/2018/05/05/28fe54b4-44c4-11e8-8569
-26fda6b404c7_story.html?noredirect=on&utm_term=.5b4f65a3bf8f.

6. Ibid.

7. Kranish and Fisher, *Trump Revealed*, p. 211.

8. Adam Davidson, "Michael Cohen and the End Stage of the Trump Presidency," *New Yorker,* April 14, 2018, https://www.newyorker.com
/news/news-desk/michael-cohen-and-the-end-stage-of-the-trump
-presidency.

9. David Ignatius, "A History of Donald Trump's Business Dealings in Russia," *Washington Post,* November 2, 2017, https://www.washing
tonpost.com/opinions/a-history-of-donald-trumps-business-dealings
-in-russia/2017/11/02/fb8eed22-ba9e-11e7-be94-fabb0f1e9ffb_story
.html?utm_term=.916ed640aac9.

10. Nathan Layne et al., "Russian Elite Invested Nearly $100 Million in Trump Buildings," Reuters Investigates, March 17, 2017, https://www
.reuters.com/investigates/special-report/usa-trump-property/.

11. Anthony Cormier and Jason Leopold, "The Trump Organization Planned to Give Vladimir Putin the $50 Million Penthouse in Trump Tower Moscow," *BuzzFeed*, November 29, 2018, https://www.buzz
feednews.com/article/anthonycormier/the-trump-organization
-planned-to-give-vladimir-putin-the.

12. House Intelligence Committee report, minority views, p. 26. https://
democrats-intelligence.house.gov/uploadedfiles/20180411_-_final_-_
hpsci_minority_views_on_majority_report.pdf.

13. House Intelligence Committee report, minority views, p. 27, March 26, 2018.

14. https://www.nbcnews.com/nightly-news/video/russian-lawyer-nata
lia-veselnitskaya-speaks-out-i-am-an-informant-1221044291570.

15. Senate Judiciary Committee testimony, *Washington Post*, May 16, 2018.

16. Veselnitskaya interview on NBC. Veselnitskaya interview, NBC News, April 27, 2018.

CHAPTER 5: **THE MISSING EMAILS**

1. https://www.nytimes.com/2017/04/22/us/politics/james-comey-elec
tion.html.

2. ABC transcript of Comey interview, p. 46. Comey Interview with
George Stephanopoulos, ABC News, April 15, 2018. https://abcnews.go
.com/Site/transcript-james-comeys-interview-abc-news-chief-anchor
/story?id=54488723.

3. James Comey, *A Higher Loyalty* (New York: Flatiron Books, 2018),
pp. 169–70.

4. Glenn Kessler and Meg Kelly, "Timeline: James Comey's Decision-
Making on the Clinton Probe," *Washington Post,* October 20, 2017,
https://www.washingtonpost.com/news/fact-checker/wp/2017/10/20
/timeline-james-comeys-decision-making-on-the-clinton-probe
/?utm_term=.33361c6b7fe7.

5. Hillary Clinton, *What Happened* (New York: Simon & Schuster, 2017),
pp. 309–10.

6. Comey interview with George Stephanopoulos, ABC News, April 15,
2018. https://abcnews.go.com/Site/transcript-james-comeys-interview
-abc-news-chief-anchor/story?id=54488723.

7. Palmieri interview with Dan Balz and Philip Rucker.

8. Ibid.

9. Hillary Clinton, *What Happened* (New York: Simon & Schuster, 2017),
p. 311.

10. *Washington Post,* Oral History of 2016. November 9, 2016.

11. Spicer oddly compared Comey and his views about Clinton to a person
trapped in a fatally flawed relationship. "It was like being told, 'I love
you, I want to spend the rest of my life with you, but I don't want to
marry you.'"

12. Dana Priest and Greg Miller, "He Was One of the Most Respected Intel
Officers of His Generation. Now He's Leading 'Lock Her Up' Chants,"
Washington Post, August 15, 2016, ttps://www.washingtonpost.com
/world/national-security/nearly-the-entire-national-security-establish
ment-has-rejected-trumpexcept-for-this-man/2016/08/15/d5072d96
-5e4b-11e6-8e45-477372e89d78_story.html?utm_term=.bc504327533f.

13. Anne Gearan, Philip Rucker, and Abby Phillip, "DNC Chairwoman
Will Resign in Aftermath of Committee Email Controversy," *Washington Post*, July 24, 2016.

CHAPTER 6: **CROSSFIRE HURRICANE**

1. Francis Elliott, "Say Sorry to Trump or Risk Special Relationship, Cameron Told," May 4, 2016, https://www.thetimes.co.uk/article/say-sorry-to-trump-or-risk-special-relationship-cameron-told-h6ng0r7xj.

2. "Our Man in London Signs Off," *Australian,* April 28, 2018.

3. Ibid.

4. Interview with participants.

5. Strzok/Page texts, p. 13. https://www.hsgac.senate.gov/imo/media/doc/Appendix%20C%20-%20Documents.pdf.

6. House Intelligence Committee, "Report on Russian Active Measures." March 22, 2018, p. 54.

7. Rosalind S. Helderman and Tom Hamburger, "Who Is Source D?" March 29, 2017, https://www.washingtonpost.com/politics/who-is-source-d-the-man-said-to-be-behind-the-trump-russia-dossiers-most-salacious-claim/2017/03/29/379846a8-0f53-11e7-9d5a-a83e627dc120_story.html?utm_term=.cc7bde4da83c.

8. Jane Mayer, "Christopher Steele, The Man Behind the Trump Dossier," *New Yorker,* March 12, 2018.

9. Comey, *A Higher Loyalty,* p. 189.

CHAPTER 7: **DEEP INSIDE THE KREMLIN**

1. https://www.cia.gov/library/center-for-the-study-of-intelligence/csi-publications/csi-studies/studies/97unclass/wagenen.html.

2. Brennan testimony, House Intelligence Committee, May 23, 2017.

3. Greg Miller, Ellen Nakashima, and Adam Entous, "The Secret Struggle to Punish Russia for Putin's Election Assault," *Washington Post,* June 23, 2017, https://www.washingtonpost.com/graphics/2017/world/national-security/obama-putin-election-hacking/?utm_term=.db222fb21f83.

4. David Rothkopf, "Obama's 'Don't Do Stupid Shit' Foreign Policy," *Foreign Policy,* June 4, 2014, http://foreignpolicy.com/2014/06/04/obamas-dont-do-stupid-shit-foreign-policy/.

5. Interview with author.

6. Greg Miller, Ellen Nakashima, and Adam Entous, "Obama's Secret Struggle to Punish Russia for Putin's Election Assault," *Washington Post,* June 23, 2017, https://www.washingtonpost.com/graphics/2017/world/national-security/obama-putin-election-hacking/?utm_term=.db222fb21f83.

7. Interview with author.

8. Miller, Nakashima, and Entous, "Obama's Secret Struggle . . ."

9. https://www.feinstein.senate.gov/public/index.cfm/press-releases ?ID=A04D321E-5F86-4FD6-AD8E-7F533E1C2845.

10. James R. Clapper, *Facts and Fears: Hard Truths from a Life Inside Intelligence* (New York: Viking, 2018), p. 2.

11. David Fahrenthold, "Trump Recorded Having Extremely Lewd Conversation About Women in 2005," *Washington Post,* October 8, 2016, https:// www.washingtonpost.com/politics/trump-recorded-having-extremely -lewd-conversation-about-women-in-2005/2016/10/07/3b9ce776 -8cb4-11e6-bf8a-3d26847eeed4_story.html?utm_term=.475e6cffa21c.

12. Eric Lipton, David E. Sanger, and Scott Shane, "The Perfect Weapon: How Russian Cyberpower Invaded the U.S.," *New York Times,* December 13, 2016, https://www.nytimes.com/2016/12/13/us/politics/russia -hack-election-dnc.html.

13. Gabriel Sherman, "Trump's Transition Team 'Is Like *Game of Thrones,'*" *New York Daily Intelligencer,* December 8, 2016, http://nymag.com /daily/intelligencer/2016/12/trumps-transition-team-is-like-game-of -thrones.html.

14. Michael Rothfeld and Joe Palazzolo, "Trump Lawyer Arranged $130,000 Payment for Adult-Film Star's Silence," *Wall Street Journal*, January 12, 2018, https://www.wsj.com/articles/trump-lawyer-arranged-130-000 -payment-for-adult-film-stars-silence-1515787678.

15. Jenna Johnson, "Donald Trump Is in a Funk," *Washington Post,* October 21, 2016, https://www.washingtonpost.com/politics/donald-trump -is-in-a-funk-bitter-hoarse-and-pondering-if-i-lose/2016/10/21/d944 b518-97a3-11e6-bb29-bf2701dbe0a3_story.html?utm_term=.c467a3e c5b6a.

16. https://www.dni.gov/files/documents/ICA_2017_01.pdf.

CHAPTER 8: **DEZINFORMATSIYA**

1. Facebook ads released by House Intelligence Committee, Q2 file from 2015, P(1)0002273.pdf on my hard drive. Listed on doc as AD ID 438.

2. "Transcript of Mark Zuckerberg's Senate Hearing," The Switch, *Washington Post,* April 10, 2018, https://www.washingtonpost.com/news /the-switch/wp/2018/04/10/transcript-of-mark-zuckerbergs-senate -hearing/?utm_term=.3b77e3981c73.

3. Facebook ads released by House Intelligence Committee, trove Q2 2015, AD ID "554."

4. Facebook ads released by House Intelligence Committee, trove Q2 2015, AD ID "555."

5. Facebook ads released by House Intelligence Committee, trove Q2 2015, AD ID "556."

6. Facebook ads released by House Intelligence Committee, trove Q2 2015, AD ID "450."

7. Craig Timberg, "Russian Propaganda May Have Been Shared Hundreds of Millions of Times, New Research Says," *Washington Post,* October 5, 2017, https://www.washingtonpost.com/news/the-switch /wp/2017/10/05/russian-propaganda-may-have-been-shared -hundreds-of-millions-of-times-new-research-says/?utm_term =.211d466e4b03.

8. Craig Timberg, Elizabeth Dwoskin, and Adam Entous, "Michael Flynn, Nicki Minaj Shared Content from This Tennessee GOP Account. But It Wasn't Real. It Was Russian," *Washington Post,* October 18, 2017, https://www.washingtonpost.com/business/technology /michael-flynn-nicki-minaj-shared-content-from-this-tennessee-gop -account-but-it-wasnt-real-it-was-russian/2017/10/18/8b92fcda-b435 -11e7-9e58-e6288544af98_story.html?utm_term=.f4de7c01b520.

9. Clemson University data provided to author.

10. Philip Bump, "At Least Five People Close to Trump Engaged with Russian Twitter Trolls from 2015 to 2017," *Washington Post,* November 2, 2017, https://www.washingtonpost.com/news/politics/wp/2017 /11/02/at-least-five-people-close-to-trump-engaged-with-russian -twitter-trolls-from-2015-to-2017/?utm_term=.7535c45dbe8b.

11. Ben Collins and Kevin Poulsen, "Michael Flynn Followed Russian Troll Accounts, Pushed Their Messages in Days Before Election," *Daily Beast,* November 1, 2017, https://www.thedailybeast.com/michael-flynn-fol lowed-russian-troll-accounts-pushed-their-messages-in-days-before -election.

12. Timberg, Dwoskin, and Entous, "Michael Flynn, Nicki Minaj . . ." https://www.washingtonpost.com/business/technology/michael-flynn -nicki-minaj-shared-content-from-this-tennessee-gop-account-but-it -wasnt-real-it-was-russian/2017/10/18/8b92fcda-b435-11e7-9e58-e62 88544af98_story.html?utm_term=.de15c37057b1.

13. https://public.tableau.com/profile/d1gi#!/vizhome/FB4/TotalReach byPage.

14. https://public.tableau.com/profile/d1gi#!/vizhome/FB4/TotalReach byPage.

15. "Transcript of Mark Zuckerberg's Senate Hearing," *Washington Post,* April 10, 2018, https://www.washingtonpost.com/news/the-switch

/wp/2018/04/10/transcript-of-mark-zuckerbergs-senate-hearing/?utm
_term=.c8e5c57ae7ba.

16. Analysis of Twitter trends attributable to Clemson researchers.

17. Craig Timberg, Elizabeth Dwoskin, Adam Entous, and Karoun Demirjian, "Russian Ads, Now Publicly Released, Show Sophistication of Influence Campaign, *Washington Post,* November 1, 2017, https://www
.washingtonpost.com/business/technology/russian-ads-now-publicly
-released-show-sophistication-of-influence-campaign/2017/11/01
/d26aead2-bf1b-11e7-8444-a0d4f04b89eb_story.html?utm_term
=.96a777d765d0.

18. Mueller indictment: https://www.justice.gov/file/1035477/download.

19. Mueller indictment.

20. Anton Troianovski, Rosalind S. Helderman, Ellen Nakashima, and
Craig Timberg, "The 21st-Century Russian Sleeper Agent Is a Troll
with an American Accent," *Washington Post,* February 17, 2018. https://
www.washingtonpost.com/business/technology/the-21st-century-rus
sian-sleeper-agent-is-a-troll-with-an-american-accent/2018/02/17
/d024ead2-1404-11e8-8ea1-c1d91fcec3fe_story.html?utm_term
=.871d9cd801d2.

21. Michael Nunez, "Former Facebook Workers: We Routinely Suppressed
Conservative News," *Gizmodo,* May 9, 2016, https://gizmodo.com/for
mer-facebook-workers-we-routinely-suppressed-conser-1775461006.

22. Alex Johnson and Matthew DeLuca, "Facebook's Mark Zuckerberg
Meets Conservatives Amid 'Trending' Furor," NBC News, May 19,
2016, https://www.nbcnews.com/tech/social-media/facebook-s-mark
-zuckerberg-meets-conservatives-amid-trending-furor-n576366.

23. Jessica Guynn and Roger Yu, "Conservative Groups Encouraged by
Meeting with Facebook's Zuckerberg," *USA Today,* May 18, 2016,
https://www.usatoday.com/story/money/2016/05/18/conservatives
-stress-thought-diversity-facebook/84550870/.

24. Louise Matsikas, "Facebook Is Killing Trending Topics," *Wired,* June 1,
2018, https://www.wired.com/story/facebook-killed-trending-topics/.

25. Nicholas Thompson and Fred Vogelstein, "Inside the Two Years That
Shook Facebook—and the World," *Wired,* February 12, 2018, https://
www.wired.com/story/inside-facebook-mark-zuckerberg-2-years-of
-hell/.

26. Robinson Meyer, "Facebook Purges Journalists, Immediately Pro-
motes a Fake Story for 8 Hours," *The Atlantic,* August 29, 2016, https://

www.theatlantic.com/technology/archive/2016/08/facebook-steps-in
-it/497915/.

27. https://docs.google.com/document/d/1QE_oWadNTAex1PkmIhHZ
vvZCEBR1-vNaMnsbBV8HayA/edit.

28. https://www.snopes.com/fact-check/pope-francis-donald-trump-en
dorsement/.

29. https://newsroom.fb.com/news/2015/01/news-feed-fyi-showing
-fewer-hoaxes/.

30. Craig Silverman, "This Analysis Shows How Viral Fake Election News
Stories Outperformed Real News on Facebook," *BuzzFeed,* November 16, 2016, https://www.buzzfeed.com/craigsilverman/viral-fake
-election-news-outperformed-real-news-on-facebook?utm_term
=.nkPROBAqb7#.ukr4PZXk95.

31. https://firstdraftnews.org/is-facebook-is-losing-its-war-against-fake
-news/.

32. Casey Newton, "Zuckerberg: The Idea That Fake News on Facebook
Influenced the Election Is 'Crazy,'" The Verge, November 10, 2016,
https://www.theverge.com/2016/11/10/13594558/mark-zuckerberg
-election-fake-news-trump.

33. https://public.tableau.com/profile/d1gi#!/vizhome/FB4/TotalReach
byPage.

CHAPTER 9: THE RUSSIAN AMBASSADOR

1. https://www.gq.com/story/inside-donald-trumps-election-night-war
-room.

2. Hillary Clinton, *What Happened* (New York: Simon & Schuster, 2017),
pp. 385–86.

3. Peter Walker, "Donald Trump Wins: Russian Parliament Bursts into
Applause upon Hearing Result," *Independent,* November 9, 2016,
https://www.independent.co.uk/news/world/americas/us-elections
/donald-trump-wins-us-election-russia-putin-result-a7406866.html.

4. Ben Rhodes, *The World As It Is: A Memoir of the Obama White House*
(New York: Random House, 2018), p. 403.

5. Greg Miller, Ellen Nakashima, and Adam Entous, "Obama's Secret
Struggle to Punish Russia for Putin's Election Assault," *Washington Post,*
June 23, 2017.

6. https://www.nbcnews.com/news/us-news/what-obama-said-putin
-red-phone-about-election-hack-n697116.

7. https://abcnews.go.com/Politics/comey-assumption-clinton-win-fac tor-email-investigation/story?id=54467459.

8. https://www.cnn.com/2016/11/17/politics/kfile-michael-flynn-social -media/index.html.

9. Spencer S. Hsu, "Comet Pizza Gunman Pleads Guilty to Federal and Local Charges," *Washington Post,* March 24, 2017, https://www .washingtonpost.com/local/public-safety/comet-pizza-gunman-to -appear-at-plea-deal-hearing-friday-morning/2017/03/23/e12c91ba -0986-11e7-b77c-0047d15a24e0_story.html?utm_term=.739bd1b7e72e.

10. Michael McFaul, *From Cold War to Hot Peace: An American Ambassador in Putin's Russia* (New York: Houghton Mifflin Harcourt, 2018), p. 100.

11. Greg Miller and Adam Entous, "Flynn Was Warned by Trump Tran- sition Officials About Contacts with Russian Ambassador," *Washington Post,* May 5, 2017, https://www.washingtonpost.com/world/national -security/flynn-was-warned-by-trump-transition-officials-about -contacts-with-russian-ambassador/2017/05/05/b552c832-3192-11e7 -8674-437ddb6e813e_story.html?utm_term=.978c7500fe5b.

12. David Filipov, Rosalind S. Helderman, and Tom Hamburger, "Explana- tions for Kushner's Meeting with Head of Kremlin-Linked Bank Don't Match Up," *Washington Post,* June 1, 2017, https://www.washingtonpost .com/politics/explanations-for-kushners-meeting-with-head-of-krem lin-linked-bank-dont-match-up/2017/06/01/dd1bdbb0-460a-11e7 -bcde-624ad94170ab_story.html?utm_term=.0993900a1fcb.

13. Michael Kranish and Jonathan O'Connell, "Jared Kushner's Trou- bles Include an Impending $1.2 Billion Company Debt," *Washington Post,* March 1, 2018, https://www.washingtonpost.com/politics/jared -kushners-troubles-include-an-impending-12-billion-company-debt /2018/03/01/3f248014-1cbb-11e8-b2d9-08e748f892c0_story.html ?utm_term=.7e084a920111.

14. Rhodes, *The World As It Is,* p. 405.

15. "From the Archives: Inside the Closed Russian Dacha on the Eastern Shore," Editorial, *Washington Magazine,* December 30, 2016, http:// washingtonlife.com/2016/12/30/from-the-archives-inside-the-closed -russian-dacha-on-the-eastern-shore/.

16. http://en.kremlin.ru/events/president/news/53678.

CHAPTER 10: **BRIEFING THE PRESIDENT**

1. Greg Miller, Greg Jaffe, and Philip Rucker, "Doubting the Intelli- gence, Trump Pursues Putin and Leaves a Russian Threat Unchecked,"

Washington Post, December 14, 2017, https://www.washingtonpost.com /graphics/2017/world/national-security/donald-trump-pursues-vladi mir-putin-russian-election-hacking/?utm_term=.09bd2a9fdab3.

2. Tom Hamburger and Rosalind S. Helderman, "Hero or Hired Gun? How a British Former Spy Became a Flash Point in the Russia Investigation," *Washington Post,* February 6, 2018, https://www.washingtonpost .com/politics/hero-or-hired-gun-how-a-british-former-spy-became -a-flash-point-in-the-russia-investigation/2018/02/06/94ea5158 -0795-11e8-8777-2a059f168dd2_story.html?utm_term=.d49c1ffdf6cf.

3. James Comey, *A Higher Loyalty: Truth, Lies, and Leadership* (New York: Flatiron Books, 2018), p. 216.

4. Ibid., p. 220.

5. Ibid., p. 221.

6. Comey memo, http://apps.washingtonpost.com/g/documents/politics /james-comeys-memos-on-his-meetings-with-trump/2913/, January 6, 2017, p. 2.

7. John Kelly, "What Lies Beneath? FBI Tunnel in Glover Park Heated Up the Cold War," *Washington Post,* February 27, 2016, https://www .washingtonpost.com/local/what-lies-beneath-fbi-tunnel-in-glover -park-heated-up-the-cold-war/2016/02/27/d722abc6-d9b9-11e5-81ae -7491b9b9e7df_story.html?utm_term=.278343c95941.

8. Matthew Nussbaum, "A History of Explaining, and Defending, Michael Flynn," *Politico,* December 1, 2017, https://www.politico.com /story/2017/12/01/history-michael-flynn-explaining-defending -274792.

9. Ashley Parker, "Flynn Told Trump Team He Might Register as a Foreign Agent," *Washington Post,* March 10, 2017, https://www.washingtonpost .com/politics/flynn-told-trump-team-he-might-register-as-a-foreign -agent/2017/03/10/7e30713a-05cb-11e7-b9fa-ed727b644a0b_story .html?utm_term=.8c76adec8697.

10. Interview with participant.

11. "Full Transcript: Sally Yates and James Clapper Testify on Russian Election Interference," *Washington Post,* May 8, 2017, https://www .washingtonpost.com/news/post-politics/wp/2017/05/08/full-tran script-sally-yates-and-james-clapper-testify-on-russian-election-inter ference/?utm_term=.7c53106daa5f.

12. Comey memo, http://apps.washingtonpost.com/g/documents/politics /james-comeys-memos-on-his-meetings-with-trump/2913/, January 28, 2017.

13. Comey memo, http://apps.washingtonpost.com/g/documents/politics /james-comeys-memos-on-his-meetings-with-trump/2913/, January 28, 2017.

14. Karen DeYoung, "Trump Administration Says It's Putting Iran 'On Notice' Following Missile Test," *Washington Post,* February 1, 2017, https:// www.washingtonpost.com/world/national-security/2017/02/01/fc 5ce3d2-e8b0-11e6-80c2-30e57e57e05d_story.html?noredirect=on &utm_term=.ae2019ab2cb2.

15. https://www.aps.org/units/fip/newsletters/201708/diplomacy.cfm.

16. Murray Waas, "Flynn, Comey, and Mueller: What Trump Knew and When He Knew It," *New York Review Daily,* July 31, 2018. https:// www.nybooks.com/daily/2018/07/31/what-trump-knew-and-when -he-knew-it/.

17. Robert S. Mueller III, *Report on the Investigation into Russian Interference in the 2016 Presidential Election*, vol. 2, Washington, D.C., March 2019, https://www.justice.gov/storage/report.pdf, p. 39 (hereafter cited as Mueller Report).

CHAPTER 11: **YOU'RE FIRED**

1. https://www.bbc.com/news/world-us-canada-40194208.

2. Karoun Demirjian et al., "Attorney General Jeff Sessions Will Recuse Himself from Any Probe Related to 2016 Presidential Campaign," *Washington Post,* March 2, 2017, https://www.washingtonpost.com/powerpost /top-gop-lawmaker-calls-on-sessions-to-recuse-himself-from-russia -investigation/2017/03/02/148c07ac-ff46-11e6-8ebe-6e0dbe4f2bca _story.html?utm_term=.75c5f615b0b7.

3. Michael S. Schmidt, "Obstruction Inquiry Shows Trump's Struggle to Keep Grip on Russia Investigation," *New York Times,* January 4, 2018, https://www.nytimes.com/2018/01/04/us/politics/trump-sessions -russia-mcgahn.html.

4. Greg Miller and Adam Entous, "Trump Administration Sought to Enlist Intelligence Officials, Key Lawmakers to Counter Russia Stories," *Washington Post*, February 24, 2017, https://www.washingtonpost.com /world/national-security/trump-administration-sought-to-enlist-intel ligence-officials-key-lawmakers-to-counter-russia-stories/2017/02/24 /c8487552-fa99-11e6-be05-1a3817ac21a5_story.html?utm_term =.c1f9a7ba1aef.

5. https://intelligence.house.gov/uploadedfiles/final_russia_investigation _report.pdf.

6. https://www.ajc.com/news/national/read-transcripts-rep-devin-nunes
-news-conferences-about-trump-surveillance/NdZ4qQv7uBnjcH9E3
HSRPJ/.

7. Comey memo, March 30, 2017.

8. Glenn Kessler, "Trump's Mixed-Up Version of the Latest Hillary Clinton E-mail Controversy," *Washington Post,* October 25, 2016, https://
www.washingtonpost.com/news/fact-checker/wp/2016/10/25/trumps
-mixed-up-version-of-the-latest-hillary-clinton-controversy/?noredi
rect=on&utm_term=.1afd57b5c7ab.

9. Philip Bump, "Here's How Unusual It Is for an FBI Director to Be
Fired," *Washington Post,* May 9, 2017, https://www.washingtonpost.com
/news/politics/wp/2017/05/09/heres-how-unusual-it-is-for-an-fbi-di
rector-to-be-fired/?utm_term=.75e6b7642037.

10. https://www.nytimes.com/2017/05/19/us/politics/trump-russia
-comey.html.

11. https://www.nytimes.com/2017/05/16/us/politics/james-comey
-trump-flynn-russia-investigation.html.

CHAPTER 12: **THE SPECIAL COUNSEL STRIKES**

1. CBS *60 Minutes*, interview with Bannon, September 7, 2017.

2. Marc Fisher and Sari Horwitz, "Born to Wealth, Raised to Lead.
Then Sharply Different Choices," *Washington Post,* February 23, 2018,
https://www.washingtonpost.com/politics/mueller-and-trump-born
-to-wealth-raised-to-lead-then-sharply-different-choices/2018/02/22
/ad50b7bc-0a99-11e8-8b0d-891602206fb7_story.html?utm_term
=.141e4692da33.

3. Ibid.

4. https://www.cnn.com/2017/05/29/politics/robert-mueller-tabor
-academy-commencement/index.html.

5. Garrett M. Graff, *The Threat Matrix: Inside Robert Mueller's FBI and the
War on Global Terror* (New York: Little, Brown, 2011).

6. http://www.law.virginia.edu/static/uvalawyer/html/alumni/uvalaw
yer/f02/mueller.htm.

7. Barton Gellman, "Is the FBI Up to the Job 10 Years after 9/11?" *Time,*
May 12, 2011.

8. Mueller Report, p. 78.

9. Greg Miller and Adam Entous, "Trump Administration Sought to Enlist Intelligence Officials, Key Lawmakers to Counter Russia Stories,"
Washington Post, February 24, 2017, https://www.washingtonpost.com

/world/national-security/trump-administration-sought-to-enlist
-intelligence-officials-key-lawmakers-to-counter-russia-stories/2017
/02/24/c8487552-fa99-11e6-be05-1a3817ac21a5_story.html?utm_
term=.396e003b887a.

10. Ashley Parker et al., "Trump Dictated Son's Misleading Statement on
Meeting with Russian Lawyer," *Washington Post,* July 31, 2017, https://
www.washingtonpost.com/politics/trump-dictated-sons-misleading
-statement-on-meeting-with-russian-lawyer/2017/07/31/04c94f96
-73ae-11e7-8f39-eeb7d3a2d304_story.html?utm_term=.928baa302f6b.

11. Mueller Report, p. 88.

12. Ibid., p. 86.

13. Ibid., p. 91.

14. Ibid., pp. 116–17.

15. Ibid., p. 101.

16. Ibid., p. 364.

17. Author interview.

18. Josh Gerstein, "George Papadopoulos's Late Night with the FBI," *Politico,* December 4, 2017.

CHAPTER 13: **"I CAN'T PUT ON THE CHARM"**

1. Rex Tillerson testimony before the House Committee on Foreign Affairs, May 21, 2019, https://www.washingtonpost.com/context/rex-till
erson-s-testimony-before-the-house-foreign-affairs-committee/cd
512b82-abb4-412f-a83f-d1deaaed127f/?utm_term=.62452767b2d6.

2. Carol E. Lee et al., "Tillerson's Fury at Trump Required an Intervention from Pence," NBC News, October 4, 2017, https://www.nbcnews
.com/politics/white-house/tillerson-s-fury-trump-required-interven
tion-pence-n806451.

3. Greg Miller, Greg Jaffe, and Phillip Rucker, "Doubting the Intelligence, Trump Pursues Putin and Leaves a Russian Threat Unchecked," *Washington Post,* December 14, 2017, https://www.washingtonpost.com
/graphics/2017/world/national-security/donald-trump-pursues-vladi
mir-putin-russian-election-hacking/?utm_term=.40b33fd20547.

CHAPTER 14: **HELSINKI**

1. https://www.newsweek.com/fundamental-human-rights-are-dimin
ishing-according-new-report-796325.

2. https://www.nytimes.com/interactive/2018/06/02/us/politics/trump
-legal-documents.html.

3. https://www.washingtonpost.com/politics/trump-says-he-would
   -speak-to-mueller-under-oath-in-russia-investigation/2018/01/24/edb
   33750-015a-11e8-8acf-ad2991367d9d_story.html?utm_term=.626
   83a9fa2db.

4. https://www.thedailybeast.com/trumps-attorney-says-no-decision-to
   -talk-to-mueller.

5. https://www.washingtonpost.com/news/the-switch/wp/2017/10/05
   /russian-propaganda-may-have-been-shared-hundreds-of-millions-of
   -times-new-research-says/?utm_term=.c9fe60d351f2.

6. https://www.thedailybeast.com/twitter-ceo-retweeted-alleged-russian
   -trolls.

7. https://www.washingtonpost.com/business/technology/russian
   -ads-now-publicly-released-show-sophistication-of-influence-cam
   paign/2017/11/01/d26aead2-bf1b-11e7-8444-a0d4f04b89eb_story.ht
   ml?utm_term=.b060b35526c2.

8. https://www.washingtonpost.com/opinions/without-the-russians
   -trump-wouldnt-have-won/2018/07/24/f4c87894-8f6b-11e8-bcd5-9d
   911c784c38_story.html?utm_term=.c51164754422.

9. https://www.lawfareblog.com/document-justice-department-releases
   -carter-page-fisa-application. Page 308 of 412.

10. https://www.vox.com/2018/6/28/17504514/house-republicans-docu
    ment-war-rosenstein-nunes-trump-mueller.

11. Alan Neuhauser, "Mueller Explains Why He Didn't Subpoena Trump,"
    U.S. News & World Report, July 24, 2019, https://www.usnews.com
    /news/national-news/articles/2019-07-24/robert-mueller-explains
    -why-he-didnt-subpoena-donald-trump.

12. https://www.washingtonpost.com/politics/a-bomb-on-trumps
    -front-porch-fbis-cohen-raids-hit-home-for-the-president/2018/04
    /09/6abb816e-3c37-11e8-974f-aacd97698cef_story.html?utm_term=
    .5d9e08a14f84.

13. https://www.washingtonpost.com/local/public-safety/manafort-or
    dered-to-jail-after-witness-tampering-charges/2018/06/15/ccc526cc
    -6e68-11e8-afd5-778aca903bbe_story.html?utm_term=.03af1bd2a728.

14. http://time.com/5338451/rod-rosenstein-russian-indictment-transcript/.

EPILOGUE

1. Shawn Boburg and Anu Narayanswamy, "Trump Has Blasted Mueller's
   Team for Political Donations. But Attorney General Nominee William P.
   Barr Has Given More Than $500,000," *Washington Post,* December 11,

2018, https://www.washingtonpost.com/investigations/trump-has-blas ted-muellers-team-for-political-donations-but-attorney-general -nominee-william-barr-has-given-more-than-500000/2018/12/11 /dce5974a-fcb0-11e8-862a-b6a6f3ce8199_story.html.

2. Michael Rothfeld, Alexandra Berzon, and Joe Palazzolo, " 'Boss, I Miss You So Much': The Awkward Exile of Michael Cohen," *Wall Street Journal,* April 26, 2018, https://www.wsj.com/articles/boss-i-miss-you-so -much-the-awkward-exile-of-michael-cohen-1524767440.

3. Michael D. Cohen testimony to the House Oversight Committee, February 27, 2019, https://docs.house.gov/meetings/GO/GO00 /20190227/108969/HHRG-116-GO00-Wstate-CohenM-20190227 .pdf.

4. Tim Mak, "How Michael Cohen Protects Trump by Making Legal Threats," NPR, May 31, 2018, https://www.npr.org/2018/05/31/615 843930/listen-how-michael-cohen-protects-trump-by-making-legal -threats.

5. Matt Zapotosky et al., "Michael Cohen Concludes His Testimony: 'I Will Not Sit Back,' " *Washington Post,* February 27, 2019, https://www .washingtonpost.com/world/national-security/michael-cohen-testi mony/2019/02/27/089664f0-39fb-11e9-a2cd-307b06d0257b_story .html.

6. David Johnston, "New Attorney General Shifts Department's Focus," *New York Times,* March 3, 1992, https://www.nytimes.com/1992/03/03 /us/new-attorney-general-shifts-department-s-focus.html.

7. Michael Tonry, *Malign Neglect: Race, Crime, and Punishment in America* (New York: Oxford University Press, 1996), p. 36.

8. William Barr memo to Rod Rosenstein, June 8, 2018, https://www .lawfareblog.com/document-william-barr-memo-obstruction-investi gation.

9. Mueller Report, p. 111.

10. Darren Samuelsohn, "New Trump-Russia Subplot: Mueller and Barr Are 'Good Friends,' " *Politico,* January 15, 2019, https://www.politico .com/story/2019/01/15/trump-russia-mueller-barr-friends-1102244.

11. Adam Goldman and Michael S. Schmidt, "Rod Rosenstein Suggested Secretly Recording Trump and Discussed 25th Amendment," *New York Times,* September 21, 2018, https://www.nytimes.com/2018/09/21/us /politics/rod-rosenstein-wear-wire-25th-amendment.html.

12. Mueller Report, p. 39.

13. *CBS This Morning,* May 30, 2019, https://twitter.com/CBSThisMorn
    ing/status/1134159718820339712.

14. Matt Zapotosky, "Trump Would Have Been Charged with Obstruction
    Were He Not President, Hundreds of Former Federal Prosecutors Assert,"
    Washington Post, May 6, 2019, https://www.washingtonpost.com/world
    /national-security/trump-would-have-been-charged-with-obstruction
    -were-he-not-president-hundreds-of-former-federal-prosecutors-as
    sert/2019/05/06/e4946a1a-7006-11e9-9f06-5fc2ee80027a_story.html.

15. Robert S. Mueller III's testimony before the House Judiciary Com-
    mittee, July 24, 2019, https://www.washingtonpost.com/politics
    /transcript-of-robert-s-mueller-iiis-testimony-before-the-house-judi
    ciary-committee/2019/07/24/7164abfe-ad96-11e9-a0c9-6d2d781
    8f3da_story.html.

16. https://www.whitehouse.gov/wp-content/uploads/2019/09/Unclassi
    fied09.2019.pdf

INDEX